GLORIOSA SUPERBA

TO MY WIFE, CHRISTINA

CLIVIA NOBILIS

THE SOUTHERN AFRICAN

WHAT FLOWER IS THAT?

TIBOUCHINA URVILLEANA

TECOMA ALATA

KRISTO PIENAAR

Struik Publishers (Pty) Ltd (a member of Struik New Holland Publishing (Pty) Ltd) 80 McKenzie Street, Cape Town 8001

Reg. No.: 1954/000965/07

First published in 2001

10 9 8 7 6 5 4 3 2 1

Copyright © in published edition 2001: Struik Publishers (Pty) Ltd
Copyright © in text 2001: Professor Kristo Pienaar

ISBN 1 86872 588 X

Cover design by Illana Fridkin
Designed by Wim Reinders, Cape Town
Illustrations by Nicci Page, Cape Town
Reproduction by Hirt & Carter Cape (Pty) Ltd
Printed and bound by Craft Print Pte Ltd

All rights reserved. No part of this publication may be reproduced, stored in a retrieval system or transmitted, in any form, or by any means, electronic, mechanical, photocopying, recording or otherwise, without the prior written permission of the copyright owner(s).

With the following exceptions, the photographs for this book were supplied by the author, Professor Pienaar. Those who made material available from their personal collections were:

Shaen Adey (Struik Image Library) – Agapanthus sp., Alstroemeria cvs 'Inca lily', Lilium sp., Scabiosa sp.
Prof. F Albers (Germany) – Orbeopsis lutea.
Trevor Barrett – Aglaonema commutatum 'Pseudobracteatum', Columnea microphylla, Crossandra infundibuliformis, Cryptostegia grandiflora, Megaskepasma erythrochlamys, Nelumbo nucifera, Stenocarpus sinuatus, Stictocardia beraviensis, Stigmaphyllon ciliatum, Vriesea x mariae.
A.J. Burger – Didelta carnosa var. carnosa, Haemanthus nelsonii, Roella ciliata, Xerophyta viscosa.
G. Dreyer (Struik Image Library) – Gazania sp.
D.I. Ferreia – Lachenalia cv.
Nancy Gardiner – Aglaonema crispum 'Malay Beauty', Aglaonema crispum 'Parrot Jungle', Aglaonema crispum 'Silver King', Alphinia zerumbet, Asarina barclaiana, Astilbe japonica, Camellia x saluenensis 'J.C. Williams', Cassia nodosa, Cerastium tomentosum, Crypthanthus bromelioides, Cynara scolymus, Episcia cupreata, Hosta crispula, Kalmia angustifolia, Kochia scoparia, Liriope muscari 'Variegata', Lithops lesliei, Lithops vanzylii, Luculia gratissima, Magnolia grandiflora, Monarda didyma, Mucuna bennettii, Myosotis scorpioides, Nigella damascena, Paphiopedilum chamberlainianum, Phacelia campanularia, Solidago virgaurea, Strongylodon macrobotrys, Syringa vulgaris, Tecomanthe venusta, Thalictrum dipterocarpum, Tigridia pavonia, Torenia fournieri, Trachelospermum jasminoides, Vriesea incurvata, Zantedescia rehmannii.
Holland Zaadunie BV, Holland – Amaranthus caudatus, Ammi majus, Lychnis chalcedonica, Nepeta cataria.
Prof W.P.U. Jackson – Castalis nudicaulis, Homeria comp tonii, Lapeirousia corymbosa, Platycodon grandiflorus, Tillandsia cyanea, Vriesea carinata.
Walter Knirr (Struik Image Library) – Disa uniflora 'Pride of Table Mountain'.
National Botanical Gardens of South Africa – Adenandra uniflora, Boophane disticha.
Jo Onderstall – Argemone mexicana, Pycnostachys urticifoloa.
Charles Rostance – Littonia modesta, Sandersonia aurantiaca.
Joan Watcham – Arum palaestinum.

BEAUMONTIA GRANDIFLORA

CERATOTHECA TRILOBA

TIBOUCHINA GRANULOSA

FOREWORD

Professor Kristo Pienaar has identified a need in horticultural literature and I am convinced that his book will be extremely valuable to all people who would like to know more about plants. The amateur gardener, for example, will find the book indispensable in identifying virtually any plant he is likely to see growing in the region and from this to be able to grow it successfully in his own home or garden; the horticulturist will find it useful for checking characteristics and valid names of plants; and the professional botanist can use it to identify horticulturally important plants at the species, variety or cultivar level.

Locally, we have a heritage of indigenous plants with a most wonderful horticultural potential. Carl Linnaeus, one of the greatest botanists who ever lived, wrote from Sweden to his friend Ryk Tulbagh, then Governor of the Cape, that if he had a choice he would rather have been Ryk Tulbagh than Croesus or Alexander the Great because of the wonderful plants in the Cape.

Gardeners are realizing to a greater extent that indigenous plants are usually better adapted to our extremes of climate and soil conditions than plants introduced from other countries. And because one of the main aims of the National Botanic Gardens of South Africa is to promote the awareness of our botanical heritage among the public, it is encouraging that more than one-third of the plants described in this book are, in fact, indigenous to South Africa.

Therefore, gardeners who wish to cultivate our indigenous flora successfully will have not only beautiful, healthy plants, suited to our conditions, but also the satisfaction of knowing that they are helping in the conservation of a precious heritage.

Prof. J.N. Eloff
Director, National Botanic Gardens of South Africa
Kirstenbosch
June 1984

ACKNOWLEDGEMENTS

In writing and compiling a book such as this, one needs encouragement, advice and assistance from many people – botanists, gardeners, horticulturists and enthusiastic colleagues.

Foremost, I offer most sincere thanks to Dinah Moffett who came to my assistance at a critical stage to research and write the majority of the entries in this book.

My gratitude also to the following, listed alphabetically rather than for the importance of their contribution: Marius de Kock, Hortulanus of the University of the Western Cape, for his help and assistance in taking the pictures of many plants on the campus and in the glass houses; Peggy Jennings of Struik for her thorough editing of the script; Rodney Moffett, Senior Lecturer in Flowering Plant Taxonomy at the University of the Western Cape, without whose specialist knowledge and assistance in identifying so many plants this book would have been impossible; Dr. John Rourke, Curator of the Compton Herbarium and his staff, especially Mrs Pauline Fairall and Miss Deirdre Snijman for identifying many of the slides and for the general information so readily given; Jac Swanepoel, San Marina Nurseries, Joostenburgvlakte, for identifying particular indoor plants, cacti and succulents; Ernst van Jaarsveld of the National Botanic Gardens at Kirstenbosch who wrote all the entries on *Plectranthus*. Ernst also assisted me in taking many photographs in the nursery at Kirstenbosch; and all the other flower-loving photographers who contributed slides.

I would like, too, to thank my wife and family who have always been so supportive and understanding of my career and my hobbies – the two, as in the case of this book, often indistinguishable.

And, of course, there are many people who have encouraged and helped me over the years to gain the knowledge necessary to even contemplate a task of this magnitude; I am grateful to all who have touched my life in this way.

I hope this book will serve as a 'thank you' to everyone mentioned above as well as to all who have ever loved flowers and to those who will come to know and love them as I do.

Kristo Pienaar
June 1984

INTRODUCTION

Most of us easily recognize a rose, a tulip or a daffodil, but how many more times have we seen a plant, admired its intricacy and beauty and wondered … 'What flower is that?' And with the seemingly limitless floral world around us in Southern Africa it is hardly surprising that even the expert botanist is frequently baffled and sent scurrying off to consult his reference works before being able to identify a particular plant. After all there are some 22 000 species of indigenous flowering plants in South Africa alone. How much more difficult then for the average gardener or even the enthusiastic amateur botanist to name correctly many of the plants widely cultivated today.

The age-old adage that one picture is better han a thousand words is never truer than when it comes to identifying a flower or a plant. For it is the colour or shape of a bloom or perhaps the foliage that first catches the eye and it is from this impression that one is able to recognize characteristics, and then be able to identify the plant.

In compiling and preparing this volume I have chosen some 1 500 species, comprising the most successful annuals, biennials, perennials, shrubs, trees, climbers, creepers, palms, indoor plants, cacti, succulents, aquatic plants, naked-seeded plants and ferns cultivated in Southern African gardens and homes, as well as some indigenous species still found growing mainly in the wild, but worthy of attention. A word of warning, however: many of our wild plants are protected by legislation or provincial ordinances and may not be picked casually without a permit. Their seeds, however, are often available from provincial conservation authorities, from the South African Botanical Society or through recognized wild flower societies and nurseries.

I have also included certain flowering species, often beautiful, which are detrimental to our indigenous flora and are regarded as noxious weeds. Their cultivation is prohibited and they should be actively destroyed. However, they have been included to help you to identify them so that you can destroy any that may be in your own garden.

PLUMERIA RUBRA

WACHENDORFIA THYRSIFLORA

ORPHIUM FRUTESCENS

WHY USE SCIENTIFIC NAMES?

The use of scientific names was devised by early botanists to overcome the problem of the same plant being known by different names, not only around the world but frequently also from one small area to another within a country. They adopted the system of binomial nomenclature – later perfected and refined by the great naturalist Linnaeus – which classified plants into genus, then species. In other words plants (and animals) receive a unique surname and first name which is recognized internationally. Often, too, plants are even further defined in terms of subspecies, varieties and cultivars.

These unique scientific names eliminate any possibility of confusion. And though the names – a *polyglot mélange* of mainly Latin and Greek and a 'smidgeon' of other languages – derive from a curious admixture, they are actually allocated according to strict taxonomic guide lines and generally pertain to definite visible characteristics of the plant. The name is always in two parts – the generic name (genus) and the specific epithet (species) is given according to botanical rules. The names are always used together when referring to species. The specific epithet often gives a clue to an aspect of the plant that is significant, for example leaf shape, habit, flower colour or even geographic origin.

Except where local study has led to newer classification, the excellent 'botanist's bible', *Hortus Third* (Bailey, 1976), as well as *Tropica* (Graf, 1978), were the ultimate arbiters in the naming of most of the plants. For the indigenous plants a checklist of species (1982 and 1983) supplied by the National Botanical Research Institute, Pretoria, was consulted.

In a land renowned for its flowering plants – and ours is, after all, a nation of gardeners – there may be favourites which were omitted through pressure of space. However, I am delighted to share with you the 1 500 species that I have chosen.

HOW TO USE THE BOOK

There is nothing more frustrating than having a comprehensive reference to hand yet not being able to find what you want. With this in mind I have attempted to make the information contained in *The Southern African What Flower is That?* as easily accessible as possible.

If you know the genus to which a plant belongs then your task is simple because the entire book has been arranged in alphabetical order according to the genus of each plant. This was done for a good reason – to avoid confusion – as a plant can have only one correct scientific (botanical) name but it could have many common names in any number of different languages. One could argue that not many weekend gardeners know much about scientific names; this is probably so, yet it is surprising how many plants are known in everyday parlance by their generic names – for example, **Agapanthus**, **Primula**, **Gladiolus**, **Dahlia**, etc.

If you know only the common name of a flower, then your task is equally simple because the comprehensive index at the back of the book has been compiled to include as many common names as possible, in both English and Afrikaans. For example, you may have heard 'Canterbury Bells' discussed in conversation and you would like to find out what it looks like, even how to grow it: look up 'Canterbury Bells' in the index and you will find it cross-referenced to **Campanula medium**, page 72. This, then, leads you directly to the page in the book where you will find 'Canterbury Bells', as well as other plants (species) in the same genus – perhaps one you like even better.

What **if you do not know a flower's name**, yet you can recognize it by sight? You could page through the book until you come to the correct photograph … but, enjoyable as this may be, it could prove frustrating and time consuming. Instead, I have devised a straightforward method of identifying the major characteristics of the flower in question that should lead you to where you are most likely to find your plants. And this is by using the 'family key'.

Some 160 families, representing over 740 genera (a family is made up of related genera) are featured in this book and 70 of the most important families are illustrated in the botanical drawings on pages 9 to 15. These botanical drawings are often more than likely the 'keys' or identification reference in finding the plant you know only by sight. Beneath the drawings are the genera which those specific characteristics represent.

Once you have found your plant you then, naturally, want to read all about it and rather than confuse a newcomer and thereby prevent his enjoyment of the world of flowers I have decided to simplify explanations. Thus, instead of lengthy instructions I have designed a sample flower entry, i.e. **Dombeya**, page 8, and you will see that all terminology used in the book is exemplified there and explained in simple terms.

One should also understand that a genus may be large, embracing 100 species or more, or very small, with only one or two species. For example, **Euphorbia** has over 2 000 species (although only a few are able to be exhibited in this book); whereas **Amaryllis** has only one species. A large genus may include plants which are annual or perennial, the size of a large tree or tiny shrub but they will always have a number of identifiable structural points in common. For example, the **Euphorbia ingens** is a tree while **Euphorbia mauritanica** is no more than a shrub, yet both have the same floral structure, and fruit, and both contain latex.

In the comprehensive index all names, scientific and common, are cross-referenced. Throughout, currently accepted botanical names are printed in bold type, synonyms in italics and common names (English and Afrikaans) in normal (roman) type face. A typical cross-reference is *Acacia elata* see **Acacia terminalis**.

I truly hope that everyone using this book will become an enthusiastic participant in the wonder and world of flowers.

YOUR GUIDE TO CULTIVATION

- 🅟 – some frost
- 🅕 – full frost
- 💧 – lots of water
- ❋ – deciduous
- ⊜ – shade-loving
- ✸ – specimen tree
- ☼ – half sun
- ⊛ – average water
- ⊛ – evergreen
- ☼ – full sun
- 💧 – little water
- 🅕 – tender to frost
- 🅦 – wind resistant

DOMBEYA

Dombeya burgessiae

HOW TO READ THE ENTRIES

Family: group of related genera with similar major characteristics.

Text: description of characteristics of the genus, geographic origins and uses as garden plants.

Species: a taxonomic group within the genus. The specific epithet is always preceded by the genus name.

Text (species): general description of the species' characteristics, plus cultivation hints.

Genus initial only: when genus previously written in full.

DOMBEYA

Sterculiaceae

A genus of evergreen and deciduous shrubs and small trees native to Africa, Madagascar and adjacent islands.

Dombeya burgessiae — Natal, Eastern Transvaal, Eastern Zimbabwe
Pink dombeya
Large bushy shrub or small tree up to 4 m. Large leaves up to 180 mm long with deep

D. rotundifolia var. rotundifolia
Northern Natal, Transvaal, East Africa and into Namibia

Wild pear or Drolpeer
Deciduous, well-shaped small tree to 5 m, occasionally more, with fragrant, creamy-

D. x tiliacea — Garden origin

Genus: group of one or many closely related plants to which species, varieties, cultivars, etc. belong, e.g. **Dombeya** and its species.

Origin: where it is believed to have originated. Guide to type of climate and environment to which plant is best suited.

Variety (var.): when species differ only in some minor definable characteristics from the rest of the species.

Common name: in English and Afrikaans; as plants are known in various areas.

Hybrid (x): The offspring of two plants of different species or genera; it does not normally occur in nature. Indicated by an x preceding the hybrid name.

FURTHER EXAMPLES

Synonym: a former taxonomic name that has since been rejected with the introduction of new facts and reclassification. Written *in italics* within brackets beneath the new name.

Synonym: genera is indicated by its initial only when reclassification retains the genera but changes the specific epithet.

Symbols: guide to gardeners for growing success. See page 7

Abutilon pictum 'Thompsonii'

Lobularia maritima
(Alyssum maritimum)

Acacia terminalis — Australia
(A. elata)

A. inapertus subsp. pendulus
Eastern Transvaal

Plumeria rubra forma lutea — Transvaal

Cultivar: The result of deliberate experimentation to breed plants with specific characteristics. The name is logically derived from (culti)vated and (var)iety. Written within single quotes.

Subspecies (subsp.): differs *slightly* from the species; has the same name as the species but the subspecific epithet (name) follows the abbreviation – subsp.

Form: when species differ only very slightly, e.g. colour of the flowers.

8

ILLUSTRATED FAMILY KEY

ACANTHACEAE

Acanthus family: Herbaceous plants mainly from the tropics. Leaves are simple, opposite; flowers are two-lipped and showy.

Acanthus
Aphelandra
Barleria
Crossandra
Dicliptera
Duvernoia
Fittonia
Hypoestes
Justicia
Mackaya
Megaskepasma
Odontonema
Pachystachys
Pseuderanthemum
Ruellia
Ruspolia
Ruttya
x Ruttyruspolia
Sanchezia
Strobilanthes
Thunbergia

AGAVACEAE

Century plant family: Rhizomatous, woody perennials some of which produce valuable fibres, such as sisal. Leaves, usually crowded at the base, are stiff, often fleshy and sharp-pointed. Flowers are lily-like and borne in racemes or panicles.

Agave
Beschorneria
Cordyline
Doryanthes
Furcraea
Phormium
Yucca

AMARANTHACEAE

Mostly herbaceous annuals with intensely coloured leaves. Inflorescences are brightly coloured, e.g. cockscomb.

Alternanthera
Amaranthus
Celosia
Gomphrena
Iresine

AMARYLLIDACEAE

Bulbous plants with lily-like flowers that are arranged mostly in umbels, but differ from Liliaceae in having an inferior ovary (below the flower parts).

Amaryllis
Boophane
Brunsvigia
Clivia
Crinum
Cyrtanthus
Eucharis
Gethyllis
Haemanthus
Hippeastrum
Hymenocallis
Leucojum
Narcissus
Nerine
Polianthes
Scadoxus
Sprekelia
Zephyranthes

APOCYNACEAE

Frangipani family: Mostly tropical and subtropical plants and shrubs. Flowers are tubular, opening with five lobes, and very fragrant.

Acokanthera
Adenium
Allamanda
Beaumontia
Carissa
Catharanthus
Chonemorpha
Mandevilla
Nerium
Plumeria
Thevetia
Trachelospermum
Vinca

APONOGETONACEAE

Waterblommetjie family: Aquatic plants with floating leaves and a dichotomous inflorescence with white flowers that also float.

Aponogeton

ARACEAE

Arum family: Tropical herbaceous plants, many of which are moist and shade-loving. Leaf forms vary greatly. Araceae are characterized by an inflorescence composed of a densely flowered spadix sub-tended by a shell-like spathe that is often coloured and showy, as in anthuriums.

Aglaonema
Alocasia
Anthurium
Arum
Caladium
Colocasia
Dieffenbachia
Dracunculus
Epipremnum
Monstera
Philodendron
Pistia
Spathiphyllum
Syngodium
Zantedeschia

ARALIACEAE

Hedera family: Trees, shrubs and climbers mostly tropical and subtropical. Leaves are often palmately lobed or divided. Ivy (Hedera) is perhaps the best known genus.

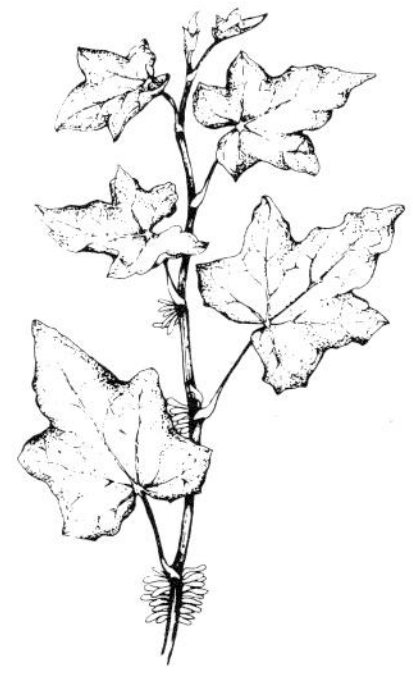

Brassaia
Cussonia
Dizygotheca
x Fatshedera
Fatsia
Hedera
Polyscias
Schefflera
Tetrapanax
Tupidanthus

ARECACEAE (=Palmae)

Palm family: Large, compound, leathery leaves and trunks often covered with old leaf bases. Flowers are insignificant.

Archontophoenix
Caryota
Chamaedorea
Cyrtostachys
Hyophorbe
Phoenix
Roystonea
Washingtonia

ASCLEPIADACEAE

Carrion or Milkweed family: Herbaceous shrubs, vines or succulents with or without a milky juice. Flowers are waxy, with an unpleasant scent and pollinated by flies and green flies, e.g. stapelia.

Asclepias
Ceropegia
Cryptostegia
Hoodia
Hoya
Microloma
Orbeopsis
Oxypetalum
Stapelia
Stephanotis
Trichocaulon

ASTERACEAE (=Compositae)

The daisy family: One of the largest in the plant kingdom and characterized by its small flowers (ray and disc florets) that combine into the typical composite head.

Achillea
Ageratum
Anthemis
Arctotheca
Arctotis
Athanasia
Bellis
Bidens
Brachylaena
Calendula
Callistephus
Centaurea
Chrysanthemoides
Chrysanthemum
Chrysocoma
Coreopsis
Cotula
Cynara
Dahlia
Dicoma
Didelta
Dimorphotheca
Dymondia
Erigeron
Eriocephalus
Eroeda
Eupatorium
Euryops
Felicia
Gaillardia
Gazania
Gerbera
Helianthus
Helichrysum
Helipterum
Kleinia
Liatris
Metalasia
Oldenburgia
Osteospermum
Pentzia
Phaenocoma
Pteronia
Rudbeckia
Santolina
Senecio
Solidago
Tagetes
Ursinia
Veronia
Wedelia
Zinnia

BALSAMINACEAE

Impatiens family: Warm-climate herbaceous plants with watery stems and attractive flowers, always with a spur. Busy Lizzie is perhaps the best known member of this family.

Impatiens

BEGONIACEAE

Begonia family: Herbaceous plants for tropical, subtropical and coastal gardens. Leaves are characteristically uneven. Rex begonias are the best known.

Begonia

BIGNONIACEAE

A family of showy climbers, shrubs and trees from tropical climates. Leaves simple or compound and the flowers tubular, trumpet-shaped, large and showy.

Bignonia
Campsis
Clytostoma
Distictis
Jacaranda
Macfadyena
Pandorea
Podranea
Pyrostegia
Rhigozum
Saritaea
Spathodea
Tecoma
Tecomaria

BRASSICACEAE (=Cruciferae)

Mustard family: Annual or perennial herbaceous plants. Flowers have four free petals, usually spreading in the form of a cross. The fruit is a pod-like capsule, called a siliqua, which splits in a characteristic manner.

Aubrieta
Brachycarpaea
Brassica
Cheiranthus
Heliophila
Iberis
Lobularia
Lunaria
Malcolmia
Matthiola

BROMELIACEAE

Pineapple family: Herbaceous plants, often epiphytes, from the warm areas of the Americas. Leaves are stiff and often fleshy and arranged in rosettes or in a tubular fashion for holding water. Inflorescences are very showy and brightly coloured.

Aechmea
Billbergia
Cryptanthus
Guzmania
Neoregelia
Tillandsia
Vriesea

CACTACEAE

Prickly pear family: Spiny succulents from tropical America with modified fleshy stems often resembling leaves. Flowers are showy with many colourful petals and stamens. They open in full sun.

Astrophytum
Cereus
Chamaecereus
Echinocactus
Echinocereus
Echinopsis
Epiphyllum
Ferocactus
Gymnocalycium
Lobivia
Mammillaria
Nopalxochia
Notocactus
Opuntia
Rhipsalidopsis
Schlumbergera
Trichocereus

CAMPANULACEAE

Campanula family: Showy bell-shaped flowers, often blue or bluish, sometimes pink or white. These are herbaceous plants from tropical and subtropical areas.

Campanula
Platycodon
Roella

CANNACEAE

Canna family: A single genus, canna, makes up this family. The plants are large, herbaceous and have a swollen underground tuberous rhizome from which the aerial stems arise. Flowers are usually large and brightly coloured, each sub-tended by a bract.

Canna

CAPRIFOLIACEAE

Honeysuckle family: Shrubs or climbers; leaves are opposite; flowers tubular, showy and fragrant.

Abelia
Lonicera
Sambucus
Symphoricarpos
Viburnum
Weigela

COMMELINACEAE

Wandering Jew family: Herbaceous, watery-stemmed, often creeping plants requiring a temperate climate. Leaves are showy and often hairy.

Callisia
Dichorisandra
Rhoeo
Setcreasea
Tradescantia
Zebrina

CONVOLVULACEAE

Morning Glory family: Twining herbaceous plants with large, funnel-shaped flowers.

Convolvulus
Dichondra
Ipomoea
Mina
Stictocardia

CRASSULACEAE

Plakkie family: Herbaceous succulent shrubs and shrublets from temperate regions. Certain species produce plantlets on the margins of their leaves.

Aeonium
Cotyledon
Crassula
Echeveria
Kalanchoe
Sedum
Tylecodon

CYPERACEAE

Reeds and Sedges: A large family of mainly perennial grass-like herbs often growing in swamps. Leaves are usually arranged in a tuft around the base of the stem.

Cyperus

ERICACEAE

Heath family: Hardwood shrubs with simple leaves and very showy flowers consisting of four or five united petals.

Erica
Kalmia
Rhododendron
(Azalea)

EUPHORBIACEAE

Euphorbia family: Mainly tropical shrubs, trees and herbaceous plants often with a milky juice (latex) which is poisonous. Flowers are regular, unisexual and the male and female may occur either on the same plant or on different plants. Some have colourful large bracts, as in poinsettias.

Acalypha
Aleurites
Breynia
Codiaeum
Euphorbia
Jatropha
Pedilanthus
Ricinus
Synadenium

FABACEAE (=Leguminosae) Subfam. Caesalpinioideae

Bauhinia family: Trees and shrubs with pinnate compound or simple bi-lobed leaves. Flowers are usually more or less zygomorphic, with five free-spreading petals. Fruit is a legume.

Bauhinia
Brownea
Caesalpinia
Cassia
Ceratonia
Cercis
Delonix
Gleditsia
Parkinsonia
Peltophorum
Saraca
Schotia

FABACEAE (=Leguminosae) Subfam. Faboideae (=Papilionoideae)

Pea family: Trees, shrubs, vines with pinnate compound leaves. Corolla consists of five petals – one large standard petal, two wing petals and two joined to form a keel. Fruit is a legume.

Bolusanthus
Calpurnia
Clitoria
Crotalaria
Cyclopia
Cytisus
Erythrina
Hardenbergia
Indigofera
Kennedia
Laburnum
Lathyrus
Lebeckia
Liparia
Lupinus
Mucuna
Phaseolus
Podalyria
Robinia
Sesbania
Spartium
Strongylodon
Sutherlandia
Tipuana
Trifolium
Ulex
Vicia
Virgilia
Wisteria

FABACEAE (=Leguminosae) Subfam. Mimosoideae

Acacia family: Trees and shrubs with pinnate compound leaves. The inflorescence is a rounded or elongated head of small sessile flowers.

Acacia
Calliandra
Dichrostachys
Mimosa

FUMARIACEAE

Dicentra family: Perennials with swollen, corm-like stocks. The flowers have an unusual and complex structure, often heart-shaped or one-spurred.

Dicentra

GERANIACEAE

'Malva' family: Herbaceous shrublets easily cultivated from cuttings. Leaves are aromatic; flowers, in umbels, are colourful and showy. Fruit is in the shape of a crane's bill.

Geranium
Pelargonium

GESNERIACEAE

Saintpaulia family: Mainly moisture and shade-loving herbaceous plants suitable for indoor conditions. Flowers are brightly coloured.

Achimenes
Columnea
Episcia
Kohleria
Saintpaulia
Sinningia
Streptocarpus

IRIDACEAE

Iris family: Herbaceous plants with corms, bulbs or rhizomes. Leaves are flattened, usually in two ranks, with parallel venation. Petals are arranged in two whorls of three each; three stamens.

Anomalesia
Antholyza
Aristea
Babiana
Chasmanthe
Crocosmia
Dierama
Dietes
Freesia
Geissorhiza
Gladiolus
Homeria
Homoglossum
Iris
Ixia
Lapeirousia
Moraea
Neomarica
Nivenia
Romulea
Schizostylis
Sparaxis
Tigridia
Tritonia
Watsonia

LAMIACEAE (=Labiatae)

Salvia family: Herbaceous and woody shrubs with opposite, aromatic leaves on square stems. Corolla of five united petals, usually two-lipped.

Ajuga
Coleus
Hemizygia
Iboza
Lavandula
Leonotis
Molucella
Monarda
Nepeta
Orthosiphon
Phlomis
Physostegia
Plectranthus
Pycnostachys
Rosmarinus
Salvia
Solenostemon
Stachys
Syncolostemon
Thorncroftia

LILIACEAE

Lily family: Bulbous herbaceous plants but tree-like in some aloes. Flowers are regular and the floral parts are in 'threes'; superior ovary; the fruit is a capsule.

Agapanthus
Albuca
Allium
Aloe
Asparagus
Aspidistra
Bulbine
Bulbinella
Chlorophytum
Dracaena
Endymion
Eucomis
Galtonia
Gasteria
Gloriosa
Haworthia
Hemerocallis
Hosta
Hyacinthus
Kniphofia
Lachenalia
Lilium
Liriope
Littonia
Muscari
Ornithogalum
Ruscus
Sandersonia
Sansevieria
Scilla
Tulbaghia
Tulipa
Veltheimia

LYTHRACEAE

Cuphea family: Herbaceous shrubs with tubular flowers.

Cuphea
Lagerstroemia

MALVACEAE

Hibiscus family: Herbaceous and woody shrubs and trees from temperate regions. Flowers are brightly coloured and widely bell-shaped. Characteristically, the stamens are united into a tube and the style is branched.

Abutilon
Alcea
Anisodontea
Hibiscus
Lagunaria
Lavatera
Malvastrum
Malvaviscus

MARANTACEAE

Arrow root family: Popular indoor tuberous plants with leaves beautifully patterned either with stripes or dark blotches.

Calathea
Maranta

MELASTOMATACEAE

Tibouchina family: Mostly tropical shrubs or trees, some of them herbaceous. Flowers are showy and the stamen filaments are elbow-shaped with sterile appendages.

Centradenia
Dissotis
Melastoma
Tibouchina

MESEMBRYANTHEMACEAE

Vygie family: Herbaceous or woody shrubs and succulents with nearly daisy-like flowers that have many petals and stamens. Flowers open in hot, sunny conditions and close at night.

Carpanthea
Carpobrotus
Cephalophyllum
Cheiridopsis
Conicosia
Conophytum
Dorotheanthus
Dracophilus
Drosanthemum
Faucaria
Fenestraria
Frithia
Glottiphyllum
Herreanthus
Lampranthus
Lithops
Pleiospilos
Sceletium
Semnanthe

MYRTACEAE

Blue gum family: Woody shrubs and trees from the tropics and subtropics. It is the colourful multiple stamens that make the inflorescence a showy one. The inflorescence is often referred to as a 'bottlebrush'.

Callisternon
Chamelaucium
Eucalyptus
Feijoa
Leptospermum
Melaleuca
Metrosideros
Myrtus
Psidium
Syzygium
Thryptomene

NYCTAGINACEAE

Bougainvillea family: Woody climbers from warm areas. Flowers are without petals and sub-tended by brightly coloured bracts.

Bougainvillea
Mirabilis
Pisonia

NYMPHAEACEAE

Water-lily family: Aquatic plants with large floating leaves and large, showy flowers that develop from a submerged rootstock.

Nelumbo
Nymphaea

OLEACEAE

Olive family: Trees, shrubs and climbers from tropical and temperate areas. Flowers are often insignificant, but sometimes showy and fragrant, as in jasmine.

Forsythia
Jasminum
Ligustrum
Syringa

ONAGRACEAE

Fuchsia family: Herbaceous and somewhat woody shrubs with very showy flowers, often hanging.

Clarkia
Fuchsia
Gaura
Oenothera

ORCHIDACEAE

Orchid family: Mostly epiphytic herbaceous plants with thick, fleshy stems. The lovely flowers have three sepals and three petals which differ notably in form — the petals form a lip or pouch. Stamens and pistils are united into a column.

Ansellia
Cattleya
Cymbidium
Dendrobium
Disa
Epidendrum
Eulophia
Odontoglossum
Paphiopedilum
Phalaeonopsis
Pterygodium
Satyrium
Vanda

OXALIDACEAE

Wood sorrel family: Tropical and subtropical annual and perennial herbaceous plants, often bulbous or tuberous. Leaves characteristically palmately compound and, in oxalis, fold downward at night and in cold weather.

Oxalis

PAPAVERACEAE

Poppy family: Mostly herbaceous annuals that have regular showy open flowers consisting of four free petals which soon fall off; there are numerous stamens and the fruit is a large capsule with special pores or valves. Coloured juice often present.

Argemone
Eschscholzia
Hunnemannia
Papaver

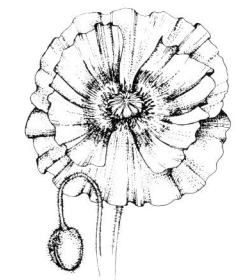

PASSIFLORACEAE

Granadilla family: Woody twiners and climbers from the tropics with simple tendrils and extraordinarily showy flowers that are referred to as passion flowers, symbolizing the crucifixion.

Passiflora

PLUMBAGINACEAE

Leadwort family: Herbaceous and slightly woody shrubs with delicate showy flowers.

Armeria
Ceratostigma
Limonium
Plumbago

POACEAE (=Gramineae)

Grass family: Leaves are parallel-veined and stems often sprout from an underground rhizome; stems have distinct nodes and internodes. The inflorescence consists of numerous spikelets.

Arundinaria
Arundo
Bambusa
Cortaderia
Miscanthus
Pennisetum
Phalaris
Rhynchelytrum

POLEMONIACEAE

Phlox family: Annual and perennial herbaceous and woody plants with brightly coloured showy, five-lobed flowers.

Cantua
Cobaea
Ipomopsis
Phlox

POLYGALACEAE

False legume family: Herbaceous plants, shrubs or small trees; inflorescence is a raceme or spike; the corolla consists of five free petals, but usually only three are present (the lowest and the two upper). The median anterior petal is keel-like and often fimbriate at the apex.

Nylandtia
Polygala

POLYPODIACEAE

Common fern family: Ferns without trunks belong to this family. Non-flowering plants that reproduce by means of spores carried in sori on the lower surface of the leaves. Leaves are often pinnate.

Asplenium
Cyrtomium
Davallia
Nephrolepis
Pellaea
Platycerium
Polypodium
Pteris
Rumohra

PORTULACACEAE

Portulaca family: Succulent herbaceous plants with short-lived colourful flowers.

Portulaca
Portulacaria

PRIMULACEAE

Primula family: Herbaceous annuals from cooler parts. Flowers are regular, five-petallate and showy.

Cyclamen
Lysimachia
Primula

PROTEACEAE

Protea family: A prominent family from the southern hemisphere. Most are trees or shrubs with flowers mainly in showy heads with a ring of colourful bracts. Flowers are normally bisexual but sometimes male and female flowers are on separate plants. The style is long and terminal, often bent inwards. The fruit is a follicle, drupe or nut.

Banksia
Grevillea
Leucadendron
Leucospermum
Mimetes
Orothamnus
Protea
Serruria
Stenocarpus
Telopea

RANUNCULACEAE

Buttercup family: Herbaceous annuals, biennials and perennials from cold climates, many of which are popular garden plants found worldwide.

Aconitum
Anemone
Aquilegia
Clematis
Consolida
Delphinium
Helleborus
Nigella
Ranunculus
Thalictrum

RESTIONACEAE

Reed family: Reed-like plants mostly from the southern hemisphere and concentrated in South Africa. They grow in clumps and the stems are green, long and wiry without functional leaf blades. Male and female flowers are on separate plants and arranged in spikes sub-tended by a large, brownish, sheath-like spathe. Reeds are used to thatch roofs.

Chondropetalum
Elegia
Willdenowia

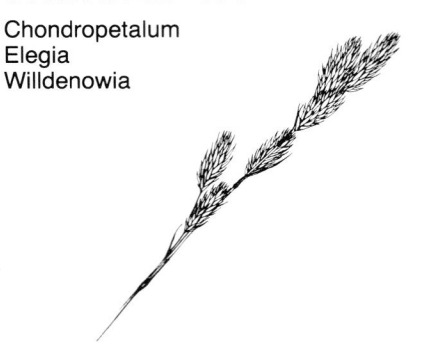

ROSACEAE

Rose family: Mostly woody shrubs and trees including the very popular garden roses and many fruit trees such as peaches, plums, pears and apricots. Flowers are characterized by being open and having numerous stamens.

Aruncus
Chaenomeles
Cliffortia
Cotoneaster
Crataegus
Duchesnea
Grielum
Kerria
Photinia
Potentilla
Prunus
Pyracantha
Raphiolepis
Rosa
Spiraea

RUBIACEAE

Coffee family: Mostly tropical shrubs and trees. Leaves are opposite and the presence of stipules is particularly characteristic. Flowers are borne in panicles or cymes or in heads with four or five fused petals.

Alberta
Burchellia
Coffea
Coprosma
Gardenia
Hamelia
Hoffmannia
Ixora
Luculia
Manettia
Mussaenda
Pavetta
Pentas
Rondeletia
Rothmannia
Warszewiczia

SAXIFRAGACEAE

Saxifraga family: Cool-climate shrubs or herbaceous indoor plants with showy foliage. Flowers of many species are showy and fragrant.

Astilbe
Bergenia
Deutzia
Escallonia
Hydrangea
Philadelphus
Saxifraga

SCROPHULARIACEAE

Antirrhinum family: Herbaceous ornamentals, and a few shrubs and climbers, which come from temperate climates of the northern hemisphere. The flowers are brightly coloured and two-lipped.

Antirrhinum
Asarina
Calceolaria
Diascia
Digitalis
Freylinia
Halleria
Hebe
Linaria
Mimulus
Nemesia
Penstemon
Phygelius
Russelia
Sutera
Torenia
Verbascum
Vernonia

SOLANACEAE

Potato family: A cosmopolitan family of herbs and a few shrubs, trees and vines. Flowers are regular and composed of five sepals and five petals variously fused and making the corolla bell-shaped or tubular. An economically important family.

Browallia
Brugmansia
Brunfelsia
Capsicum
Cestrum
Cyphomandra
Fabiana
Jochroma
Nicotiana
Nierembergia
Petunia
Physalis
Salpiglossus
Schizanthus
Solandra
Solanum
Streptosolen

STRELITZIACEAE

Bird of Paradise family: Herbaceous or tree-like genera in this family that is related to the banana. Stems are formed by the sheathing leaf bases. Leaves grow in two ranks with a thick midrib and long petioles. Flowers are irregular, very showy and borne in long-stalked cincinni (a scorpioid cyme) enclosed in a large, boat-shaped bract.

Heliconia
Ravenala
Strelitzia

TROPAEOLACEAE

Nasturtium family: Fast-growing, soft herbaceous plants often climbing or twining. Flowers are brightly coloured and showy, with one sepal forming a long nectar spur.

Tropaeolum

VERBENACEAE

Verbena family: Herbaceous plants, shrubs, trees and climbers mostly from the tropics and subtropics with their leaves opposite. Flowers are irregular and arranged in racemose or cymose inflorescences. Corolla is tubular and four to five-lobed.

Aloysia
Callicarpa
Caryopteris
Citharexylum
Clerodendrum
Duranta
Holmskioldia
Lantana
Petrea
Verbena
Vitex

VIOLACEAE

Violet family: Perennial (rarely annual) shrubs and small herbaceous ornamental plants including violets and pansies. Showy flowers with one petal spurred.

Viola

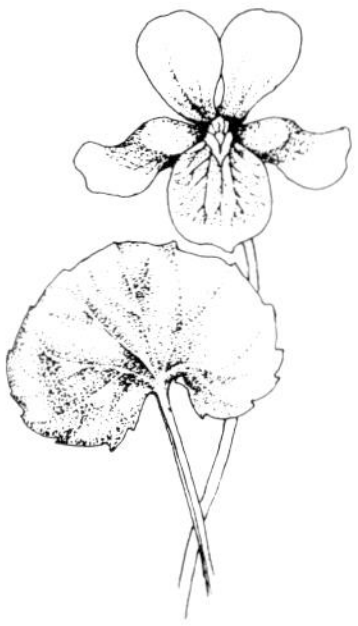

VITACEAE

Grape family: Mostly woody vines with branched tendrils. Leaves are simple or compound and often have exceptionally bright autumn colouring. Flowers are insignificant.

Cissus
Cyphostemma
Parthenocissus
Rhoicissus

ZINGIBERACEAE

Ginger family: Tropical rhizomatic herbs with cane-like stems and irregular flowers with a unique and complicated structure, usually showy.

Alpinia
Hedychium

BIBLIOGRAPHY

Adamson, R.S. & Salter, T.M. 1950. *Flora of the Cape Peninsula*. Juta, Cape Town.
Bailey, L.H. 1976. *Hortus Third*. Macmillan, New York.
Baker, H.A. & Oliver, E.G.H. 1977. *Ericas in Southern Africa*. Purnell, Cape Town.
Botanical Research Institute, 1982 & 1983. Numerical List of Species in the National Herbarium, Pretoria.
Coates Palgrave, K. 1981. *Trees of Southern Africa*. Struik, Cape Town.
Court, D. 1981. *Succulent flora of Southern Africa*. A.A. Balkema, Cape Town.
Dyer, R.A. 1975. *The genera of Southern African flowering plants*. Vol. 1. Dicotyledons. Dept. of Agric. Tech. Services, Pretoria.
Dyer, R.A. 1976. *The genera of Southern African flowering plants*. Vol. 2. Gymnosperms and Monocotyledons. Dept. of Agric. Tech. Services, Pretoria.
Graf, A.B. 1978. *Tropica*. Roehrs Co., New Jersey.
Heywood, V.H. Ed. 1978. *Flowering plants of the world*. Oxford, Oxford University Press.
Hunt, P. 1970. *Encyclopedia of gardening. 1-84*. Marshall Cavendish, London.
Kruger, T.J. 1973. *Bome, struike en rankplante*. Kruger, Ermelo.
Sheat, W.G. 1982. *The A-Z of gardening in South Africa*. Struik, Cape Town.
Vogts, M. 1982. *Suid-Afrika se Proteaceae*. Struik, Cape Town.

Abelia floribunda

ABELIA
Caprifoliaceae

A genus of deciduous or evergreen flowering shrubs native to Asia and Mexico, abelias are useful, popular ornamentals which are grown as specimen shrubs for their graceful habit, glossy foliage and sprays of white, pink or mauve flowers which have colourful sepals that remain on the plants after the blossoms fall. The flowers of several species have a warm, light fragrance which is particularly noticeable on still summer evenings. Abelias can be trimmed to make a stout hedge, and an attractive one too, for the new growth in many species is a rich, reddish-bronze. These are tough, adaptable plants that are drought, wind, and often frost resistant, and will grow in full sun or semi-shade. Propagate by cuttings.

Abelia floribunda   Mexico
Mexican abelia
Evergreen shrub to 3 m with drooping sprays of small, rosy pink flowers in summer. The persistent calyces are brick-red, and the foliage turns a bronzy shade in winter, making this a most colourful shrub for many months of the year.

A. floribunda 'Francis Mason'

A. x grandiflora

A. floribunda 'Francis Mason'
A striking, bright yellow variegated leaf form of the above.

A. x grandiflora   Garden hybrid
Glossy abelia
Evergreen shrub to 2 m; small white flowers tinged with pink in summer, with persistent, purplish sepals.

ABUTILON

Abutilon megapotamicum 'Variegata'

A. pictum

A. x *hybridum*

A. pictum 'Thompsonii'

ACACIA

Acacia ataxacantha

A. baileyana

ABUTILON
Malvaceae

A genus of perennials, soft-wooded shrubs, and occasionally annuals, of widespread distribution found in the warmer regions of the world. Abutilons are grown for their lovely, drooping, lantern-like flowers in shades of red, orange, pink, yellow and white, often netted and veined in darker colours, and sometimes with showy protruding stamens. In warm climates these plants bloom throughout all but the coldest months of the year. Abutilons need protection from the wind and do well planted against a sunny wall. Grow in enriched soil, and prune these somewhat lanky plants regularly and heavily.

Abutilon x hybridum — Garden hybrid
Chinese lantern
Soft-wooded shrubs to 3 m; flowers in various shades and patterns in summer.

A. megapotamicum 'Variegata' — Brazil
Chinese lantern
Shrub to 2 m with flowers resembling fuchsias with red calyces, yellow petals and purplish, protruding stamen columns. Can be grown indoors in cold climates as a hanging basket plant.

A. pictum — Brazil
Flowering maple
Shrub or small tree to 5 m with maple-like leaves and yellow or orange flowers veined crimson, in summer.

A. pictum 'Thompsonii' — Garden origin
As above, with leaves marbled gold.

ACACIA
Fabaceae (=Leguminosae) Subfam. Mimosoideae

A large genus of quick-growing and often very ornamental trees and shrubs native to the dry tropical and temperate regions of the world. Form and habit vary tremendously, as do the shape and colour of the leaves, but all species bear minute yellow or creamy flowers clustered together in fluffy balls or spikes. These are very decorative and usually sweetly scented. Most acacias are drought resistant and will grow in any soil.

Acacia ataxacantha — Southern Africa
Flame acacia or Vlamdoring
Shrub or small tree to 10 m which bears cream flower spikes in late summer. Young fruit pods are flaming red, fading to brown.

A. baileyana — Australia
Bailey's wattle
Spreading, ornamental evergreen tree to 10 m or more, with most attractive fern-like foliage. Masses of bright yellow flowers like little balls are carried in decorative sprays in winter.

CONTINUED

ACACIA

A. caffra

A. cyclops

A. podalyriifolia

A. cultriformis

A. karroo

A. robusta

A. saligna

A. caffra   Transvaal, Natal, Eastern Cape
Common hook-thorn or Haakdoring
Tree up to 12 m; bark is dark brown to black. Flowers are produced on creamy-white spikes in spring.

A. cultriformis   New South Wales
Knife-leaf wattle
Small tree seldom higher than 3 to 3,5 m. Leaves are grey-green, 10 to 20 mm long, triangular and with a firm texture. Yellow flowers in small balls are borne in masses in spring.

A. cyclops   Australia
Rooikrans
Large shrub or small tree to 5 m. It is identifiable by the twisted, flattened seed pods and especially the bright red seed stalk encircling the seed in the pod (hence the common name, rooikrans, meaning red-rimmed). *Acacia cyclops* has become a serious pest plant and has spread along almost the entire coastline of the Cape Province as well as inland, suppressing and replacing the indigenous vegetation. Like the Port Jackson willow, this acacia should not be cultivated as it seeds itself freely.

A. karroo   Southern Africa
Sweet thorn or Soetdoring
Tree to 15 m bearing golden yellow, strongly sweet-scented flowers in profusion during the summer months. The long, silvery white thorns are also decorative. This fast-growing tree has many uses: the foliage, flowers and seed pods are eaten by stock, the large quantities of nectar and pollen make it a good 'bee tree', the bark has several uses, and the wood is hard and heavy. *Acacia karroo* is protected in the northern Cape and parts of the Orange Free State.

A. podalyriifolia   Australia
Pearl acacia
Quick-growing ornamental shrub or tree reaching 4 m with most attractive silvery leaves and sprays of fragrant yellow flowers in winter and early spring. Unfortunately these very showy trees tend to become top-heavy in good soil and blow over easily, so either plant in a protected spot or be prepared to stake in areas where strong winds blow.

A. robusta   Southern Africa
Splendid acacia or Enkeldoring
Flat-topped tree to 25.m. Bears white flowers during winter and spring.

A. saligna   Australia
Port Jackson willow
Shrub to small tree, introduced from Australia where it is known as weeping wattle. *Acacia saligna* has become a serious

A. schweinfurthii

A. xanthophloea

A. terminalis

Acalypha hispida

pest plant, especially in the south-western Cape where it invades and suppresses the indigenous flora. As it seeds itself freely, it is difficult to eradicate and should not be cultivated.

A. schweinfurthii　　　Southern Africa
🌸🌱🌳
River climbing acacia or Rivierrankdoring
Shrub or small spreading tree, but most frequently a climber. Flowers, as white or pale cream balls, are borne in summer.

A. terminalis　　　Australia
(*A. elata*)
🌸🌱🌳☀🌊
Cedar wattle
This tree is quick growing to 20 m. It produces pale yellow flower balls in summer.

A. xanthophloea
🌱🌊🌳☀🌸　　East and south-east Africa
Fever tree or Koorsboom
Well-shaped tree to 15 m. Characteristic of the bark is its pale green-yellow colour. Yellow flower balls are borne in spring.

ACALYPHA
Euphorbiaceae

A large genus of highly ornamental shrubs, and occasionally annuals and trees, native to the tropical and subtropical regions of the world, acalyphas are grown for their colourful, decorative foliage. They are particularly striking when grown in full sun against a white wall. Although acalyphas are adaptable plants, and fairly wind and drought resistant, for best results plant them in good soil and water regularly. Prune in early spring and propagate from cuttings in autumn.

Acalypha hispida　　　New Guinea, Malaysia
🌱🌳☀🌸🌊
Chenille plant or Red-hot cat's tail
Shrub to 5 m in its natural habitat, usually to 2 m in cultivation. This is the only species bearing flowers of note; produced in summer, these hang in showy, drooping spikes of red or purple up to 500 mm long.

CONTINUED

ACALYPHA

A. wilkesiana 'Godseffiana'

A. wilkesiana 'Macrophylla'

A. wilkesiana 'Marginata'

A. wilkesiana 'Obovata'

A. wilkesiana 'Tricolor'

A. wilkesiana 'Godseffiana'	South Pacific
A. wilkesiana 'Macrophylla'	
A. wilkesiana 'Marginata'	
A. wilkesiana 'Obovata'	
A. wilkesiana 'Tricolor'	

Copperleaf, Beefsteak plant or Fijian firebush

Shrubs to 15 m in their natural habitat, usually to 2 m in cultivation, these are grown for their magnificently showy foliage.

ACANTHUS

Acanthus mollis

Acanthaceae

A genus of perennials and sub-shrubs native to the Mediterranean region and extending into tropical and subtropical Africa and Asia, of which one species, *Acanthus mollis*, is widely cultivated.

Acanthus mollis — Southern Europe

Bear's breeches, Wild rhubarb or Artist's acanthus

These are large perennials with tall flower spikes to 2 m high. The dark green, glossy leaves are large and decorative, and inspired notable ornamental features in Greek and Roman art and architecture. The striking flower spikes bear white, creamy-grey and purple-flushed flowers in spring and summer. These handsome plants do best in full shade or filtered sunlight, and in rich, well-drained soil, with ample water. Once established, however, they will withstand considerable neglect and adverse conditions. Propagate by seeds or division of the clumps in spring.

ACHILLEA

Achillea millefolium 'Rosea'

ACHIMENES

Achimenes grandiflora

ACOKANTHERA

Acokanthera oblongifolia

A. oblongifolia (fruit)

ACHILLEA
Asteraceae (=Compositae)

A genus of usually aromatic, herbaceous perennials native to the northern temperate regions, with daisy-like flowers in white, pink or yellow. These are useful plants as ground covers or for borders and rock gardens, growing in any soil in full sun, flowering throughout spring and summer. Easily propagated by division or by seed. The name is from Achilles, Greek hero of the Iliad who supposedly used the plant to heal his wounds.

Achillea millefolium 'Rosea'   Europe, Western Asia
Yarrow or Milfoil
Aromatic perennial to 1 m; pink flowers in spring and summer. Dried leaves and flowers have been used medicinally.

ACHIMENES
Gesneriaceae

Showy, deciduous, herbaceous perennials native to Central America and Jamaica, these are greenhouse plants which make good stoep plants in warm areas, being particularly suited to hanging baskets where their glossy leaves and brightly coloured funnel-shaped flowers are shown to advantage. Grow in light, well-drained soil and water regularly. The name is from the Greek *cheimaino*, to suffer from the cold.

Achimenes grandiflora   Central America
Hot water plant
Stems to 500 mm long; reddish-purple flowers in summer.

ACOKANTHERA
Apocynaceae

A genus of shrubs and small trees native to Arabia and east and southern Africa with several species indigenous to South Africa. Grown as ornamentals for their handsome, leathery, dark green foliage and fragrant white to pink flowers, it should be borne in mind that most species are extremely poisonous in all, or some of their parts. The sap, rendered down to a sticky gum, was used by the Bushmen as a quick-acting, deadly poison to tip their arrows.

Acokanthera oblongifolia   Eastern Cape, Natal, Transvaal and Swaziland
Bushman poison tree, African winter sweet or Gifboom
Poisonous, evergreen shrub or small tree to 7 m, occasionally more. All parts of this easily grown plant are potentially poisonous. Leaves are a glossy dark green and the fragrant flowers, which appear in spring, are white, or slightly flushed with pink. These are followed by purplish-black shiny berries, which are at their most toxic when unripe. For this reason, it is wise to prune this shrub immediately after flowering, to prevent fruit forming.

ACRIDOCARPUS

Acridocarpus natalitius

ADENANDRA

Adenandra fragrans

A. uniflora

ADENIUM

Adenium boehmianum

A. multiflorum

ACRIDOCARPUS
Malpighiaceae

A genus of about 30 species found mainly in tropical and subtropical Africa, with one species in Madagascar, one in New Caledonia in the Pacific, and one indigenous to South Africa, *Acridocarpus natalitius*. It is the fruit which gives the plant both its generic and common name; it is a winged nut which resembles a dark reddish-brown moth. Acridocarpus is from the Greek *akris*, grasshopper and *karpos*, fruit.

Acridocarpus natalitius — Transkei and Natal coastal belt, into Southern Moçambique
Moth fruit or Feather climber
An evergreen scrambling shrub, becoming a strong climber under forest conditions, and occasionally growing into a small tree up to 5 m in height. In its natural habitat, it grows in riverine bush, along forest margins and in moist kloofs. Leaves are green and leathery, and the striking flowers are a deep, rich yellow, carried in sturdy spikes. Easily grown from seed or cuttings, this plant is believed to have magical powers by the people of its native habitat.

ADENANDRA
Rutaceae

A genus of small indigenous evergreen shrubs with a neat habit and tiny aromatic leaves. In winter and spring they bear most attractive, glossy pink, red or white flowers which look like fine porcelain. These plants are often found growing in the mountains, and need regular water, well-drained soil and full sun, making them ideal plants for the rock garden. Propagate by seed but be prepared to wait a few years for the flowers, as the plants are slow growing.

Adenandra fragrans — South-western Cape
Anysboegoe
A neat little shrub bearing pink flowers in spring.

A. uniflora — South-western Cape
China flower or Betsie
Shrub 0,5 to 1 m. White flowers striped with pink, from mid-winter to early summer. This plant needs water in winter, and well-drained soil. It does well in a rockery.

ADENIUM
Apocynaceae

A genus of strange-looking, deciduous, succulent shrubs with smooth, fleshy, swollen stems and branches, native to tropical Africa, Arabia and Socotra, with four species indigenous to the hottest parts of South Africa. The starry flowers appear in masses after the leaves have fallen, completely transforming the appearance of the plant. Carried in clusters at the tips of the branches, the flowers are white, edged with crimson and very striking. Suitable only for hot areas, these extremely drought-resistant, slow-growing plants should be planted in well-drained soil and full sun. The name is from Aden, home of some species.

Adenium boehmianum — Namibia
Impala lily
Long-tubed flowers with light pink petals and deep pink throats; flowers in autumn.

ADIANTUM

AECHMEA

A. obesum

Adiantum capillus-veneris

Aechmea fasciata

A. raddianum

A. fulgens var. *discolor*

A. multiflorum East Africa, Transvaal lowveld, Zululand
(*Adenium obesum* var. *multiflorum*)
Impala lily or Sabie star
Shrub to 1,5 m; white starry flowers with bright, cerise-pink margins, borne in winter and spring.

A. obesum East Africa, Southern Arabia
The corolla lobes are downy, bright cerise at the margins, fading to pink towards the centre; lobes are rounded terminally with a short sharp point. Winter flowering.

ADIANTUM
Adiantaceae

A large genus of dainty ferns of widespread distribution, but mainly from tropical America. Most often grown as indoor plants, and particularly attractive in hanging baskets, the delicate and graceful maidenhair ferns have fine, wiry black, purple or bronze stems and sprays of tiny flat leaflets, like pale green confetti.

Adiantum capillus-veneris All tropical regions of the world
Maidenhair or Venus-hair fern
Height and spread to 300 mm.

A. raddianum Brazil
Maidenhair fern
Height and spread to 450 mm. This is the maidenhair fern used by florists.

AECHMEA
Bromeliaceae

Evergreen epiphytes from tropical America normally grown as house plants and in greenhouses for their unusual foliage and showy inflorescences. Leaves are arranged in a rosette and shaped to capture and hold water.

Aechmea fasciata Brazil
Vase plant or Urn plant

A. fulgens var. discolor Brazil
Coral berry

23

AEONIUM AGAPANTHUS

Aeonium arboreum

Agapanthus africanus

A. caulescens subsp. *angustifolius*

A. arboreum 'Atropurpureum'

A. campanulatus subsp. *campanulatus*

A. inapertus subsp. *hollandii*

AEONIUM
Crassulaceae

This is a genus of herbaceous succulents and sub-shrubs from Madeira, the Canary Islands and adjacent North Africa, well suited to hot, dry conditions. The glossy green leaves are carried in rosettes at the end of the branches. Small flowers which are usually yellow, but also pink or white, are carried in dense showy pyramidal spikes. Grow these tough, wind-resistant plants in full sun and well-drained soil.

Aeonium arboreum Morocco
Shrub to 1 m, with green foliage and yellow flowers in spring.

A. arboreum 'Atropurpureum' Morocco
Shrub to 1 m; leaves purple, and yellow flowers in spring.

AGAPANTHUS
Liliaceae

A genus of indigenous rhizomatous perennials bearing large heads of blue flowers above clumps of strap-like leaves in summer. These useful and popular plants will grow almost anywhere, but in order to flower well they need adequate water. The name is from the Greek *agape*, love and *anthos*, flower. Propagate by division of the clumps.

Agapanthus africanus Southern Africa
A. campanulatus subsp. *campanulatus*
A. caulescens subsp. *angustifolius*
A. inapertus subsp. *hollandii*
A. inapertus subsp. *pendulus*
A. orientalis 'Albidus'
A. orientalis 'Nanus'
A. praecox

A. inapertus subsp. *pendulus*

AGATHOSMA

AGAVE

A. orientalis 'Albidus'

Agathosma ovata

Agave americana

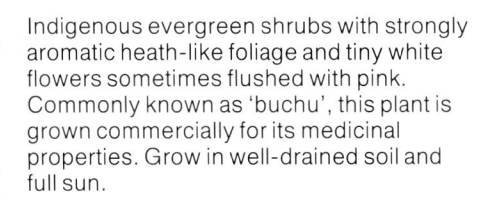

A. orientalis 'Nanus'

A. americana 'Marginata'

A. praecox

AGATHOSMA
Rutaceae

Indigenous evergreen shrubs with strongly aromatic heath-like foliage and tiny white flowers sometimes flushed with pink. Commonly known as 'buchu', this plant is grown commercially for its medicinal properties. Grow in well-drained soil and full sun.

Agathosma ovata South-western Cape
Buchu or Boegoe
Shrub to 1,75 m, flowering in spring.

AGAVE
Agavaceae

A genus of large, sculptured, evergreen succulents with rosettes of long, fleshy, sword-shaped leaves, tipped and edged with wicked spines. Native to the Americas but naturalized in other parts of the world, including South Africa. Most species are slow growing and, having taken a number of years to reach the flowering stage, flower once and die. However, numerous offsets are produced to form new plants.

Agave americana Mexico
Century plant or Garingboom
Large ornamental succulent with grey-green leaves up to 2 m long forming huge clumps, and flower spikes up to 10 m high. Although the common name suggests that these plants take a hundred years to come into bloom, this is not quite so, ten years being nearer the mark.

A. americana 'Marginata' Mexico
Century plant or Bontblaargaringboom
Succulent, leaves to 2 m edged with yellow; flower spikes to 10 m.

CONTINUED

AGAVE

A. attenuata

A. parryi

AGERATUM

Ageratum houstonianum

AGLAONEMA

Aglaonema commutatum 'Pseudobracteatum'

A. crispum 'Malay Beauty'

A. attenuata — Mexico
Succulent to 1 m; drooping flower spikes to 4 m.

A. parryi — Mexico
Stemless, leafy rosette; leaves 300 mm long and 100 mm wide with a terminal spine. Inflorescence nearly 3 mm high. Flowers red in bud and creamy-yellow when open.

AGERATUM
Asteraceae (= Compositae)

The soft, misty-blue ageratums belong to a genus of annuals and shrubs native to Central and South America and the West Indies. Only the annual species are commonly cultivated. These are useful in the mixed border or for bedding, while the dwarf, compact cultivars are ideal for carpeting, edging and window-boxes. Grow in ordinary garden soil and full sun.

Ageratum houstonianum — Mexico
Floss flower or Pussyfoot
Annual to 300 mm with fluffy flower heads of powder blue or bluish-mauve flowers in spring and summer. A white-flowered cultivar exists.

AGLAONEMA
Araceae

These are evergreen perennials from tropical Asia bearing flowers similar to arum lilies although less showy. These plants are grown chiefly for their foliage which is often attractively mottled with green and gold. Usually greenhouse plants, they can be grown on stoeps out of direct sunlight in warm areas.

Aglaonema commutatum
'Pseudobracteatum' — Philippine Islands
Glossy, lance-shaped leaves, 300 mm long, green with patches of white and grey-green. Also known as the cv. 'White Rajah'.

A. crispum 'Malay Beauty' — Philippine Islands
Painted drop-tongue
Height to 1 m. Yellowish-green leaves.

A. crispum 'Parrot Jungle' — Philippine Islands
As above but leaves are wider and margins wavy; midrib dark green.

AJUGA

ALBERTA

A. crispum 'Parrot Jungle'

Ajuga reptans

Alberta magna

A. crispum 'Silver King'

A. reptans 'Atropurpurea'

A. magna

A. crispum 'Silver King'   Philippine Islands
As above but leaves are narrow, creamy-yellow with green patches.

AJUGA
Lamiaceae (=Labiatae)

Creeping perennials which make a dense and attractive ground cover. Ajugas spread by runners and are easy to propagate by division. They need regular water and good drainage.

Ajuga reptans   Europe
Carpet bugle
Ground cover with dainty spikes of blue flowers to 100 mm in early summer. These will flower under trees in filtered shade, making a sheet of intense blue that is most effective when the plants are grown beneath flowering shrubs and trees which bloom at the same time.

A. reptans 'Atropurpurea'   Europe
Carpet bugle
As above, with bronzy-purple leaves and dark purple flowers.

ALBERTA
Rubiaceae

A small genus of evergreen trees and shrubs found in Madagascar except for one species, *Alberta magna,* which is indigenous to South Africa and a protected plant.

Alberta magna   Transkei, Natal, Zululand
Natal flame tree, Breekhout or Natalvlamboom
A slow-growing tree to 13 m with glossy dark green leaves that show off the striking scarlet flowers which appear in the spring. The flowers have showy, brilliant red bracts which remain long after the flowers themselves have fallen, making the tree most ornamental for many months. A good tree for small gardens at the coast, it does not thrive inland.

ALBUCA

Albuca altissima

A. cooperi

Albuca species

ALBUCA
Liliaceae

A genus of bulbs native to Africa and Arabia but which are mainly indigenous to South Africa. Usually fragrant, yellow, green or white flowers are carried in loose spikes above the leaves that are normally strap-shaped. However, one species, *Albuca spiralis,* has leaves that coil like springs in a most attractive and charming fashion, making the plant worth growing for this alone. These are not the showiest of our bulbs but nevertheless worth a place in the garden as a contrast to more brilliant flowers. Furthermore, once well established they will withstand considerable neglect. The flowers have an unusual shape. Three of the petals point forward forming a tube, while the other three point outwards, thus making these plants easily identifiable.

Albuca altissima South-western Cape
Slymstok or Kamiemie
Bulb to 1 m. Flower is white with a green stripe, up to 25 mm long and borne in spring.

A. cooperi South-western Cape
Geldbeursie or Blougif
Perennial bulb with spikes of green, yellow and white flowers, to 500 mm high in the spring.

Albuca species South-western Cape
Bulb to 1,5 m; white flowers with dark green stripes are borne in spring.

ALCEA

Alcea rosea

ALCEA
Malvaceae

A genus of mostly biennials, or short-lived perennials, native to the Mediterranean regions and Central Asia, these are the popular hollyhocks. Their tall flower spikes bear double or single flowers in warm shades of red, pink, purple, apricot, white and yellow. All that these tough, adaptable plants need is protection from the wind; grow them at the back of a sheltered border, among shrubs in a protected corner, or against a wall. For windy gardens there are dwarf cultivars that do not need staking. Grow in full sun and ordinary garden soil, watering regularly.

Alcea rosea
(Althea rosea)
Hollyhock or Stokroos
Biennial with flower spikes to 3 m in summer.

ALEURITES

Aleurites fordii

ALLAMANDA

Allamanda cathartica 'Hendersonii'

A. neriifolia

ALLIUM

Allium christophii

ALEURITES
Euphorbiaceae

A genus of six species from the tropics, these are mostly trees with latices. Aleurites are grown mainly for their seeds which yield valuable oils but they are also useful for shade. Propagate from seed and hardwood cuttings.

Aleurites fordii   Asia
Tung-oil tree
Tree to 12 m, usually less in cultivation. Flowers 30 mm across, are white with red veins at the base of the petals. This tree is the source of tung-oil and an excellent specimen tree.

ALLAMANDA
Apocynaceae

A genus of evergreen sprawling, climbing shrubs, native to tropical America. Allamandas thrive in rich, damp soil in warm climates. Grown for their funnel-shaped yellow or purple flowers, they also make a luxuriant cover for walls and stout fences.

Allamanda cathartica 'Hendersonii'   South America, Guyana
Golden trumpet vine
Vigorous, fast-growing, climbing or sprawling shrub to 3 m with large yellow trumpet-shaped flowers up to 120 mm across in summer.

A. neriifolia   Brazil
Golden trumpet bush
Sprawling shrub to 1,5 m. The yellow flowers, streaked with orange in the throat, are profusely borne in summer.

ALLIUM
Liliaceae

A large genus of rhizomatous or bulbous plants, of widespread distribution in the northern hemisphere, includes onions and garlic which are strongly odorous when bruised. There are a number of highly ornamental species producing large round heads of flowers in a wide range of bright colours, including many pinks, blues, yellows and whites. Alliums are easy to grow, requiring ordinary garden soil which should be well drained. Most species thrive in full sun.

Allium christophii   Asia Minor, Iran
Stars-of-Persia
Umbels of starry lilac flowers to 750 mm high in summer.

ALOCASIA

Alocasia sanderana

A. cuprea

ALOCASIA
Araceae

A genus of rhizomatous perennials from tropical Asia grown for their large ornamental leaves which are often variegated. The flowers resemble those of arum lilies and although not very colourful, are ornamental and unusual, and ideal for sophisticated flower arrangements. Some species have delightfully fragrant flowers. Alocasias are usually grown in greenhouses, but will grow outdoors in warm subtropical gardens, where they need a damp, shady spot.

Alocasia cuprea   Borneo
Giant caladium
Leaves are up to 450 mm long and 300 mm wide, the upper surface an iridescent purple or pale green with darkly marked veins, the lower surface purplish-red. The summer flowers have a purplish tube and a green spathe.

A. macrorhiza   East Indies
Elephant's ear, Giant alocasia or Olifantsoor
Huge perennial; leaves to 2 m long. Yellow-green flowers in summer.

A. macrorhiza

A. sanderana   Philippine Islands
Large greenish-black leaves with a metallic sheen, silvery veins and margins, and purple undersides. Flower spathes, creamy-white, up to 100 mm long, appear in summer.

ALOE

Aloe arborescens

A. ciliaris

ALOE
Liliaceae

Striking indigenous ornamental plants native to Asia, but chiefly Africa. Aloes range from small trees and large, sprawling shrubs, to miniature perennials suitable for the smallest patio or courtyard. Although they will survive long droughts and grow in poor soil, aloes flower best when given reasonably good soil and water at the

A. distans

Aloe hybrid

A. ferox

A. plicatilis

A. reynoldsii

correct time. Excellent accent plants, they are ideal for rockeries and are useful for dry, windy corners of large gardens.

Aloe arborescens Southern Africa, widespread
This species is most variable, depending on locality, although usually it is seen as a dense, shrubby bush to 3 m. Sickle-shaped leaves are carried in large rosettes. Flowers, usually red, sometimes yellow or orange, appear in winter.

A. ciliaris Eastern Cape
Climbing aloe or Klimaalwyn
Fast-growing climber to 5 m; does well against a fence. It flowers all year round.

A. distans South-western Cape, near Saldanha Bay
Jewelled aloe
Up to 1 m. Best in a glasshouse if grown outside its natural environment.

A. ferox Cape Province, Lesotho, Natal
Bitter aloe, Bergaalwyn or Bitteraalwyn
Single stem, densely covered in old dead leaves. Late summer flowering. Flowering season extremely variable because it is widespread over so many different climatic areas.

Aloe hybrid South Africa
Many aloes hybridize in nature when they grow and flower together. Most hybrids are hardy, drought resistant and sun-loving.

A. plicatilis South-western Cape mountains
Fan aloe, Bergaalwyn, Tongaalwyn or Waaieraalwyn
Average height 2,5 m but it may reach 4,5 m. Easily recognized by its pleated, fan-like leaves at the end of the branches. Spring flowering.

A. reynoldsii Transkei
Height to 450 mm. Leaves are 'H'-spotted and the very slender, branched inflorescences carry yellow flowers.

CONTINUED

ALOE

A. striata

A. variegata

A. thorncroftii

A. striata — Southern and eastern Cape
Good garden aloe up to 1 m with attractive foliage. Winter/spring flowering.

A. thorncroftii — Eastern Transvaal mountains
Very decorative; grows and flowers well in cultivation. Spring flowering.

A. variegata — Cape, Orange Free State, Southern and south-western Africa
Partridge aloe, Kanniedood or Bontaalwyn Small aloe to 250 mm. Leaves spotted white. Does well in cultivation in a well-drained spot. It requires only small amounts of water. Winter/spring flowering.

A. wickensii — Northern Transvaal
Stemless or short-stemmed plant forming large clumps of leaves to 1,5 m high. Buds are red but flowers are yellow, giving a bi-coloured effect. Easily grown in cultivation. Winter flowering.

N.B. Aloes are protected plants in all provinces and may not be picked or dug up from the veld.

A. wickensii

ALOYSIA

Aloysia triphylla

ALOYSIA
Verbenaceae

Lemon-scented verbena is the most commonly cultivated species in this genus of aromatic shrubs native to the warm parts of the Americas.

Aloysia triphylla — South America
Lemon verbena
Shrub to 3 m, grown chiefly for the delightful lemon scent of its leaves when crushed. This is a good plant to grow next to a stoep, path, or gateway where the scent may be enjoyed by passers-by. Tiny blue-white flowers are carried on dainty spikes in summer. This shrub will grow in all but the coldest climates, and in any soil. It has an untidy habit and needs regular trimming. This provides an opportunity to collect the leaves, dry them, and use them in pot-pourri, or for making refreshingly scented sachets.

ALPINIA

Alpinia purpurata

A. zerumbet

ALSOPHILA

Alsophila dregei

ALPINIA
Zingiberaceae

A large genus of perennials from tropical Asia grown for their showy inflorescences and striking foliage, alpinias are best suited to warm subtropical regions; elsewhere, they are best treated as greenhouse plants. Alpinias need rich soil, semi-shade, and ample water in the growing period; after flowering, the plants should be cut back to ground level and water withheld during winter. Propagate by division.

Alpinia purpurata Pacific Islands

Red ginger or Rooigemmer
Perennial to 5 m, forming large leafy clumps. The showy, sometimes drooping flower spikes are up to 1 m long and consist of small white flowers enclosed in brilliant red bracts. These appear in summer. This plant reproduces itself in an unusual way; small plantlets appear between the flower bracts and as the flower dies, the stem droops to the ground, enabling the new plants to take root.

A. zerumbet East Asia

Shell flower, Shell ginger, Pink porcelain lily or Skulpgemmer
Perennial to 4 m, with drooping flower spikes of white, waxy, pink-flushed bracts which enclose fragrant red, yellow and brown variegated flowers. This is a slightly hardier species than most alpinias.

ALSOPHILA
Cyatheaceae

A large genus of mostly tropical evergreen tree ferns with a number of strictly protected species indigenous to South Africa. They make handsome ornamentals with their large, arching fronds carried at the tops of sturdy trunks.

Alsophila dregei Tropical Africa

Common tree fern or Boomvaring
Specimen tree to 5 m. Found in shady kloofs or along the banks of streams in nature, these are well suited to waterside planting in the garden. This fern is now known as *Cyathea dregei*.

ALSTROEMERIA

Alstroemeria aurantiaca

A. psittacina

ALSTROEMERIA
Alstroemeriaceae

Quick-spreading, fibrous-rooted perennials from South America which bear spikes of showy, trumpet-shaped flowers in shades of red, violet, yellow and white throughout the summer months. Grown outdoors in rich, moist soil and semi-shade in warm climates, alstroemerias can also be grown in greenhouses. Propagate by seed or division, but do not disturb unnecessarily.

Alstroemeria aurantiaca Chile

Peruvian lily or Chilean lily
Summer-flowering perennial to 1 m. Flowers in the species are orange and yellow, spotted and streaked with dark red; a number of cultivars include shades of white, pink, yellow and brick-red.

A. psittacina

As above, but flowers are pink-yellow with dark purple dots.

ALTERNANTHERA

Alternanthera ficoidea 'Bettzickiana'

ALTERNANTHERA
Amaranthaceae

The cultivated species in this large genus of cosmopolitan distribution are grown as neat, evergreen, perennial ground covers with attractively variegated foliage, usually in shades of pink, yellow and green. Widely used in formal bedding schemes, they make good edging plants and are ideal for rockery pockets or small containers on sunny stoeps and patios. Grow in good soil in full sun and propagate by cuttings or division. Trim the plants regularly to keep them neat and tidy.

Alternanthera ficoidea 'Bettzickiana'
Central and South America
Calico plant, Joseph's coat or Joyweed
Ground cover to 250 mm.

AMARANTHUS

Amaranthus caudatus

A. tricolor 'Splendens'

AMARANTHUS
Amaranthaceae

A cosmopolitan genus of coarse annuals, including a number of weeds and a few species used as food plants in Asia, garden amaranthus are grown for their brightly coloured leaves and to a lesser extent their flowers. Useful in the shrub or mixed border, these plants do not require good soil; in fact leaf colours are brighter when the plants are grown in poorer soil. Grow in full sun. Propagate from seed.

Amaranthus caudatus Tropical regions

Love-lies-bleeding
Up to 1,75 m long; drooping or erect spikes of red flowers appear in summer.

A. tricolor 'Splendens' Tropical regions

Joseph's coat
Height 1,25 m. Leaves dark red, with lighter, brilliant red leaves at the tips of the shoots. Foliage plant.

AMARYLLIS

Amaryllis belladonna

AMMI

Ammi majus

ANCHUSA

Anchusa capensis

AMARYLLIS
Amarylidaceae

There is one species in this genus, the spectacular *Amaryllis belladonna*, indigenous to the winter rainfall areas of the western Cape.

Amaryllis belladonna Western Cape
🅕 ⊛ ☼
March lily or Belladonna lily
Bulb to 750 mm. Large clusters of strongly sweet-scented, pale to dark pink, trumpet-shaped flowers up to 90 mm across and 120 mm long are carried on dark red stems which appear out of the bare earth, before the leaves, in late summer. However, amaryllis do not flower regularly each year. In their natural habitat, the loveliness of the flowers is enhanced by the fact that they often appear against a background of sun-scorched vegetation and dry earth. Plant the bulbs in mid-summer, before the flowers appear, and water regularly until the leaves start to die down, then withhold water until the flower buds appear. Soil should be enriched and well drained.

AMMI
Apiaceae (=Umbelliferae)

A small genus of perennials, native to the Mediterranean regions, Chile and Brazil, of which only one, *Ammi majus,* is commonly cultivated, usually as an annual.

Ammi majus Mediterranean regions
⊛ ☼
Queen Anne's lace or Lace plant
Annual to 750 mm grown for its flat, dainty, lacy heads of tiny white flowers which are most decorative and widely used by florists. Foliage is fine and feathery. Very useful in the mixed border where the delicate flowers contrast well with bolder, brighter blooms. Grow in ordinary garden soil in full sun.

ANCHUSA
Boraginaceae

A genus of coarse annuals and perennials native to Europe, Asia Minor and Africa, these quick-growing perennials are best treated as annuals. Useful for their rich blue colouring, anchusas grow easily in well-drained garden soil and full sun.

Anchusa capensis Cape Province,
🅕 ⊛ ☼ Lesotho, Orange Free State
Cape forget-me-not
Biennial best treated as an annual. Bright blue flowers to 600 mm in spring. This is one of two indigenous species.

ANEMONE

Anemone coronaria

ANIGOZANTHOS

Anigozanthos flavidus

ANISODONTEA

Anisodontea scabrosa

A. x hybrida

ANEMONE
Ranunculaceae

This is a genus of perennials native to the northern temperate regions, some of which, including the popular spring-flowering *Anemone coronaria,* are tuberous-rooted. Anemones are grown for their showy flowers in shades of blue, red, white and a wide range of pinks. The name is from the Greek *anemos,* meaning wind, and *mone,* meaning habitation.

Anemone coronaria Mediterranean region
Poppy anemone
Height 200 mm. Tuberous plants with showy red, white and blue spring flowers, widely planted as a spring 'bulb'.

A. x hybrida Garden hybrid

ANIGOZANTHOS
Haemodoraceae

A genus of tall, evergreen, drought-resistant perennials from south-western Australia, with sword-shaped leaves and strange red, purple, green or yellowish flowers. Grow in well-drained soil in full or semi-shade. Propagate by root division.

Anigozanthos flavidus Western Australia
Kangaroo paw
Perennial to 1,5 m, with greenish-yellow flowers in spring.

ANISODONTEA
Malvaceae

A genus of indigenous evergreen soft-wooded shrubs and perennials belonging to the same family as hibiscus and bearing flowers which look like miniature hibiscus flowers, in shades of red, pink and yellow. None are especially showy, but are suitable for the herbaceous border, or for containers on patios and stoeps. They grow in ordinary garden soil, need regular watering and occasional pruning.

Anisodontea scabrosa Southern and eastern Cape and Transkei
Mallow
Shrub to 2 m with pink flowers, petals marked with darker stripes appearing mainly in spring and summer; but in its natural habitat, it can be seen at other times of the year as well.

ANOMALESIA

Anomalesia cunonia

ANSELLIA

Ansellia gigantea var. *nilotica*

ANTHEMIS

Anthemis cupaniana

A. tinctoria

ANOMALESIA
Iridaceae

There are two species in this genus of indigenous cormous perennials found in the winter rainfall area of the Cape.

Anomalesia cunonia South-western Cape
Bright crimson flowers to 35 mm long carried on 450 mm stems. A mountain species, requiring enriched, well-drained soil.

ANSELLIA
Orchidaceae

A genus of epiphytic orchids from tropical Africa, the eastern Transvaal and Natal. Stems are cane-like and the leaves are two-ranked. The flowers are borne terminally in a long inflorescence and the sepals and petals are similar. Best suited for glasshouse conditions, these plants are the largest amongst the South African orchids.

Ansellia gigantea var. **nilotica** Natal, Eastern Transvaal
Easily grown on coarse bark but they need frequent water and food during the growing season. Yellow, brown-spotted flowers are borne on a branched spike in spring.

ANTHEMIS
Asteraceae (=Compositae)

From the Mediterranean regions and surrounding areas come these annual and perennial spreading plants which form dense clumps of feathery, aromatic leaves. The small, daisy-like flowers are profusely borne in summer and autumn. Easy to grow in any soil provided drainage is good, they are excellent for arrangements.

Anthemis cupaniana Italy
Camomile or Dog fennel
Aromatic, cushion-forming perennial growing to 1 m across and 200 mm high, with grey leaves and white flowers in summer.

A. tinctoria Mediterranean regions
Golden camomile
Bushy biennial to 1 m, golden yellow flowers in summer.

ANTHOLYZA   ANTHURIUM

Antholyza plicata

Anthurium andraeanum

A. scherzeranum

A. ringens

A. andraeanum 'Album'

ANTHOLYZA
Iridaceae

Formerly a genus containing many species, of which *Antholyza ringens* is one of the few remaining.

Antholyza plicata Namaqualand and South-western Cape
Cormous perennial to 450 mm. Red flowers up to 40 mm long with silvery bracts, in spring.

A. ringens South-western Cape coast
Rat's tail, Rotstert or Hanekam
Small bulbous plant with strongly ribbed leaves resembling those of *Babiana*. Scarlet flowers up to 40 mm long in spring. The inflorescence is interesting for the 'bird perch' which is provided to facilitate pollination.

ANTHURIUM
Araceae

A large genus of more than 600 species of perennial, often epiphytic plants, native to tropical America; anthuriums are evergreen greenhouse and indoor plants grown for their ornamental leaves and especially their highly glossy, showy and elegant flower spathes. Specialist advice on their growing requirements is recommended for the novice anthurium grower.

Anthurium andraeanum Colombia
Flamingo lily or Oilcloth flower
Perennial to 1 m; heart-shaped leaves. Brilliant, glossy scarlet flower spathes borne in spring.

A. andraeanum 'Album'
As above, but with milky white flower spathe.

A. crystallinum Colombia
Crystal anthurium
Height to 750 mm. Leaves netted with silvery veins. Green flower spathes in spring.

A. crystallinum

A. scherzeranum Guatemala, Costa Rica
Pigtail plant or Varkstertanthurium
Smaller plant to 300 mm. Spathe variable in colour with coiled spadix, hence the common name. It flowers all year round.

ANTIGONON

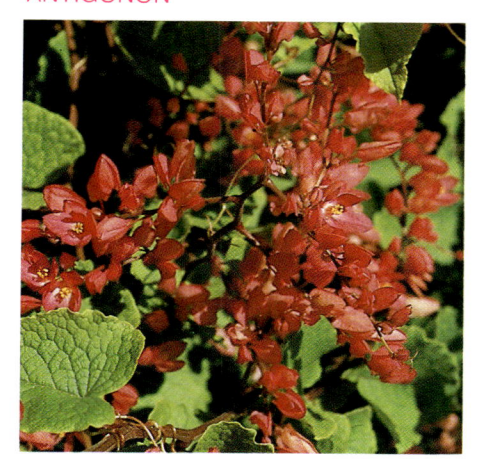

Antigonon leptopus

ANTIRRHINUM

Antirrhinum majus

APHELANDRA

Aphelandra squarrosa

ANTIGONON
Polygonaceae

There are only two or three species in this genus of fast-growing creepers from tropical Central America which are grown for their sprays of tiny pink, red, white or yellowish flowers. Easily grown in warm climates and doing well against a sunny wall in cooler ones, these climbers can be propagated from seeds or cuttings.

Antigonon leptopus   Mexico
Coral creeper or Koraalranker
Fast-growing, dainty and most showy creeper climbing by tendrils in its natural habitat, with masses of intensely pink flowers in summer. Ideal for patios and pergolas.

ANTIRRHINUM
Scrophulariaceae

A genus of annuals and perennials of widespread distribution of which one, *Antirrhinum majus,* the familiar snapdragon, is commonly cultivated as a garden annual. From the Greek *anti,* like, and *rhinos,* snout, referring to the shape of the flowers.

Antirrhinum majus   Mediterranean region
Snapdragon or Leeubekkie
Annuals, from dwarf varieties to 650 mm, in a wide range of colours from red through to yellow, white and mauve, which flower in winter and spring in warm climates, and in spring and summer in cooler ones.

APHELANDRA
Acanthaceae

Perennial evergreens from tropical America which make good stoep and greenhouse plants, with their striking ornamental leaves and showy spikes of sculptured-looking flowers in red, yellow and orange.

Aphelandra squarrosa   Brazil
Zebra plant or Saffron spike
Perennial to 1 m, bearing yellow flower spikes above dark green leaves broadly veined in silvery white, in summer.

APONOGETON

Aponogeton distachyos

A. junceus

AQUILEGIA

Aquilegia caerulea

ARBUTUS

Arbutus unedo

APONOGETON
Aponogetonaceae

A genus of aquatic tropical and subtropical perennials, several of which are indigenous to South Africa. Useful for ponds and water gardens.

Aponogeton distachyos   Western Cape
Cape pondweed, Water hawthorn or Waterblommetjie
Quick-growing aquatic plants with scented white flowers, the buds of which are used in traditional Cape stews. They have an unlimited spread over the surface of the water and produce flowers in winter and spring.

A. junceus   South Africa
Waterblommetjie
As above, but flowers less showy.

AQUILEGIA
Ranunculaceae

A genus of most attractive, dainty, delicate-looking perennials, native to the temperate regions of the northern hemisphere, often grown as annuals in South Africa. The blue-green lacy foliage resembles that of a maidenhair fern and the star-shaped, spurred flowers come in a wide range of colours, often bi-coloured. Grow them in light shade in rich, well-drained soil.

Aquilegia caerulea   Rocky Mountains of North America
Columbine
Perennial or annual to 0,75 m. Flowers, in a variety of colours, are borne in spring.

ARBUTUS
Ericaceae

Grown for their colourful fruit as well as their flowers, the evergreen shrubs and trees in this genus are native to western North America and the Mediterranean region. The bell-shaped flowers are white and pink, and the edible fruits are orange or red. Grow arbutus in well-drained soil and protect them from wind. Propagate from seeds or cuttings.

Arbutus unedo   Southern Europe, Ireland
Strawberry tree or Aarbeiboom
Slow-growing evergreen tree to 10 m, with glossy foliage and drooping sprays of tiny white or pinkish bell-shaped flowers borne in the autumn. These are followed by strawberry-like edible fruits which are yellow, orange and finally scarlet.

ARCHONTOPHOENIX

Archontophoenix cunninghamiana

ARCHONTOPHOENIX
Arecaceae (=Palmae)

A genus of two Australian feather palms, these are among the fastest growing of cultivated palms. The young plants make particularly good container subjects.

Archontophoenix cunninghamiana
Australia
King palm, Piccabeen palm or Koningspalm
Tall, straight trees to 20 m with lilac flowers borne in summer.

ARCTOTHECA

Arctotheca calendula

ARCTOTHECA
Asteraceae (=Compositae)

A genus of about six species in Africa and Australia, with four indigenous to South Africa. These are low-growing perennial, spreading plants which make good ground covers under adverse conditions but are not exactly showy, and are more commonly regarded as weeds than garden flowers, especially by farmers.

Arctotheca calendula   South-western Cape
Cape weed or Cape dandelion
Height up to 100 mm, spreading over 400 mm. A perennial with yellow daisy flowers that bloom all year round, depending on climate. Leaves are green with white undersides.

ARCTOTIS

Arctotis breviscapa

A. fastuosa

ARCTOTIS
Asteraceae (=Compositae)

A genus of annuals and perennials found growing wild from Africa to Australia, with a number of species indigenous to South Africa. The cultivated species usually have grey-green foliage and large daisy-like flowers up to 100 mm across. The flowers come in a wide range of colours in both bright and pastel shades. These plants will grow in poor soil, with regular water, full sun and good drainage being their most important requirements. These are ideal as rockery plants or as ground covers. Propagate by division, cuttings or seed; many species self-seed freely.

Arctotis breviscapa   Namaqualand, South-western Cape
Gousblom
Annual, orange flowers in spring.

A. fastuosa   Namaqualand, South-western Cape
Namakwaland gousblom or Bitter gousblom
Annual to 600 mm. Deep orange flowers, with dark brown rings at the base of the petals, are produced in spring.

CONTINUED

ARCTOTIS

A. hirsuta

A. stoechadifolia

A. hirsuta Namaqualand, South-western Cape
Gousblom
Annual to 400 mm. Flowers are white, yellow and orange and sometimes marked with purple at the base of the petals. Spring flowering.

A. stoechadifolia Namaqualand, South-western Cape
Trailing arctotis
Perennial, trailing plant. Dark pink flowers, reddish on the underside of the petals, are borne in spring.

ARDISIA
Myrsinaceae

Evergreen shrubs native to the tropical and subtropical regions of the world, except Africa. They grow in moist shady places outdoors, except in areas of heavy frost. Some species make attractive indoor plants.

Ardisia crispa Asia, from India to Japan
Coral Berry or Koraalbessie
Shrub to 1,5 m but very slow growing as a pot plant. Ardisias have a neat symmetrical habit, glossy, decorative foliage and clusters of delightfully fragrant white or pink flowers which are followed by shiny, brilliant red berries that remain on the plants for many months.

Ardisia crispa

ARGEMONE
Papaveraceae

A genus of annuals and perennials native to the Americas, grown as annuals in the garden. Most species have extremely prickly foliage and poppy-like flowers. They will grow in full sun and in any soil.

Argemone mexicana West Indies, Central America
Mexican poppy
Annual to 1 m, with attractive blue-grey leaves which are very prickly. The yellow poppy flowers bloom in spring and grow up to 60 mm across. Self-seeding and a *troublesome weed* in warm areas.

Argemone mexicana

ARISTEA

ARISTOLOCHIA

Aristea major

Aristolochia durior

A. elegans

A. gigantea

ARISTEA
Iridaceae

A genus of evergreen perennials native to tropical and southern Africa growing in large, leafy clumps and producing spikes of brilliant blue flowers. Grow in enriched soil and full sun. Once established, these plants do not readily recover from being moved. If they need to be divided, they must be kept moist throughout the transplanting process.

Aristea major   Western Cape
(*A. thyrsiflora*)
Tall aristea or Blou suurknol
Large clumps up to 2 m bearing 300 mm spikes of intensely blue star-shaped flowers. Can be grown as a waterside plant, or in full shade. They are spring/summer flowering.

ARISTOLOCHIA
Aristolochiaceae

A large genus of shrubs and climbers from the tropics bearing strangely shaped flowers in muted colours. They are outdoor plants in most climates, but need protection from frost. They require rich soil, high humidity and partial shade.

Aristolochia durior   North America
Dutchman's pipe
Quick-growing, deciduous woody climber to 10 m. Flowers are brownish-purple, shaped like curved pipes and appear in summer.

A. elegans   Brazil
Calico plant or Oupa-se-pyp
Creeper to 6 m. Fragrant reddish-purple flowers with white thread-like markings appear in summer.

A. gigantea   Brazil
Giant Dutchman's pipe or Reuse oupa-se-pyp
Creeper to 10 m with large heart-shaped leaves. Large bell-shaped, purple-red flowers up to 200 mm across and 300 mm long are borne in summer.

ARMERIA

Armeria maritima

ARUM

Arum palaestinum

ARUNCUS

Aruncus dioicus

ARMERIA
Plumbaginaceae

These perennial, evergreen, low-growing, tufted herbaceous plants are ideal as rockery specimens or as border plants. They will grow in any soil but flourish in a well-drained, sunny spot. Propagate by seed or division of the clumps.

Armeria maritima   Widespread
Thrift or Sea pink
Armeria maritima forms a dense little clump to 200 mm high; grassy leaves are 100 mm long; deep pink papery flowers grow in heads to 30 mm across in spring/summer.

ARUM
Araceae

Grown for its striking flowers and clumps of arrow-shaped and often variegated leaves, this small genus of tuberous perennials is native to Europe and Asia. It does not include the plant commonly referred to in South Africa as the arum lily, which belongs to the genus *Zantedeschia*. Grow arums in rich, moist soil and full shade. Propagate by offsets.

Arum palaestinum   Israel
Black calla, Solomon's lily or Jerusalem lily
Tuberous perennial to 375 mm, with flower spathes up to 200 mm long. Flowers are dark purple on the inner surface and green on the outer surface, with a purple-black spadix, making this a most unusual and striking inflorescence. Flowers are produced in spring.

ARUNCUS
Rosaceae

A small genus of tall perennials native to the northern hemisphere. Its broad, fern-like leaves are suitable for moist, shady places with rich soil. The name is said to come from a Greek word meaning goat's beard, which the plumes of the tiny creamy flowers resemble.

Aruncus dioicus   Europe, Asia,
(*A. sylvester*)   North America
Goat's beard
Perennial to 2 m with most attractive plumes of tiny, creamy-white flowers growing up to 400 mm long in summer.

ARUNDINARIA

Arundinaria disticha

A. variegata

ARUNDINARIA
Poaceae (=Gramineae)

Native to North America and Eastern and Southern Asia, these large, perennial woody grasses of rhizomatous habit thrive next to water but will grow very well elsewhere. Many of them are rampant growers, but the dwarf species are suitable for small gardens. Propagate by division. Arundinaria comes from the Latin *arundo,* meaning reed or cane.

Arundinaria disticha　　　　　　Japan
Dwarf fern-leaf bamboo
Dwarf foliage plant to 0,75 m. Leaves are bright green and stems are tinged with purple.

A. variegata　　　　　　　　　　Japan
Dwarf white-striped bamboo
Dwarf to 1 m with white-striped leaves.

ARUNDO

Arundo donax var. *versicolor*

ARUNDO
Poaceae (=Gramineae)

A small genus of tall perennial reeds native to the tropics and subtropics of Africa and Asia. They form large, leafy clumps, making striking accent plants for large gardens.

Arundo donax var. **versicolor**　　　Spain
(*A. donax* var. *variegata*)
Spanish reed, Giant reed or Spaansriet
Perennial grass to 6 m with leaves striped white. Graceful, feathery cream panicles are borne in autumn.

ASARINA

Asarina barclaiana

ASARINA
Scrophulariaceae

A small genus of climbing perennials native to North America and Europe, with showy flowers looking like snapdragons (antirrhinums) in shades of purple, blue, pink and white. Not very vigorous, these plants adapt well to hanging baskets and window-boxes.

Asarina barclaiana　　　　　　Mexico
(*Maurandia barclaiana*)
Summer-flowering creeper to 3 m with showy, mauve flowers which turn purple with age.

45

ASCLEPIAS

Asclepias fruticosa

A. physocarpa

ASCLEPIAS
Asclepiadaceae

A large genus of perennial plants of worldwide distribution, some of which are commonly regarded as weeds. Two species have unusual ornamental seed pods that are useful in flower arranging.

Asclepias fruticosa Southern Africa
Wild swans, Gansies or Milkweed
Spindly shrub to 2 m with ovoid seed pods of a clear, pale green, closely covered with prickles and narrowed and curved at the tip to give them the shape of a tiny swan. Pods are borne in autumn.

A. physocarpa Southern Africa
Wild cotton, Wildekapok or Milkweed
Spindly shrub to 2 m with rounded pale green, slightly prickly pods which burst open to reveal a mass of white silky threads. Pods appear in early summer.

ASPARAGUS

Asparagus aethiopicus

A. densiflorus

ASPARAGUS
Liliaceae

A large genus of evergreen perennials native to Africa and Asia. Mostly climbers and shrubs, many of them indigenous and often referred to as ferns, these plants are grown chiefly for their decorative foliage, although some species have attractive flowers and showy berries. Many species will grow in full or semi-shade as well as full sun, and make decorative house or stoep plants. Others are creepers, and some shrubby varieties, especially the spreading species, look good in rockeries as they add a leafy luxuriance. The delicious edible asparagus also belongs to this genus.

Asparagus aethiopicus Cape Province
Spreading shrub with dense, feathery foliage and pinkish-mauve flower spikes which appear almost all year round.

A. densiflorus Natal
A small, woody, erect bush to 750 mm; cladophylls are linear, flattened and three or more form at a node, giving the plant a compact appearance.

A. densiflorus 'Myers'

A. densiflorus 'Sprengeri'

A. densiflorus 'Myers' Natal
Asparagus fern, Plume asparagus, Foxtail fern or Katstert
Erect-growing form with foxtail-shaped fronds up to 450 mm long and 60 mm across. Foliage plant.

A. densiflorus 'Sprengeri' Natal
Emerald fern, Emerald feather or Basket asparagus
Graceful drooping stems up to 1 m long covered in fine, needle-like foliage. Popular for hanging baskets. Foliage plant. The generic name for South African species, *Asparagus*, has changed to *Protasparagus*.

ASPIDISTRA

Aspidistra elatior

ASPLENIUM

Asplenium nidus

ASTER

Aster novi-belgii

A. tradescantii

ASPIDISTRA
Liliaceae

A small genus of evergreen herbaceous plants native to Asia. Only one of these, *Aspidistra elatior*, is commonly grown as an indoor, shade or stoep plant.

Aspidistra elatior Japan
◉ ⊛ ✿ Ⓕ
Bar room plant, Parlour palm or Cast-iron plant
Clumps of tough, leathery leaves up to 200 mm across and 750 mm high which grow straight out of the soil. These plants will survive in the most unsuitable conditions, such as dark, sunless rooms, and they will endure considerable neglect; hence the name cast-iron plant. However, plant in good soil and water regularly for best results. Foliage plant.

ASPLENIUM
Polypodiaceae

A large genus of ferns of cosmopolitan distribution which can be grown outdoors, in greenhouses or as house plants.

Asplenium nidus Tropical Asia, Polynesia
⊛ ◉
Birds' nest fern or Voëlnesvaring
Fern to 1,25 m. Large, striking plants, their erect-flaring bright green fronds with wavy margins will grow 400 to 800 mm long in good conditions; width 100 to 200 mm.

ASTER
Asteraceae (=Compositae)

A very large genus of perennials, and occasionally annuals, biennials and shrubs of cosmopolitan distribution, ideal for growing in bold clumps in the mixed border. The daisy-like flowers are borne in dense spikes of varying height but can reach 1,5 m in good conditions. Colours range from white to every shade of purple, mauve, blue, pink and deep pink to crimson. Grow Michaelmas daisies in good garden soil and water well. Flowering season varies from mid-summer into winter. The rapidly increasing clumps are easily divided in autumn or spring.

Aster novi-belgii Temperate regions of
Ⓕ ⊛ ✿ ☼ the northern hemisphere
Michaelmas daisy, Star wort or Frost flower
Rhizomatous, summer and autumn-flowering perennial to 1,5 m with mauve to purple flowers to 50 mm across. This is the parent strain of most garden hybrids.

A. tradescantii North America
Ⓕ ⊛ ✿ ☼
Perennial to 1 m; white flowers, 150 mm across in summer.

47

ASTILBE

Astilbe japonica

ASTILBE
Saxifragaceae

Many of the original species in this genus have colourless, inconspicuous flowers, hence the name which comes from the Greek, meaning no brightness. However, numerous very showy cultivars have now been raised, and if conditions are right, they are well worth growing for their most attractive feathery plumes of minute flowers in white, pink and crimson. They need a cool, shady spot and deep, rich, moist soil, and can be grown next to water where their perennial, fern-like foliage is attractive all the year round. Astilbes are native to East Asia and North America.

Astilbe japonica — Japan
Goat's beard or Florist's spiraea
Height 600 mm; pink flowers in dainty, feathery spikes are borne in spring.

ASTROPHYTUM

Astrophytum myriostigma

ASTROPHYTUM
Cactaceae

Succulents with one globular, ridged stem which becomes cylindrical with age. The large yellow flowers are borne singly, although in a long succession. These plants need well-drained soil and a dry climate and can also be grown indoors very successfully.

Astrophytum myriostigma — Mexico
Bishop's cap
Succulent up to 600 mm, but usually only about 150 mm. The stem is in the shape of a bishop's mitre. Yellow fragrant flowers appear in spring.

ATHANASIA

Athanasia crithmifolia

A. parviflora

ATHANASIA
Asteraceae (=Compositae)

These are strongly aromatic indigenous shrubs, rather spindly in appearance and therefore best grown in clumps.

Athanasia crithmifolia — South-western Cape
Coulter bush or Klaaslouwbossie
Shrub to 1 m; grey-green foliage with yellow flowers arriving in spring.

A. parviflora — South-western Cape
Coulter bush or Kouterbossie
Quick-growing shrub reaching up to 3 m. Its tiny yellow flowers are carried in large, flat heads in late spring.

48

AUBRIETA

Aubrieta deltoidea

AUCUBA

Aucuba japonica 'Variegata'

AUBRIETA
Brassicaceae (=Cruciferae)

A small genus of mat-forming, creeping, evergreen perennials native to the mountainous regions from southern Europe to Asia Minor. Grown for their masses of colourful spring flowers, the dense, low-growing mounds of foliage make excellent ground covers, rockery plants, and edging plants for flowerbeds. Propagate from cuttings or seeds and trim after flowering. These are cool-climate plants, not suited to tropical and subtropical areas.

Aubrieta deltoidea Sicily, Greece, Asia Minor
Purple rock cress
A variable species usually about 150 mm high, sometimes to 300 mm. Rosy lilac to purple flowers appear in spring.

AUCUBA
Cornaceae

A small genus of hardy evergreen shrubs, native to temperate Asia from the Himalayas to Japan, which are grown for their ornamental foliage and colourful berries. Useful for growing in the shade under large trees, they need rich, moist and well-drained soil. Easily propagated from cuttings or seed. The name is from *aokiba,* the Japanese name for the plant.

Aucuba japonica 'Variegata' Garden origin
Gold-dust tree
Shrub to 3 m with large, yellow-spotted leaves.

BABIANA

Babiana disticha

B. stricta var. *stricta*

B. rubrocyanea

B. villosa

BABIANA
Iridaceae

Small, indigenous cormous plants bearing spikes of fragrant star-shaped flowers in a wide range of colours, although mostly blue, often with contrasting centres. Easily recognized by their strongly ribbed, slightly hairy leaves, these plants are ideal for rockery pockets, or other sunny spots. The name comes from the Afrikaans *bobbejaan*, baboon, a reference to the fact that baboons dig up and eat the corms.

Babiana disticha South-western Cape
Cormous herb to 300 mm in height. Flowers have light blue petals, yellow at the base.

B. rubrocyanea South-western Cape
Wine cup, Bobbejaantjie or Kelkiewyn
Small bulb to 200 mm. Flowers are intense blue with scarlet centre in spring.

B. stricta var. **stricta** South-western Cape
Bobbejaantjie
Slightly taller variety, with erect flower stalks and leaves spreading like a fan.

Flowers are variable, pale to deep blue or mauve and appear in spring.

B. villosa South-western Cape
Crimson babiana or Rooibobbejaantjie
Height to 250 mm; showy cup-shaped flowers, usually in shades of deep red with conspicuous black anthers, that appear in spring.

BAEOMETRA

Baeometra uniflora

BAEOMETRA
Liliaceae

Only one species, *Baeometra uniflora*, in this genus which is endemic to the south-western Cape.

Baeometra uniflora South-western Cape
A geophyte with an ovoid corm, 10 mm in diameter and covered by thin, brown tunics. Stems are solitary with sheathing leaves in two ranks. Inflorescence is a spike or raceme with erect flowers in spring. Petals are yellow inside, purple at the base and red or with a red streak outside. Plant them in a mass in clayish soil in a rockery pocket for a superb display.

BAMBUSA

Bambusa glaucescens

B. vulgaris

BAMBUSA
Poaceae (=Gramineae)

Tall, tropical grasses with graceful evergreen leaves, often variegated, forming large dense clumps. Easily propagated by clump division.

Bambusa glaucescens China
(*Bambusa multiplex*)

Hedge bamboo or Oriental hedge
Variable species reaching 3 m in height which makes them useful for hedges, ornamental planting and as pot plants. Leaves are green. Foliage plant.

B. vulgaris Tropics, worldwide

Common bamboo or Bamboes
Open clumps growing to 20 m high and up to 125 mm in diameter with fresh green leaves. Easily grown, they spread to form huge clumps; often used as a windbreak.

BANKSIA

Banksia ericifolia

BANKSIA
Proteaceae

Evergreen flowering shrubs and small trees mostly indigenous to Australia, banksias bear striking, large, dense flower spikes in shades of red and yellow. As members of the protea family they need similar growing conditions and climate. They were named in honour of Sir Joseph Banks, 1743-1820, a patron of natural history.

Banksia ericifolia Australia

Shrub or small tree to 5 m bearing golden yellow flower spikes up to 250 mm long in springtime.

B. integrifolia Australia

Tree to 10 m; pale yellow flower spikes 150 mm long are borne in spring.

B. serrata Australia

Tree to 3 m; flower spikes to 150 mm long, with blue-grey flowers at first, later yellowish, borne in summer.

CONTINUED

BANKSIA

B. integrifolia

B. serrata

BARLERIA

Barleria obtusa

B. repens 'Rosea'

BARLERIA
Acanthaceae

A genus of evergreen tropical and subtropical shrubs with blue, white or red flowers. The one most commonly found in South African gardens is the indigenous *Barleria obtusa*.

Barleria obtusa Subtropical regions of Eastern Cape, Natal and Transvaal
Bush violet or Bosviooltjie
Small herbaceous shrubs growing to 1 m with an equal spread, bearing masses of violet-blue flowers in autumn. This blue contrasts well with the tints of autumn leaves and berries and is intensified if the shrubs are planted in semi-shade. This useful plant seeds itself easily and may also be grown from cuttings.

B. repens 'Rosea' Garden origin
Small herbaceous shrub growing to 500 mm, bearing rose-pink flowers.

BAUHINIA

Bauhinia blakeana

B. galpinii

BAUHINIA
Fabaceae (=Leguminosae) Subfam. Caesalpinioideae

Spectacularly showy flowering trees. Large orchid-like flowers massed on bare branches in spring characterize this genus of trees, shrubs and creepers which are widespread in the warm, temperate and tropical regions of the world. The leaves are distinctive, two-lobed, almost butterfly-shaped in some species. Quick growing, adaptable to most climates except extremes of heat and frost, bauhinias will grow in most garden soils.

Bauhinia blakeana China
Evergreen tree to 13 m but usually nearer 3 m, bearing purple flowers in winter up to 150 mm across. This is the only bauhinia that does not set seed and must be propagated vegetatively. It is thought that all cultivated plants originated from a single tree, possibly a hybrid, found in the province of Canton, China.

BEAUMONTIA

B. variegata

Beaumontia grandiflora

B. purpurea

B. galpinii   Zululand, Transvaal, Zimbabwean and East African lowveld
Pride-of-de-Kaap or Vlam-van-die-Vlakte
Rambling, spreading shrub, occasionally a spreading small tree, 3 to 5 m high. Flowers are bright salmon-pink to bright brick-red. The flowering season is variable from summer to late autumn.

B. purpurea   India to Malaysia
Butterfly tree, Orchid tree or Orgideëboom
Tree to 10 m, occasionally higher. Flowers range in shades of mauve and purple, borne in spring.

B. variegata   India, China
Orchid tree
Tree to 10 m. The flowers, which grow to 120 mm across, are found in shades of purple, pink and white and are produced in spring.

B. variegata 'Candida'   India, China
As above, but with pure white flowers in spring.

B. variegata 'Candida'

BEAUMONTIA
Apocynaceae

Large woody evergreen vines that are tender to frost and need good, deep soil. Prune immediately after flowering.

Beaumontia grandiflora   Himalayas
Nepal trumpet flower or Herald's trumpet
A climber to 3 m bearing fragrant white trumpet-shaped flowers up to 100 mm long and 100 mm across which appear in spring.

BEGONIA

Begonia caffra

B. dregei

B. masoniana

B. coccinea

B. x elatior

B. rex-cultorum

BEGONIA
Begoniaceae

This huge genus of over 1 000 species has given rise to over 10 000 recorded hybrids. This gives some idea of the popularity and variety of these plants. Begonias can be broadly divided into bedding plants, indoor plants and foliage plants, but many species are suitable for all three uses. Bedding begonias are valued for their profusion of flowers borne for months at a time; the indoor begonias are known for their large, exquisite flowers, while the foliage plants have asymmetrical leaves in a wonderful variety of shapes and colours. Some begonias have specialized requirements and specialist advice is recommended.

Begonia caffra — Subtropical forests of Transvaal, Natal
A vigorous, fibrous-rooted perennial to 700 mm. Foliage plant.

B. x semperflorens-cultorum

B. coccinea — Brazil
Angel-wing begonia
Fibrous-rooted, herbaceous plants sending up cane-like stems to 1 m; leaves up to 150 mm long with wavy red margins. Drooping red flowers bloom in summer.

B. dregei — Subtropical forests of Transvaal, Natal, Eastern Cape
A very showy foliage plant to 300 mm. Leaves are glossy green, ovate and asymmetrical; the lower parts of the veins are purplish-red.

B. x elatior — Garden hybrid
Tuberous-rooted plant; suitable for indoor culture as well as outdoors. Its flowering season is variable. Height variable.

B. masoniana — China
Iron cross plant or Ysterkruisbegonia
Foliage plant; variable in height and spread with variegated leaves to 100 mm across.

B. rex-cultorum — Garden origin
Rex begonia or Koningsbegonia
A common rhizomatous, this very attractive foliage begonia is of complex hybrid origin. Leaves are mostly obliquely ovate, zoned, marbled, blotched or spotted in various patterns of green, purple, red, brown, grey or silver. Rex begonias need rich, well-drained soil and glasshouse conditions.

B. x *tuberhybrida*

Bellis perennis

B. x *tuberhybrida* 'Pendula'

Berberis thunbergii 'Atropurpurea'

B. x semperflorens-cultorum
Garden hybrid
Bedding begonia, Wax begonia or Wasbegonia
Bushy plants with mottled and variegated foliage and profusely borne flowers. This species makes excellent bedding plants for sun or shade, yet equally good indoor plants. Flowering is variable over many months of the year.

B. x tuberhybrida
Garden hybrid
Knolbegonia
Tuberous begonias; a large and variable species, some of which can be planted outdoors for summer flowering, although indoors the flowering is variable.

B. x tuberhybrida 'Pendula'
Garden hybrid
As above, but with pendent flowers.

BELLIS
Asteraceae (=Compositae)

Herbaceous perennial daisies usually grown as annuals or biennials. Useful small bedding or edging plants because they send up large double daisy flowers in all shades of pink and white from a neat rosette of green leaves. They grow in full sun or semi-shade in many South African gardens, and tend to seed themselves well.

Bellis perennis
Britain
English daisy, Bachelor's button or Engelse madeliefie
Neat plants bearing spring flowers in pink and white to 150 mm. Considered a weed in Europe and North America.

BERBERIS
Berberidaceae

From *berberys*, the Arabic name. This is a genus of deciduous or evergreen spiny shrubs useful for small hedges as well as specimen bushes because of their attractive spring flowers, autumn fruits, and the often unusual brilliant autumn colouring of their leaves.

Berberis thunbergii 'Atropurpurea'
Japan
Barberry or Japanese barberry
Deciduous, dense, compact and most ornamental shrubs which grow to 1,5 m with dark purple leaves, turning brilliant scarlet in autumn. Will grow in semi-shade.

BERGENIA

Bergenia cordifolia

BERZELIA

Berzelia lanuginosa

BESCHORNERIA

Beschorneria yuccoides

BERGENIA
Saxifragaceae

A genus of herbaceous perennials native to temperate Asia, forming large clumps and usually grown as ground covers. They are evergreen in most areas and adaptable to semi-shade. Bergenias send up spikes of pink or white flowers which are useful as cut flowers, especially as they often appear in winter although the flowering season varies according to climate. Propagate by division of the clumps; feed and water well for best results.

Bergenia cordifolia Siberia, Mongolia

Ground cover with large leaves up to 200 mm long; pink flowers on spikes to 300 mm long which are borne in early spring.

BERZELIA
Bruniaceae

Evergreen indigenous shrubs with fine feathery leaves and clusters of creamy-white, tiny, fluffy pompom flowers at the tips of the branches. A marsh or stream-side plant, its presence is considered to be an indication of perennial water in its natural habitat. However, it does not necessarily have to be planted near water in the garden as long as it is well watered.

Berzelia lanuginosa Southern and western Cape

Kolkol or Vleiknopbos

Shrub to 2 m with needle-like foliage and showy creamy-white to yellow pompom flowers borne on dense spikes in spring/summer.

BESCHORNERIA
Agavaceae

A small genus of evergreen rhizomatous perennials with fleshy, sword-shaped leaves forming stemless rosettes from which arise flower spikes with colourful bracts and rather dull-coloured flowers. Native to Mexico, these plants need well-drained soil and full sun. Propagate from offsets.

Beschorneria yuccoides Mexico

Evergreen to 2 m, with much-branched flower spikes in summer, carrying green tubular flowers to 50 mm long, with showy, bright red flower bracts.

BETULA

Betula pendula

BETULA
Betulaceae

Graceful, most ornamental deciduous trees with attractively coloured bark in some species. Foliage is pale green turning to a clear yellow in autumn. Native to the colder regions of the world, they are not suited to warm climates but make ideal specimen trees in areas where they will grow.

Betula pendula Europe and Asia Minor
Silver birch or Silwerberk
Ornamental tree growing to 20 m with drooping branches and white bark flaking off in layers. Catkins are borne in spring.

BIDENS

Bidens formosa

B. sulphureus

BIDENS
Asteraceae (=Compositae)

Free-flowering annuals up to 1 m. Flowers are mostly in shades of pink, red or white and foliage is fine and feathery. Easily grown from seed sown *in situ*, it is frequently seen as a roadside weed in warmer areas. The common name comes from the Greek, *kosmos*, meaning beautiful.

Bidens formosa Mexico
(*Cosmos bipinnatus*)
Cosmos or Kosmos
Annual to 1 m. Pink, red and white flowers appear in spring/summer.

B. sulphureus Mexico
Annual to 1 m. Orange-yellow flowers are produced in spring/summer.

BIGNONIA

Bignonia capreolata

BIGNONIA
Bignoniaceae

Only one species, *Bignonia capreolata*, a woody, evergreen climber, is left in this once large genus.

Bignonia capreolata Eastern North America
Cross vine, Trumpet flower or Trompetblom
Vigorous climber to 12 m. Leaflets are ovate; tendrils are branched; funnel-shaped flowers are yellow and brown-red growing to 50 mm long in spring.

BILLBERGIA

Billbergia nutans

B. pyramidalis

BIXA

Bixa orellana

B. orellana (fruit)

BOLUSANTHUS

Bolusanthus speciosus

BILLBERGIA
Bromeliaceae

A genus of stemless epiphytic plants as easily grown out of doors as inside. They vary in their requirements according to species.

Billbergia nutans — Brazil
Friendship plant or Queen's tears
If grown indoors, this plant needs strong light; outdoors, filtered sun. Leaves grow to 450 mm and flower spikes to 300 mm. The drooping, summer-flowering bracts are bright rose. Flowers have yellowish-green, blue-edged petals. They are lovely as cut flowers.

B. pyramidalis — Brazil
Very showy. Leaves to 1 m. Flower spikes are a dense pyramid of red flowers tipped with violet and blue stigmas that are produced in spring/summer.

BIXA
Bixaceae

There is only one species in this genus, *Bixa orellana*.

Bixa orellana — Tropical America
Lipstick plant or Annatto tree
Shrub or small tree to 3 m; evergreen. Its large leaves grow to 180 mm. Pink flowers, borne in summer, are followed by ornamental red spiny fruits.

BOLUSANTHUS
Fabaceae (=Leguminosae) Subfam. Faboideae (=Papilionoideae)

Only one species in this genus, the indigenous *Bolusanthus speciosus*. Named in honour of Harry Bolus, 1834-1911, a famous South African amateur botanist.

Bolusanthus speciosus — Hot regions of Transvaal, Swaziland and Moçambique
Tree wistaria, Elephant's wood or Van Wyk's hout
Handsome deciduous tree with gracefully arching and drooping branches bearing 150 mm long sprays of purple pea-flowers, resembling those of wistaria in the spring. It reaches 12 m in its natural habitat but is slow growing and seldom reaches 10 m in gardens. *Bolusanthus* will grow in areas of frost if well protected.

BOOPHANE

Boophane disticha

B. disticha

BOOPHANE
Amaryllidaceae

Indigenous bulbs best left undisturbed once established. The bulbs are large, reaching a diameter of 300 mm, although usually about 200 mm, and said to be poisonous to cattle; hence the common name in Afrikaans. The correct pronunciation is in four syllables: Bo-oph-an-e.

Boophane disticha All provinces of South Africa except south-western Cape
Fan-leaved boophane, Red posy or Gifbol
Bulb to 300 mm. Wine-red, lily-like flowers are borne in spring in a globe-shaped umbel up to 180 mm across. After the flowers die, the leaves appear in a neat, decorative fan. In some climates the flowers have an unforgettable, bittersweet fragrance. These bulbs need good drainage, especially in winter rainfall areas where they also need summer watering.

BOUGAINVILLEA

Bougainvillea x buttiana 'David Lemmer'

B. x buttiana 'Lady Mary Baring'

B. x buttiana 'Killie Campbell'

B. glabra 'Formosa'

BOUGAINVILLEA
Nyctaginaceae

Vigorous, woody climbing plants from tropical and subtropical South America. Usually very thorny, they grow luxuriantly on strong supporting walls or pergolas, can be trained as standard specimens or trimmed to make a stout hedge. The 'flowers' are actually the colourful flower bracts which make brilliant displays in summer in shades of magenta, crimson, red, pink, salmon, orange and cream, and there are bi- and multi-coloured varieties. Bougainvilleas thrive in warm climates, flowering best in full sun, but need protection from frost. Young plants do not transplant well, nor must they be over watered. Once established, they are drought resistant. These flowers are useful in dried flower arrangements as the bracts fade to most attractive pastel shades.

Here are some of the many lovely cultivars.
Bougainvillea x buttiana 'David Lemmer'
B. x buttiana 'Killie Campbell'
B. x buttiana 'Lady Mary Baring'
B. glabra 'Formosa'

BRACHYCARPAEA

Brachycarpaea juncea (pink)

B. juncea (mauve)

BRACHYCARPAEA
Brassicaceae (=Cruciferae)

Only one species in this genus, *Brachycarpaea juncea*.

Brachycarpaea juncea   Namaqualand, South-western and southern Cape
🌣 ❀ ❁ ☀ Ⓦ
Bergriet or Ridderspoor
A shrubby indigenous perennial, very similar to Spanish broom in habit, it is covered in mauve, pink, blue or white flowers in spring. Height to 1 m. Plant in well-drained soil.

BRACHYCHITON

Brachychiton discolor

BRACHYCHITON
Sterculiaceae

Tall shrubs and trees native to Australia. They are grown for their symmetrical ornamental shape, lovely flowers and attractive foliage. Some species have particularly brilliant foliage.

Brachychiton acerifolium   Queensland,
🌣 ❀ ❁ ❃ ☀ Ⓦ   New South Wales
Flame tree or Vlamboom
This tree reaches 30 m in its native habitat, but is seldom higher than 13 m in South Africa. It is a good specimen tree growing in a neat pyramidal shape with large maple-like leaves, but it is when this tree flowers that it is truly spectacular. The leaves fall in late winter or spring and the bare branches are covered in bright red, bell-shaped flowers, making the tree seem brilliantly aflame. In some districts flame trees flower at the same time as jacarandas, making an unforgettable combination. But be warned: these trees can be erratic in flowering and may not put on their breathtaking display every year.

B. populneus

B. acerifolium

B. discolor   North Australia, Queensland,
🌣 ❀ ❁ ❃ ☀ Ⓦ   New South Wales
Queensland lace-bark or Lace-bark tree
Tree to 15 m with rusty pink flowers in the spring.

B. populneus   Australia
🌣 ❀ ❁ ❃ ☀ Ⓦ
Kurrajong
A sturdy tree with a dense, heavy crown. Leaves are 75 mm long, glossy and glabrous. Flowers are small, in short panicles, greenish-yellow and reddish inside.

BRACHYLAENA

Brachylaena discolor subsp. *transvaalensis*

BRASSAIA

Brassaia actinophylla

BRASSICA

Brassica oleracea

BRACHYLAENA
Asteraceae (=Compositae)

A genus of evergreen shrubs and trees, several of which are indigenous to South Africa. They are unusual because they are among the few plants in the daisy (Asteraceae) family to reach the size of trees. Foliage is attractive: leaves are dark green on top and felted silvery white beneath; flowers are thistle-like and cream-coloured. These are tough, quick-growing trees which thrive in any normal garden soil.

Brachylaena discolor subsp. transvaalensis Natal coastal belt, Eastern Transvaal and Moçambique
Wild silver oak, Wildevaalbos or Bitterblaar
Shrub or small tree 4 to 10 m in height, sometimes reaching 30 m. The creamy-white, thistle-like flowers are produced in sprays in autumn to spring, depending on the locality.

BRASSAIA
Araliaceae

A genus of trees and shrubs native to Asia, Australia and the Pacific Islands, of which one species, *Brassaia actinophylla*, is cultivated.

Brassaia actinophylla Australia
(*Schefflera actinophylla*)
Australian umbrella tree or Sambreelboom
Tree to 10 m with leaves shaped exactly like umbrellas, and spikes of small red flowers that stand out above the foliage. A good specimen tree in subtropical areas, it can also be kept pruned as a shrub, or grown indoors as a container plant. Grow in deep, rich soil and propagate by cuttings.

BRASSICA
Brassicaceae (=Cruciferae)

This genus includes cabbage, cauliflower, broccoli, etc. as well as turnips, swedes, mustard and numerous other vegetables, most of which have been in cultivation for so long their native origin is lost. Although many economy-minded gardeners grow the vegetable brassicas in odd corners of their flower gardens, the species most commonly seen is *Brassica oleracea*, or ornamental kale, grown for its attractive foliage which is often crimped or frilly. Found in most attractive shades of purple, pink and white, it is a useful plant for winter colour both in the garden and in floral arrangements, although not a pleasant-smelling addition.

Brassica oleracea Europe
Ornamental kale or Curly kale
Annual foliage plant of variable size and spread, providing colourful foliage in winter. Feed and water well.

BREYNIA

Breynia disticha 'Roseo-picta'

BROWALLIA

Browallia americana

B. speciosa

B. speciosa 'Major'

BREYNIA
Euphorbiaceae

A genus of shrubs and trees from the Pacific Islands of which only *Breynia disticha* is commonly cultivated.

Breynia disticha 'Roseo-picta'
(*Phyllanthus nivosus*)   Pacific Islands

Snowbush, Foliage flower, Leaf plant, Ice-cream bush or Roomysbossie
Shrub to 1 m. Grown for its most attractive green, white and pink mottled leaves carried on dark red stems, which are often scandent. A striking foliage shrub or bedding plant, it does well only in warm, subtropical areas.

BROWALLIA
Solanaceae

A genus of annual and perennial plants usually treated as annuals, best grown in damp, rich soil and semi-shade. Flowers of blue, violet and white are up to 50 mm across.

Browallia americana   Tropical American lowlands

Bush violet or Bosviooltjie
Garden annual to 600 mm, bearing bluish-purple flowers with pale yellow eyes in summer.

B. speciosa   Colombia

Amethyst flower, Sapphire flower or Saffierblom
Attractive herbaceous plant with sprawling slender branches profusely blooming with dark purple flowers.

B. speciosa 'Major'   Colombia

Bush violet or Bosviooltjie
Height to 1,25 m. The summer-borne sapphire flowers grow to 50 mm and larger. Graceful in hanging baskets.

BROWNEA

Brownea coccinea

BRUGMANSIA

Brugmansia x *candida*

BRUNFELSIA

Brunfelsia pauciflora 'Eximia'

B. pauciflora 'Magnifica'

BROWNEA
Fabaceae (=Leguminosae) Subfam. Caesalpinioideae

A genus of mostly small, spreading evergreen trees from the tropics and suitable for similar warm, damp and humid climates. Browneas are favourites grown for their showy red or pink flowers.

Brownea coccinea — Venezuela
Scarlet flame bean or Rooivlamboontjie
This short-spreading tree with drooping branches and leaves bears masses of flame-red flower clusters in the spring.

BRUGMANSIA
Solanaceae

A genus of shrubs and small trees, mainly evergreen, they are fast growing, usually from 3 to 6 m. Grown for their large bell or trumpet-shaped flowers which are extraordinarily fragrant at night, they are often referred to as daturas. The flowers and seeds of this plant are poisonous.

Brugmansia x candida — Ecuador
(*Datura cornigera*)

Moonflower, Angel's trumpet or Maanblom
Small tree from 3 to 6 m, with velvety grey-green leaves and many large, usually 200 to 300 mm long, pendent, trumpet-shaped flowers of white or cream, rarely yellow or pink. Very strongly scented at night.

BRUNFELSIA
Solanaceae

Evergreen shrubs and small trees grown for their abundant flowers which are exquisitely scented in most species. Unfortunately the scent has been lost in some hybrids. They are native to tropical America. These shrubs do best in warm, frost-free regions. They do well in semi-shade as well as full sun.

Brunfelsia pauciflora 'Eximia' — Brazil

Yesterday, Today and Tomorrow or Verbleikblom
Shrub to 2,5 m, evergreen but in some climates sheds its leaves shortly before flowering. Grown for the exquisitely scented flowers which literally cover the bush from late winter to early spring if the right conditions prevail. The flowers are violet-mauve when they open and fade to pale mauve and then white, on successive days. The flowers can be up to 70 mm across.

B. pauciflora 'Magnifica'

Shrub to 3 m, covered in large blue-violet flowers edged with white in spring.

BRUNIA

Brunia nodiflora

B. neglecta

B. stokoei

BRUNSVIGIA

Brunsvigia orientalis

BRUNIA
Bruniaceae

Indigenous evergreen shrubs with heath-like foliage and massed flower heads of fluffy pompoms. These fragrant flowers open after the first rains and new buds appear soon afterwards but do not open until the following winter. In other words, these velvety small globes are carried on the plant for a year and are most attractive and useful in floral arrangements. Native to the south-western Cape mountains, these shrubs need good drainage.

Brunia neglecta   South-western Cape
Shrub to 1,5 m, with silvery white flower heads borne in winter.

B. nodiflora   South-western Cape
Stompie or Fonteinbossie
Shrub to 1 m with attractive brown-pink pompom flower heads.

B. stokoei   Southern Cape
Rooistompie
Shrub to 2 m or more, with attractive silver, velvety buds opening into fluffy red flowers.

BRUNSVIGIA
Amaryllidaceae

Indigenous plant with a large bulb up to 300 mm long. The brunsvigia sends up a stout leafless peduncle to 450 mm, which carries a large umbel up to 600 mm in diameter and this bears up to 60 pink-red or crimson trumpet-shaped flowers. The umbel and stem usually break off in one piece after flowering and blow around the veld like tumbleweed. These flower heads can be rescued and made into unusual indoor decorations. Brunsvigias are slow growing, resent being moved, and must not be watered in their dormant period.

Brunsvigia orientalis   South-western Cape, Coastal districts
Candelabra flower or Kandelaarblom
Bulb, dormant in summer, sends up a flower stalk from the bare ground to 450 mm bearing an umbel up to 600 mm in diameter which consists of up to 60 crimson flowers. The leaves, half as broad as they are long, appear after the flowers and lie flat on the ground. Needs climate and soil closely matching that of its natural habitat. The flowers are borne in autumn.

BUDDLEJA

Buddleja davidii

B. madagascariensis

B. salviifolia

BULBINE

Bulbine frutescens

BUDDLEJA
(*Buddleia*)
Loganiaceae

A large genus of free-flowering evergreen or deciduous shrubs or small trees. The very fragrant flowers are borne in large, colourful trusses or spikes. The foliage is sage-like and the leaves are dark green on top and silvery white beneath, adding to the attraction of the shrub. These quick-growing shrubs need good drainage and full sunlight, and can be heavily pruned in late winter. The plant is named after Reverend Adam Buddle, the English botanist. The common name, butterfly bush, refers to the attraction that the flowers have for butterflies and hence unfortunately, for caterpillars.

Buddleja davidii — China
Butterfly bush, Summer lilac or Somerlila
Vigorous shrub to 4 m. Spikes of fragrant lilac flowers with an orange 'eye' are up to 250 mm long and produced in summer/autumn. It is the parent plant of many named varieties.

B. madagascariensis — Madagascar
Straggling shrub to 6 m; panicles of orange flowers are borne in winter.

B. salviifolia — South Africa, all provinces
Sage wood, Winter buddleia or Wildesalie
Shrub or small tree to 5 m, bearing cream to lilac flowers with orange throats in dense panicles up to 150 mm long, borne on tips of 'weeping' branches, in winter/spring.

BULBINE
Liliaceae

Perennial rhizomatous plants with succulent leaves and flowers of yellow or white on spikes up to 300 mm long. Filaments of the stamens are characteristically hairy or sometimes only the inner three are hairy. Easily grown and drought resistant, bulbines are adaptable to semi-shade.

Bulbine frutescens — South-western Cape
Stalked bulbine or Katstert
Succulent to 600 mm with spikes of yellow flowers growing to 100 mm. A vigorous, spreading plant which seeds itself freely and can be grown easily from cuttings. Spring/summer/autumn flowering.

BULBINELLA

Bulbinella floribunda

BURCHELLIA

Burchellia bubalina

BULBINELLA
Liliaceae

A genus of rhizomatous perennials, native to New Zealand and South Africa and grown for their poker-shaped spikes of densely packed, tiny, star-shaped flowers in shades of orange, yellow and white, which make excellent cut flowers. These plants will resist heavy frost, and consequently are most useful for gardens in cold areas. Good drainage is essential, especially in summer rainfall areas and this makes them perfect assets to the rock garden. Propagation is by seed or root division. Take care not to let the roots dry out during autumn when the plants are dormant for a short while.

Bulbinella floribunda South-western Cape
Cat's tail, Katstert or Seeroogkatstert
Perennial, forming clumps to 450 mm. Flowers are carried on stems to 750 mm long with flower spikes to 200 mm in length. Flowers are yellow, orange, cream or white and are produced in late winter or early spring. This species is a waterside plant in its natural habitat, but must have a dry season in summer.

BURCHELLIA
Rubiaceae

Only one species in this genus. It is indigenous to a stretch up the coast from the southern Cape through Natal and inland into the eastern Transvaal. Its name commemorates Dr W.J. Burchell, the nineteenth century plant collector and author of the famous *Travels into the interior of southern Africa*.

Burchellia bubalina Cape, Natal, Transvaal
Wild pomegranate or Wildegranaat
Excellent garden tree with a neat habit and glossy leaves with showy scarlet to orange flowers that bloom from late spring into summer. Height 2 to 3 m and occasionally more. Slow growing but flowering even from the time it is still very small. The common name, wild pomegranate, refers to its resemblance to the pomegranate, although it is not of the same family.

CAESALPINIA

Caesalpinia gilliesii

C. pulcherrima

CAESALPINIA
Fabaceae (=Leguminosae) Subfam. **Caesalpinioideae**

A genus of tropical and subtropical deciduous trees and shrubs grown for their attractive finely divided foliage and unusual showy flowers. Named after Andreas Caesalpini, an Italian botanist.

Caesalpinia gilliesii   Argentina, Uruguay
Bird of paradise or Paradysblom
A straggly shrub or small tree growing up to 3 m with equal spread, it has pale green, finely-cut, fern-like foliage and spikes of showy bright yellow flowers in summer with brilliant silky red stamens protruding, giving the impression of a dainty bird perched on the branches. These plants are not always deciduous in warm areas.

C. pulcherrima   West Indies
Pride of Barbados or Trots-van-Barbados
Thorny shrub to 3 m in height with dainty fern-like foliage and summer flowers of orange-scarlet with yellow margins and red stamens to 50 mm long.

CALADIUM

Caladium x hortulanum

CALADIUM
Araceae

These popular indoor and outdoor plants, grown for their beautifully-marked foliage, are among the 15 species contained in this genus of tuberous perennials from tropical America. The large, arum-like leaves are truly spectacular and marked with red, pink, green, silver and bronze, resembling an artist's palette. Grow in enriched soil and keep moist. Propagate by seed or division.

Caladium x hortulanum   Garden hybrid
Gorgeously-marked leaves, splashed and blotched with red, rose-pink, salmon-pink, white and green make these highly ornamental indoor plants, and also suitable for a warm, shady patio.

CALATHEA

Calathea insignis

C. ornata 'Roseo-lineata'

CALATHEA
Marantaceae

Perennial tuberous plants grown for their brilliantly marked foliage, either indoors or in a warm greenhouse. The name comes from the Greek *Kalathos*, meaning basket, referring to its leaves which are used for basket weaving in the plant's native habitat. Calatheas need warmth and high humidity.

Calathea insignis   Brazil
Rattlesnake plant or Ratelslangplant
A foliage plant with unusually beautiful leaves that have alternately large and small dark green blotches, not unlike the markings on a rattlesnake. They grow to 600 mm in height.

C. ornata 'Roseo-lineata'
Pot or greenhouse foliage plant to 1 m; leaves to 600 mm, green above, purple beneath. Marked with rose-pink lines along the lateral veins bearing spikes of violet flowers 150 mm long.

CALCEOLARIA

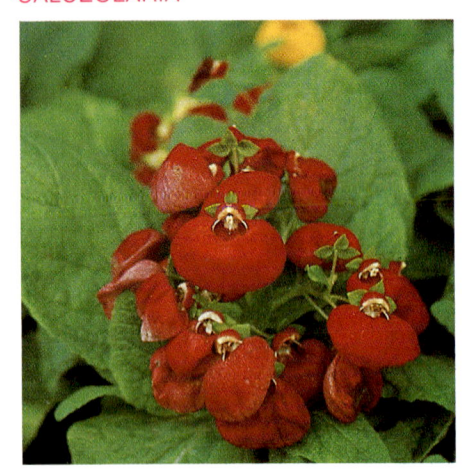

Calceolaria crenatiflora

C. crenatiflora

CALCEOLARIA
Scrophulariaceae

From the Latin *calceolus*, a slipper, referring to the shape of the flower. A genus of annual and perennial herbaceous and shrubby plants, sometimes with variegated leaves. The fleshy flowers are shaped like little purses in colours of bright yellow, red, orange and rust, usually mottled and bi-coloured. Most commonly grown as pot plants for stoeps, greenhouses and indoors; they can also be used as bedding plants in shady spots.

Calceolaria crenatiflora — Chile
Slipper flower, Purse flower, Ladies purses or Pantoffelblom
Perennial to 600 mm. Summer flowers 25 mm across are yellow with rusty orange spots. This is the parent plant of many cultivars.

CALENDULA

Calendula officinalis

CALENDULA
Asteraceae (=Compositae)

Easy, quick-growing annuals for colour in winter gardens. Through hybridization there is a great variety in flower forms and colours, which range from deep orange to yellow, apricot and cream. Do not overfeed — these European weeds thrive in poor soil.

Calendula officinalis — Mediterranean regions and Central Europe
Pot marigold, English marigold or Gousblom
Annual to 250 mm. The name, pot marigold originates from the fact that the flowers are used as a herb in cooking. They bloom in winter/spring.

CALLIANDRA

Calliandra brevipes

C. tweedii

CALLIANDRA
Fabaceae (=Leguminosae) Subfam. Mimosoideae

Evergreen shrubs and trees from the tropics, with finely-cut, acacia-like foliage and beautiful dainty flowers consisting of a puff of silky stamens. Aptly named, calliandra comes from the Greek *kallos*, beauty and *andros*, stamens.

Calliandra brevipes — Brazil
(*C. selloi*)
Powder puff tree, Fairy duster or Poeierkwas
Summer-flowering shrub; variable in height with silky, pinky white stamens which are darker pink at the tips, looking like a powder puff.

C. tweedii — Brazil
Mexican flame bush or Meksikaanse vlambos
Shrub to 2 m; summer flowers consist of a puff of brilliant red stamens.

CALLICARPA

Callicarpa dichotoma

CALLISIA

Callisia elegans 'Nana'

CALLISTEMON

Callistemon citrinus 'Splendens'

C. macropunctatus

CALLICARPA
Verbenaceae

Evergreen or deciduous shrubs and small trees native to the tropical and subtropical regions of America and Asia. The name comes from the Greek *kallos*, beauty and *karpos*, fruit.

Callicarpa dichotoma　　　China to Japan
Beauty berry
Shrub to 1,5 m; purplish leaves, pink flowers, and attractive glossy, deep lilac or violet berries that are borne in dense clusters against the stem in autumn.

CALLISIA
Commelinaceae

A genus of sprawling plants similar to the related tradescantias, they make very easy-to-grow and easy-to-propagate indoor plants. For best results grow them in hanging baskets.

Callisia elegans 'Nana'　　　Mexico
Dwarf-striped inch plant.

CALLISTEMON
Myrtaceae

An Australian genus of small evergreen trees and shrubs, known as bottle-brush trees because of the way in which the flowers with their long, profuse, coloured stamens are clustered round and down the stem in the fashion of a narrow brush. These shrubs grow easily and some species are particularly drought resistant. Prune well to increase flowering; can be used as hedge plants.

Callistemon citrinus 'Splendens'　Australia
Bottlebrush
Shrub or small tree to 3 m; very floriferous producing bright red 'bottle brushes' up to 120 mm long in spring/summer and again in autumn.

C. macropunctatus　　　South Australia
(*C. coccineus*)
Shrub to 1,5 m producing dull red 'bottle brushes' in late spring. Leaves narrow to 60 mm long.

CONTINUED

CALLISTEMON

C. viminalis

CALLISTEPHUS

Callistephus chinensis

CALODENDRUM

Calodendrum capense

C. viminalis Australia
Weeping bottlebrush or Treurbottelborsel
Shrub or small tree to 4 m with graceful willow-like branches and pinky bronze young growth borne in the spring with scarlet flowers.

CALLISTEPHUS
Asteraceae (=Compositae)

One species only in this genus – the popular summer annuals known as China asters. Good bedding plants but useful, too, as cut flowers, asters come in many varied forms and sizes and all shades of purple, blue, pink, mauve, white and even pale yellow. Easily grown from seed; they do best in full sun.

Callistephus chinensis China

China aster or Chinese aster
Herbaceous annual to 0,75 m; many cultivars varying in height, size and form of blooms appearing in summer.

CALODENDRUM
Rutaceae

Only one species, *Calodendrum capense*, in this African genus.

Calodendrum capense
Forests of Transvaal to Natal and Western Cape
Cape chestnut, Kaapse kastaiing or Wildekastaiing
Small evergreen tree growing to 7 m high in gardens. Leaves are simple and large. Flowers, in terminal heads, are striking with pale pink petals conspicuously dotted with maroon glands. Plant in rich, well-drained soil.

CALPURNIA

Calpurnia aurea

CAMELLIA

Camellia japonica cv.

C. x saluenensis 'J.C. Williams'

CAMPANULA

Campanula carpatica

C. glomerata

CALPURNIA
Fabaceae (=Leguminosae) Subfam. Faboideae (=Papilionoideae)

This is a small genus of six or seven species of trees and shrubs native to India and Africa with several species indigenous to South Africa. The plants in this genus look like a yellow-flowered form of keurboom (*Virgilia*) with their feathery foliage and long, pendent sprays of yellow pea-flowers. They are fairly drought resistant but need to be watered well for best results.

Calpurnia aurea   Eastern Cape coastal belt, Transkei, Natal, Eastern Transvaal
Wild laburnum, Golden tassel tree or Wildegeelkeur
Shrub or small, bushy tree to 4 m; can be occasionally taller in nature; yellow flowers mainly in summer.

CAMELLIA
Theaceae

This genus is the source of the tea we drink but it is for the exquisite waxy flowers that these deservedly popular ornamental shrubs are grown. Glossy evergreen foliage makes the plants attractive at all times and they flower from the time they are 450 mm high. In their natural habitat they are sub-shrubs that prefer a slightly acid, well-drained soil, rich in leaf mould. Grow in filtered shade, for the petals can be burnt around the edges by the hot afternoon sun. Try to screen the plants from prevailing hot dry winds.

Camellia japonica cv.   Japan
Common camellia or Japonika
Camellias can reach the size of large trees but are usually slow-growing shrubs to several metres. Flowers come in shades of pink, red, white, variegated, mottled and marbled. There are over 2 000 named cultivars and all flower in winter/spring.

C. x saluenensis 'J.C. Williams'   Garden hybrid
Compact shrub bearing large semi-double pink flowers with prominent gold stamens.

CAMPANULA
Campanulaceae

A large genus of annual and perennial herbaceous plants providing many species – and hundreds of named cultivars – suitable for flowerbeds, rockeries and mixed borders. The name comes from the Latin *campanula,* meaning a little bell, because many species have bell-shaped flowers. Colours are mainly shades of blue from purple through to white, and sometimes rose-pink. The combinations make these most attractive and useful garden plants and they are able to grow in semi-shade as well as sun.

Campanula carpatica   Carpathian mountains of eastern Europe
Tussock bellflower or Klokblom
Clump-forming perennial to 450 mm but usually half this height; lilac-blue flowers are borne in spring.

C. glomerata   Eurasia
Clustered bellflower
Erect perennial to 1 m with blue or white flowers that grow in dense clusters in summer.

CONTINUED

CAMPANULA

C. trachelium

C. medium

C. medium   Southern Europe
Canterbury bells or Canterburyklokkies
Tall, to 1 m, annual or biennial; bell-shaped flowers of purple, blue and white in summer.

C. trachelium   Eurasia
Nettle-leaved bellflower
Erect perennial to 1 m; blue-purple bell-flowers appear in summer.

CAMPSIS

Campsis grandiflora

CAMPSIS
Bignoniaceae

A genus of two vigorous deciduous creepers which achieve their climbing success by means of their aerial rootlets clinging to bricks, wood or any other support. These fast-growing creepers cover large areas and are most beautiful. The flowers, borne in showy clusters, bloom for a long period. Both species grow and flower best in full sun.

Campsis grandiflora   China
Chinese trumpet creeper or Ranktrompet Creeper, to 6 m; scarlet to orange flowers, up to 50 mm across, are produced in summer in terminal clusters.

CANNA

Canna x generalis 'Confetti'

C. indica

CANNA
Cannaceae

Tall rhizomatous perennials. Very useful and popular in home gardens and as striking massed plantings in parks and public places. Most cultivated cannas are hybrids in a range of brilliant warm colours, some having purple-bronze foliage, as well as the usual green. Easily grown, these are greedy feeders, needing enriched soil and copious water to look their best. They are easily propagated too, by dividing the rhizomes, each piece with a bud. Cut back after flowering.

Canna x generalis 'Confetti' Garden hybrid
Summer-flowering perennials.

C. indica   Tropical America
Indian shot or Kanna
Rhizomatous perennial to 1,2 m; leaves green, flowers bright red with orange lip, spotted with red; flowers in summer.

CANTUA

Cantua buxifolia

CAPSICUM

Capsicum annuum

CARISSA

Carissa bispinosa

C. edulis

CANTUA
Polemoniaceae

A small genus of shrubs and trees native to Andean South America and grown for their showy trumpet-shaped flowers. *Cantua* is the Peruvian name for *Cantua buxifolia*.

Cantua buxifolia North Chile, Peru, Bolivia
Sacred (or magic) flower of the Incas, Magic flower or Towerblom
Shrub to 3 m. Pinkish-red flowers, striped red with purple anthers borne in spring. Plant in enriched well-drained soil.

CAPSICUM
Solanaceae

A genus of shrubby perennials usually grown as annuals for eating and flavouring or as ornamental garden plants. Its flowers are insignificant but the shiny fruits are most decorative, changing colour as they ripen from green through cream to yellow, orange then brilliant red. One bush will often bear fruits displaying all these colours simultaneously. These plants, which have many cultivars, are easily raised from seed and grow in full sun and any soil, provided they get adequate water.

Capsicum annuum Tropical America
Ornamental chilli, Red pepper, Sierrissie or Rooirissie
Small bushes of varying size with fruits of varying shape and colour produced after flowering in early summer.

CARISSA
Apocynaceae

Indigenous evergreen shrubs and trees, with handsome glossy foliage and fragrant starry white jasmine-like flowers followed by ornamental edible scarlet to crimson oval fruits. Carissas are most attractive ornamental shrubs as specimens but they also make excellent impenetrable hedges, particularly as they are well armed with thorns.

Carissa bispinosa Cape, Natal, Transvaal
Num-num or Noem-noem
Thorny shrub to 1,25 m; white flowers up to 20 mm across and red fruits 20 mm long are borne in late summer.

C. edulis Transvaal, Namibia, Botswana
Num-num or Noem-noem
A dense shrub to 1,5 m grown in semi-shade. Masses of pure white flowers, 20 mm across, appear in spring. These are followed by small red fruit.

CONTINUED

CARISSA

C. macrocarpa

C. macrocarpa — Natal coast
Amatungulu, Natal plum, Natalpruim or Grootnoemnoem
Thorny shrub to 3 m; white flowers grow to 50 mm across and red fruits 25 mm across and almost 50 mm long. This shrub will grow happily next to the beach in Natal or thrive just as well in the semi-shade of the coastal bush. Although very much at home in its native conditions, it flourishes in the winter rainfall area.

CARPANTHEA

Carpanthea pomeridiana

CARPANTHEA
Mesembryanthemaceae

Two species of succulent herbaceous plants, indigenous to South Africa, belong in this genus but only one, *Carpanthea pomeridiana*, grows in gardens.

Carpanthea pomeridiana — Cape Province
Vetkousie
The whole plant body is covered with white hairs. The leaves are narrow and the yellow flowers are distinguished from those of *Dorotheanthus* by their densely petalled nature. Suitable for planting in a rock garden pocket.

CARPOBROTUS

Carpobrotus deliciosus

C. edulis

CARPOBROTUS
Mesembryanthemaceae

A genus of succulent plants found in Australia and the Americas as well as in South Africa. These are tough, evergreen trailing plants which spread rapidly to make a ground cover on soils and slopes where little else will grow. The fleshy leaves are three-sided, growing upwards from the stems. Flowers are followed by tart, edible fruits.

Carpobrotus deliciosus — Eastern Cape coast
Tough ground cover, bearing brilliant purple flowers and purplish fruit in spring.

C. edulis — South-western Cape coast
Hottentot fig, Sour fig, Hotnotsvy, Gouna, Perdevy or Suurvy
Ground cover, bearing yellow flowers which turn pink with age, to 80 mm across that are produced in spring.

C. muirii — Riversdale, southern Cape
Real sour fig, Ware suurvy or Suurvy
Ground cover; best species for eating. Flowers 100 mm across; borne in spring.

CARYOPTERIS   CARYOTA

C. muirii

Caryopteris incana

C. quadrifidus

Caryota mitis

C. sauerae

CARYOPTERIS
Verbenaceae

A genus of small shrubs and herbaceous perennials. Its blue flowers are carried in dense clusters in autumn. Best grown in warm areas, it needs a warm sunny spot in cooler areas.

Caryopteris incana　　　　China, Japan
Blue spiraea
Shrub to 1,75 m with blue flowers in autumn.

C. quadrifidus　　　　Clanwilliam
Branches to 1 m long. Glistening pink flowers are borne singly in spring.

C. sauerae　　　　Saldanha Bay
Elandsvy
Deep pink flowers and the largest of all species. It flowers in spring.

CARYOTA
Arecaceae (=Palmae)

A small genus of ornamental palms from tropical Asia, distinguished from all other palms by the 'fish-tail' at the tip of the leaves. The name comes from the Greek *karyotis*, a word first used by the Greeks for cultivated dates. Caryotas do not produce dates.

Caryota mitis　　　　Burma, Malaysia, Java, Philippine Islands
Fish-tail palm, Clustered fishtail palm or Visstertpalm
Palm tree from 4 m to 10 m high consisting of a cluster of stems 100 mm in diameter. Ornamental tree.

CASSIA

Cassia artemisioides

C. corymbosa

C. didymobotrya

C. multijuga

C. nodosa

CASSIA
Fabaceae (=Leguminosae) Subfam. **Caesalpinioideae**

A large genus which includes trees and shrubs, among which are some very showy species suitable for garden planting. Native to the tropics and subtropics, cassias are fast growing, often drought and frost resistant. They put on a spectacular display of flowers, in a warm yellow, the loveliest being *Cassia corymbosa*, or Autumn cassia.

Cassia artemisioides Australia
Wormwood cassia, Feathery cassia or Silwerkassia
Shrub to 1,2 m. Silky grey leaves make this an attractive plant all year round; sulphur-yellow flowers are borne in winter.

C. corymbosa Northern Argentina, Uruguay, Southern Brazil
Woody shrub or small tree to 3 m with bright green leaves. Large clusters of yellow flowers cover the tree in autumn.

C. didymobotrya Tropical Africa, Natal
Peanut butter cassia or Grondboontjiebotterkassia
Shrub to 3 m. Evergreen, occasionally semi-deciduous in cold areas. Its showy spikes of yellow flowers open from dark brown buds and give off a scent like peanut butter in summer/autumn.

C. multijuga Brazil and Guyana
Tree to 3 m. Fast growing it is inclined to become top-heavy and blow over and therefore needs staking protection from wind. The golden yellow flowers in winter show up well against the dark green leaves.

C. nodosa Eastern Himalayas to Malay Peninsula
Pink-and-white-shower
This can become a large tree; leaflets grow in 8 to 12 pairs; flowers, in dense racemes, are first pale but become dark pink; three of the stamen filaments are thickly swollen in the middle.

CASSINE

Cassine crocea

CASTALIS

Castalis nudicaulis

CASTANEA

Castanea sativa

CASSINE
Celastraceae

Several species in this genus of evergreen trees and shrubs, native to the tropical and subtropical regions of the world, are indigenous to South Africa. Parts of some species are used by the tribal Africans for medicinal purposes, and the wood is used for making small implements. Different species have differing habitats, and this should be taken into consideration when planting cassines in the garden.

Cassine crocea   Southern and eastern Cape, Transkei and Natal
Saffraan
Spreading tree to 13 m usually found in coastal bush. Small greenish flowers appear in summer and autumn. These are followed by oval berries which ripen to pale yellow.

CASTALIS
Asteraceae (=Compositae)

This genus consists of three perennial species of daisy similar to *Dimorphotheca* but separated from them by small botanical details. Not quite as showy as some indigenous daisies, their permanent clumps are useful in dry sunny rockeries with well-drained soil.

Castalis nudicaulis   Cape Province
Ox-eye daisy or Wit-margriet
Low-growing clumps to 300 mm bearing white daisy flowers with purple on the undersides of the petals and yellow centres; borne in spring.

CASTANEA
Fagaceae

This is the chestnut genus. The most popular species in South Africa, and grown in many parts of the country, is *Castanea sativa*. A slow-growing deciduous tree, it rarely exceeds 18 m in cultivation.

Castanea sativa   Europe
Spanish or European chestnut or Europese kastaiing
Leaves 150 to 250 mm long with coarse spreading teeth. Fruit 40 mm across with a prickly, dehiscent involucre enclosing one to three brown edible nuts.

CATHARANTHUS

Catharanthus roseus

C. roseus 'Albus'

CATHARANTHUS
Apocynaceae

A small genus of herbaceous annuals and perennials native to the tropics of Africa and Asia.

Catharanthus roseus Madagascar to India
Periwinkle, Madagascar periwinkle, Vinca or Kanniedood
A most tough and adaptable plant often seen growing as a weed. Spindly in poor conditions, it becomes a luxuriant small bush to 600 mm when cared for. The catharanthus' glossy foliage and rose-pink, phlox-like flowers grow up to 40 mm across and can be counted on to provide blooms in an otherwise unimaginative garden. Often referred to as *Vinca*, this plant has medicinal properties yet is poisonous to stock. Mainly summer flowering, but scattered flowers are produced throughout the year.

C. roseus 'Albus'
Same as above, with white flowers in summer; poisonous to stock.

CATTLEYA

Cattleya x hybridum

CATTLEYA
Orchidaceae

These striking, showy flowers characterize the thousands of hybrids that have been raised from parent plants in this genus of about 60 species of epiphytic orchids native to tropical America. The waxy, long-lasting flowers come in a variety of shapes, colours and sizes, the largest being up to 200 mm across. Provided their fairly specialized requirements are met, cattleyas are not difficult to grow; however novice orchid growers should get specialist advice.

Cattleya x hybridum Garden hybrid

CEANOTHUS

Ceanothus x delilianus 'Gloire de Versailles'

C. papillosus 'Roweanus'

CEANOTHUS
Rhamnaceae

A genus of small trees and shrubs native to western North America, ceanothus include many ornamentals, most of which have deep blue flowers, making them invaluable assets in the garden, particularly the many decorative hybrids. There are both evergreen and deciduous varieties and they will grow in a wide range of climatic conditions, although best in cooler regions away from the tropics.

Ceanothus x delilianus United States
'Gloire de Versailles'
Evergreen shrub 1 m to 2 m; spikes of sky-blue flowers cover the plant in summer.

C. papillosus 'Roweanus' North America
Wart leaf
Evergreen shrub, sometimes sprawling, to 1 m or more, with tiny leaves and abundant spikes of blue flowers, making an exciting display in spring.

CELOSIA

Celosia argentea 'Pyramidalis'

C. cristata

CELOSIA
Amaranthaceae

Perhaps the brightest, most brilliant colours in the summer garden are provided by these tropical weeds, now cultivated as rewarding, colourful annuals. Excellent for a mixed border, or for bedding in blocks of one dramatic colour. There are two distinct species, one sending up dense, glossy, grass-like plumes, and the other compact, contorted, crested heads looking as if they were made of crushed velvet ribbon. Colours are brilliant magenta, scarlet, bronze, pink, and rich shades of yellow, gold and orange. Easy to grow in full sun.

Celosia argentea 'Pyramidalis' Tropical Asia
Summer flowering.

C. cristata Tropical Asia
Cockscomb or Hanekom
Summer flowering.

CELTIS

Celtis africana

CELTIS
Ulmaceae

A genus of about 70 species, usually deciduous and native to temperate regions. Leaves are asymmetrical at the base and rough above. Flowers are very insignificant.

Celtis africana Widespread in all
(*C. kraussiana*) four provinces
White stinkwood or Witstinkhout
One of the best indigenous shade trees to 10 m high; will tolerate varied climatic conditions and grow in almost any soil. Excellent specimen tree on the lawn. It is not related to the common stinkwood.

CENTAUREA

Centaurea cineraria

C. cyanus

CENTAUREA
Asteraceae (=Compositae)

A large genus containing many ornamental plants. Some flowering annuals and foliage plants are suitable for bedding and others, the larger perennials, mostly with silvery foliage are usually found in large mixed borders and shrubberies. The name apparently originated from a Greek myth – the plant was said to have healed a wounded centaur.

Centaurea cineraria Southern Europe
Dusty miller
Perennial foliage plant to 750 mm spreading up to 2 m with most attractive ash-grey foliage. Its flowers are thistle-like and purple, appearing in summer. A tough plant easily grown in any soil in the sun, but it improves with good soil and water, provided drainage is good. Grown from cuttings.

C. cyanus
Cornflower
Flowers in shades of blue, mauve, crimson, pink and white are produced in summer. Dwarf and tall varieties are in cultivation.

CENTRADENIA

Centradenia grandiflora

C. rosea

CENTRADENIA
Melastomataceae

Centradenias are grown for their showy coloured leaves and flowers. They are native to Central America. Compost-rich, well-drained soil is essential for successful growth.

Centradenia grandiflora   Mexico, Central America
Shrub to 1,5 m with long curved leaves, red on the underside, bearing rose-pink flowers in spring.

C. rosea
Glossy green leaves and deep pink flowers in summer.

CEPHALOPHYLLUM

Cephalophyllum alstonii

C. procumbens

CEPHALOPHYLLUM
Mesembryanthemaceae

A genus of indigenous dwarf succulents with the familiar 'vygie' flowers. The stems trail along the ground sending up tufts of leaves that look like chubby fingers. Native to Namibia, Namaqualand, the northern Cape, and the drier districts of the southern Cape, these plants must have good drainage and be kept dry in summer if they are to flower.

Cephalophyllum alstonii   Ceres, Southern Karoo
Slow-growing succulents spreading over 600 mm, bearing blue-green leaves about 50 mm long. The ruby-red flowers with violet stamens are exceptionally showy and grow up to 50 mm or more across in spring.

C. procumbens   South-western Cape
Dwarf succulent with greyish-pink leaves, purplish beneath and golden yellow flowers up to 50 mm across.

CERASTIUM

Cerastium tomentosum

CERASTIUM
Caryophyllaceae

A genus of herbaceous annuals and perennials referred to in the United States by the delightful name of Mouse-Ear Chickweek. Only one is commonly grown in South African gardens, *Cerastium tomentosum*.

Cerastium tomentosum   Mountains of Italy and Sicily
Snow-in-Summer
This is an excellent perennial ground cover or rockery plant forming a dense mat of most attractive silvery grey foliage up to 100 mm high, sending up masses of white flowers in summer. Easily propagated by root division and easily grown in well-drained soil. It flowers best in full sun.

CERATONIA

Ceratonia siliqua

C. siliqua

CERATONIA

Fabaceae (=Leguminosae) Subfam. Caesalpinioideae

A genus with one species of evergreen tree. The name ceratonia comes from the Greek *keration*, meaning a horn or pod, referring to the shape of the pods.

Ceratonia siliqua   Eastern Mediterranean
Carob, St John's bread, Locust bean or Karob
An evergreen tree to 12 m. Leathery leaves and red and yellow flowers in summer are carried on drooping sprays to 150 mm long, followed by leathery seed pods up to 80 mm long with edible pulp. They make good trees for dry, hot areas but need protection from frost when young.

CERATOSTIGMA

Ceratostigma willmottianum

CERATOSTIGMA

Plumbaginaceae

A genus of herbaceous perennials and small shrubs, both deciduous and evergreen, useful for their true blue flowers.

Ceratostigma willmottianum   Western China and Tibet
Chinese plumbago
Deciduous shrub to 1 m. Pale blue plumbago-like flowers. Leaves turn red in autumn.

CERATOTHECA

Ceratotheca triloba

CERATOTHECA

Pedaliaceae

A small genus of herbaceous perennials and annuals indigenous to southern and tropical Africa, of which only *Ceratotheca triloba* is commonly cultivated.

Ceratotheca triloba   Eastern Cape, Natal, Transvaal
Wild foxglove
Tall annual to 2 m with aromatic leaves and summer-bearing, foxglove-like flowers streaked with purple and carried on tall spikes. Easily grown from seed, these plants do best in areas of heavy summer rain.

CERCIS

Cercis siliquastrum

C. siliquastrum

CERCIS
Fabaceae (=Leguminosae) Subfam. Caesalpinioideae

These deciduous shrubs and small trees are planted for their spectacular displays of blossom in late winter and early spring.

Cercis siliquastrum Eastern Europe, Western Asia
Judas tree (i.e. Judaean Tree) or Judasboom
Although this tree reaches over 30 m when found in nature, it is slow growing and seldom reaches 5 m when cultivated. However it makes a most attractive deciduous specimen tree, with pretty rounded pink pea-flowers in spring. These are followed by long-lasting decorative seed pods. This is a tough tree, resistant to drought, heat and frost, but produces its best results when given adequate water.

CEREUS

Cereus hildmannianus

C. peruvianus 'Monstrosus'

CEREUS
Cactaceae

A genus of ribbed, cylindrical cacti, mostly erect but some sprawling, varying in height from tree-like, branched species to small compact pot plants. All have spines, all are night flowering and the flowers are usually large and often fragrant.

Cereus hildmannianus Brazil
Tree-like to 6 m, branched. White flowers grow up to 200 mm long in summer. Cultivate in full sun and keep dry in resting period.

C. peruvianus 'Monstrosus' Garden origin
Curiosity plant
Shrubby, to 3 m, sometimes almost tree-like with stout branches that are irregularly ridged. Flowers are white and slightly fragrant and produced in summer.

CEROPEGIA

Ceropegia woodii

CEROPEGIA
Asclepiadaceae

A genus of tropical climbers or sprawling shrubs, some of which are indigenous to South Africa. Mostly they are grown as greenhouse or indoor plants. The name *Ceropegia* has an attractive meaning in Greek – *keros*, wax, and *pege*, fountain, referring to the waxy appearance of the flowers and their curious shape.

Ceropegia woodii Zimbabwe, Transvaal, Natal
Necklace vine, Rosary vine, String of hearts or Halssnoer-ranker
Slender, trailing plants sending up stems to 1 m long from a corm. Heart-shaped dark green leaves are marbled with white and very decorative, pinkish flowers are borne in summer. An indoor plant, happy in sun or shade, it needs to be damp in summer. Very attractive if planted in a hanging basket or hanging pot.

CESTRUM

Cestrum aurantiacum

C. diurnum

C. elegans

C. elegans 'Smithii'

C. nocturnum

CESTRUM
Solanaceae

Flowering shrubs and small trees from tropical America, they are both deciduous and evergreen. Their tubular flowers come in a wide range of colours, except blue. Plants grow well in most soils.

Cestrum aurantiacum Guatemala
A scrambling shrub or small tree 2 m to 6 m with leaves aromatic when crushed. Very floriferous tubular orange flowers about 25 mm long, followed by fruits like small white marbles, are borne in summer.

C. diurnum West Indies
Shrub or small tree to 5 m. Flowers produced in summer, are fragrant in the day time and greeny white to yellow. The fruit is glossy black.

C. elegans Mexico
Scrambling shrub to 3 m, spreading nearly as much and needing occasional pruning for shape. Flowers, borne in open, pendent clusters in summer, are crimson to purple-red. The fruit is red.

C. elegans 'Smithii'
As above. Rose-pink flowers bloom continuously in summer.

C. nocturnum
Night cestrum
Scandent or spreading shrub to 4 m. Summer-bearing, greenish-cream flowers are borne in clusters and very fragrant at night. The fruit is white.

CHAENOMELES

Chaenomeles speciosa

C. speciosa 'Umbilicata Nana'

CHAENOMELES
Rosaceae

A genus of three species of deciduous or semi-evergreen shrubs from eastern Asia usually grown for the spectacular displays of late winter and spring blossoms. There are numerous cultivars and hybrids giving a colour range from white through all the pinks to red-orange, as well as single, double and semi-double flowers. They are easy-to-grow plants that can be trimmed into a neat hedge which will burst into a mass of blossoms at the end of winter.

Chaenomeles speciosa China
(*C. lagenaria*)
Japanese flowering quince or Japanse blomkweper
Shrub to 3 m, spreading, with erect thorny branches. Flowers are usually red, although also pink and white, and up to 50 mm across. Delightful yellow fruits up to 60 mm long, look like small quinces, and are deliciously fragrant.

C. speciosa 'Umbilicata Nana'
As above, but dwarf almost spineless shrub with small single red flowers.

83

CHAMAECEREUS

Chamaecereus sylvestri

CHAMAECYPARIS

Chamaecyparis obtusa 'Crippsii'

CHAMAEDOREA

Chamaedorea cataractarum

C. elegans

CHAMAECEREUS
Cactaceae

There is only one species in this genus, *Chamaecereus sylvestri*, a small cactus from Argentina with slender stems which lie on the ground with their tips turning upward and forming low clumps. This is a very adaptable plant which grows well indoors on a sunny windowsill or fills a rockery pocket outdoors equally satisfactorily. Propagation is easy: the finger-shaped stems detach themselves from the main plant from time to time and send out new roots from their bases. These can be planted to form new clumps.

Chamaecereus sylvestri　　　Argentina
Peanut cactus or Grondboontjiekaktus
Perennial, 50 mm to 75 mm high and spreading; pale green stems with soft white spines. It has red, funnel-shaped flowers in spring to 50 mm in length and across.

CHAMAECYPARIS
Cupressaceae

Evergreen, erect and highly variable these pyramidal or columnar trees, native to North America and Asia, reach a height of over 35 m in these habitats; however, the many dwarf cultivars make excellent small ornamental trees. The foliage is in the form of flattened sprays of tiny scale-like leaves which may be gold, yellow, bronze or blue-green as well as dark green. The foliage is dense from the ground up making the trees attractive from a height of 300 mm and upwards.

Chamaecyparis obtusa 'Crippsii'　　　Japan
Golden cypress, Hinoki cypress or Goue sipres
Small foliage tree to 5 m with a spread to 4 m; slow growing with golden leaves.

CHAMAEDOREA
Arecaceae (=Palmae)

More than 100 species of dioecious palms from tropical rain forests of which a number are commonly cultivated as indoor specimens. Woody stems and somewhat arching pinnate leaves and delightful small orange-yellow flowers in dainty sprays make these palms most popular. Chamaedoreas normally grow to 1 m, and can tolerate dry air but flourish best when it is moist.

Chamaedorea cataractarum　　　Mexico
Lovely indoor palm with erect pinnate leaves.

C. elegans　　　Mexico, Guatemala
Parlour palm or Good-luck palm
Most popular, delightfully small palm for the indoor garden. It bears orange-yellow flowers on erect sprays but, because the sexes are on different plants, a single specimen can not fruit. Well-drained soil, with regular watering and liquid feedings, is essential for a healthy specimen.

C. geonomiformis

C. seifrizii

C. geonomiformis   Honduras
Leaves are deeply two-cleft at apex, otherwise undivided.

C. seifrizii   Yucatan Peninsula
Can withstand more sun than most chamaedoreas.

CHAMELAUCIUM

Chamelaucium uncinatum

CHAMELAUCIUM
Myrtaceae

The heath-like evergreen shrubs in this genus are native to Western Australia, where they thrive in dry, sandy soil. One species is widely cultivated, *Chamelaucium uncinatum*.

Chamelaucium uncinatum   Western Australia
Geraldton wax plant or Geraldton-wasplant Shrub to 5 m or more in its natural habitat but usually about half this in cultivation. Leaves are narrow and needle-like, and the waxy, white flowers come in shades of pink, lilac and white, in spring. Grow in well-drained soil and do not over water.

CHASMANTHE

Chasmanthe floribunda

C. floribunda var. *duckittii*

CHASMANTHE
Iridaceae

Indigenous cormous plants from winter rainfall areas which send up bright green sword-shaped leaves to 1 m, and orange, red and yellow spikes of flowers to 1,5 m. They are easy to grow from rapidly multiplying corms planted in autumn.

Chasmanthe floribunda   South-western Cape
Piempiempie, Suurknol or Rooi-Afrikaner Cormous plant to 1,5 m. Orange-red flowers are produced in winter/spring.

C. floribunda var. duckittii
                             South-western Cape
As above. A form with yellow flowers.

CHEIRANTHUS

Cheiranthus cheiri

CHEIRIDOPSIS

Cheiridopsis herrei

C. serrulata

CHIRONIA

Chironia baccifera

C. baccifera (fruit)

CHEIRANTHUS
Brassicaceae (=Cruciferae)

These free-flowering annual or perennial herbaceous plants are excellent for bedding or mixed borders as they flower in late winter and early spring in a range of warm colours from yellow, orange and brown to pink, red and burgundy and their fragrant, sometimes double flowers are often multi-coloured.

Cheiranthus cheiri   Southern Europe
Wallflower, English wallflower or Muurblom Perennial to 750 mm; a bushy plant with yellow to yellow-brown fragrant flowers in spring.

CHEIRIDOPSIS
Mesembryanthemaceae

A large genus of about 100 species of clump-forming succulents to be found from Namibia and Namaqualand to the south-western Cape. Leaves are in pairs, often dissimilar, one pair fully opened while the next pair remains joined almost its entire length. Very showy vygie-like flowers are borne in colours of yellow, pink or orange in spring. They need sandy soil.

Cheiridopsis herrei   Namaqualand
Leaves are short and very succulent with tips tinged with pink-purple. Rewarding to grow.

C. serrulata   Namaqualand
Leaves grey-green, spotted and tapering. Large bright yellow flowers in spring.

CHIRONIA
Gentianaceae

Named after Chiron, the Greek centaur, who was the legendary father of medicine, this is a genus of moisture-loving indigenous evergreen perennials, with pinkish-mauve flowers.

Chironia baccifera   South African summer rainfall coastal regions, also inland
Wild gentian, Christmas berry or Bitterbos Small bushes to 450 mm with summer-blooming, bright pink starry flowers followed by long lasting pea-sized, scarlet berries.

CHLOROPHYTUM

Chlorophytum capense

C. comosum 'Picturatum'

C. comosum 'Vittatum'

C. comosum 'Variegatum'

CHLOROPHYTUM
Liliaceae

Evergreen, rhizomatous perennials suitable for both indoor and outdoor cultivation. These plants often have their green, almost grass-like leaves striped with white, yellow or cream. Flowers are usually white and insignificant, borne on long arching flower spikes which produce new tufts of leaves at the tips where they usually touch the ground. These tufts then take root which make these plants good, quick-spreading ground covers, especially under trees. They are also pretty and graceful in hanging baskets.

Chlorophytum capense   South Africa
Evergreen perennial; clumps of leaves about 600 mm high send up loosely branched spikes of white flowers in summer.

C. comosum 'Picturatum'   South Africa
Hen-and-chickens, Spider plant or Hen-en-kuikens
Foliage plant for shade or filtered sun, indoors or out. Leaves to 300 mm long with central yellow stripe.

C. comosum 'Variegatum'
Foliage plant; leaves to 300 mm long, margined with white.

C. comosum 'Vittatum'
Leaves with white or cream central stripe. Popular for hanging baskets.

CHONDROPETALUM

Chondropetalum tectorum

CHONDROPETALUM
Restionaceae

A genus of reeds or rushes arising from rhizomatous roots in tufts or clumps, many of them indigenous to South Africa. Many have tough or wiry stems and are widely used in thatching.

Chondropetalum tectorum   South-western Cape
Thatching reed, Dakriet or Olifantsriet
Reed to 1,5 m. Flowering stems with terminal heads of brown inflorescences in autumn. Useful in dried floral arrangements.

CHONEMORPHA

Chonemorpha fragrans

CHRYSANTHEMOIDES

Chrysanthemoides monilifera

CHRYSANTHEMUM

Chrysanthemum frutescens 'Mary Wootten'

C. maximum

CHONEMORPHA
Apocynaceae

Vigorous climbers from tropical Asia sprouting clusters of fragrant creamy-white flowers.

Chonemorpha fragrans India, Malaysia

Malayan jasmine or Maleisiese jasmyn
A climber with large leaves up to 150 mm long, its fragrant funnel-shaped, creamy-white flowers grow up to 60 mm in length and 100 mm in width in late spring/summer.

CHRYSANTHEMOIDES
Asteraceae (=Compositae)

These indigenous evergreen shrubs and small trees range in height from 1 to 6 m. The six sub-species cover a wide variety of habitats from the south-western Cape into Zimbabwe but occur mainly in frost-free or light frost areas. Quick growing, drought and wind resistant, these shrubs make good windbreaks or edges, especially at the coast.

Chrysanthemoides monilifera

Southern Africa, coastal and temperate regions
Bush-tick berry, Boetabessie or Bietou
A spreading shrub bearing bright yellow daisy flowers in winter/spring followed by edible purple berries which give this variety its common name. The specific name, *monilifera* means 'bearing a necklace' which comes from the fact that the fruit is arranged in neat circles on the plant.

CHRYSANTHEMUM
Asteraceae (=Compositae)

This is a large genus of most important garden plants that includes several species not usually referred to as chrysanthemums. The ones most commonly recognized as chrysanthemums are the *morifolium* hybrids, the huge, perfect blooms seen in florists or as perennial border plants, usually making a brilliant autumn display in gardens. Also well known are the annual chrysanthemums, including *Chrysanthemum coronarium*, and the Feverfew chrysanthemums, those tough little plants with strongly aromatic foliage and small white daisy flowers with yellow centres. The Pyrethrum chrysanthemums are grown for their daisy-like flowers in shades of pink, white and mauve, but also as an important source of the insecticide pyrethrum. Well known too, are the Marguerites, or daisy bushes, *Chrysanthemum frutescens*, which sometimes grow as high as 2 m with a spread double their height. They are perennials with daisy-like flowers in many shades of white, yellow, red and pink. Finally there are the perennial daisies generally referred to as Shasta daisies.

CISSUS

C. frutescens cv.

C. morifolium cv.

C. morifolium 'Sungold'

Chrysanthemum frutescens cvs.
Bushy woody perennials, easily propagated by cuttings. Flowers are profuse in late winter and spring coming in shades of yellow, pink, red and white.

C. frutescens 'Mary Wootten' Garden origin
As above.

C. maximum
Shasta daisy which flowers in summer.

C. morifolium cvs. China
Florist's chrysanthemum or Krisant Extremely variable in habit and bloom but usually flowers in summer/autumn.

C. morifolium 'Sungold' Garden origin

Cissus rhombifolia 'Ellen Danica'

CISSUS
Vitaceae

This is a genus of creepers and shrubs native to the tropical and subtropical regions of the world, with a number of species indigenous to South Africa. Grown for their ornamental foliage, they are suitable for growing outdoors or on stoeps in warm climates, and indoors or in greenhouses where it is cooler. The climbing species are attractive on an indoor trellis, or in hanging baskets. Easily grown, they are propagated from cuttings.

Cissus rhombifolia 'Ellen Danica' Central and South America
Venezuela treebine or Venezuela-wildedruif Creeper, climbing by trendrils.

89

CISTUS

Cistus crispus

C. x purpureus

C. incanus

C. vaginatus

CISTUS
Cistaceae

From the Greek *kistos*, rock rose, this is a genus of useful shrubby, herbaceous plants native to the drier Mediterranean regions and excellent for rockeries and sunny borders. The foliage is grey-green and the flowers are like slightly crumpled single roses which appear in succession for a long flowering period, although each flower lasts only a day.

Cistus crispus Portugal to Italy, and western North America
Rock rose or Kliproos
Perennial to 600 mm. Rose-coloured flowers to 50 mm across appear in summer.

C. incanus Mediterranean regions
Rock rose or Kliproos
Shrubby perennial to 1 m with rose-pink flowers up to 70 mm across that bloom in summer.

C. x purpureus Garden hybrid
Shrub to 1,2 m with flowers up to 75 mm across with petals of purple with a yellow base and deep red blotches.

C. vaginatus Canary Islands
Rock rose or Kliproos
Shrub to 2 m with summer-blooming pink flowers to 50 mm across.

CITHAREXYLUM

Citharexylum quadrangulare

CITHAREXYLUM
Verbenaceae

A genus of deciduous shrubs or small trees native to the American tropics with glossy light green leaves which turn a rich glowing orange before they fall. The flowers are tiny, white and insignificant in appearance but very fragrant, especially on warm still evenings.

Citharexylum quadrangulare West Indies
Fiddlewood
Foliage tree to 7 m. Colourful autumn foliage.

CLARKIA

Clarkia amoena subsp. *whitneyi*

C. unguiculata

CLARKIA
Onagraceae

Discovered in the Rocky mountains of North America by Captain William Clarke, these are a genus of now popular garden annuals, good for the mixed border and for cut flowers. Bearing tall spikes of single or double flowers in every shade of pink, from purple to white, clarkias need good drainage and protection from dry, searing winds. They are quick growing from seed.

Clarkia amoena subsp. **whitneyi**
(Godetia whitneyi)   Washington, Oregon interior

Satin flower or Satynblom
Erect annual to 2 m with lavender flowers, some with dark central spot, borne in summer.

C. unguiculata   California

Satin flower or Satynblom
Annual to 1 m, flowers are purple, mauve, pink or salmon and bloom in summer.

CLEMATIS

Clematis brachiata

C. x *jackmanii* 'Rubra'

CLEMATIS
Ranunculaceae

A large genus, including herbaceous perennials. The small-flowered woody vines are used as creepers, and the large-flowered vines are used extensively in the development of ornamental hybrids grown for their exceptionally beautiful flowers.

Clematis brachiata   Natal, Transvaal

Traveller's joy or Klimop
A deciduous climber or scrambler extending to 5 m and bearing masses of small creamy-white, fragrant flowers which bloom in late summer.

C. x **jackmanii** 'Rubra'

Climber to 3 m with spectacular flowers to 150 mm across, in purplish-red and produced in summer.

CLEOME

Cleome spinosa

CLEOME
Capparaceae

A large genus of mainly tropical and subtropical annuals, perennials and shrubs of which *Cleome spinosa*, a spidery-like flowered variety is the most frequently cultivated.

Cleome spinosa

Spider flower
Height 1 to 1,5 m and summer/autumn flowering.

91

CLERODENDRUM

Clerodendrum glabrum

C. thomsoniae

C. splendens

C. ugandense

CLERODENDRUM
Verbenaceae

A large genus of evergreen and deciduous trees, climbers and shrubs which are native to the tropics and subtropics. Grown for their often fragrant showy flowers, these plants need warm frost-free winters and plenty of water in summer if they are to blossom as spectacularly as they are capable of doing.

Clerodendrum glabrum   Southern Africa, Transkei, into Natal, Transvaal and northwards
White cat's whiskers
Shrub or small tree to 10 m. Flowers are fragrant and borne in dense, rounded heads of white tinged with pink. Flowers arrive in late winter at the coast, late summer inland.

C. splendens   Sierra Leone
Evergreen shrub to 2 m, often scrambling, with shining green leaves and very showy scarlet flowers which form in clusters in summer.

C. thomsoniae   West Africa
Bleeding heart vine
Climber to 4 m. Very showy spring flowers with large white heart-shaped calyx, scarlet petals and long white stamens peeping out of the calyx. Unless the climate is highly suitable, best grown indoors.

C. ugandense   Tropical Africa
Oxford and Cambridge bush
Shrub to 3 m. Bi-coloured blue flowers in summer, hence the common name.

CLIVIA

Clivia miniata var. *miniata*

C. miniata var. *citrina*

CLIVIA
Amaryllidaceae

Strictly protected plants. Clivias are a small genus of indigenous plants with fleshy, often bulbous roots, strap-shaped evergreen leaves and umbels of showy orange, red and yellow flowers. They thrive best in shady situations and grow well under trees. They also make good pot plants for stoeps and shady patios. Do not divide unnecessarily as they resent disturbance.

Clivia miniata var. **miniata**   Natal
Bush lily, Fire lily, St John's lily or Boslelie
Showy rounded umbels of orange spring flowers carried up to 750 mm high, followed by red berries.

C. miniata var. **citrina**
As above, but flowers are yellow.

CLYTOSTOMA

CODIAEUM

Clytostoma callistegioides

Codiaeum variegatum var. *pictum* 'Elaine'

C. nobilis

C. variegatum var. *pictum* 'Excurrens'

C. nobilis   Natal

As *Clivia miniata*, but flowers are drooping, curved and narrower, found in colours of red and yellow, tipped with green.

CLYTOSTOMA
Bignoniaceae

A small genus of vigorous evergreen, climbing shrubs native to tropical South America and grown for the showy trumpet-shaped flowers carried in masses at the tips of long, drooping stems. These quick-growing creepers climb by means of tendrils, thus needing support. They are semi-deciduous in frosty areas.

Clytostoma callistegioides   Brazil, Argentina

Argentinian trumpet vine, Violet trumpet vine or Trompetblom
Creeper to 3 m. Flowers to 75 mm long and wide in mauve streaked with violet and blooming in summer.

CODIAEUM
Euphorbiaceae

A small genus of shrubs and trees native to Malaysia and the Pacific Islands. Only one species *Codiaeum variegatum*, is cultivated for its strikingly coloured and variegated foliage. Codiaeums make good stoep plants although they can also do well out of doors in tropical and warmly temperate regions provided they are kept damp. Plant in rich, well-drained soil and water regularly. Often referred to erroneously as crotons.

Codiaeum variegatum var. *pictum* 'Elaine'
C. variegatum var. *pictum* 'Excurrens'
C. variegatum var. *pictum* 'Gloriosum'
C. variegatum var. *pictum* 'Gloriosum superbum'
C. variegatum var. *pictum* 'Gold Spot'

Foliage plants.

CONTINUED

CODIAEUM

C. variegatum var. *pictum* 'Gloriosum'

C. variegatum var. *pictum* 'Gloriosum superbum'

C. variegatum var. *pictum* 'Gold Spot'

COFFEA

Coffea arabica

COFFEA
Rubiaceae

There are about 40 species in this genus but to most people two are of vital importance, both as a source of coffee which is extracted from their seeds. Native to tropical Africa and Asia, these evergreen shrubs or trees make acceptable ornamentals with attractive flowers and fruits. The name is from the Arabic *quahouch*, the name for coffee.

Coffea arabica　　　　Tropical Africa
Coffee, Common coffee, Arabian coffee or Koffieboom
Shrub to 5 m, large glossy green leaves and white, fragrant flowers which are followed by red fruits containing two seeds, the coffee 'beans'. Propagate by these seeds or cuttings, but these shrubs are only suited to outdoors and should be planted in really warm, tropical regions.

COLEONEMA

Coleonema album

C. aspalathoides

COLEONEMA
Rutaceae

Indigenous evergreen shrubs with aromatic, feathery, heath-like foliage and tiny pink or white flowers borne in profusion in late winter and spring. These plants are native to the south-western Cape, but grow well elsewhere. They are wind resistant at the coast, and need full sun to flower properly. These self-seeding shrubs can be pruned to fit a large rockery pocket, or grown in the shrub border. The flowers last well in water.

Coleonema album　　　　South-western Cape
Cape May, Klip buchu or Klipboegoe
Bushy shrub to 1 m with pale yellow-green foliage and masses of tiny white flowers in winter and spring.

C. aspalathoides　　　　South-western Cape
A dense shrub to 1 m with small glossy dark green ovate leaves 10 mm long. Its flowers, in light pink, grow profusely in late winter and early spring.

C. pulchellum

Coleus x *hybridus*

COLEUS

COLLETIA

Colletia cruciata

C. x *hybridus*

COLEUS
Lamiaceae (=Labiatae)

These popular annual or perennial herbaceous plants are grown for their strikingly ornamental colourful foliage. Native to the tropics, they will only grow outdoors in similar climates, but they are good house and greenhouse plants and most suitable for stoep containers. The leaves are found in every shade of purple, red and pink, as well as yellow and green, usually very vivid, and variegated. Plant in rich, well-drained soil. Reproduction by stem cuttings in spring and summer.

Coleus x hybridus Garden hybrid
Painted nettle, Flame nettle or Josefskleed

COLLETIA
Rhamnaceae

Strange-looking, spiny, stiff, evergreen shrubs from South America are contained in this genus. Leaves are non-existent, usually replaced by their fierce spines, and branches that are flattened and triangular-shaped. The white, bell-shaped flowers are often fragrant. Grow these curiosities in well-drained soil in full sun.

Colletia cruciata South America
Anchor plant or Ankerplant
Shrub to 3 m with yellowish-white flowers in autumn.

C. pulchrum

C. pulchellum South-western Cape
Bushy shrub to 1,5 m with needle-shaped leaves and masses of dark pink flowers in winter and spring.

C. pulchrum South-western Cape
Confetti bush or Konfettibos
Bushy shrub to 1,2 m or more. Pink, confetti-like flowers are produced in profusion in winter and spring.

COLOCASIA

Colocasia esculenta 'Euchlora'

COLUMNEA

Columnea microphylla

C. x *banksii*

COMBRETUM

Combretum bracteosum

C. microphyllum

COLOCASIA
Araceae

A genus of tropical plants of variable height with large ornamental leaves, suitable for borders or patio tubs and as waterside plants where they give an effect of tropical luxuriance. If grown in areas of frost, the tubers should be lifted and stored during winter when they are semi-dormant.

Colocasia esculenta 'Euchlora'　　　　Tropical Asia
Elephant's ear or Olifantsoor
Perennial. Size depends on conditions but they can reach 1 m or more. Dark green leaves with violet margins and stems, the flower spathe, borne in summer, is similar to an arum.

COLUMNEA
Gesneriaceae

Named in honour of an Italian nobleman, Fabius Columna, author of the earliest botanical book which was illustrated using copper plates. It was published in Naples in 1592. This is a fairly large genus, with a large number of cultivated species. Native to tropical America, these epiphytic shrubs and vines are grown for their trailing sprays of showy flowers, which are best displayed when the plants are grown in hanging baskets, usually in greenhouses, but also out of doors in warm subtropical humid climates. Water well in the growing season, less after flowering.

Columnea x banksii
A branching herbaceous shrublet with pendulous stems ideally suited to a hanging basket. Leaves are greenish-bronze, small and ovate, and two-lipped scarlet flowers with yellowish stripes at the mouth are produced.

C. microphylla　　　　Central America
Perennial with long, pendulous stems with scarlet and yellow flowers in summer.

COMBRETUM
Combretaceae

A large genus including trees, shrubs and climbers, native to the tropics and suitable for warm, frost-free gardens.

Combretum bracteosum　　　Natal, Transkei
Hiccough creeper, Hiccup nut or Hikranker
A straggling, evergreen semi-woody shrub that climbs all over itself and will only succeed in temperate and subtropical coastal regions. Orange-red flowers in compact, nearly globular, spikes are borne in late spring.

C. microphyllum　　　　Tropical Africa
Flaming creeper, Burning bush or Vlamklimop
A vigorous climber to a great height, it will need pruning. Its summer flowers are coral-red and very showy, especially as the plant frequently drops its leaves before bearing orange-pink fruit. Extremely popular in the eastern Transvaal and Natal.

CONICOSIA

CONOPHYTUM

Conicosia pugioniformis

Conophytum apiatum

C. circumpunctatum

C. jacobsenianum

C. minutum

CONICOSIA
Mesembryanthemaceae

A small genus of annual, biennial and perennial succulents indigenous to South Africa, with large silky 'vygie' flowers. Good for growing in dry, sandy soil as ground covers, or in well-drained rockery pockets in full sun.

Conicosia pugioniformis
South-western Cape
Evergreen succulent to 200 mm, grey-green cylindrical leaves and shining, silky yellow flowers up to 100 mm across are borne in spring. Propagate by division.

CONOPHYTUM
Mesembryanthemaceae

Strictly protected, this large genus of indigenous dwarf succulents is most interesting in the way that it resembles a cluster of pebbles. Each plant consists of two fleshy, rounded leaves (often well camouflaged to resemble the surroundings), with a slit between them through which the vygie-like flower appears. Native to the driest regions of the winter rainfall area, these plants are best grown indoors in full sun and should be very sparingly watered. It is highly illegal to remove them from the veld, as is the case with most indigenous plants. Plant in well-drained soil.

Conophytum apiatum	North-western Cape
C. circumpunctatum	North-western Cape
C. jacobsenianum	North-western Cape
C. minutum	North-western Cape

CONSOLIDA

Consolida ambigua

CONSOLIDA
Ranunculaceae

Ranunculas or larkspurs are popular garden annuals, grown for their tall spikes of flowers in a wide variety of colours in the pink, blue and purple range. Native to the Mediterranean regions, and spreading into Central Asia, larkspurs make good bedding and border plants, growing in ordinary, preferably enriched garden soil and full sun.

Consolida ambigua   Mediterranean
(*Delphinium ajacis*)
Larkspur or Ridderspoor
Annual to 600 mm with fine lacy foliage; flowers in shades of blue, pink and white are borne in spring and summer.

CONVOLVULUS

Convolvulus cneorum

C. mauritanicus

CONVOLVULUS
Convolvulaceae

Annual and perennial trailing or climbing shrubby plants native to the temperate regions. They grow so easily they tend to become weeds. Variable in size and spread, their flowers also vary in size. Colours are sometimes white and pink but mainly found in shades of blue and mauve. They make good ground covers in a variety of situations.

Convolvulus cneorum   Southern Europe
Silver bush
Small shrub to 1 m with silvery leaves and pinkish-white flowers borne in summer.

C. mauritanicus   North Africa
Prostrate perennial; good for rockeries, borders and tubs; blue flowers with white throats are borne in summer.

COPROSMA

Coprosma x kirkii

C. repens

COPROSMA
Rubiaceae

Robust evergreen shrubs and small trees native to Australasia and the Pacific Islands and grown for their tough, leathery, highly glossy, often variegated foliage. These drought-resistant plants make excellent windbreaks and hedges especially at the coast, as they will grow in poor, sandy soil. Female plants bear ornamental berries if male plants are nearby.

Coprosma x kirkii   Hybrid origin
Sprawling foliage shrub used as ground cover to 450 mm.

C. repens   New Zealand
Mirror plant, Looking-glass plant or Spieëlplant
Will grow as a prostrate shrub or as a small tree to 8 m. Berries are orange. This foliage plant can be trimmed into a hedge.

C. repens 'Marble Chips'   New Zealand
Leaves are irregularly margined in yellow-white and speckled white.

CORDYLINE

COREOPSIS

C. repens 'Marble Chips'

Cordyline australis

Coreopsis grandiflora

C. repens 'Variegata'

C. terminalis

C. robusta

C. repens 'Variegata'   New Zealand
Leaves are very glossy green marked with yellow blotches.

C. robusta   New Zealand
A larger leafed species to 3 m. Insignificant flowers are followed by masses of yellow-red berries.

CORDYLINE
Agavaceae

A genus of shrubby or tree-like tropical evergreens grown chiefly for their striking foliage, although they do bear spikes of insignificant fragrant greenish-white or yellow-green flowers in summer. Grow outdoors in semi-shade in warm climates but in containers on stoeps and sheltered patios where winters are cold.

Cordyline australis   New Zealand
Cabbage tree, Palm lily, Grass palm or Palmlelie
Outdoors, this tree will grow to 30 m; however, in a container it will remain under 1 m high for several years. Tiny white fragrant flowers are borne on branched spikes in summer.

C. terminalis   Eastern Asia
Ti tree, Good luck plant or Tree of kings
Foliage shrub to 3 m; leaves 750 mm long, coloured and variegated; flowers are insignificant.

COREOPSIS
Asteraceae (=Compositae)

Annual and perennial herbaceous plants with daisy-like flowers that bloom for many weeks in summer. They grow well in any garden soil.

Coreopsis grandiflora   North America
Perennial to 500 mm high. Bright yellow single and double flower varieties.

99

CORTADERIA   COTONEASTER

Cortaderia selloana

Cotoneaster amoenus

C. franchetii

C. conspicuus

C. frigidus

C. horizontalis

CORTADERIA
Poaceae (=Gramineae)

Only one species in this genus is commonly cultivated here – the popular and striking Pampas grass, *Cortaderia selloana*. The name is from the Argentinian *cortadera*, meaning pampas grass. Bird-lovers will derive much pleasure from watching birds strip the silky plumes to line their nests, although gardeners may be less delighted. These are useful in dried floral arrangements.

Cortaderia selloana Brazil, Argentina, Chile
Pampas grass or Pampasgras
Large ornamental grass clumps spreading over 3 m with plumes reaching 4 m or more in summer. Plumes are silvery white, cream or dusty pink. Very striking; worth feeding and watering well. They are good windbreak plants.

COTONEASTER
Rosaceae

It is fair to say there is a place for the cotoneaster in every garden. It is a large genus of ornamental shrubs and small trees, both evergreen and deciduous. Cotoneasters are grown for a multitude of reasons – their attractive form, as specimens, as hedges or windbreaks, as ground covers or rockery plants. Although some species are quite attractive, flowers are on the whole insignificant, while others have good autumn colouring. All, however, are grown for their brilliantly coloured, roughly pea-sized autumn berries. For the bird-lover, these shrubs are a must, as they attract a variety of birds to the garden, and the berries are so numerous that they last for weeks in spite of the birds' attentions.

Cotoneaster amoenus   China
An evergreen, erect and compact shrub to 3 m; red berries are borne in autumn.

C. conspicuus   Tibet
Evergreen to 2 m, spreading as much. Flowers are white with red-purple anthers and profuse red berries.

C. franchetii   China, Burma
Evergreen to 3 m; arching branches have a graceful habit. Leaves are felted on the underside giving a silvery appearance to the shrub. Flowers are inconspicuous but profuse red-orange berries are brilliant.

COTULA

COTYLEDON

C. hupehensis

Cotula turbinata

Cotyledon orbiculata

C. x watereri 'Cornubia'

C. tomentosa

C. frigidus — Himalayas
🇫 ⊕ ♣ ☼ 🇼
Deciduous or semi-evergreen shrub or small tree to 6 m. Whitish flowers; bright red berries appear in autumn.

C. horizontalis — China
🇫 ⊕ ♣ ☼ 🇼
Herringbone cotoneaster
Semi-evergreen to 1 m with branches spreading horizontally; arched side branches are geometrically arranged making this shrub very striking if trained against a white wall. The leaves are glossy dark green and tiny pink pretty flowers produce red berries in autumn/winter.

C. hupehensis — China
🇫 ⊕ ♣ ☼ 🇼
Deciduous shrub to 2 m with graceful arching branches. Leaves are felted beneath. The insignificant flowers are followed by bright red berries in autumn.

C. x watereri 'Cornubia' — Garden hybrid
🇫 ⊕ ♣ ☼ 🇼
Evergreen or partly evergreen shrub to 6 m. White flowers produce red berries in autumn.

COTULA
Asteraceae (=Compositae)

Aromatic herbaceous annuals, biennials and perennials with fine, dissected foliage. Flower heads are solitary. Fairly common in the south-western Cape.

Cotula turbinata — South-western Cape
⊕ ☼ 🇼
Ganskos
Annual growing to 450 mm.

COTYLEDON
Crassulaceae

Indigenous evergreen succulents, some cotyledons grow tall enough to be classed as shrubs. They make wonderful rockery plants in hot, dry places, with their fleshy, decorative leaves and spikes of aloe-like flowers, and are easily propagated by planting pieces of the stems in the ground; even the leaves can grow roots. Some species make good container plants on sunny patios or in a hot corner by a swimming pool. Always make certain drainage is good.

Cotyledon orbiculata — South-western Cape and Namaqualand. Widespread
⊕ ♣ ☼ ⊕ 🇼
Pig's ear or Varkoor-plakkie
This is a highly variable species, usually a small shrub. Leaf sizes and shape are also variable but usually grey-green with a shiny red margin. Flowers are bell-shaped in orange, pink or red and carried on branched spikes in summer.

C. tomentosa — Little Karoo
⊕ ♣ ☼ ⊕ 🇼
Dwarf shrub with felty leaves and pink flowers borne in summer.

CRASSULA

Crassula capitella subsp. *thyrsiflora*

C. coccinea

C. multicava

C. ovata

C. rubricaulis

C. perfoliata

CRASSULA
Crassulaceae

From the Latin *crassus*, thick, referring to the fleshy leaves. These evergreen succulents are largely indigenous to southern Africa, and range from dwarf types to shrubs several metres high. As well as being good garden plants, crassulas are very suitable as house and stoep plants. Apart from the decorative leaves of many species, the flowers are often very showy. Easily grown from stem and leaf cuttings.

Crassula capitella subsp. **thyrsiflora** Namaqualand
Foliage plant; shrub with shiny orange leaves.

C. coccinea South-western Cape mountains
Red crassula or Klipblom
Erect stems to 600 mm bearing umbels of the most brilliant crimson-red flowers in late summer.

C. multicava Widespread
This species is perhaps the most common one in our gardens. It will flourish equally well in semi-shade or full sun. Dainty pink inflorescences are borne in late spring and summer.

C. ovata South-eastern Cape, Little Karoo
(*C. argentea*; *C. portulacea*)
Pink joy, Beestebul or Plakkies
Large, rounded bush to 2 m high or more with dense foliage and fleshy leaves clustered in rosettes. Tiny pale pink starry flowers grow in clusters covering the entire bush at times. The flowering season is variable, depending on climate, but it is usually from winter through to summer. An excellent rockery plant, it is easily propagated by stem cuttings.

C. perfoliata Eastern Cape
Shrub to 750 mm with red or pink flowers.

C. rubricaulis Southern Cape
Small shrub to 300 mm bearing pink flowers.

C. rupestris Namaqualand, Little Karoo and Eastern Cape
Spreading shrub to 500 mm with brownish-red to purple leaves with red or yellow margins. A very showy succulent with pale pink flowers in spring.

CRATAEGUS

C. rupestris

Crataegus x grignonensis

C. laevigata

C. subulata

C. phaenopyrum

C. x prunifolia

C. subulata   Vanrhynsdorp along mountains to Port Elizabeth
Sparsely branched small shrub to 400 mm. Creamy-white flowers in dense heads carried on long, erect peduncles in late spring.

CRATAEGUS
Rosaceae

Mostly thorny, deciduous small trees and shrubs native to North America, Europe and northern Asia. Crataegus are commonly known as hawthorns. Good ornamental trees, they are grown for their spring blossoms, showy autumn fruits and often good autumn colouring. The name is from the Greek *krataigas,* meaning flowering thorn.

Crataegus x grignonensis   Garden hybrid
Shrub or small tree to 6 m. White flowers and red berries are both freely borne in autumn.

C. laevigata   Europe
(*Crataegus oxyacantha*)
English hawthorn or White thorn
Small tree to 8 m. White flowers; berries are a deep red.

C. phaenopyrum   North America
Washington thorn
White flowers, with showy shiny bright red berries.

C. pubescens forma *stipulacea*

C. x prunifolia
Shrub or small tree; white flowers with red berries.

C. pubescens forma **stipulacea**   Mexico
Mexican Hawthorn or Skaapvrug
Tree to 10 m. White flowers and orange fruit.

103

CRINUM

Crinum bulbispermum

C. macowanii

C. campanulatum

C. moorei

CRINUM
Amaryllidaceae

A genus of bulbs including several indigenous species which make good garden plants with widespread distribution throughout the tropics and temperate regions of both Americas, Australia, Asia and Africa. Best left undisturbed, the huge (up to 150 mm long) bulbs give rise to large clumps of strap-like leaves, usually evergreen, and then showy, lily-like flowers in shades of pink and white. Some species have red stripes down the petals. The name is from the Greek *krinon*, lily.

Crinum bulbispermum — Southern Africa
Orange River lily or Oranjerivierlelie
Large bulbous plant; many leaves, 70 to 100 mm wide and 1 m long; a peduncle 1 m long bearing 15 or more flowers arranged in a terminal umbel. Flowers are white to pink, red striped down the centre of petals. This is the floral emblem of the Orange Free State.

C. campanulatum — Eastern Cape
Water crinum, Vlei lily or Vleilelie
In nature, this plant grows in shallow ponds which dry up in winter, making it an excellent plant for garden ponds and water gardens. Its flowers are pink or white, sometimes streaked with red, and carried on stems up to 450 mm long. Spring flowering.

C. macowanii — Northern Transvaal, Transvaal, Natal
Sabie crinum or Sabielelie
Spring-bearing flowers are open and more bell-shaped than trumpet-shaped in pink or white striped with red.

C. moorei — Eastern Cape
Moore's crinum, Cape Coast lily or Boslelie
This crinum prefers a shady spot, and combines well with agapanthus; they both flower at the same time, in summer. It produces flower stalks almost 1 m high and carries heads of graceful, nodding pink lily flowers up to 100 mm across.

CROCOSMIA

Crocosmia masonorum

CROCOSMIA
Iridaceae

A small genus of indigenous cormous plants grown for their graceful arching sprays of orange-red, star-shaped flowers held on wiry stems. Crocosmias are perfect for brightening up any shady spot in the garden, and are particularly exquisite in flower arrangements. These plants are best left undisturbed to form large clumps, only being moved when they become overcrowded.

Crocosmia masonorum
(*Tritonia masonorum; Montbretia*) — Pondoland (Transkei)
Golden swans
Showy sprays of brilliant orange flowers up to 50 mm across and 750 mm high are produced in summer.

104

CROSSANDRA / CROTALARIA

C. paniculata

Crossandra infundibuliformis

Crotalaria agatiflora

C. capensis

C. paniculata South Africa
Falling stars
Flower stems up to nearly 1 m in height with sprays 300 mm long bearing starry, bright orange flowers in spring/summer.

CROSSANDRA
Acanthaceae

A genus of shrubs and perennials native to Asia, Africa and Madagascar, grown for their spikes of showy flowers. The commonly grown species, both outdoors or as a house plant, is *Crossandra infundibuliformis*.

Crossandra infundibuliformis
India and Sri Lanka
Firecracker flower
Shrub to 1 m, with glossy, drooping leaves, and tubular, bright orange or salmon-pink flowers in summer.

CROTALARIA
Fabaceae (=Leguminosae) Subfam. Faboideae (=Papilionoideae)

Herbaceous annuals and perennials, shrubs and small trees make up this large genus. Widespread in the warmer regions of the world, there are several species indigenous to southern Africa. The garden varieties are grown for their yellow pea-flowers, which in some species resemble a fluttering bird attached to the stem by its beak. The name comes from the Greek *krotalon*, a castanet, referring to the way in which the seeds rattle in the dried pods.

Crotalaria agatiflora East and Central Africa
Bird flower, Canary bird bush or Voëltjiebos
Shrub or small tree. Large yellow flowers, in spring, are tinged purplish-brown and look like birds hanging on to the stems.

C. capensis From the southern Cape up east coast into Moçambique and Zimbabwe
Cape laburnum, Cape rattlepod or Kaapse klapperpeul
Shrub or small tree to 3 m bearing bright yellow flowers in spring. Quick growing

105

CRYPTANTHUS

Cryptanthus bromelioides

CRYPTOSTEGIA

Cryptostegia grandiflora

CUNONIA

Cunonia capensis

CRYPTANTHUS
Bromeliaceae

The plants in this genus form dwarf, flattened rosettes of stiff, prickly-margined leaves often called 'earth stars' or 'starfish plants' because of the shape. The leaves are handsomely marked, mottled and striped, making them most attractive house plants. Flowers are insignificant. The name is from the Greek *kryptos*, hidden, and *anthos*, flower, as the flowers are hidden inside the bracts. Native to Brazil, they will grow outdoors in warmer climates as well as indoors.

Cryptanthus bromelioides Brazil
Pink cryptanthus
Foliage plant with leaves to 175 mm long and 50 mm wide, that are green above and silvery beneath. White flowers are on inflorescences 150 mm high.

CRYPTOSTEGIA
Asclepiadaceae

A few species of woody evergreen vines from tropical Africa and Madagascar are contained in this genus, only one of which is commonly cultivated.

Cryptostegia grandiflora Tropical Africa
Rubber vine or Rubberklimop
Vigorous climber with large glossy leaves and showy lilac-purple flowers up to 75 mm across and carried in clusters in summer.

CUNONIA
Cunoniaceae

A small genus, of which only one species, the indigenous *Cunonia capensis,* is cultivated.

Cunonia capensis South-western Cape up the east coast into Natal
Red alder or Rooiels
Striking evergreen tree growing up to 30 m in favoured habitats but far less in cultivation, thereby making an attractive garden tree. Flowers, showy, creamy-white and carried in dense spikes up to 140 mm long, are borne in autumn.

CUPHEA

Cuphea hyssopifolia

C. ignea

CUSSONIA

Cussonia spicata

C. micropetala

CUPHEA
Lythraceae

Native to the warmer regions of the Americas, this genus consists of herbaceous perennials and evergreen small shrubs. It is such an easily grown rockery and border plant, which flowers for most months of the year, that it is perfect for the amateur unenthusiastic gardener who likes success.

Cuphea hyssopifolia Mexico
False heather or Elfin herb
Small shrub to 600 mm. Flowers are green and purple, pink or white and appear in spring/summer.

C. ignea Mexico, Jamaica
Cigarette bush, Cigar flower, Firecracker plant or Sigaretplant
Useful and popular small shrub to 750 mm. Flowers grow as long, bright red tubes to 250 mm with tips of violet and white. Plant in a sheltered spot in frosty areas. Spring/summer flowering.

C. micropetala Mexico
Bushy shrub to 600 mm. Flowers are bright red, tipped with greenish-yellow, and appear in summer.

CUSSONIA
Araliaceae

Indigenous to southern Africa and the adjacent islands of the Indian Ocean, this is a genus of trees grown for its distinctive shape and ornamental foliage. Several species make good trees for small townhouse gardens or courtyards as they have tall single trunks similar to palm trees. Topped with a crown of dramatic foliage, they give an impression of tropical luxuriance.

Cussonia spicata Widespread except the northern Cape
Cabbage tree, Umbrella tree or Kiepersol
Fast-growing tree, 3 to 10 m tall with large leaves crowded at the ends of the branches. Greenish flowers on spikes resembling candelabra are borne in summer.

107

CYCAS

Cycas circinalis

C. revoluta

CYCAS
Cycadaceae

These plants are among the most primitive of living seed plants, remnants of an ancient cycad flora that was once an important part of the Earth's vegetation. With their thick stubby stems carrying rosettes of large stiff ornamental leaves, they resemble palms, but are naked-seeded and related to the conifers. Male plants produce terminal cones. In female plants the 'cone' consists of a loose rosette of megasporophylls, each bearing several naked seeds.

Cycas circinalis   Tropical Asia
Sago palm or Fern palm
Very slow growing, but decorative from an early age, they reach 6 m in their natural habitat, but far less in cultivation.

C. revoluta   Southern Japan
Japanese sago palm, Japanese fern palm or Japanse varingpalm
Ornamental foliage with large, twisting leaves, hence the specific name. Slow growing to 3 m.

CYCLAMEN

Cyclamen persicum cv.

CYCLAMEN
Primulaceae

A small genus of tuberous deciduous perennials native to Central Europe and the Mediterranean regions, with exquisite dainty flowers in every shade of pink, mauve and white, often bi-coloured, or blotched and marbled. One species, *Cyclamen persicum*, and its numerous hybrids, is commonly grown in South Africa as a container plant suitable for shady stoeps and windowsills out of direct sunlight.

Cyclamen persicum cv.   Eastern Mediterranean
Florist's cyclamen or Siklaam
Cormous plant. This species has fragrant flowers although many of the named cultivars are scentless. All, however, have large, particularly lovely flowers that bloom in late winter.

CYCLOPIA

Cyclopia genistoides

CYCLOPIA
Fabaceae (=Leguminosae) Subfam. Faboideae (=Papilionoideae)

A genus of indigenous evergreen shrubs of which only one, *Cyclopia genistoides*, is found in cultivation.

Cyclopia genistoides   South-western Cape to Langkloof
Bush tea, Honey tea or Heuningtee
Small shrub to 1 m with thin, needle-like leaves and small yellow pea-flowers. As the common name indicates, the stalks, leaves and flowers are dried and used to make an aromatic, refreshing tea. In nature this plant is often found near rivers; therefore plant in good soil and water well for best results. It flowers from late winter and through spring to mid-summer.

CYMBIDIUM

Cymbidium cv.

Cymbidium cv.

Cymbidium cv.

Cymbidium cv.

Cymbidium cv.

CYMBIDIUM
Orchidaceae

A genus of terrestrial, semi-epiphytic and epiphytic orchids native to tropical Asia and Australia, from which many thousands of hybrids have been raised. Popular as greenhouse plants, they need direct, but filtered sunlight. Cymbidiums produce erect or arching stems carrying up to 30 large, long-lasting flowers in a wide range of colours.

Cymbidium cvs.

CYNARA

Cynara scolymus

CYNARA
Asteraceae (=Compositae)

A genus of coarse, thistle-like perennials native to the Mediterranean region and Canary Islands. These large plants have attractive silvery grey foliage which make them useful in mixed borders or rock gardens. Flowers, found in shades of purple and mauve, resemble large thistles yet make surprisingly good cut flowers. These are adaptable plants and will grow in most climates and soils, but for best results one should feed and water them well. Propagate from seed, or from suckers or sideshoots.

Cynara scolymus   Mediterranean region

Globe artichoke or Artisjok
Tall perennial to 1,5 m. Edible flower buds become mauve-blue flowers in summer.

109

CYPERUS

Cyperus alternifolius

C. papyrus

CYPERUS
Cyperaceae

Both annuals and perennials are included in this large genus, but it is the rhizomatous perennials that are cultivated for their ornamental foliage, particularly as waterside or aquatic plants, seen around pools.

Cyperus alternifolius   Madagascar, Mauritius
Umbrella sedge or Sambreelbiesie
This foliage plant sends up clumps of stems to over 1 m in favourable conditions, each stem bearing a graceful crown of grass-like needle leaves, radiating like the spokes of an umbrella. It is best in semi-shade close to water. It can also be grown in ponds, as an aquatic, where it multiplies rapidly.

C. papyrus   North and tropical Africa
Papyrus, Egyptian reed, Papirus or Papierriet
This foliage plant, the paper plant of the ancient Egyptians, will send up stems to over 2 m that are crowned with a mop-like head of thread-like flower spikelets. Although usually seen as a waterside or quick-spreading aquatic plant, *Cyperus papyrus* will grow anywhere in the garden.

CYPHOMANDRA

Cyphomandra betacea

CYPHOMANDRA
Solanaceae

Perennials, shrubs and trees comprise this genus from tropical America, of which only one species, *Cyphomandra betacea*, is cultivated. This same species has become naturalized in the eastern regions of Zimbabwe, the eastern Cape, and possibly Natal.

Cyphomandra betacea   Peru
Tree tomato or Boomtamatie
Quick-growing tree which will fruit within two years from seed, reaching a height of 2 to 3 m. Leaves are large, felty and grey-green; flowers are pinkish-white, fragrant, and not very showy; fruit is orange-red, egg-shaped, and up to 50 mm long. Edible as well as ornamental, the fruit can be used raw in salads, for jam and chutney or added to stews and curries. It flowers in spring, followed by fruits in summer.

CYPHOSTEMMA

Cyphostemma currorii

C. juttae

CYPHOSTEMMA
Vitaceae

Vines, shrubs and small trees are included in this genus of plants native to the tropics and subtropics. Grown for their foliage and decorative, sometimes poisonous, fruits, they can be found in every imaginable form, from pot plants to ground covers, to rockery plants or unusually small trees.

Cyphostemma currorii   Northern Africa and Namibia
Cobas or Kobas
A thickset succulent ornamental tree reaching a height of 7 m in nature, but probably far less in cultivation. Leaves are thick and fleshy with poisonous red fruit in grape-like bunches borne in late summer.

C. juttae   Northern Africa, Namibia and northwards
Bastard cobas or Basterkobas
Small, succulent ornamental tree usually up to 2 m, occasionally to 4 m. Huge swollen trunk, bearing a spreading crown of branches at the top, is ornamental in an unusual way. Flowers borne in early summer are inconspicuous but the fruit is red, and later purple.

CYRTANTHUS

Cyrtanthus falcatus

C. mackenii var. *mackenii*

C. brachyscyphus

C. elatus

CYRTOMIUM

Cyrtomium falcatum

CYRTANTHUS
Amaryllidaceae

Commonly known as fire lilies, this is a genus of indigenous bulbs, some of which burst into bloom after fires and make brilliant splashes on the blackened veld. As well as red, they also come in shades of cream, yellow and orange. The flowers are borne in loose umbels at the tips of hollow stalks which vary from a few millimetres to 600 mm high. The name comes from the Greek *kyrtos*, curved and *anthos*, flower, referring to the graceful, drooping way the flowers curve away from the stems.

Cyrtanthus falcatus   Eastern Cape
Green-red flowers to 60 mm long borne in spring.

C. mackenii var. **mackenii**   Natal south coast
Ifafa lily or Ifafalelie
Fragrant ivory flowers up to 50 mm long, reaching 300 mm above the ground, bloom in late winter/early spring.

C. brachyscyphus   Eastern Cape mountains and Natal
Kleinrooipypie
Small, bright red, scentless flowers in spring.

C. elatus   South Africa
Red flowers in spring.

CYRTOMIUM
Polypodiaceae

A genus of tropical ferns with firm arching fronds of leathery glossy foliage which make lovely ornamental indoor plants, but also grown outdoors in warm climates. Some species are indigenous to South Africa.

Cyrtomium falcatum   South Africa, Asia
Holly fern
Foliage plant with stiff, erect fronds to 750 mm long with glossy, dark green leaves.

111

CYRTOSTACHYS

CYTISUS

Cyrtostachys lakka

Cytisus x *praecox* 'Albus'

CYRTOSTACHYS
Arecaceae (=Palmae)

A genus of handsome ornamental palms native to Malaysia and the adjacent Pacific Islands. Suitable for cultivation only in the tropics.

Cyrtostachys lakka Malaysia, Borneo
Sealing-wax palm or Lipstick palm
Foliage plant; palm to 5 m or more and slender. Leaves to 1,75 m long with leaf stalks of orange-red.

CYTISUS
Fabaceae (=Leguminosae) Subfam. Faboideae (=Papilionoideae)

A genus of deciduous and evergreen shrubs from the Mediterranean regions grown for their yellow, red or white pea-flowers which cover the plants in spring. These adaptable shrubs will grow in poor soil, under most conditions. Propagate from seeds or cuttings and prune the bushes hard after flowering.

Cytisus x praecox 'Albus' Garden hybrid
Bridal broom or Bruidsbesem
Shrub to 2 m, with attractively drooping branches and masses of small white flowers borne in early spring.

DAHLIA
Asteraceae (= Compositae)

This amazing genus of tuberous perennials, so universally popular, is from Central America and it is from this very genus that the 11 groups of garden dahlias come. Dahlias come in a fascinating array of shapes and sizes, and in virtually every colour except blue; many are even multi-coloured. Plants come in 11 sizes, from dwarf varieties suitable as border, bedding and rockery plants to tall bushes suitable for mixed borders, and to the other extreme of tree dahlias. Wonderfully colourful in the garden, dahlias are among the finest cut flowers. The successful cultivation of dahlias requires a certain amount of time and effort, and novice gardeners should consult a nurseryman or a reliable gardening book. Named after Andreas Dahl, 1751-1789, Swedish botanist, pupil of Linnaeus.

Dahlia imperialis Central America
Tree dahlia
Herbaceous to woody perennial growing to 4 m. Unbranched except at the flowering tips, leaves grow up to 750 mm long and

DAHLIA

Dahlia imperialis

D. pinnata cv.

D. pinnata cv.

D. pinnata cv.

D. pinnata cv.

D. pinnata 'Pompon'

flowers, up to 100 mm across, are white, mauve or rosy purple and bloom in summer.

D. pinnata cvs.
The 'garden dahlias', with tuberous roots, form an herbaceous bush to 1,5 m with showy flower heads in summer, in many forms, sizes and colours.

D. pinnata 'Pompon'
Small, round double flower heads are ball-shaped. Ray florets are cupped or tubular.

DAIS

Dais cotinifolia

D. cotinifolia

DAIS
Thymelaeaceae

Only one species in this very small genus is cultivated, the indigenous *Dais cotinifolia*.

Dais cotinifolia Transkei, Natal, Eastern Transvaal escarpment
Pompon tree or Kannabas
A very attractive, semi-deciduous shrub or tree, usually fairly neat and small in gardens, but capable of reaching 13 m where conditions suit it. The tree is often completely covered with blossoms in spring. The flower heads are pink to mauve and globes are about 40 mm in diameter, with a particularly lovely fragrance, especially at dusk.

113

DELONIX

Delonix regia

D. regia

DELPHINIUM

Delphinium x *elatum*

D. grandiflorum

DELONIX
Fabaceae (=Leguminosae) Subfam. Caesalpinioideae

There are three species in this genus of tropical trees, of which one, *Delonix regia*, is widely cultivated. From the Greek *delos*, conspicuous and *onyx*, claw, referring to the shape of the petals.

Delonix regia — Madagascar
Poinciana or Flamboyant
As the common name implies, these are among the showiest of trees, quick growing, with delicate, acacia-like foliage and spectacular displays of scarlet flowers in early summer. Growing to 10 m, these trees, with their flat crowns, can spread over twice their height. Very tender to frost, flamboyants thrive only where conditions are truly subtropical.

DELPHINIUM
Ranunculaceae

Perhaps the most beautiful blues in the garden are provided by the plants in this genus of annuals, biennials and perennials native to the temperate regions of the northern hemisphere. Many hybrids have been raised from the original 'blue' species. As well as the traditional intense 'delphinium blue', the shades now go into mauves, reds, pinks, purples, whites and yellows. Plants vary in size from the magnificent tall spires of the perennial, *Delphinium* x *elatum*, to the low-growing annual cultivars of *Delphinium grandiflorum*. Delphiniums are certainly worth taking trouble over. Give them deep, rich, moist but well-drained soil and full sun and you will reap a magnificent harvest. The name comes from the Greek *delphin*, a dolphin, referring to the shape of the flower buds.

Delphinium x elatum — Garden hybrid
Pacific hybrids
Perennials from 1 to 2 m high with tall central spikes of semi-double flowers, surrounded by shorter spikes. Summer flowering, they range through brilliant blues to purple, pink, yellow and white, often with contrasting centres. Protect delphiniums from wind; or stake.

D. grandiflorum — Siberia, China
Butterfly delphinium or Blue butterfly
Perennials usually grown as annuals, up to 450 mm, often less, that flower in springtime.

DENDROBIUM

Dendrobium phalaenopsis

DEUTZIA

Deutzia gracilis

D. scabra 'Plena'

DIANTHUS

Dianthus x *allwoodii*

D. barbatus

DENDROBIUM
Orchidaceae

Some of the loveliest orchids belong to this genus of about 900 species which are widespread in Asia, Australia and the Pacific Islands. The colour and shape of the flowers differ greatly, but many are borne on the most graceful, delicate sprays. Because the natural habitat varies so greatly, from the hottest tropics to the Himalayas and Tibet, and north to Korea and Japan, cultivation requirements also vary. However, it is worthwhile finding out the exact requirements of a particular species from an expert, as they are easy to grow if conditions are right; the flower displays are more than rewarding.

Dendrobium phalaenopsis
Australia, New Guinea
These are greenhouse plants of a specialist culture. Stems grow to 600 mm or more and produce flower sprays 600 mm long with up to 18 flowers over 60 mm across in rose, purple and pink, with dark purple throats. They flower in late spring to late autumn.

DEUTZIA
Saxifragaceae

The bridal wreaths are one of the most ornamental free-flowering shrubs from temperate Asia and the mountains of Central America. Usually deciduous, they produce masses of dainty blossoms carried on graceful arching or drooping sprays in the spring. Flowers are somtimes white but delicately flushed with pink or can be pink, deep rosy pink and lavender. Grow in good soil in semi-shade and prune hard after flowering. Propagate by division, layering and cuttings.

Deutzia gracilis
Japan
Slender deutzia
Low-growing shrub, wide spreading and bearing lovely pure white flowers in spring.

D. scabra 'Plena'
Japan
Bridal wreath
Shrub to 2,3 m with masses of double flowers in spring. These are white, delicately tinged with purplish-pink on the outside.

DIANTHUS
Caryophyllaceae

This genus of annuals, biennials and perennials, found from Portugal to Japan, includes some of the most richly scented flowers in the world. South Africa, too, has a few species, which are not cultivated. The best known species in this genus is the popular florist's carnation, *Dianthus caryophyllus*; other species are the *Dianthus barbatus*, the border perennial known as Sweet William and usually grown as a biennial, *Dianthus chinensis*, the annual dianthus, and the low-growing perennial pinks, including *Dianthus* x *allwoodii*. All *Dianthus* species require full sun and very good drainage and grow easily from seed or tip cuttings. The name is from the Greek *dios*, a god or divinity, and *anthos*, a flower; thus divine flower, or flower of the gods.

Dianthus x allwoodii
Garden hybrid
Pinks
A tufted perennial in all shades of red, pink, mauve and white, 150 mm to 400 mm in summer.

CONTINUED

DIANTHUS

D. caryophyllus

D. chinensis 'Heddewiggii'

DIASCIA

Diascia integerrima

DICENTRA

Dicentra spectabilis

D. barbatus — Mountains of southern Europe
Sweet William or Baardangelier
Biennial to 400 mm; flowers are purple through pinks to white in summer.

D. caryophyllus — Mediterranean region
Carnation, Clove pink, Divine flower or Angelier
Short-lived perennial to 1 m. Flowers grow up to 80 mm across in all colour shades except blue, often mottled or striped.

D. chinensis 'Heddewiggii' — China
Rainbow pink, Japanese pinks or Japanse grasangelier
Annual to 400 mm. Pink-mauve flowers.

DIASCIA
Scrophulariaceae

There are about 50 species in this genus of small, dainty plants, both annual and perennial, and all are indigenous to South Africa. Most species are recognizable by the 'spurs' underneath each flower. Colours are reds, pinks and mauves, often with darker throats and a yellow blotch on each. The perennial varieties are showier than the annuals and are useful in rockeries or at the front of a border in full sun. The name comes from the Greek *diaskeo*, to adorn, referring to the very decorative flowers.

Diascia integerrima — South-western Cape to Natal
Twinspur or Pansies
Perennial up to 450 mm. Pink flowers 20 mm across are borne in summer for several months from October onwards.

DICENTRA
Fumariaceae

Many species in this genus are native to the colder regions of North America and Asia and grow best in semi-shade. These herbaceous perennials bear dainty, unusually shaped flowers hanging from arching stems, above pretty, lacy foliage. Good, rich soil is essential for successful flowering. From the Greek *di*, two, *kentron*, a spur, referring to the spurs on the petals.

Dicentra spectabilis — Japan
Bleeding hearts, Lyre plant, Lady's locket or Dutchman's breeches
Perennial to 450 mm. Flowers are rosy red and white in spring.

DICHONDRA

Dichondra micrantha

DICHORISANDRA

Dichorisandra thyrsiflora

DICHROSTACHYS

Dichrostachys cinerea subsp. *africana*

DICHONDRA
Convolvulaceae

There are nine species in this genus of low-growing, creeping, prostrate perennial ground covers native to both Americas, eastern Asia and Australasia, but only one, *Dichondra micrantha*, is commonly cultivated. This is a most attractive ground cover, making a dense mat of pretty, rounded leaves, useful in sun and semi-shade; the flowers are insignificant.

Dichondra micrantha North America, Asia
(*D. repens*)
Wonderlawn
Ground cover that can serve as a lawn substitute for light-traffic areas.

DICHORISANDRA
Commelinaceae

Herbaceous perennials native to tropical America and requiring warm, moist, shaded conditions. Often grown as greenhouse plants for their tropical foliage which is sometimes variegated; some species have showy purple or blue flower spikes as well.

Dichorisandra thyrsiflora Brazil
Perennial to 1,5 m with glossy green leaves and spikes of blue-violet flowers borne in summer/autumn.

DICHROSTACHYS
Fabaceae (=Leguminosae) Subfam. Mimosoideae

A small genus of shrubs and small trees which extends from Australia through southern Asia to Africa and South Africa. Only one species is widespread in South Africa, *Dichrostachys cinerea* subsp. *africana*.

Dichrostachys cinerea subsp. **africana**
Widespread in Central Africa, Transvaal, Northern Cape and Natal
Sickle bush or Sekelbos
A summer-flowering shrub or small tree growing to 3 m and resembling the indigenous acacias. Drooping flowers like fluffy catkins come in shades of pink and yellow and make a lovely ornamental asset to a garden.

DICLIPTERA

Dicliptera suberecta

DICOMA

Dicoma zeyheri

DIDELTA

Didelta carnosa var. *carnosa*

D. spinosa

DICLIPTERA
Acanthaceae

A genus of herbaceous shrubs native to the tropics and temperate regions. Also called jacobinias.

Dicliptera suberecta   Uruguay
(*Jacobinia suberecta*)
Shrubby perennial to 300 mm with greyish velvety leaves, and red-orange tubular flowers. A good stoep plant, it is also suitable for warm rockeries as it flowers all season.

DICOMA
Asteraceae (=Compositae)

A genus of herbaceous perennials, most of which are found in Africa, with about 25 species in South Africa. It is widespread but has not yet reached the south-western Cape.

Dicoma zeyheri   Zululand, Transvaal
Maagwortel or Jakkalsbos
This small summer-flowering perennial has thistle-like flower heads growing to 300 mm high. The silvery green, prickly leaves make good flower arrangements.

DIDELTA
Asteraceae (=Compositae)

Many of the famous photographs of Table Mountain, taken from across the bay, feature spectacular sheets of yellow daisies growing on the sand dunes. These are *Didelta carnosa*, one of two species which make up this genus of plants indigenous to the western Cape, Namaqualand and Namibia.

Didelta carnosa var. **carnosa**   Western Cape, Namaqualand
Seegousblom, Duinegousblom or Perdeblom
Perennial up to 1 m with green leaves and yellow daisy flowers, 40 to 70 mm across, that bloom late spring/summer.

D. spinosa   Namaqualand, Clanwilliam
Perdebos
An erect branched shrub to 2 m. Leaves bright green to 70 mm long and 60 mm wide. Flower heads 40 to 70 mm across in yellow to orange appear in early spring.

DIEFFENBACHIA

Dieffenbachia amoena

D. maculata 'Rudolph Roehrs'

D. maculata

DIEFFENBACHIA
Araceae

A genus of evergreen shrubby perennials from tropical America grown for their large decorative leaves, often strikingly variegated. They make good indoor and stoep plants that require plenty of light, but not direct sun. They are poisonous and the bitter sap causes the tongue to swell to such a size that speech is impossible – hence the common name 'Dumb cane'.

Dieffenbachia amoena Tropical America
Dumb cane
Poisonous evergreen foliage plant with leaves to 600 mm, green and blotched with cream.

D. maculata Central and South America
Spotted dumb cane
Poisonous foliage plant variable to 3 m; oblong or lance-shaped leaves that are heavily spotted with white.

D. maculata 'Rudolph Roehrs' Central and South America
Yellow leaf dumb cane
Poisonous foliage plant mutant of *Dieffenbachia maculata* with leaves mostly creamy-white, or pale apple-green with fine splotches of white.

DIERAMA

Dierama pendulum

DIERAMA
Iridaceae

Dainty drooping bells carried on long, slender, grass-like stems, arching at the tips with the weight of the flowers. This makes 'wand' flowers easily recognizable in their natural habitat, the mountain ranges of eastern Africa from Kenya to the eastern Cape. These are cormous plants, more or less evergreen, which form clumps of grass-like leaves best left undisturbed once established in the garden. In their mountain habitat they grow in rich, moist soil and partial shade with plenty of movement in the air about them; these conditions should be provided in the garden. Increase by division, but only when necessary as the plants resent disturbance.

Dierama pendulum Eastern Cape
Zuurberg Harebell, Wand flower, Fairy bells or Grasklokkie
An evergreen cormous perennial forming large clumps of leaves up to 1 m high, with flower stems much taller, carrying pink or mauve flowers in late spring or early summer.

DIETES

Dietes bicolor

D. grandiflora

DIETES
Iridaceae

About five species make up this genus of indigenous, rhizomatous iris-like plants with the evergreen sword-like foliage forming large clumps. These tough, drought-resistant plants will thrive in semi-shade as well as full sun, often where little else will grow. Dietes will tolerate both wind and frost, and seed themselves freely. The flowers, carried on wiry, arching stems, are dainty and although each bloom usually lasts only a day, new flowers open continually during flowering spells.

Dietes bicolor   Eastern Cape
Peacock flower, Yellow wild iris, Uintjie or Poublom
Clumps 750 mm high. Late spring yellow flowers reach about 50 mm across; alternate petals are blotched brown and orange.

D. grandiflora   Eastern Cape, Natal and into East Africa
Wild iris or Wilde iris
Leaves to 1 m or more. White flowers up to 100 mm across last several days in summer.

DIGITALIS

Digitalis purpurea

DIGITALIS
Scrophulariaceae

The name of this genus comes from the Latin *digitus*, a finger, referring to the way the flowers resemble the finger of a glove. They are most commonly known, however, as foxgloves. Native to Europe, Central Asia and the Mediterranean regions, many striking garden varieties have been raised from the original species. Tall perennials, usually treated as biennials, foxgloves are hard to beat for accent plants in mixed borders or elsewhere in the garden, and there are dwarf varieties available as well. These plants, which seed themselves freely, are best in semi-shade and need rich soil and ample water.

Digitalis purpurea   Western Mediterranean
Foxglove or Vingerhoedjie
Biennial to 1,25 m. Very showy spring and summer flowers are purple, pink, white and cream, and spotted inside.

DILATRIS

Dilatris pillansii

DILATRIS
Haemodoraceae

A genus of five species of South African herbaceous perennials with rootstocks. Leaves are rigid, glabrous and linear-oblong. Flowers are borne in racemes, corymbs or pseudo-umbellate panicles in spring. They need well-drained soil and must be left undisturbed.

Dilatris pillansii   South-western Cape
Rooiwortel
Flower stalk up to 1 m.

DIMORPHOTHECA

Dimorphotheca pluvialis

D. sinuata

DIONAEA

Dionaea muscipula

DIOSCOREA

Dioscorea bulbifera

DIMORPHOTHECA
Asteraceae (=Compositae)

About seven species make up this genus of annuals and perennials indigenous to South Africa, although the species native to the winter rainfall area of the Cape and particularly Namaqualand are the best known. Most species have glossy, shining flower petals, so that when they flower in masses in the wild, the sheets of colour they create have a shimmering brilliance. Although not actually scented, some species have a warm, fresh fragrance.

Dimorphotheca pluvialis South-western Cape, Namaqualand and Namibia
Cape daisy, Rain daisy or Witbotterblom
Late winter/spring flowering annual, varies in height but usually low growing. Flower petals are snowy white above, violet below.

D. sinuata Namaqualand
Namaqualand daisy, Botterblom or Jakkalsblom
Annual, rather sprawling, to 300 mm high with orange flowers that bloom in late winter/spring.

DIONAEA
Droseraceae

Only one species, *Dionaea muscipula*, in this carnivorous genus of low-growing, perennial, herbaceous plants from North America. Lately they have become available in South Africa and grown as a curiosity.

Dionaea muscipula North and South Carolina, United States
Venus's flytrap or Venusvlieëvanger
Leaves grow in a basal rosette to 250 mm long. Petioles are flat, winged and the terminal leaf blade is two-lobed. Lobes are hinged and fringed with hair-like, stiff outgrowths and with three sensitive hairs on the upper surface of each lobe. The lobes come together amazingly quickly when the sensitive hairs are touched and any insect settling on them is immediately 'caught'. Digestive glands secrete enzymes and later absorb the digested materials as a complementary source of nitrogenous nutrition. These plants normally occur on soils poor in nitrogen. To grow, these curious plants need specialized attention and conditions.

DIOSCOREA
Dioscoreaceae

Named after Pedianos Diascorides, an ancient Greek physician and authority on medicinal herbs. This large genus includes species whose tubers are a source of medicinal drugs and others that are important sources of food in the tropics. Commonly known as yams, these quick-growing, twining plants produce large, edible tubers that are cooked and eaten like potatoes. Some species make ornamental stoep and indoor plants.

Dioscorea bulbifera Tropical East Asia
Air potato or Yam
Twining foliage plant, bearing large edible aerial tubers.

DIOSMA

Diosma ericoides

DIOSPYROS

Diospyros kaki

DISA

Disa uniflora

D. uniflora 'Kirstenbosch Pride'

DIOSMA
Rutaceae

A genus of heath-like, small shrubs indigenous to the Cape, mainly the south-western districts extending into the eastern Cape Province. The name comes from the Greek, meaning divine odour, and most species have delightfully aromatic foliage and tiny fragrant flowers. Diosmas need similar growing conditions to ericas.

Diosma ericoides South-western Cape
Breath of heaven
Bushy shrub to 600 mm; spring flowers are tiny, white and flushed with pink, and very fragrant.

DIOSPYROS
Ebenaceae

This is a genus of widely distributed deciduous and evergreen trees and shrubs, some grown as ornamentals, others for their fruit persimmons, and still others for timber, especially ebony. Flowers are insignificant, the ornamental species being grown for their pleasing shape and glossy foliage which has showy autumn colouring. The fruits of the edible varieties are also attractive, going orange to dark red when ripening. These are easily grown trees in most soils but climatic requirements vary according to species.

Diospyros kaki Japan
Japanese persimmon or Persimmon
Spreading tree up to 15 m with fruit to 75 mm in diameter, borne in autumn and coloured orange to orange-red. It is the most popular fruit in Japan and China, where it is much cultivated.

DISA
Orchidaceae

A genus of terrestrial orchids indigenous to southern Africa and Madagascar. The South African species occurs mostly in a wide coastal belt from the south-western Cape, through the eastern Cape and into Natal. Some species are also found in inland mountainous areas. Only a few are found in cultivation, and of these, *Disa uniflora* is the best known, although notoriously difficult to grow outside its natural habitat, where it is strictly protected.

Disa uniflora South-western Cape mountains
Red disa, Pride of Table Mountain or Rooidisa
Strictly protected and the flower emblem of the Cape Province. This tuberous perennial grows to 600 mm; very showy flowers up to 100 mm across in brilliant carmine-red are produced in late winter/spring. Consult a specialist about where to plant.

D. uniflora 'Kirstenbosch Pride'
(*D. uniflora* x *D. cardinalis*)
As above. Flowers are orange-red.

DISSOTIS

Dissotis canescens

D. canescens

DISSOTIS
Melastomataceae

A genus of herbaceous perennials or small shrubs native to tropical and southern Africa, of which two, *Dissotis princeps* and *Dissotis canescens*, are indigenous to South Africa. Both species have hairy leaves and spikes of showy flowers. Found near perennial water in nature, these make good plants for a water garden, although they will grow elsewhere in a garden if kept constantly moist.

Dissotis canescens   North-eastern Transvaal, Natal, Transkei
Dwarf glory bush or Kalwerbossie
Shrub to 1,5 m. Flowers, up to 50 mm across in varying shades of purple and pink, are produced in late summer/autumn.

DISTICTIS

Distictis buccinatoria

D. laxiflora

D. x riversii

DISTICTIS
Bignoniaceae

A genus of about nine species of evergreen woody climbers, native to the West Indies and tropical America. Distictis are grown for their showy sprays of large, brightly coloured flowers. Vigorous and spreading, these vines cling with tendrils to surfaces such as brick or stone.

Distictis buccinatoria   Mexico
(*Phaedranthus buccinatorius*; *Bignonia cherere*)
Mexican blood-trumpet
A climber to 4 m bearing large clusters of flowers in bright shades of red in summer.

D. laxiflora   Mexico
Creeper to 4 m with flowers opening in purple then fading to nearly white and growing up to 80 mm across; in summer.

D. x riversii
(*D. buccinatoria* x *D. laxiflora*)
Flowers resemble those of *Distictis laxiflora* but twice as large; also summer flowering.

DIZYGOTHECA

Dizygotheca elegantissima

DODONAEA

Dodonaea angustifolia

D. angustifolia 'Purpurea'

DOMBEYA

Dombeya burgessiae

D. rotundifolia var. *rotundifolia*

DIZYGOTHECA
Araliaceae

A genus of shrubs and small trees native to the South Pacific Islands. Their particularly attractive and unusual juvenile foliage is retained permanently when grown as indoor plants, which is why they are so popular.

Dizygotheca elegantissima
New Caledonia
False aralia or Valsaralia
Foliage plant; 1 to 2 m; with thread-like, serrated drooping leaflets; reddish when young, then turning dark green with a prominent reddish midrib.

DODONAEA
Sapindaceae

These shrubs and small trees are native to the tropical and subtropical regions of the world, but mostly Australasia. Grown for their foliage, they make excellent hedge and windbreak plants.

Dodonaea angustifolia
New Zealand
Sand olive, Hop bush, Ysterhout or Sandolien
Shrub or small tree growing to 4 m; flowers are greenish and insignificant but are followed by attractive sprays of papery winged seeds; a tough, wind-resistant plant that flowers in summer.

D. angustifolia 'Purpurea'
New Zealand
Purple hop bush or Perssandolien
Shrub or small bushy tree to 4 m with decorative foliage in shades of purple-bronze, varying with the season. They display attractive sprays of papery seeds, cream-coloured and topped with red or purple in summer; good for dried arrangements. This shrub is striking when planted against a sunny, white wall.

DOMBEYA
Sterculiaceae

A genus of evergreen and deciduous shrubs and small trees native to Africa, Madagascar and adjacent islands. Dombeyas are grown for their ornamental habit and showy clusters of fragrant flowers in shades of pink and white. Easily grown, fairly drought resistant, but needing shelter from wind and frost, they will grow in semi-shade as well as full sun.

Dombeya burgessiae
Natal, Eastern Transvaal, Eastern Zimbabwe
Pink dombeya
Large bushy shrub or small tree up to 4 m. Large leaves up to 180 mm long with deep or pale pink flowers or white ones in large rounded heads; autumn/early winter flowering.

DOROTHEANTHUS   DORYANTHES

D. x *tiliacea*

Dorotheanthus bellidiformis

D. wallichii

D. bellidiformis

Doryanthes excelsa

D. rotundifolia var. **rotundifolia**
Northern Natal, Transvaal, East Africa, into Namibia
Wild pear or Drolpeer
Deciduous, well-shaped small tree to 5 m, occasionally more, with fragrant, creamy-white flowers in clusters that cover the tree in late winter/spring before the leaves appear.

D. x tiliacea Garden hybrid
Shrub or small tree to 3 m; pink flowers in ruffled dense umbels that bloom in summer.

D. wallichii East Africa, Madagascar
Shrub or small tree to 5 m; flowers are deep pink or red, carried in dense umbels in winter.

DOROTHEANTHUS
Mesembryanthemaceae

Named after Frau Dorothea Schwantes, wife of a German botanist. This small genus of dwarf succulent annuals is indigenous to the south-western Cape and Namaqualand and includes the brilliant Bokbaaivygie, *Dorotheanthus bellidiformis*.

Dorotheanthus bellidiformis
South-western Cape
Livingstone daisy or Bokbaaivygie
Annual 100 to 120 mm high. Ideal for edging rockeries, bedding and massed displays, the plants are completely covered with brilliant, glistening springtime flowers in all shades of red, pink, purple, orange, apricot and cream. Easily grown from seed. Spring flowering.

DORYANTHES
Agavaceae

From the Greek *dory*, a spear, and *anthos*, a flower, because the flower stem is like the shaft of a spear. This is a genus of two or three species of succulents native to Australia. Resembling the agaves in size and habit, they make striking accent plants in the garden but should be planted in semi-shade and watered well.

Doryanthes excelsa Australia
Spear lily, Giant lily or Gymea lily
Leaves to 2,5 m long with flower spikes to 4 m. Lily-like bright red flowers in round clusters 30 mm across that appear in spring.

125

DRACAENA

Dracaena deremensis 'Warneckii'

D. hookerana

D. marginata 'Tricolor'

DRACAENA
Liliaceae

A genus of evergreen foliage plants from the tropics. Some are suitable for growing outdoors in partial shade in warmer climates while others are best as indoor or stoep plants.

Dracaena deremensis 'Warneckii'
Tropical Africa
Striped dracaena
Foliage plant, growing to 5 m but less indoors; leaves grow to 600 mm long and 50 mm wide, with white stripes.

D. hookerana Tropical Africa, Kei River in South Africa
Foliage plant, growing to 2 m or more; leaves are white margined; greenish flowers and orange berries appear at irregular times.

D. marginata 'Tricolor' Madagascar
Foliage plant to 2 m; leaves are grey-green, with pale red margins.

DRACOPHILUS

Dracophilus dealbatis

DRACOPHILUS
Mesembryanthemaceae

Small cushion-like succulents with rough, bluish-green leaves. Flowers are white or pink. Grow in well-drained, coarse sandy soil to secure success.

Dracophilus dealbatis Northern Namaqualand
Short stems with four leaves each growing to 40 mm long and 15 mm across; an excellent specimen for the miniature rock garden.

DRACUNCULUS

Dracunculus vulgaris

DROSANTHEMUM

Drosanthemum bicolor

D. speciosum

DUCHESNEA

Duchesnea indica

DRACUNCULUS
Araceae

Two aptly named plants from the Greek word for a little dragon, with handsome foliage and positively arresting flowers, belong in this genus from the Mediterranean region. Grow them outdoors in semi-shade, in rich, well-drained soil.

Dracunculus vulgaris
Mediterranean region
Dragon lily or Draaklelie
Tuberous perennial to 1 m, with deeply divided, fan-shaped leaves and most striking, almost heraldic-looking flower spathes which are green on the outside and purple inside, with a long, deep purple spadix. These flowers give off a carrion-like smell when in full bloom in summer, attracting flies for pollination purposes.

DROSANTHEMUM
Mesembryanthemaceae

A genus of evergreen succulents indigenous to South Africa and commonly referred to as 'vygies' or ice-plants which bear brilliantly coloured flowers that often completely cover the foliage in spring. Excellent plants for rockeries, or as spreading ground covers. They will grow in poor soil but need full sun and good drainage. The name is from the Greek, meaning dew-flower, referring to the tiny glistening dots on the leaves which sparkle like dew.

Drosanthemum bicolor
South-western Cape
Bushy plant to 600 mm, spreading as much again. Flowers produced in spring are yellow in the centre and orange to purple towards the tips of the shiny petals.

D. speciosum
South-western Cape
Height and spread is 600 mm. Flowers are orange or red with a green or yellow central zone and are borne and found in spring.

DUCHESNEA
Rosaceae

Of these two small, spreading perennials from southern Asia, only one, *Duchesnea indica*, is cultivated.

Duchesnea indica
India
(*Fragaria indica*)
Indian strawberry, Mock strawberry or Wildeaarbei
Quick-growing, drought-resistant ground cover, spreading by runners, with strawberry-like leaves and bright yellow flowers up to 50 mm across throughout spring and summer. These are followed by fruits which resemble tiny strawberries, but which are quite tasteless. Grow in full sun or semi-shade, and propagate by division. Duchesneas self-seed freely in favourable conditions.

DURANTA

Duranta repens

D. repens 'Variegata'

DURANTA
Verbenaceae

A genus of quick-growing evergreen shrubs or small trees from Central America, sometimes thorny and useful as hedges or windbreaks as well as being decorative ornamental specimens. The dainty sprays of forget-me-not flowers in various shades of mauve and blue are followed by long-lasting dense, drooping spikes of very showy orange berries. Durantas seed themselves fairly freely and grow in any soil. In some climates they are semi-deciduous. This plant has become naturalized in some parts of southern Africa.

Duranta repens　　　　Central America
Golden dewdrop, Pigeon berry, Sky flower or Forget-me-not tree
Shrub or small tree to 3 m with blue flowers in spring, followed by orange berries.

D. repens 'Variegata'　　　Central America
As above, although leaves are variegated cream.

DUVERNOIA

Duvernoia adhatodoides

DUVERNOIA
Acanthaceae

Only three or four species make up this genus of evergreen shrubs and small trees native to tropical and southern Africa. Only one is cultivated, *Duvernoia adhatodoides*, found in the coastal forests of the Transkei and Natal. The common name, pistol bush, comes from the way in which the ripe seed pods burst open with a loud crack, throwing the seeds some distance from the parent plant.

Duvernoia adhatodoides　　Natal, Transkei
Pistol bush
Shrub to 3 m, with showy, fragrant white flowers in summer up to 30 mm long; they have purple markings in the throat.

DYMONDIA

Dymondia margaretae

DYMONDIA
Asteraceae (=Compositae)

There is only one South African species in this genus, *Dymondia margaretae*, which is found in the Bredasdorp district of the Cape.

Dymondia margaretae　　Southern Cape
Silver carpet
A prostrate evergreen herbaceous perennial with tiny blue-grey leaves which make a neat attractive ground cover. Its tiny yellow flowers, borne in spring, are insignificant. Fairly drought resistant, it needs good drainage.

ECHEVERIA

Echeveria elegans

E. x hybrida

ECHINOCACTUS

Echinocactus grusonii

ECHEVERIA
Crassulaceae

Drought-resistant succulents, usually forming charming, symmetrical rosettes of neat, fleshy leaves, are contained in this genus of shrubs and perennials from the drier regions of the Americas, especially Mexico. The waxy leaves are often attractively coloured in muted shades of grey, red and pink, while spikes of red, pink and yellow flowers appear at various times of the year. These are ideal plants for the dry rockery, as ground covers, or as container plants. Echeverias will grow in full sun or semi-shade, but the soil must be well drained and kept fairly dry. They are easily propagated by offsets and cuttings. The name of the genus commemorates a Mexican botanical artist, Atanasio Echeveria.

Echeveria elegans Mexico
Mexican snowball
Leaves 30 to 70 mm long, corolla pink-red with yellow tips.

E. x hybrida Hybrid origin
Echeverias hybridize readily with each other, as well as with other succulents, making positive identification difficult. However, this means that the gardener may have the pleasure of discovering a completely new species in his window-box, rockery or patio garden.

ECHINOCACTUS
Cactaceae

The name of this genus comes from the Greek *echinos*, a hedgehog, and *cactus*, referring to the numerous spines found in this genus of 16 species, native to Mexico and south-western United States. These cacti are cylindrical and grow very large in their native habitat – literally the size and shape of barrels – but in containers they grow slowly for many years.

Echinocactus grusonii Mexico
Golden barrel cactus, Mother-in-law's chair or Skoonmoederstoel
Ribbed stems to 1 m in diameter and 1,5 m tall in nature; round and smaller in cultivation. It is covered in long, arching yellow spines which grow along the well-defined ribs. Brilliant yellow flowers grow up to 50 mm across in spring.

ECHINOCEREUS

Echinocereus melanocentrus

E. pectinatus var. *neomexicanus*

ECHINOCEREUS
Cactaceae

A genus of ribbed cacti. Spiny flowers are solitary and last for several days. As with all succulents, they must be grown in well-drained soil and full sun.

Echinocereus melanocentrus Mexico
This is apparently a variety of *Echinocereus pectinatus*.

E. paectinatus var. neomexicanus
(E. dasyacanthus)
Arizona, Mexico
Rainbow cactus or Reënboogkaktus
Flowers are mostly yellow.

ECHINOPSIS

Echinopsis multiplex

ECHINOPSIS
Cactaceae

This South American genus includes some of the most commonly cultivated cacti. It is popular for its large, delicate-looking, often fragrant flowers, which last for nearly two days. These plants are spherical but grow cylindrical with age, and are strongly ribbed, with spines growing along the ribs.

Echinopsis multiplex Brazil
Easter lily cactus, Sea urchin cactus or Hedgehog cactus
This cactus produces one or more cylindrical, ribbed stems up to 200 mm high and 150 mm across, with yellow spines. Very showy, fragrant spring-blooming flowers are rose-pink coloured, reaching 200 mm in length.

ECHIUM

Echium fastuosum

ECHIUM
Boraginaceae

A genus including shrubs, herbaceous perennials and annuals, native to the Mediterranean regions, Canary Islands and Madeira. One of these, *Echium vulgare*, has become a serious pest plant worldwide but others are useful garden shrubs, flowering best in poor soil but needing full sun and good drainage.

Echium fastuosum Canary Islands
Pride of Madeira or Tower of jewels
This very striking, ornamental grey-leafed shrub sends up showy flower spikes in spring to a height of 450 mm, well above the foliage. These spikes consist of tightly packed, tiny, brilliant blue flowers with crimson anthers. Although these plants are somewhat short-lived, they seed themselves freely so that replacements are usually available to the gardener.

EICHHORNIA

Eichhornia crassipes

EICHHORNIA
Pontederiaceae

A small genus of rhizomatous aquatic plants. Some are actually floating, with their showy flowers usually borne on spikes. Native to tropical America, it is named after J.A.F. Eichhorn, a nineteenth century Prussian statesman.

Eichhornia crassipes   Tropical America
Water hyacinth or Waterhiasint
Aquatic plants kept afloat by their inflated leaf stems, these are a *serious pest* in the tropics where they block waterways. They must therefore not be planted where they can drift away and establish themselves elsewhere. Attractive flower spikes of lilac flowers, borne in summer, are spotted with yellow and make these useful pond plants.

EKEBERGIA

Ekebergia capensis

EKEBERGIA
Meliaceae

A genus of trees, shrubs and dwarf shrubs native to tropical and southern Africa and Madagascar. Both deciduous and evergreen, the species *Ekebergia capensis* is most commonly grown.

Ekebergia capensis   From the Transkei, into Natal, Eastern Transvaal and Zimbabwe
Cape ash or Essenhout
A medium to large tree, evergreen, or semi-deciduous in cold areas. Usually about 10 m high with a spreading crown, making it a good shade tree. Leaves are compound, glossy and dark green while the flowers are insignificant but sweetly scented; fruit is berry-like, bright red and attractive to birds. The flowers appear in spring, followed by fruit in summer or autumn.

ELAEAGNUS

Elaeagnus pungens 'Aureo-variegata'

ELAEAGNUS
Elaeagnaceae

A genus of shrubs and small trees, both evergreen and deciduous. The *Elaeagnus* is native to southern Europe and Asia and is grown for its fragrant silvery white flowers and red berries, as well as for the decorative foliage of several cultivars.

Elaeagnus pungens 'Aureo-variegata'   China, Japan
An evergreen thorny shrub growing to 5 m. Its leaves have a large yellow blotch in the middle. White flowers are produced in summer; berries are silvery when young but turn brown, then red.

131

ELEGIA ENCEPHALARTOS

Elegia capensis

Encephalartos altensteinii

E. horridus

E. frederici-guilielmi

E. latifrons

ELEGIA
Restionaceae

A genus of reeds native to South Africa, Australia and New Zealand. The South African species range from Namaqualand to the southern and eastern Cape.

Elegia capensis South-western Cape
Foliage plant with unusual feathery reeds to 2,5 m. Plant in sandy soil.

ENCEPHALARTOS
Zamiaceae

South Africa's own 'living fossils' are represented in this genus of 28 species popularly referred to as cycads. Native to tropical as well as southern Africa, these are strictly protected plants which lend a tropical and exotic touch to any garden, yet are not difficult to grow. The difficulty lies in obtaining them. However, the lucky gardener who does acquire one is advised to get expert advice on its cultivation. There are separate male and female plants.

Encephalartos altensteinii Eastern Cape coast from East London, Wild Coast to Natal border
Eastern Cape cycad or Oos-Kaapse broodboom
Shrub or tree to 4 m, occasionally to 7 m, looking very like a palm tree. Its huge, stiff compound leaves, sometimes curved, grow to 3,5 m. Clusters of yellowish-green cones develop terminally on the trunk.

E. frederici-guilielmi Eastern Cape interior, Transkei interior
White-haired cycad or Withaarbroodboom
Height to 4 m; trunk thick, to 600 mm in diameter. Leaves go up to 1 m with their under-surfaces white and woolly. Cones are also woolly, but not showy nor yellow-grey to brown as in *Encephalartos altensteinii*.

E. horridus Eastern Cape
Underground stem or short stem to 300 mm. Leaves to 600 mm long are an intense glaucous blue; cones are brownish-red.

E. latifrons Albany district of the eastern Cape
Albany cycad or Albany broodboom
Often branched; to 3 m with leaves up to 1,5 m long. Cones are dark green to bluish-green.

ENDYMION

ENSETE

E. transvenosus

Endymion hispanicus

Ensete ventricosum (South Africa)

E. ventricosum (Tropical Africa)

E. transvenosus — Northern and north-eastern Transvaal
Modjadji cycad or Modjadji-broodboom
One of the largest cycads in the world, usually 5 m to 8 m high, occasionally reaching 13 m. Leaves grow to 2,5 m in length. These plants are from the land of the legendary Rain Queens, Modjadji, in the north-eastern Transvaal.

ENDYMION
Liliaceae

The famous English bluebell belongs to this very small genus of three or four species of bulbous plants native to western Europe and North Africa. Bluebells are unlikely to form sheets of blue in South African conditions as they do in Europe, but they are worth growing for the note of blue they introduce to the spring border or shaded rockery.

Endymion hispanicus — Western Europe
Spanish bluebell
Height about 450 mm; campanulate flowers appear in the spring and are carried on spikes. White, blue and pink-flowered cultivars are available.

ENSETE
Musaceae

The plants in this small genus are similar to banana trees, but instead of edible fruits they produce showy inflorescences. Native to tropical Asia and Africa, one species is, however, indigenous to the northern Transvaal.

Ensete ventricosum (South Africa) — Northern Transvaal
Wild banana or Wildepiesang
Large leafy tree 6 to 12 m tall; leaves 2 to 5 m long and 1 m wide with pink-red midrib. Late spring flowers droop in spikes 2 to 3 m long with showy dark red bracts.

E. ventricosum (Tropical Africa) — Ethiopia
Abyssinian banana
As above but with a yellowish-green midrib and green flower bracts.

133

EPIDENDRUM

Epidendrum x obrienianum

EPIPHYLLUM

Epiphyllum chrysocardium

EPIPREMNUM

Epipremnum aureum

EPIDENDRUM
Orchidaceae

Although the name comes from the Greek meaning 'growing on trees', there is a wide variety of habits in this large genus of about 1 000 species. Native to tropical and subtropical America, the genus includes a group of long-stemmed orchids for the open garden, known as reed or cane orchids, of which *Epidendrum x obrienianum* is one.

Epidendrum x obrienianum   Garden hybrid
Scarlet orchid, Butterfly orchid or Baby orchid
Perennial ground orchid to 1 m or more. Suitable for borders or rockeries, its dainty, long-lasting scarlet orchid flowers are borne at the tips of long graceful stems all year round. Good for cut-flower arrangements.

EPIPHYLLUM
Cactaceae

Cacti from the jungle, not from the desert, make up this genus of about 16 species that are native to the American tropics. They are epiphytic and suited to indoor as well as outdoor cultivation and best grown in semi-shade in frost-free areas. The flowers are often strikingly showy and fragrant and come in a wide range of colours, often with decorative stamens.

Epiphyllum chrysocardium   Mexico
Pure white summer flowers extending 300 mm in length and 200 mm across.

EPIPREMNUM
Araceae

Tropical creepers which climb to great heights in their natural habitat, South East Asia. These foliage plants make attractive specimens for containers indoors and on stoeps in warm climates but they are best grown with a type of trellis for climbing.

Epipremnum aureum   South Pacific Islands
(*Scindapsus aureus*)
Golden Ceylon creeper
Foliage plant. Height variable with leaves to 300 mm long that are dark green and blotched golden yellow.

EPISCIA

Episcia cupreata

ERICA

Erica bauera

E. cerinthoides

E. blenna

E. conspicua

EPISCIA
Gesneriaceae

Greenhouse, stoep and indoor plants grown for their decorative foliage and flowers, episcias are a small genus of spreading perennials from tropical America. The cultivated species often have variegated leaves, with contrasting veining. Flowers are red-pink, orange, purple and white. Propagate by cuttings and division.

Episcia cupreata — South America
Flame violet or Vlamviooltjie
Spreading perennial to 100 mm high, leaves reddish coppery-green or clear green, sometimes variegated with silver, and showy red, or occasionally yellow flowers.

ERICA
Ericaceae

Over 600 species of ericas in the south-western Cape and roughly another 20 species in the eastern Cape, Natal and eastern Transvaal, mostly growing along the escarpment, make this the largest genus of flowering plants in South Africa. Ericas, or heaths, are also native to Europe and the Mediterranean region. These evergreen shrubs have needle-like foliage and vary in size from spreading ground covers to shrubs several metres in height, while the flowers come in an endlessly fascinating variety of colours, shapes and sizes. Some species are easily grown in gardens and these are the ones usually available from nurseries, while others will not thrive outside their particular habitat. Ericas need good drainage, a light, sandy, well-composted soil, no lime and no manure unless it is well rotted in compost.

Erica bauera — Southern Cape
Bridal heath, Albertinia heath or Albertiniaheide
Shrub to 1 m, tube-shaped pink or white flowers up to 20 mm long produced at all times of the year. Easily cultivated species.

E. blenna — Southern Cape
Lantern heath or Lanternheide
Upright shrub to 1,3 m; lantern-shaped flowers are bright orange with green tips and usually borne in spring, but occasionally in other seasons.

E. cerinthoides Widespread in South Africa
Rooihaartjie
Fire-resistant shrub to 1,8 m, usually less, with woolly tubular flowers in shades of red, occasionally white. A variable species.

E. conspicua — South-western Cape
Flowering in April.

E. fastigiata — Shaw's Pass, Cape Province
Jasmine heath or Trompetheide
Flowering in early summer.

E. patersonia — South-western Cape
Mealie heath or Mielieheide
Foliage bright green; the dense elongated cluster of yellow flowers is suggestive of a mealie cob.

CONTINUED

ERICA

E. fastigiata

E. speciosa

E. patersonia

E. versicolor

E. regia

E. vestita

E. regia   Southern Cape
Upright shrub to 2 m; tubular flowers up to 18 mm long and variable in colour; red, white with red tips, or white, purple, and red. Chiefly spring flowering.

E. speciosa   Duiwelskop Pass, Cape Province
Flowering in April.

E. versicolor   Swellendam to Knysna
Flowering in April.

E. vestita   Southern and south-western Cape
Erect shrub to 1 m with a compact habit and tubular flowers to 25 mm long, in shades of red and pink, or white. These appear from early spring to mid-winter; an easily cultivated species.

ERIGERON

Erigeron karvinskianus

ERIGERON
Asteraceae (=Compositae)

A wide range of annual, biennial and perennial herbaceous, almost cosmopolitan species, belong to this genus. They bloom mostly in spring and early summer and their delightful flower heads stay attractive for long periods. Although they will grow easily from seed, division of the perennial clumps is advisable. Grow in rich, well-drained soil and water carefully.

Erigeron karvinskianus   Mexico to Venezuela
This herbaceous perennial shrub to 400 mm with its solitary small flower heads, 15 to 20 mm across in white to reddish-purple, makes an excellent display in early to late summer.

136

ERIOCEPHALUS

Eriocephalus africanus

EROEDA

Eroeda capensis

ERYTHRINA

Erythrina caffra

E. crista-galli

ERIOCEPHALUS
Asteraceae (=Compositae)

The name is from the Greek *erion*, wool, and *cephalus*, head, referring to the woolly seed heads. This is a genus of indigenous, aromatic, usually silvery or silky shrubs, with tiny white daisy flowers which are followed by fluffy white seed heads like tufts of cotton wool. These can be dried for decoration. Only one species is cultivated, *Eriocephalus africanus*.

Eriocephalus africanus
South-western Cape
Wild Rosemary or Kapokbossie
Branching shrub to 2 m, with pleasantly aromatic foliage and tiny purple-centred daisy flowers in winter, followed by woolly seed heads. Best grown in light, well-drained soil.

EROEDA
Asteraceae (=Compositae)

A small genus of low-growing, hardy shrubs indigenous to the south-western and eastern Cape. Prickly foliage. A good rockery specimen.

Eroeda capensis
South-western Cape
Height to 600 mm with golden yellow summer flowers.

ERYTHRINA
Fabaceae (=Leguminosae) Subfam. Faboideae (=Papilionoideae)

A genus of mostly deciduous trees and shrubs widespread in the tropical and subtropical regions of the world. Erythrinas are grown for their showy flowers which appear on bare branches in winter and spring before the new leaves appear. Several species are indigenous to southern Africa.

Erythrina caffra
Coastal belt from eastern Cape through Transkei into Southern Natal
Coast erythrina or Kuskoraalboom
Medium to large deciduous tree usually about 9 to 12 m in height, reaching 20 m in favourable conditions. An easily grown, good garden tree with brilliantly showy spikes of flowers in spring, usually scarlet in colour.

E. crista-galli
South America
Coral tree or Koraalboom
A tree to 6 m with long drooping sprays of crimson flowers that bloom in spring/summer.

CONTINUED

ERYTHRINA

E. humeana

E. latissima

E. variegata var. *orientalis*

E. lysistemon

E. humeana Coastal belt from eastern Cape through Natal to Moçambique, Northern Natal, Eastern Transvaal and lowveld
Dwarf erythrina or Kleinkoraalboom
Shrub or small tree sometimes reaching 4 m but usually less, bearing brilliant scarlet flowers in summer.

E. latissima Eastern Cape, Natal, Eastern and northern Transvaal
Broad-leaved coral tree, Woolly coral tree or Breëblaarkoraalboom
Tree to 8 m and conspicuous for its grey corky bark and large leaves. Large inflorescences appear in spring although relatively fewer than either *Erythrina caffra* or *Erythrina lysistemon*.

E. lysistemon Natal, Transvaal
Common coral tree or Gewone koraalboom
Small to medium tree usually about 6 m in height, bearing scarlet flowers in spring. This is the most popular species.

E. variegata var. **orientalis** Philippine Islands, Indonesia
A spreading tree to 20 m with leaves variegated in bright yellow along the veins. Scarlet flowers abound in spring.

E. zeyheri Highveld areas of Transvaal, Orange Free State
Ploegbreker
Large underground tuberous stem and roots; 500 mm high shoots, armed with short prickles, grow out annually and die off in winter. Leaflets are large and protected by prickles; inflorescences on long, erect, reddish peduncles carry racemes of bright red flowers in late spring. Propagate by seed only.

E. zeyheri

ESCALLONIA

Escallonia x *langleyensis*

E. rubra var. *macrantha*

ESCALLONIA
Saxifragaceae

These useful garden shrubs belong to a genus of evergreen shrubs and trees from South America, mainly the Andean region. They are tough, wind, drought and frost resistant, and make good trimmed or untrimmed hedges as well as specimen plants. The attractive foliage is dense, dark and glossy, and the flowers are decorative in shades of white, pink and red. Escallonias will grow in sun or shade.

Escallonia x langleyensis Garden hybrid
Shrub, usually low growing, but reaching 2,5 m, with attractive dark green toothed leaves and arching sprays of purplish-pink flowers in summer.

E. rubra var. macrantha Chile
Shrub to 5 m. Red to rose-red flowers, up to 20 mm across, bloom in summer.

ESCHSCHOLZIA

Eschscholzia californica

E. californica

ESCHSCHOLZIA
Papaveraceae

A small genus of annual or perennial herbaceous plants native to western North America, eschscholzias are usually grown as self-seeding annuals in the garden.

Eschscholzia californica California
Californian poppy or Kaliforniese-papawer Bushy annuals to 500 mm with red, orange, yellow and cream flowers, sometimes bi-coloured or double in summer. Very showy, easily grown in well-drained soil.

EUCALYPTUS

Eucalyptus calophylla

E. erythrocorys

EUCALYPTUS
Myrtaceae

Here is a genus of evergreen trees and a few shrubs, mostly indigenous to Australia and Tasmania, which has become a characteristic part of the South African landscape. Very useful trees for the farmer, and of considerable economic value as forestry trees, most species of eucalyptus are too tall and too large for garden purposes, but the species mentioned below are smaller, useful for shade and as ornamentals. It is the colourful stamens in the flowers that make them showy.

Eucalyptus calophylla Western Australia
White flowering gum or Witbloekom Evergreen tree to 15 m with a spreading crown and masses of fluffy white, or occasionally pink flowers in summer.

E. erythrocorys Western Australia
Red helmet
Small tree to 10 m with fluffy yellow-green flowers in summer. Young flowers have bright scarlet caps which drop off to reveal the yellow stamens.

CONTINUED

EUCALYPTUS

E. ficifolia

EUCHARIS

Eucharis grandiflora

EUCOMIS

Eucomis autumnalis subsp. *autumnalis*

E. ficifolia   Western Australia
Red flowering gum
Small tree to 10 m with very showy flowers in shades of red in summer.

EUCHARIS
Amaryllidaceae

Usually grown in the greenhouse, the Amazon lily, *Eucharis grandiflora*, is the most popular species in this small genus from tropical America.

Eucharis grandiflora   South America

Amazon lily, Eucharist lily or Madonna lily
Coming from the Andes of Colombia and Peru, this somewhat unpredictable bulb sends up flower spikes to 600 mm high, which bear loose clusters of graceful daffodil-like, strongly fragrant white flowers up to 75 mm across, at irregular intervals. Grow in rich soil, and feed and water well for this rewarding plant really lives up to its generic name which is from the Greek word meaning 'very pleasing and filled with grace'.

EUCOMIS
Liliaceae

A small genus of indigenous bulbs with a widespread distribution, the eucomis bears erect, densely packed flower spikes topped with a tuft of leaves. This unusual feature is referred to in the name, which comes from the Greek *eukomes*, meaning beautiful-haired.

Eucomis autumnalis subsp. **autumnalis**
(*E. undulata*)   South Africa

Pineapple flower or Wildepynappel
Flower spikes of green, white or yellow growing to 750 mm are borne in summer and resemble a pineapple – hence the popular name.

E. autumnalis subsp. **clavata**   South Africa
(*E. clavata*)

As above. Summer flowering.

E. comosa var. **comosa**   Natal,
                                Eastern Transvaal
Flower spikes to 1 m bearing blooms of white, tinged pink or purple, in summer with attractive greenish-purple seed pods.

EULOPHIA

EUONYMUS

E. autumnalis subsp. *clavata*

Eulophia speciosa

Euonymus japonica

E. comosa var. *comosa*

E. japonica 'Aureo-marginata'

EULOPHIA
Orchidaceae

A genus of mostly terrestrial orchids with worldwide distribution, eulophias are large plants with leathery leaves.

Eulophia speciosa South and east coastal areas of South Africa. The most common species in cultivation. The flowers are bright yellow with a purplish lip, produced in summer.

EUONYMUS
Celastraceae

A genus of deciduous or evergreen trees and shrubs, and occasionally ground covers or creepers, cultivated for their foliage, and in some species, also for their autumn berries. Although native chiefly to Asia, a few species are found elsewhere in the world. The evergreen species with their glossy, leathery leaves make good hedges and windbreaks as they are resistant to wind even at the coast. The deciduous varieties have showy autumn foliage.

Euonymus japonica Japan
Spindle tree
Evergreen shrub or tree to 5 m; glossy dark green leaves. Flowers are insignificant but the fruits, produced in autumn, are very showy with salmon-pink berries that split to reveal colourful orange seeds.

E. japonica 'Aureo-marginata' Japan
Spindle tree
Foliage plant, slow-growing shrub to 3 m. Leaves are edged with yellow.

CONTINUED 141

EUONYMUS | EUPATORIUM | EUPHORBIA

Eupatorium cannabinum var. *plenum*

Euphorbia caput-medusae

E. japonica 'Aureo-variegata'

E. sordidum

E. cooperi

E. japonica 'Aureo-variegata'
Warm temperate areas. Glossy leaves are deep green with creamy-yellow centres.

EUPATORIUM
Asteraceae (=Compositae)

A genus of mainly perennial herbaceous plants and shrubs of widespread distribution but mostly native to tropical America. The eupatorium's flowers, in shades of pink and mauve, are carried as showy, flattened heads, often fluffy, like large ageratums.

Eupatorium cannabinum var. plenum
Europe, Asia, North Africa
Hemp agrimony
Perennial to 1,2 m with dense heads of double pink flowers in summer.

E. sordidum Mexico
Semi-woody shrub to 1,5 m; leaves are ovate to 100 mm long and toothed. Flower heads are pinkish-violet, fragrant and resemble small dainty powder puffs; a lovely specimen for a special spot, either in full or half sun.

EUPHORBIA
Euphorbiaceae

There is an immense and fascinating variety of form and habit in this genus of over 2 000 species (over 200 in South Africa alone). They include annual and perennial herbaceous plants, creepers, succulents, shrubs and trees. Distribution is worldwide but mainly in the temperate regions, with many species, mostly succulents, indigenous to South Africa. All species have a white milky sap, which is usually irritating to the skin and eyes, and is often poisonous. Flowers are inconspicuous, but in many species they are surrounded by large, colourful bracts which make up the 'flower'.

Euphorbia caput-medusae
South-western Cape
Medusa's head or Vingerpol
Spineless, dwarf succulent to 300 mm which secretes a poisonous sap; interesting creamy-green flowers in summer.

142

E. curvirama

E. heterophylla

E. ingens

E. grandicornis

E. mauritanica

E. marginata

E. cooperi   Natal, Transvaal and Central Africa
Lesser candelabra tree or Transvaalse kandelaarnaboom
Spiny, succulent tree to 7 m with branches that spring from the trunk like a candelabra. This makes a striking accent plant. The sap is very poisonous. The fruit is reddish-brown and quite showy.

E. curvirama   Eastern Cape
Cape candelabra tree or Kaapse kandelaarnaboom
Spiny, candelabra-shaped succulent tree to 5 m.

E. grandicornis   Transvaal, Pongola
Cow's horn, Transvaal candelabra tree or Transvaalse kandelaarnaboom
Succulent, spiny, much-branched shrub to 2 m. Tiny yellow flowers are borne in summer.

E. heterophylla   Subtropical and tropical America
Mexican fire plant or Annual poinsettia
Annual to 1 m. Bracts are green but red at the base of the blade and borne in summer.

E. ingens   Natal, Transvaal, Zimbabwe
Candelabra tree or Naboom
Specimen tree, densely branched to 10 m with a spreading, rounded crown. The sap is poisonous.

E. marginata   North America
Snow-on-the-mountain or ghostweed
Foliage plant; annual to 600 mm, sometimes to 1 m; very attractive leaves with broad white margins; poisonous sap.

E. mauritanica   Cape, Natal and Namibia
Yellow milk bush, Gifmelkbos or Jakkalskos
Succulent, spineless much-branched shrub to 2 m. Yellow flowers are borne in spring. Poisonous sap.

E. milii var. **splendens**   Madagascar
(*E. splendens*)
Christ thorn or Christusdoring
Slow-growing, much-branched, very spiny shrub to 1,5 m. Branches are silvery grey, showing up the brilliant red flowers borne mainly in winter, but also throughout the year. It makes an impenetrable small hedge.

CONTINUED

EUPHORBIA

E. milii var. *splendens*

E. pulcherrima (pink)

E. pulcherrima (standard red)

E. pulcherrima (cream)

E. pulcherrima 'Plenissima'

E. pulcherrima cv.

E. pulcherrima　　　　　　　　　　Mexico
Poinsettia or Karlienblom
Shrub to 3 m with equal spread. Brilliant scarlet bracts resembling petals are borne in winter after the leaves have fallen. Also comes in pink and creamy-yellow cultivars. The most popular Christmas flower in North America and Britain.

E. pulcherrima 'Plenissima'　　Garden origin
Flaming sphere or Dubbelkarlienblom
Poinsettia with double flowers are borne in autumn/winter. Small and shrub-like.

E. pulcherrima cv.　　　　　　Garden origin
Small poinsettia or Dwergkarlienblom
Excellent indoor popular poinsettia to 400 mm, flowering in autumn/winter.

EURYOPS

Euryops pectinatus

E. spathaceus

EURYOPS
Asteraceae (=Compositae)

Indigenous evergreen, quick-growing shrubs with yellow daisy-like flowers which often cover the bush when conditions are right. Best in winter rainfall areas, these plants are drought, wind and frost resistant, needing well-drained soil.

Euryops pectinatus　　South-western Cape
Grey-leaved euryops or Wolharpuisbos
Shrub to 1 m with yellow winter/spring flowers.

E. spathaceus　　Humansdorp, South Africa
Shrub to 1 m with equal spread; foliage blue-green with yellow flowers in autumn/winter.

E. speciosissimus　　South-western Cape
Clanwilliam marguerite or Harpuisbos
A branched shrub to 1 m; flower heads bright yellow, 50 mm across, on stalks 100 to 200 mm long in springtime.

EXACUM

E. speciosissimus

Exacum affine

E. tenuissimus

E. virgineus

E. tenuissimus South-western Cape, Namaqualand
🄵 ⊕ ♣ ☼ 🅆
Grootharpuisbos
Shrub to 1,5 m with yellow flowers 30 mm across, in winter/spring.

E. virgineus Southern and eastern Cape
🄵 ⊕ ♣ ☼ 🅆
Heuningmargriet
Shrub to 1,5 m with small honey-scented, yellow flowers in masses; winter/spring.

EXACUM
Gentianaceae

A genus of annuals, biennials and perennials native to Europe and Asia which make most attractive free-flowering indoor plants.

Exacum affine Socotra (Gulf of Aden)
⊛ ⊛
German violet or Persian violet
Fragrant blue-lilac flowers with prominent yellow anthers in summer.

145

FABIANA

Fabiana imbricata

FAGUS

Fagus sylvatica 'Atropunicea'

X FATSHEDERA

x *Fatshedera lizei*

x *F. lizei* 'Variegata'

FABIANA
Solanaceae

These are evergreen, heath-like shrubs from temperate South America. One species is cultivated, *Fabiana imbricata*.

Fabiana imbricata   Chile
False heath or Valsheide
Spreading, graceful shrub to 2,6 m, with tubular white flowers profusely borne in spring and early summer. Grow in any soil and prune regularly after flowering. Propagate by cuttings taken in spring or autumn.

FAGUS
Fagaceae

Only a few species of this deciduous tree genus are suitable for cultivation. Because of their very attractive foliage, both in summer and autumn, they are popular specimens, especially in cooler moist areas. Light, gravelly, limestone soil is essential for best results.

Fagus sylvatica 'Atropunicea'   Europe
(*F. sylvatica* 'Cuprea')
Copper beech or Koperbeuk
A much-prized large specimen tree with most attractive copper-red foliage, it will probably only succeed on the highveld.

X FATSHEDERA
Araliaceae

This is a hybrid genus developed from crossing the shrub *Fatsia japonica* with an ivy, *Hedera*. The resulting evergreen climber has dark green glossy leaves shaped like five-pointed stars. It will grow in sun or shade outdoors but also makes a good indoor plant, although it needs support at all times. There is one species, x *Fatshedera lizei*.

x Fatshedera lizei   France, Garden hybrid
Tree ivy
Foliage plant; climber which varies in height according to conditions but reaches about 2 m.

x F. lizei 'Variegata'   Garden hybrid
As above but leaves are white margined.

FATSIA

Fatsia japonica

FAUCARIA

Faucaria felina

Faucaria sp.

FEIJOA

Feijoa sellowiana

FATSIA
Araliaceae

There is only one species in this genus, an evergreen shrub or small tree with large, fan-shaped leaves, useful for creating a striking tropical effect near water or next to a shady patio. Fatsias need good soil and protection from the wind. They can also be grown on stoeps or indoors.

Fatsia japonica   Japan
Can reach 6 m but usually less than 3 m. Their glossy leaves grow up to 400 m across and have spikes of cream-coloured flowers in summer, followed later by black fruits.

FAUCARIA
Mesembryanthemaceae

A genus of dwarf indigenous succulents. An almost stemless plant, it forms unusual clumps of fleshy, boat-shaped, toothed leaves, which are unusual and ornamental. The name is from the Latin *fauces*, throat, a reference to the throat-like appearance of the pairs of leaves.

Faucaria felina   Cape Province, Eastern Karoo
Tierbekvygie
Leaves with pronounced 'teeth' along the edges; its yellow 'vygie' flowers appear in the spring.

Faucaria sp.
As above.

FEIJOA
Myrtaceae

This genus has two species, but only one, *Feijoa sellowiana*, is cultivated.

Feijoa sellowiana   South America
Pineapple guava or Pynappelkoejawel
Evergreen shrub or tree which grows to 6 m in its native habitat but is usually only 2 to 3 m in cultivation. Its leathery leaves are shiny green above and grey below. White flowers tinged with red or purple sprout masses of showy purple-red stamens, and reddish-green, edible fruit in summer.

FELICIA

Felicia heterophylla

F. amelloides

FELICIA
Asteraceae (=Compositae)

Truly sky-blue flowers are rare in the garden, but several species of felicia have daisy flowers of a clear, intense blue, as well as shades of mauve, pink and white. This genus of annuals and small herbaceous shrubs is native to Africa and western Arabia but most species are found in the south-western Cape. The name comes from the Latin, *felix*, meaning cheerful, a reference to the bright flowers.

Felicia amelloides — Widespread in the Cape Province
Blue daisy, Blue marguerite, Bush felicia or Bloumargriet
Bushy shrub to 1 m with equal spread; sky-blue flowers with bright yellow centres bloom all year, mainly spring. Felicias will grow in semi-shade as well as sun. Easily propagated by seed and cuttings, they make good rockery plants.

F. fruticosa subsp. *fruticosa*
As above but flowers are more delicate and a paler blue.

F. fruticosa subsp. *fruticosa*

F. heterophylla — South-western Cape, Namaqualand
Bushy annual to 350 mm, bearing deep blue flowers with purplish centres.

FENESTRARIA

Fenestraria aurantiaca

F. rhopalophylla

FENESTRARIA
Mesembryanthemaceae

Two species make up this indigenous genus of fascinating, tiny succulents which are unique in the way they have adapted to their semi-desert environment. These plants form clumps of small pebble-like leaves which have a translucent patch at the tips. When the plant is almost buried in the sand in its natural habitat, the clear tops allow sunlight to penetrate to the chlorophyll-bearing tissue in the leaves. Soil must be three-quarters sand, and watered sparingly.

Fenestraria aurantiaca — Port Nolloth
Window plant or Vensterplant
Dwarf succulent to 50 mm, usually less, forming cushions up to 100 mm across; leaves are grey-green and flowers yellow, up to 50 mm across, borne in summer.

F. rhopalophylla — Namibia
Baby toes
Dwarf succulent, usually 30 to 40 mm high, forming spreading clumps; leaves are grey-green and flowers white, up to 40 mm across and borne in autumn.

FEROCACTUS

Ferocactus setispinus

FERRARIA

Ferraria crispa var. *crispa*

FICUS

Ficus elastica

F. elastica 'Variegata'

FEROCACTUS
Cactaceae

The name of this genus comes from the Latin *ferus*, wild, and *cactus*. The plants are attractive with ferocious, often brightly coloured spines. Native to Mexico and south-western America, these ribbed, round cacti become cylindrical with age and grow tall in their native habitat, but because they are slow growing they make excellent container plants. The flowers are showy, in shades of red, orange and yellow and sometimes bi-coloured. Easily grown outdoors in the rock or cactus garden, they must be protected from frost.

Ferocactus setispinus Mexico, Texas
Strawberry cactus or Aarbeikaktus
Stems are flabby and grow to 300 mm high and 120 mm thick; spines are white or brown; flowers, yellow with red centres grow to 75 mm and are borne from spring to autumn.

FERRARIA
Iridaceae

Cormous, herbaceous plants with stout, usually branched short stems. Lower leaves are firm, narrow and spathe-like. Flower segments are free, spreading and the margins greatly crisped. Plant in well-drained soil, full sun.

Ferraria crispa var. **crispa** Stilbaai, southern Cape
Spider flower or Spinnekopblom
Suitable for a special sunny pocket in the rock garden.

FICUS
Moraceae

A large and varied genus of evergreen and deciduous trees, shrubs and creepers native to the tropics and subtropics, with many species indigenous to southern Africa. Included in the genus is the common fig which bears edible fruit, but most species are grown only for their ornamental foliage. It is interesting that the two indoor species described below grow to great heights outdoors but will grow sufficiently slowly indoors to make excellent container plants. Gardeners are warned that most species have vigorous, invasive root systems.

Ficus elastica Himalayas, Burma
Indian rubber tree or Rubber plant
Foliage plant. Tree to 30 m in its natural habitat but it is most commonly cultivated as an indoor plant. Leaves are ornamental, growing to 300 mm in length, dark green and glossy above and reddish beneath.

F. elastica 'Variegata' Garden origin
As above but leaves are light green and margined in white or yellow.

CONTINUED

FICUS

F. lyrata

F. pumila

F. natalensis

F. nitida

F. sur

F. lyrata Tropical Africa
Fiddle-leaf fig or Fiddle leaf
Foliage plant with large violin-shaped leaves; mostly grown as an indoor plant.

F. natalensis Central and eastern Transvaal, Natal and Eastern Cape
Common wild fig or Gewone wildevy
A medium-sized evergreen shade tree. Its edible fruits are borne from July to January.

F. nitida
One of the best specimen trees, up to 5 m, for the average garden. A quick grower in good garden soil.

F. pumila Japan
Creeping fig or Tickey creeper
This fast-growing creeper grows to any height and will cling to any support with its suckers. Young growth is often an attractive bronzy red.

F. sur Coastal belt from eastern Cape,
(F. capensis) Natal into eastern Transvaal and northwards
Foliage and shade tree to 30 m but usually about 12 m. It is a good shade tree but only for large gardens because the surface roots take up considerable space. Large reddish figs, 30 to 40 mm in diameter, are borne in branched clusters low on the main branches.

FITTONIA

Fittonia verschaffeltii

FITTONIA

Acanthaceae

Fittonia has two species of ornamental low-growing or creeping foliage plants and both are native to the moist forests of South America. They are suitable as stoep or indoor plants in warm areas and greenhouse plants elsewhere, and are easily grown from stem cuttings.

Fittonia verschaffeltii Colombia to Peru
Mosaic plant, Silver net plant or Mosaïekplant
A creeping perennial to 300 mm. The oval leaves grow to 100 mm long and are dark green with rosy red veins.

FOENICULUM

Foeniculum vulgare

FORSYTHIA

Forsythia x *intermedia* 'Spectabilis'

FORTUNELLA

Fortunella margarita

FOENICULUM
Apiaceae (=Umbelliferae)

There are two or three species in this genus of short-lived perennials, usually grown as annuals. Foeniculums are native to Europe and the Near East. Only one species, *Foeniculum vulgare*, is cultivated. Its seeds and leaves are used for food flavouring or garnishing, while the leaf bases are used for cooking as a vegetable and in salads. This tall, feathery-leafed plant, with its flat heads of yellow flowers, can be seen growing wild in parts of South Africa. The generic name is the Latin for fennel.

Foeniculum vulgare　　　Southern Europe
🄵 ⊛ ⊛ ☼
Fennel or Vinkel
Perennial to 1,5 m with delicate, thread-like, blue-green leaves and yellow flowers borne in spring.

FORSYTHIA
Oleaceae

Named in honour of the royal gardener of Chelsea Physic Garden, William Forsyth, 1737-1804, this is a small genus of deciduous shrubs native to eastern Asia, except for one species which is native to eastern Europe. The bright yellow flowers are borne profusely on bare branches before the leaves appear, making them spectacularly showy in early spring.

Forsythia x intermedia 'Spectabilis'
🄵 ⊛ ⊛ ☼ 🅆　　　　　　Garden hybrid
Shrub to 3 m; branches are arching and spreading; flowers, over 25 mm long in bright golden yellow, are very showy and seen in late winter/early spring.

FORTUNELLA
Rutaceae

The attractive aromatic fruits of the kumquats make delicious preserves, but it is mainly as highly decorative, neat ornamentals that these evergreen shrubs and small trees are grown. They make perfect container plants for small gardens or sunny patios with their glossy, slightly aromatic leaves, sweet-scented white flowers and bright orange fruits, which hang on the trees for many weeks. Cultivated as citrus, kumquats belong in a small genus probably native to eastern Asia and Malaysia.

Fortunella margarita　　　Probably south-eastern China but known
🄵 ⊛ ⊛ ☼　　　　　　only in cultivation
Oval kumquat, Ngami kumquat or Koemkwat
Shrub or small tree to 5 m but remaining small when grown in a container, with oval-shaped orange-yellow fruits, ripening in autumn.

FREESIA

Freesia x *hybrida*

F. x *hybrida*

F. x *hybrida*

F. x *hybrida*

FREESIA
Iridaceae

A genus of indigenous cormous plants with heavily fragrant flowers from which numerous hybrids have been raised. They come in a wide range of brilliant colours although the scent of some of the hybrids has been diminished and is even absent. The showy flowers are borne on wiry, arching stems, which make them useful for flower arrangements. Freesias are easily flattened by rain or wind, so some form of shelter and staking is advisable. Careful watering is required.

Freesia x hybrida — Originally south-western Cape
Kammetjies
Spring flowering.

FREYLINIA

Freylinia lanceolata

F. visseri

FREYLINIA
Scrophulariaceae

An African genus of six species of shrubs and small trees of which four are indigenous to South Africa. Although not often cultivated, *Freylinia lanceolata* makes a good garden subject.

Freylinia lanceolata — South-western and southern Cape
Heuningklokkiesbos
Shrub or small tree to 5 m with willow-like leaves and drooping heads of creamy-golden flowers that have a strong honey fragrance. In nature this is a waterside plant. It flowers in spring, and then at intervals all year.

F. visseri — North-western Cape
Low-growing, very attractive shrub with drooping branches. Tubular mauve-pink flowers appear in terminal clusters in spring. Propagate by hardwood cuttings, 80 to 120 mm long, in summer and grow the shrubs in well-prepared sandy soil.

FRITHIA

FUCHSIA

Frithia pulchra

Fuchsia x *hybrida*

F. x *hybrida*

F. magellanica

F. triphylla

FRITHIA
Mesembryanthemaceae

There is one species in this genus, *Frithia pulchra*, found in the Magaliesberg range in the Transvaal.

Frithia pulchra　　　Magaliesberg, Transvaal
Fairy elephant's feet
Stemless succulent with club-shaped, grey-green leaves up to 20 mm long, with 'windows' at the tips; flowers, up to 20 mm across, are found in magenta and white or all white in summer.

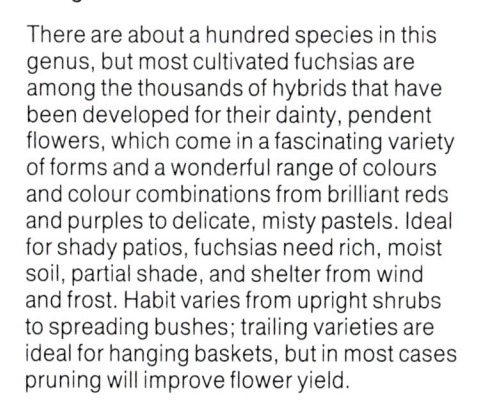

FUCHSIA
Onagraceae

There are about a hundred species in this genus, but most cultivated fuchsias are among the thousands of hybrids that have been developed for their dainty, pendent flowers, which come in a fascinating variety of forms and a wonderful range of colours and colour combinations from brilliant reds and purples to delicate, misty pastels. Ideal for shady patios, fuchsias need rich, moist soil, partial shade, and shelter from wind and frost. Habit varies from upright shrubs to spreading bushes; trailing varieties are ideal for hanging baskets, but in most cases pruning will improve flower yield.

Fuchsia x hybrida　　　Garden hybrid
(*F. fulgens* x *F. magellanica*)
Spring/summer flowers.

F. magellanica　　　Southern Chile, Argentina
Shrub to 4 m, sometimes sprawling; flowers are red and purplish-red produced in spring/summer.

F. triphylla　　　Haiti, San Domingo
Honeysuckle fuchsia or Kanferfoeliefuchsia
Small shrub to 600 mm with red flowers produced in summer/winter.

FURCRAEA

Furcraea foetida

FURCRAEA
Agavaceae

There are about 20 species in this genus from tropical America. Leaves are sword-shaped in basal rosettes resembling *Agave*.

Furcraea foetida Mauritius, St. Helena
Mauritius hemp, Green aloe or Mauritiusvlas
This plant is without a trunk. Leaves up to 2,5 m long are arranged in a basal rosette; inflorescences grow to 7 m tall and are branched, with a delicate appearance. Bulbils, which are vegetative propagules that can develop into plantlets, develop on the inflorescence and fall to the ground in late winter.

GAILLARDIA

Gaillardia aristata

G. x grandiflora

G. pulchella 'Lorenziana'

GAILLARDIA
Asteraceae (=Compositae)

A small genus of annuals and perennials native to the Americas, although the cultivated species are all from North America. The common name is 'blanket flower' because the colours of the flowers resemble the bright oranges, reds and yellows of the blankets traditionally worn by Red Indians. Good cut flowers, gaillardias have a long flowering season but need good drainage and full sun for best results. Easily grown from seed.

Gaillardia aristata United States and Canada
Blanket flower
Perennial to 750 mm. Flowers of purple and yellow are borne in summer.

G. x grandiflora Garden hybrid
Blanket flower
Vigorous perennials, easily propagated from seed or by division of clumps. Flowers are red, yellow and orange and some are bi-coloured, but all are borne in summer.

G. pulchella 'Lorenziana' United States
Blanket flower
Annual to 600 mm. Flower heads are pompom-shaped and come in shades of dark red or red and yellow in summer/autumn.

GALTONIA GARDENIA

Galtonia candicans

Gardenia cornuta

G. cornuta (fruit)

G. jasminoides 'Veitchii'

G. thunbergia

G. thunbergia

GALTONIA
Liliaceae

A small genus of bulbs, indigenous to South Africa, which are closely related to the hyacinths. Flowers are white or green, carried on tall spikes. Native to the Drakensberg mountains, they need good soil, full sun and a dry winter. Only one species, *Galtonia candicans*, is commonly found in cultivation, where it is best planted in clumps for maximum effect.

Galtonia candicans — Natal, Orange Free State and Northern Cape mountains
Berg lily, Cape hyacinth or Berglelie
Stout flower spikes to 1,2 m. White pendent, bell-shaped, fragrant flowers are borne in summer.

GARDENIA
Rubiaceae

Heavily fragrant, waxy, opulent-looking flowers are the hallmark of this genus of shrubs and small trees native to tropical and subtropical Asia and Africa. Handsome, evergreen shrubs with tough glossy leaves, gardenias do best in rich, slightly acid soil, and need plenty of water. Named after an American eighteenth century botanist, Dr Alexander Garden.

Gardenia cornuta — Zululand and Swaziland
Natal gardenia or Natalkatjiepiering
Small tree, 4 to 5 m in height; shiny light green leaves crowded at the ends of branchlets. Spring flowers are fragrant white, ageing to yellow; a long corolla tube opens in five spreading lobes. Fruit is ovoid, yellow when mature.

G. jasminoides 'Veitchii' — China
Common gardenia or Katjiepiering
Evergreen shrub to 2 m or more, with equal spread. It bears fragrant white flowers, in double and single forms, in summer. They are excellent as cut flowers.

G. thunbergia — Coastal strip from the eastern Cape through into Mozambique
Witkatjiepiering or Wildekatjiepiering
Slow-growing evergreen shrub or small tree to 5 m but usually only about 2 m high. Snowy white, heavily perfumed, saucer-shaped flowers up to 80 mm across are produced in summer.

155

GASTERIA

Gasteria batesiana

G. acinacifolia

G. excelsa

G. excelsa

G. transvaalensis

GASTERIA
Liliaceae

About 50 species make up this genus of indigenous succulents grown for their interesting variety of leaf shapes and textures, but equally for their spikes of red or pink inverted bell-shaped flowers. The plants are mostly stemless with the leaves either forming rosettes, or rising out of the ground in pairs, making them useful for rockery pockets and container plants on sunny windowsills and stoeps. The name comes from the Greek *gaster*, meaning belly, probably an allusion to the pot-bellied shape of the flowers.

Gasteria batesiana Piet Retief, south-eastern Transvaal
Leaves tuberculate and spirally arranged.

G. acinacifolia South coast, Cape Province
Exceptionally large gasteria with leaves spirally arranged. Inflorescence divided into several almost lateral racemes.

G. excelsa South Africa, Kei River area
Succulent. Brown-spotted leaves 300 mm long in spiral rosettes to 450 mm high. Pink flowers are borne in summer.

G. transvaalensis Transvaal
Succulent. A northern gasteria with white-dotted green leaves forming a rosette. Pink flowers appear in summer.

GAURA

Gaura lindheimeri

GAZANIA

Gazania hybrid

Gazania hybrid

Gazania hybrid

G. krebsiana

GAURA
Onagraceae

Tall graceful spikes of flowers, showy when allowed to grow in large clumps at the back of a mixed border, or as accent plants elsewhere in the garden, gauras belong to a genus of annuals and perennials native to North America. Flowers are usually white tinged with pink, but there is one yellow species. These are tough, accommodating plants, easily propagated by division if perennials or by seed if annuals.

Gaura lindheimeri   North America
Rosy pink flowers on spikes to 1,2 m are borne in summer.

GAZANIA
Asteraceae (=Compositae)

For brilliant colour in sunny places in the garden, gazanias are hard to beat. The petals often have a satiny texture adding extra intensity to the colours which include countless shades of red, pink, orange, yellow, cream and white. The petals are sometimes bi-coloured striped longitudinally, or have spots or blotches at the base, enhancing the attractiveness of the flower. Gazanias are basically of two types, clump-forming or trailing. All are easily propagated from seed and self-sow freely, or they may be propagated by division. Ideal for rockeries, borders, edgings and ground covers, the plants in this genus are mostly indigenous, although a few species are found in tropical Africa. Apart from full sun, their chief requirement is good drainage.

Gazania hybrids   Namaqualand and South-western Cape
Clump-forming to about 150 mm. Leaves are green and grey beneath. Flowers come in an endless variety of colours and markings as well as seasons. They flower in winter and spring and sporadically in summer and autumn.

G. krebsiana   South-western Cape
Botterblom or Gousblom
Flowers up to 80 mm across have dark, intense red petals blotched at the base with a brown patch containing a white or black dot. Very showy and found in winter/spring.

G. lichtensteinii   North-western Cape, Karoo
An annual reaching a height of 200 mm. Petals are yellow with a black dot at the base and are borne in summer.

G. rigens var. **rigens**   South-western Cape
Rankbotterblom
Good ground cover in trailing form with green and silvery white leaves and clear, long-stalked yellow flowers, borne in spring/summer.

G. rigens var. **uniflora**   South-western Cape
As above but flowers are small and short-stalked.

CONTINUED

GAZANIA

G. lichtensteinii

G. rigens var. *rigens*

G. rigens var. *uniflora*

GEISSORHIZA

Geissorhiza radians

G. tulbaghensis

GEISSORHIZA
Iridaceae

These low-growing cormous plants with small, but often brilliantly coloured flowers, are found in the Cape coastal belt from Namaqualand to the Eastern Province. An entirely South African genus, geissorhiza require a moist situation, which may be allowed to dry out in summer, when the plants are dormant.

Geissorhiza radians South-western Cape
Wine cups or Kelkie-wyn
Corm to 150 mm high with ribbed leaves and wiry stems bearing cup-shaped flowers up to 30 mm across. These are coloured a deep wine-red at the base of the petals, then a faint white line separates this colour from the intense purple of the upper half of the petals. The colours are jewel-like in their intensity, making these plants most attractive which no doubt contributes to the fact that they are rare, and therefore strictly protected.

G. tulbaghensis Tulbagh area
As above but flowers are creamy-yellow and greyish-brown at the base of the petals.

GELSEMIUM

Gelsemium sempervirens

GELSEMIUM
Loganiaceae

There are three species in this genus of evergreen climbers, one native to eastern Asia and two found in eastern North America. One species, *Gelsemium sempervirens*, is commonly cultivated.

Gelsemium sempervirens North and Central America
Yellow jessamine, Carolina jasmine or False jasmine
Evergreen creeper with glossy green leaves and fragrant yellow flowers up to 35 mm long, which appear for many months in winter and spring. Useful as a light creeper or as a ground cover.

GERANIUM

Geranium sanguineum

G. palmatum

G. incanum

GERBERA

Gerbera jamesonii

G. jamesonii hybrids

GERANIUM
Geraniaceae

Plants in this genus have circular, flat or saucer-shaped flowers with five equal-sized petals, whereas the flowers of pelargoniums, which are frequently called geraniums, have five petals of unequal size and shape. The foliage differs too. Geraniums have finer, lacier foliage with more deeply cut leaves than the pelargoniums. Geraniums are native to the temperate regions of the world or mountainous regions of the tropics. Several species are indigenous to South Africa. There are annual and perennial varieties with a few growing as large as shrubs. Geraniums need good drainage and make good rockery plants and ground covers. In very hot areas they may prefer partial shade.

Geranium incanum   South-western and southern Cape
Carpet geranium or Bergtee
Perennial to 300 mm, with finely cut, lacy foliage; flowers in shades of pink, lavender or mauve are produced in spring and summer.

G. palmatum   Canary Islands
(*G. anemonifolium*)
Biennial to 800 mm; leaves pinnately toothed and with long petioles; inflorescences are terminal and profusely branched. Flowers are pink-purple and borne in summer.

G. sanguineum   Europe
Crane's bill
Perennial to 450 mm. Flowers are dark red, purple or mauve and are borne in summer.

GERBERA
Asteraceae (=Compositae)

Only one species in this genus is commonly cultivated: the well-known Barberton daisy, indigenous to the eastern Transvaal. From this herbaceous perennial with its scarlet single flowers have been raised double and single hybrids in a wide range of colours from crimson through all shades of red, pink, orange and yellow, to cream. The long-lasting daisy flowers are carried on tall graceful stems, making them superb cut flowers. Propagate from fresh seed, or by division of the clumps when necessary, as they resent being disturbed. Plant in good, composted, well-drained soil, and water well in summer. These are ideal rockery plants.

Gerbera jamesonii   Eastern Transvaal
Barberton daisy or Transvaal daisy
Perennial which forms clumps up to 600 mm across, bearing flowers on stems 450 mm long or more. Red flowers up to 100 mm across are borne in spring. This is the sporting emblem of northern Transvaal.

G. jamesonii hybrid
As above.

GETHYLLIS

Gethyllis ciliaris

G. ciliaris (fruit)

GETHYLLIS
Amaryllidaceae

A genus of indigenous bulbs with the delightful common name of kukumakranka, these little plants produce tufts of somewhat grass-like leaves in winter, which usually die down before the fragrant flowers appear in late spring or summer. These are followed in autumn by heavily scented, cylindrical fleshy fruits which are edible, and occasionally are used to flavour liqueur brandy in country districts. Native to the Cape, from Namaqualand to Uitenhage, they have spread into Namibia as well.

Gethyllis ciliaris   South-western Cape
Kukumakranka or Koekemakranka
Creamy-yellow flowers in summer. Fruits appear above the ground in autumn.

GINKGO

Ginkgo biloba

GINKGO
Ginkgoaceae

There is only one species, *Ginkgo biloba*, in this genus of nearly extinct gymnospermous plants.

Ginkgo biloba   South-eastern China, now widespread
Maidenhair tree or Nooienshaarboom
An attractive deciduous tree, remarkably resistant to air pollution. Male and female plants are separate. Leaves distinctly bi-lobed. The ginkgo prefers good rainfall and rich soil, and does well in temperate and cold climates.

GLADIOLUS

Gladiolus alatus

GLADIOLUS
Iridaceae

The plants in this genus vary from the small, dainty and sometimes hauntingly fragrant indigenous species to the magnificent, colourful, stately spikes of huge flowers which hybridists have raised from these original species. Gladiolus is a genus of cormous perennials native to Europe and the Mediterranean regions, the Near East, and to tropical and southern Africa. Although found mainly in the winter rainfall areas, various indigenous species are found in the summer rainfall areas as well, and all are fairly easily grown under their native conditions. The massive garden hybrids have rather specialized requirements and it is worth finding out what these are before planting is undertaken.

Gladiolus alatus   South-western Cape
Kalkoentjie or Rooikalkoentjie
Perennial cormous plant to 350 mm, it has sword-shaped leaves and red and yellow bi-coloured flowers in spring.

160

GLEDITSIA

G. cardinalis x *G. carmineus*

G. carneus

Gleditsia triacanthos

G. x *hortulanus*

G. dalenii

G. cardinalis x G. carmineus South-western Cape
A most beautiful hybrid.

G. carneus South-western Cape
Painted lady or Bergpypie
This species varies greatly from one locality to another and has been used in hybridization.

G. x hortulanus
Height up to 1,5 m. All commercially grown hybrids with large flowers which come in all shades, except blue, in the summertime.

G. dalenii Transvaal, Zimbabwe
Parrot gladiolus
Flower stems to 1 m high, bearing in autumn hooded flowers of bi-coloured scarlet and yellow blooms.

GLEDITSIA
Fabaceae (=Leguminosae) Subfam. Caesalpinioideae

About 12 species of deciduous trees make up this genus, all usually armed with thorns. Leaves are pinnately compound. Only the well-known honey locust, *Gleditsia triacanthos*, is normally cultivated as a specimen or shade tree.

Gleditsia triacanthos Eastern America
Honey locust
A valuable deciduous tree to 8 m, found in areas of little rainfall. Masses of long yellow-brown pods are produced during autumn.

161

GLORIOSA

Gloriosa superba

G. rothschildiana

GLORIOSA
Liliaceae

A small genus of five or six species of tuberous, perennial, weak-stemmed plants which support themselves by the tendrils at the tips of the leaves. The flowers are most decorative, striking yet delicate, with reflexed, wavy-edged petals and conspicuous anthers. These plants are native to Asia and Africa, with one species indigenous to South Africa. Scramblers in nature, they prefer semi-shade, protection from wind, and need a trellis or similar support in the garden. Gloriosa lilies make excellent, long-lasting and most attractive cut flowers. The bulbs are poisonous.

Gloriosa rothschildiana Tropical Africa
Scrambling to over 2 m. Flowers, crimson with yellow margins and base, and up to 80 mm across are borne in summer.

G. simplex Tropical Africa and Asia
(*G. virescens*)
Growing to over 1 m in height; flowers produced in summer are greenish, changing to yellow or red.

G. simplex

G. superba Northern and eastern Transvaal and northwards into Central Africa
Flame lily
Height to 2 m; flowers red, orange or yellow, deepening in colour with age; some are bi-coloured. Summer flowering. This was the floral emblem of the former Rhodesia.

GLOTTIPHYLLUM

Glottiphyllum parvifolium

GLOTTIPHYLLUM
Mesembryanthemaceae

Dwarf succulents indigenous to South Africa comprise this genus. The name is from the Greek *glotta*, tongue, and *phyllon*, leaf, referring to the leaf shape of these almost stemless, clump-forming plants which freely produce large 'vygie'-like flowers in the spring. Native to the drier areas of the Cape, these succulents are good for well-drained rockery pockets.

Glottiphyllum parvifolium Little Karoo
Dwarf succulent with large yellow flowers in spring.

GOMPHRENA

GREVILLEA

Gomphrena globosa

Grevillea banksii 'Forsteri'

G. punicea

G. juniperina 'Rubra'

G. glabrata

GOMPHRENA
Amaranthaceae

Only one species in this genus is generally cultivated, the popular *Gomphrena globosa*, an easily grown annual with papery pompom-like flower heads. Good for bedding and long-lasting as cut flowers, they are useful for dried arrangements as the flowers retain their colour if dried correctly. These free-flowering plants grow well in any soil, in full sun.

Gomphrena globosa Tropical Africa and Asia
Globe amaranth
Annual to 450 mm; flowers are purple, pink, orange, white or variegated and are borne in summer.

GREVILLEA
Proteaceae

A large genus of evergreen trees and shrubs native to Australia and Malaysia, it was named in honour of Charles F. Greville, 1749-1809, founder of the Royal Horticultural Society. There is a great variety of form and foliage in this genus but all have showy, wiry, spidery flower clusters. The plants can be used as specimen shrubs or hedges, shade trees or windbreaks, and some species can be grown indoors as foliage plants. One of these is *Grevillea robusta*, silky oak or silver oak, familiar as a very large tree but adaptable to living indoors where its fine, feathery, often red-tipped foliage can be appreciated.

Grevillea banksii 'Forsteri' Australia
Shrub or small tree to 6 m; red or white spring flowers in terminal spikes up to 150 mm long.

G. glabrata Western Australia
Scandent shrub to 2,5 m, with drooping sprays of dainty creamy-white flowers that are borne in spring. Rich in nectar, they attract many bees.

G. juniperina 'Rubra' Australia
A very popular cultivar with a horizontal branching habit. It is drought resistant. Flowers are coral-red over a long period.

G. punicea Australia
Red spider flower
Shrub to 1,5 m; bright red or pink flowers are borne in spring.

CONTINUED

GREVILLEA

G. robusta

G. rosmarinifolia

GREWIA

Grewia occidentalis

GREYIA

Greyia radlkoferi

G. sutherlandii

G. robusta — Australia
Silver oak or Silky oak
Large tree to 25 m which drops its fern-like, silver-backed leaves just before flowering. Showy golden orange flower spikes appear in spring and are rich in nectar.

G. rosmarinifolia — Australia
Dense shrub growing to a height of 2 m with an equal spread. Spidery pink-red flowers are borne in summer.

GREWIA
Tiliaceae

A genus of evergreen shrubs, climbers and small trees, native to Asia and Africa with several species indigenous to South Africa. Only one is commonly cultivated in gardens, *Grewia occidentalis*.

Grewia occidentalis — Widespread in South Africa, excluding the northern Cape
Cross-berry or Kruisbessie
A rather sprawling shrub or small tree to 6 m in height. Starry flowers in summer come in shades of pink and mauve with prominent, massed showy, yellow stamens. The fruit is square in shape, divided into four lobes; hence the common name. Grewias will grow in semi-shade.

GREYIA
Greyiaceae

Named in honour of Sir George Grey, famous governor of the Cape in the nineteenth century, this is a genus of three indigenous species. These deciduous shrubs or small trees bear spikes of brilliant red flowers with numerous protruding red anthers, making the whole inflorescence resemble a bottlebrush. Easily grown from seed or cuttings, these plants are fairly drought resistant.

Greyia radlkoferi — Eastern Transvaal
Transvaal bottlebrush or Transvaalse baakhout
Shrub or small tree to 5 m with showy spikes of scarlet flowers in winter and spring, before or with the young leaves.

G. sutherlandii — Transkei and Natal interior, and into the southern Transvaal
Natal bottlebrush or Natalse baakhout
Shrub or small tree to 7 m; most ornamental, and quick growing. Red flowers flourish in the spring on spikes up to 120 mm long, and are very showy. Colourful autumn foliage is attractive.

GRIELUM

Grielum humifusum

GUNNERA

Gunnera manicata

GUZMANIA

Guzmania lingulata var. *major*

G. lingulata var. *minor*

GRIELUM
Rosaceae

Annual, dwarf herbaceous plants from Namaqualand and the south-western Cape. Propagated mainly by seed, and grown in enriched, well-drained soil. Flowers appear solitary.

Grielum humifusum Namaqualand, Clanwilliam
Herbaceous creeping annual bearing lemon-yellow flowers, 20 to 30 mm across, in spring.

GUNNERA
Gunneraceae

A genus of herbaceous perennials, native to the tropical and temperate regions and grown for their ornamental foliage. Some species grow to gigantic proportions, forming clumps of enormous rhubarb-like leaves, while the smaller kinds form decorative cushions or rosettes of leaves. Flowers are insignificant, but the larger species carry huge inflorescences which are quite ornamental. These are waterside plants, needing good, moist soil. The larger species are suited only to very large gardens.

Gunnera manicata Colombia
Waterside foliage plant with leaves growing to nearly 3 m across in nature but less in cultivation, although still very large. Plants grow to 3 m high with inflorescences up to 1 m long and 300 mm across. Rust-coloured flowers are produced in summer.

GUZMANIA
Bromeliaceae

Named after one Anastatio Guzman, a Spanish apothecary and naturalist, this is a genus of perennial epiphytic and terrestrial plants from tropical America. Grown for their ornamental foliage and colourful flower spikes, these are good indoor plants and suitable for shady stoeps in warmer, humid regions. They require moisture, humidity and good drainage, and plenty of light, but not direct sunlight.

Guzmania lingulata var. **major** Tropical America
Scarlet star
Epiphyte with bold, rising inflorescence of recurving scarlet red bracts surrounding the small white flowers.

G. lingulata var. **minor** Tropical America
Orange star
Foliage plant. Epiphyte with narrow, stiff, strap-like leaves to 450 mm long, producing tiny white flowers with smaller, showy scarlet bracts.

GYMNOCALYCIUM

Gymnocalycium gibbosum 'Nigrum'

G. mihanovichii 'Rubra'

GYPSOPHILA

Gypsophila elegans

G. elegans 'Grandiflora Alba'

GYMNOCALYCIUM
Cactaceae

A genus of low, round cacti with shallow ribs and usually developing a protrusion or 'chin' below the areole. Spines are slightly curved and rather sparse and the flowers are large for the size of the plants. These little cacti are native to South America and make excellent house plants, although they can be grown outdoors in frost-free areas. For better growth a variety of cultivars are usually grafted on night-blooming *Hylocereus undatus*.

Gymnocalycium gibbosum 'Nigrum'
Argentina
Strongly tubercled stem with nearly black spines. Flowers are white and 80 mm long.

G. mihanovichii 'Rubra'
Paraguay
Ruby ball
Strikingly colourful red, pink and yellow small globe cactus which lacks chlorophyll and must therefore be grafted on to the top of a green cactus stock.

GYPSOPHILA
Caryophyllaceae

Popular with florists, flower arrangers and gardeners for their airy sprays of tiny flowers, gypsophilas are native mainly to the Mediterranean regions. The genus includes a few small shrubs as well as annuals and perennials, several of which are grown for their misty effect in rock gardens and borders. Although the name, from the Greek, *gypsos*, meaning chalk, and *phileo*, to love, indicates that the plants grow best in chalky soils, gypsophilas will tolerate other soils provided they are well drained. Grow in full sun and propagate by seed or division.

Gypsophila elegans
Much-branched annual, 200 to 600 mm high; inflorescence a panicle of cymes, flowers white, not more than 7 mm across. Much used in floral arrangements.

G. elegans 'Grandiflora Alba'
As above but flowers large, white.

HAEMANTHUS
Amaryllidaceae

The name of this genus comes from the Greek *haima*, blood, and *anthos*, flower, a reference to the deep red flowers of some species. Plants in this genus are native to tropical and southern Africa, with several species indigenous to both the summer and winter rainfall areas. Haemanthus are bulbous plants sending up stout flower stalks bearing dense heads of flowers which are sometimes rounded like a puff-ball, or shaped like a shaving brush. In nature, they grow in good soil in partial shade with a cool root-run. Good drainage is important, with plenty of water in the growing season.

HAEMANTHUS

Haemanthus coccineus

H. humilis

HALLERIA

Halleria elliptica

HAMELIA

Hamelia chrysantha

Haemanthus coccineus — South-western Cape
April fool, Maartblom, Veldskoenblaar or Skeerkwas
A 'brush' of brilliant coral-red flowers, surrounded by scarlet, waxy bracts, appears before the leaves. Flower heads are carried up to 250 mm above ground and are up to 75 mm across. It flowers in autumn.

H. humilis — Transvaal
As above. Pale pink flowers take the form of large heads.

HALLERIA
Scrophulariaceae

A small genus of evergreen shrubs and small trees native to southern and tropical Africa and Madagascar. All have red tubular flowers in drooping clusters followed by berries which are very attractive to birds. These are drought-resistant shrubs and trees which will grow in any soil and are able to withstand all but the most severe frost.

Halleria elliptica — South-western Cape
Wild fuchsia
A much branched shrub to 2,5 m. Orange-red flowers are produced in autumn.

HAMELIA
Rubiaceae

This is a genus of evergreen shrubs and small trees native to Central America and the West Indies and suited to subtropical and frost-free regions. Flowers are tubular, in shades of red, orange and yellow, followed by berries which are quite showy in some species.

Hamelia chrysantha — Jamaica
Firebush or Vuurbos
Height 1,5 to 2 m, with a spread to 1,5 m. Orange flowers in spring/summer and autumn are followed by black berries.

HARDENBERGIA

Hardenbergia comptoniana

HAWORTHIA

Haworthia comptoniana

H. cymbiformis

H. cooperi var. *leightonii*

H. herbacea

HARDENBERGIA
Fabaceae (=Leguminosae) Subfam. Faboideae (=Papilionoideae)

Showy sprays of pea-shaped flowers in an especially lovely shade of blue-violet, pink or white characterize the three species in this genus of dainty evergreen creepers and sub-shrubs from Australia. As they are not too vigorous and will grow in semi-shade as well as full sun, they are ideal for shady patios. Plant in light, enriched soil that is well drained. Prune in winter if necessary.

Hardenbergia comptoniana Australia
Australian lilac or Sarsaparilla vine
A dainty evergreen creeper to 3 m, its flower sprays grow to 150 mm long. Flowers are a beautiful blue-violet and can be seen in spring.

HAWORTHIA
Liliaceae

A genus of succulents indigenous to South Africa and grown for their interesting and varied foliage. Some species are similar to the stemless aloes to which they are closely related, and form attractive cushions or rosettes of leaves, while others have longer stems. Leaves are often dotted, mottled, ridged and striped and the flowers are greenish-white and inconspicuous. These plants are ideal for drier rockery pockets, and make good container plants. Propagate from offsets, and cultivate like other succulents.

Haworthia comptoniana Karoo
Leaves are dark purplish-green with reddish stripes.

H. cooperi var. **leightonii** Eastern Cape
Greyish-green rosettes of leaves distinguished by their reddish veins.

H. cymbiformis Eastern Cape
Dwarf succulent. Leaves are boat-shaped and translucent at the tips.

H. herbacea Robertson, Karoo
Stemless rosette composed of up to 80 leaves; margins toothed and keel often with a double row of spines.

H. reinwardtii Eastern Cape
Stem to 150 mm, and branches freely. Leaves are dark green dotted white with reddish tips and clasp round the stem.

H. venosa subsp. **recurva** Widespread in the Cape Province, Orange Free State and Namibia
A stemless rosette of dark green leaves with tessellate veining.

HEBE

H. venosa subsp. *recurva*

Hebex andersonii 'Variegata'

H. salicifolia

H. reinwardtii

H. speciosa

H. speciosa cv.

HEBE
Scrophulariaceae

Most species in this genus are native to New Zealand, although they are also found in South America and New Guinea. They are evergreen shrubs with glossy leaves, and bear attractive spikes of small flowers in shades of purple, blue, mauve, pink and white. Tolerant of frost, these shrubs need regular water, and do well in coastal gardens where they are wind resistant. Fast growing, they can be pruned hard and used as hedge plants.

Hebe x andersonii 'Variegata' Garden hybrid
Shrub to 2 m. Leaves are variegated cream and the flowers are lavender-blue.

H. salicifolia
Shrub to 1,5 m which produces light pink flowers on open spikes in summer.

H. speciosa New Zealand
Winter-flowering shrub to 1,75 m. Purple flowers are produced on spikes up to 100 mm long.

H. speciosa cv. Garden origin
As above, but flowers are purple-pink.

169

HEDERA

Hedera canariensis 'Gloire de Marengo'

H. helix 'Bulgaria'

H. helix 'Marmorata'

H. helix 'Aureo-variegata'

H. helix 'Star'

HEDERA
Araliaceae

Extremely useful plants as creepers, ground covers and indoor specimens, the ivies belong to a small genus of about five species. However, most of these species mutate freely and numerous cultivars have arisen, with immensely varied and ornamental foliage. Native to Europe, Asia and North Africa, ivies are adaptable to a wide variety of conditions, soils and climate. They will cling to any support by means of strong rootlets on the stems, quickly forming a dense cover. When the plants reach the top of their support they produce stiff, rootless, shrubby stems which then produce greenish, insignificant flowers and black fruits.

Hedera canariensis 'Gloire de Marengo'
Ⓕ ⓒ ⓢ ☼ Ⓦ   Europe
Algerian ivy, Canary ivy or Madeira ivy
Vigorous creeper to great heights; young stems and leaf stalks are purplish-red. Will grow in full sun, full shade and semi-shade.

H. helix 'Aureo-variegata'   Europe,
Ⓕ ⓒ ⓢ ☼ Ⓦ   West Asia, North Africa
English ivy
Creeper; ground cover or indoor plant. Leaves are variegated creamy-yellow.

H. helix 'Bulgaria'   Europe, West Asia,
Ⓕ ⓒ ⓢ ☼ Ⓦ   North Africa
Leaves are dark green with creamy-white veins. Excellent ground cover.

H. helix 'Marmorata'   Europe, West Asia,
Ⓕ ⓒ ⓢ ☼ Ⓦ   North Africa
Ground cover; leaves are small, triangular and mottled like marble.

H. helix 'Minima Luzi'   Europe, West Asia,
Ⓕ ⓒ ⓢ ☼ Ⓦ   North Africa
Leaves are small, somewhat wavy with yellow centres and green margins that come in a delicate form and are extremely decorative.

H. helix 'Minima Luzi'

H. helix 'Star'   Europe, West Africa,
Ⓕ ⓒ ⓢ ☼ Ⓦ   North Africa
Bushy; leaves are slender, five-lobed and star-like.

HEDYCHIUM

Hedychium coccineum

H. coronarium

H. gardneranum

HELIANTHUS

Helianthus annuus

H. debilis

HEDYCHIUM
Zingiberaceae

About 50 species of rhizomatous perennials from tropical Asia and the Himalayas comprise this genus. Ginger lilies are grown for their lush, tropical-looking foliage and their showy, delightfully sweet-scented flowers. They need rich soil and plenty of water. These tall, clump-forming plants prefer semi-shade, and are suitable for growing in containers on stoeps and shady patios. The flowers are useful in floral arrangements. Propagate by division of the rhizomes. The name comes from the Greek *hedys,* meaning sweet, and *chios,* meaning snow, referring to the fragrant white flowers of some species.

Hedychium coccineum　　　　　India

Red ginger lily, Scarlet ginger lily or Rooigemmerlelie
Perennial to 2 m. Leaves grow to 500 mm in length and 50 mm across. Dense flower spikes to 250 mm long produce red flowers with showy pink stamens in spring and early summer.

H. coronarium　　　　　Tropical Asia

Garland flower, Butterfly lily, White butterfly lily or Witgemmerlelie
Perennial to 2 m. Leaves grow to 600 mm in length. Very fragrant white flowers tinged with yellow, up to 75 mm across and carried on spikes 150 mm long, are produced in summer.

H. gardneranum　　　　　India

Kahili ginger, Ginger lily, Yellow ginger or Geelgemmerlelie
Perennial to nearly 3 m with large glossy leaves. Yellow flowers with prominent red stamens are carried on spikes up to 250 mm long and borne in summer.

HELIANTHUS
Asteraceae (=Compositae)

The name of this genus comes from the Greek *helios,* the sun, and *anthos,* flower. It is a genus of annuals and perennials native to the Americas, which includes the largest daisies in the world, the giant *Helianthus annuus,* the common sunflower, an important economic plant. There are numerous cultivars of this and other species, which make good garden subjects, as well as many flower forms and several colours available, besides the traditional golden yellow. Sunflowers are quick growing, easily raised from seed, or propagated by division, and grow in any soil. Best results are obtained by feeding and watering well.

Helianthus annuus　　　　　North America

Annual to 3 m with flowers up to 300 mm or more across, borne in summer.

H. debilis　　　　　North America

Bushy annual to 2 m; flowers grow to 75 mm across in summer.

CONTINUED　　　　　171

HELIANTHUS

H. decapetalus 'Multiflorus'

H. tuberosus

H. decapetalus 'Multiflorus'   Garden origin
Thin-leaf sunflower
Perennial to 2 m; 'double' flower heads up to 180 mm across are borne in summer.

H. tuberosus   North America
Jerusalem artichoke or Jerusalemartisjok
Perennial to 4 m producing edible tubers; flowers to 80 mm across are borne in summer.

HELICHRYSUM

Helichrysum argyrophyllum

H. bracteatum

H. petiolare

H. pinifolium

HELICHRYSUM
Asteraceae (=Compositae)

Many of the species in this large genus are indigenous to South Africa but they are equally numerous in Australia and New Zealand as well as being widespread in the rest of Africa, Asia and southern Europe. The genus includes annuals, perennials and shrubs, some of which bear the glossy, papery flowers commonly known as Everlastings, that are found in a wide range of colours; some flowers are bi-coloured and in double as well as single forms. There is considerable variation of form and habit within the genus and the different species can be grown as annuals, which, when dried successfully, keep their colour for winter decoration, or as rockery plants or ground covers. All need full sun, good drainage, and will grow in any soil. The origin of the name is rather lovely, from the Greek *helios*, sun, and *chrysos*, gold.

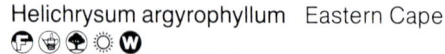

Helichrysum argyrophyllum   Eastern Cape
Golden guinea everlasting
Dense ground cover with silvery foliage and yellow flowers in summer.

H. bracteatum   Australia
Straw-flower, Everlasting, Immortelle or Strooiblom
Perennial usually grown as an annual to 1 m, papery flowers in shades of red, orange, pink, yellow and white in summer.

H. petiolare   Southern Cape
Licorice plant or Kooigoed
Shrubby, spreading perennial to 1,2 m with felty, silvery white foliage and cream or ivory flowers in summer.

H. pinifolium   South-western Cape
Scantily branched sub-shrub with erect, leafy stems; yellow flowers.

172

HELICONIA

H. retortum

Heliconia humilis

H. psittacorum

H. splendidum

H. mariae

H. rostrata

H. retortum South-western Cape, Blouvbergstrand
An erect or somewhat spreading sub-shrub to 400 mm high.

H. splendidum Eastern Transvaal
Dense-growing, erect shrubby perennial with silver-grey foliage.

HELICONIA
Strelitziaceae

This is a genus of plants closely related to the banana family, native to tropical South America, and suitable only for really warm, moist areas. They are grown for their lush foliage and brilliant inflorescences which consist of brightly coloured, boat-shaped bracts that enclose the small insignificant flowers. These plants make large clumps and do well in semi-shade, in rich, moist soil. They also make good waterside plants. Propagate by division of the rhizomes.

Heliconia humilis Northern South America
Lobster's claw or Kreefklou
Stems to 2,5 m; leaves to nearly 2 m long and 250 mm wide. Bracts, red, with green tips and edges, appear in summer.

H. mariae Northern South America to Honduras
Beefsteak heliconia
Huge plant with stems to 3 m long and leaves 3 m long and up to 750 mm wide. The whole plant reaches heights up to 8 m. Dark crimson flower bracts are borne on long, drooping inflorescences in summer.

H. psittacorum Northern South America
Parrot flower
Stems are 2 m with narrow leaves to 300 mm. Inflorescences are erect with green or orange flower bracts that are borne in summer.

H. rostrata Argentina to Peru
Hanging lobster claws
Stems are to 2 m but less in cultivation. Leaves are over 1 m long, and up to 300 mm wide. Drooping inflorescences to 600 mm bear flowers of red shading to yellow, in summer.

HELIOPHILA

Heliophila coronopifolia

HELIOTROPIUM

Heliotropium arborescens

HELIPTERUM

Helipterum eximium

HELIOPHILA
Brassicaceae (=Cruciferae)

Usually recognized by the intense blue of their flowers, heliophilas are also found in shades of pink, yellow, and white. This is an indigenous genus, with several of the species well known in the south-western Cape and Namaqualand for their spectacular displays in springtime. The shimmering drifts of blue seen in the veld are hard to capture in the garden but several species are suitable for annual borders or rockery pockets. Grow in full sun and well-drained soil. As well as the annual species that are raised from seed, there are a few shrubby species not often cultivated.

Heliophila coronopifolia   South-western Cape
'Sporrie'
Spring-flowering annuals to 600 mm, with bright to pale blue flowers with a light centre, up to 12 mm across.

HELIOTROPIUM
Boraginaceae

A genus of shrubby perennials and annuals widespread in the tropical and temperate regions of the world, with fragrant blue, purple, pink or white flowers. The species most often cultivated is *Heliotropium arborescens*, which has heavily fragrant flowers used in perfume. These are rather sprawling plants which need pinching back and regular pruning to keep in shape. This shrub needs a warm protected position and will do well in a container next to a patio. Plant in good soil and water well.

Heliotropium arborescens   Peru
Heliotrope or Cherry pie
Perennial or shrub to 1,25 m bearing fragrant flowers that vary from purple and heliotrope to white and are carried in flat heads mainly in summer.

HELIPTERUM
Asteraceae (=Compositae)

A genus of annuals, perennials, sub-shrubs and shrubs native to South Africa, Australia and Tasmania, with papery 'everlasting' daisy flowers. The flowers, in shades of pink, yellow and white, usually appear in spring and summer but can be dried and used for winter flower arrangements. Easily raised from seed, these plants will grow well in poor soil as long as it is well drained.

Helipterum eximium   South-western Cape
Cape everlasting, Straw flower or Rooisewejaartjie
An erect sub-shrub to 1 m high with woolly grey leaves; red flowers are borne in summer.

HEMEROCALLIS

Hemerocallis aurantiaca

H. lilioasphodelus

HEMIZYGIA

Hemizygia transvaalensis

HERREANTHUS

Herreanthus meyeri

HEMEROCALLIS
Liliaceae

About 15 species make up this genus of clump-forming perennials which occur from Central Europe to China and Japan. The trumpet-shaped flowers last only a day, hence the name, from the Greek *hemero,* a day, and *kallos,* beauty; however, numerous buds are carried on each wiry flower spike so the plants are in flower for many weeks at a time. Day lilies come in shades of yellow, orange, red, purple and brown and in numerous combinations of these colours. They are easy to grow in any soil and any position, except in deep shade, and are propagated by dividing the clumps.

Hemerocallis aurantiaca China
Day lily
Deciduous rhizomatous perennial with orange flowers up to 100 mm, in summer.

H. lilioasphodelus Eastern Siberia to Japan
(*H. flava*)
Yellow day lily or Geeldaglelie
Rhizomatous perennial with yellow flowers up to 100 mm across in spring/summer.

HEMIZYGIA
Lamiaceae (=Labiatae)

Herbaceous shrublets of which 20 species are found widespread in Transvaal and Natal. Leaves are opposite and flowers bilabiate. They need rich, well-drained soil.

Hemizygia transvaalensis Transvaal
Small shrublet to 750 mm; pink flowers are arranged in long terminal racemes in late spring.

HERREANTHUS
Mesembryanthemaceae

There is only one species in this genus named after Dr Hans Herre, curator at the Stellenbosch University botanic garden from 1925-1962. This is *Herreanthus meyeri,* a dwarf succulent native to the Richtersveld in northern Namaqualand, and therefore needing very little water in cultivation. This rare plant produces fragrant, milky white 'vygie' flowers.

Herreanthus meyeri Namaqualand
Dwarf succulent with bluish-green, rather geometrical leaves that turn up at the tip. White flowers are produced in spring.

175

HIBBERTIA   HIBISCUS

Hibbertia scandens

Hibiscus rosa-sinensis cv.

HIBBERTIA
Dilleniaceae

A genus of evergreen shrubs and creepers native to Australia, Tasmania and Malaysia. Flowers are usually in shades of yellow with a prominent tuft of anthers. These are shrubs for warm climates, and *Hibbertia scandens* grows on sand dunes in its native habitat and therefore is a good choice for sandy coastal gardens. The plant is named after George Hibbert, an early nineteenth century patron of botany.

Hibbertia scandens　　　　　　Australia
Golden guinea plant or Guinea gold vine
Shrubby, scandent climber to 2,75 m, bearing golden yellow flowers in summer/autumn.

HIBISCUS
Malvaceae

Widely grown for their superb flowers, the plants in this genus are native to every continent except Europe. Although the genus includes annuals, perennials and trees, the exceptionally showy flowering shrubs are the reason hibiscus are usually grown. As well as making a striking show of colour when in bloom, the individual blossoms are flamboyantly lovely, especially the cultivars of *Hibiscus rosa-sinensis*. Most commonly cultivated species are easy to grow and adaptable to a wide range of conditions.

Hibiscus rosa-sinensis cvs.　　　　China
Hawaiian hibiscus, Rose-of-China or Hibiskus
The species is an erect-growing shrub or bushy small tree to 3 m or more with dark green glossy leaves. The flowers are found in all shades except blues and mauves and are often bi-coloured, blotched, striped etc.; they can be single or double, and are enhanced by a showy anther column. Best suited to warm coastal regions where they make excellent seaside hedges, but adaptable elsewhere, they are even grown in semi-shade. Semi-deciduous in some regions, they are spring and summer flowering.

H. rosa-sinensis 'Cooperi'　　　　China
As above, foliage variegated.

H. rosa-sinensis 'Princess Marina'　　China
As above. Often with single and double flowers on the same plant.

H. schizopetalus　　　Tropical East Africa
Japanese lantern
Shrub to 3 m. Its slender drooping branches bear delicate pink flowers with a showy stamen column, on long pendent stems in summer.

H. syriacus　　　　　　　　Eastern Asia
Rose-of-Sharon
Erect shrub or small tree to 3 m or more. Its double or single flowers in shades of white, mauve, purple and lavender-blue, usually with a crimson base to the petals, are borne in summer.

H. rosa-sinensis cv.

H. rosa-sinensis 'Cooperi'

H. tiliaceus

H. rosa-sinensis cv.

H. rosa-sinensis 'Princess Marina'

H. vitifolius

H. rosa-sinensis cv.

H. syriacus

H. schizopetalus

H. tiliaceus Tropical and subtropical coastal areas, worldwide
Tree hibiscus, Mahoe coast hibiscus or Wilde Katoenboom
Evergreen tree to 6 m. Yellow flowers with dark throats, the colour deepening with age to orange, are borne in summer.

H. vitifolius Eastern Transvaal
Annual to 1 m and prefers wet places in full sun.

HIPPEASTRUM

Hippeastrum x hybrida

H. x hybrida

HIPPEASTRUM
Amaryllidaceae

Closely related to amaryllis, the bulbous plants in this genus are native mainly to tropical America. Most cultivated specimens are hybrids with large showy trumpet flowers in all shades of red and pink, also yellow and white, with flowers often veined, striped and blotched in contrasting colours. The flowers, which are up to 225 mm across, appear before the strap-like leaves, carried in a cluster at the top of a stout stem up to 600 mm high. Easily grown in the garden, hippeastrums are perhaps most successful as container plants. They are quite spectacular on patios, stoeps or windowsills when they are in full bloom.

Hippeastrum x hybrida
Flowering season variable.

HOFFMANNIA

Hoffmannia ghiesbreghtii

H. refulgens

HOFFMANNIA
Rubiaceae

These evergreen foliage plants belong to a genus native to South and Central America. The leaves are prominently ribbed and veined, dark green above and in shades of purple and red beneath. Flowers are red or yellow, but not as showy as the leaves. These plants are best suited to the greenhouse in cold areas but in warmer climates they are suitable for house and stoep culture.

Hoffmannia ghiesbreghtii   Guatemala
Tall taffeta plant
Foliage plant. Shrub to 1,2 m; leaves are to 300 mm long, dark green above and purple beneath. Flowers are yellow with a red spot.

H. refulgens   Central America, Mexico
Taffeta plant
Foliage plant. Small shrub to 300 mm with leaves to 150 mm long, green above and wine-red beneath; flowers are red.

HOLMSKIOLDIA

Holmskioldia sanguinea

H. tettensis

HOLMSKIOLDIA
Verbenaceae

Colourful flower calyces like tiny Chinese hats characterize the plants in this genus of shrubs and small trees native to India, Madagascar and Africa; several species are indigenous to South Africa. The drooping flowers are sometimes in a contrasting colour to the calyx, adding to the attractiveness of the flowers so suitable for flower arranging. Both evergreen and deciduous species are found, although this tends to be variable, depending on climate. These shrubs are easy to grow in any garden soil.

Holmskioldia sanguinea
Himalayan foothills
Chinese hat plant, Parasol flower or Sambreelblom
Shrub 2 to 3 m. Flowers are red with brick-red and orange calyces. They are spring/summer flowering.

H. tettensis   Central Africa
Shrub to 1,5 m. Flowers borne in summer are blue with mauve calyces.

HOMALOCLADIUM

Homalocladium platycladum

HOMALOCLADIUM
Polygonaceae

There is only one species in this genus, *Homalocladium platycladum*, a shrub native to the Solomon Islands in the Pacific.

Homalocladium platycladum
Solomon Islands
Centipede plant, Tapeworm plant, Ribbon bush or Lintwurmplant
Decorative plant. Shrub to 4 m in nature but only about 2 m in cultivation. The cladodes (leaf-like stems) are non-fleshy. Small insignificant flowers are produced at the nodes.

HOMERIA

Homeria comptonii

H. elegans

HOMERIA
Iridaceae

Some species in this genus are showy enough to grow in the garden, while others are considered noxious weeds by stock farmers. This genus of cormous perennials has yellow, orange, salmon-pink or lilac flowers, most of which are only open for a day, although the flowering spike bears a number of flowers in succession. Easily grown in any soil, homerias often self-seed freely. Propagate either by this method or by offsets.

Homeria comptonii
South-western Cape
Cormous perennial with open, six-petalled flowers in yellow and orange-red. Plant in well-drained soil.

H. elegans
Southern Cape
Painted homeria or Poublom
Spring flowers up to 100 mm across, usually bright yellow, or with the petals splashed with orange and green, or with alternate pink and greenish-blue petals.

HOMOGLOSSUM

Homoglossum watsonium

HOMOGLOSSUM
Iridaceae

This is a genus of about 10 species of cormous plants, indigenous to the southern and south-western Cape, closely related to the indigenous gladiolus and having similar requirements in cultivation.

Homoglossum watsonium
Southern and south-western Cape
Red Afrikaner or Rooi-afrikaner
Up to 400 mm high and autumn flowering. This plant is now known as *Gladiolus watsonius*.

179

HOODIA

Hoodia bainii

H. triebneri

HOODIA
Asclepiadaceae

Leafless perennial herbaceous succulents restricted to the arid regions of Namibia, the Karoo and the north-western Cape. Stems are many-angled and prickly. Flowers are large, flat and showy.

Hoodia bainii　　　　　Namaqualand, Karoo
Bitterghaap
A bushy species with long spines; flowers, 60 to 75 mm across, are greyish-green tinged pink and borne in October.

H. triebneri
Reddish flowers show five distinct petals. This plant is also known as *Hoodiopsis triebneri*.

HOSTA

Hosta crispula

HOSTA
Liliaceae

Grown for their luxuriant, decorative foliage, plantain lilies are hardy herbaceous perennials from the Far East. The glossy, corrugated leaves are often variegated and form large, neat ornamental clumps. Some species have showy flowers, in shades of mauve and white, which are carried on spikes above the foliage. Both leaves and flowers are useful for floral decoration. Hostas are shade and water-loving plants, and will grow in good, moist soil under tall trees, as well as next to ponds and pools. Propagate by division.

Hosta crispula　　　　　　　　　Japan

Perennial to 1 m. Leaves are up to 200 mm long, with white margins. Flowers are lavender, up to 50 mm long, and carried on a loose spike in summer.

HOYA

Hoya carnosa

H. carnosa 'Variegata'

HOYA
Asclepiadaceae

Popular indoor and greenhouse plants are included in this genus of evergreen, shrubby climbers native to East Asia, the Pacific Islands and Australia. Suitable for growing out of doors in warm, frost-free areas, these plants produce rounded heads of waxy, star-shaped flowers which are sweetly fragrant. Dead flower heads should not be pruned as new flowers form on the remains of the old ones.
Propagation is by layering or from cuttings.

Hoya carnosa　　Southern China to Australia

Wax plant, Honey plant or Wasplant
Shrubby climber to 3 m. Flowers are pink with red centres and borne in spring.

H. carnosa 'Variegata'　　　　Garden origin

Variegated wax plant or Bontblaarwasplant
As above but leaves margined white.

HUNNEMANNIA

Hunnemannia fumariifolia

HYACINTHUS

Hyacinthus orientalis cv.

HYDRANGEA

Hydrangea macrophylla var. *macrophylla*

H. macrophylla var. *macrophylla*

HUNNEMANNIA
Papaveraceae

There is only one species in this genus, *Hunnemannia fumariifolia,* a herbaceous perennial closely related to eschscholzia and native to Mexico.

Hunnemannia fumariifolia   Mexico
Mexican tulip poppy
Perennial, grown as an annual, reaching up to 600 mm high, with silvery grey foliage and bright yellow summer flowers up to 75 mm across. These plants require a warm position in full sun, and well-drained soil. Propagate by seeds.

HYACINTHUS
Liliaceae

The one species in this genus is a bulbous plant native to the Mediterranean region and Asia Minor. The name has its origin in the Greek myth in which Apollo accidentally killed Hyakinthos, and hyacinths sprang up where his blood was shed. There are many named cultivars, and colours are every shade of blue and mauve, pink, red, white and yellow. Intensely fragrant, hyacinths are used in perfume production. Often grown in containers indoors, they are also effective planted in drifts under deciduous trees for early spring flowering in cool climates. Bulbs require special treatment and careful handling before planting, so buy from a reliable source and get specialist advice if necessary.

Hyacinthus orientalis cv.
                         Mediterranean region
Hyacinth or Hiasint
Plant is 150 mm to 250 mm high. Flowers are in all usual colours and produced in spring.

HYDRANGEA
Saxifragaceae

One species in this genus is familiar to most gardeners, for who has not admired the widely grown, spectacular, and much loved common hydrangea, or Christmas rose? However, there are over 20 species in the genus, native to the Americas and eastern Asia, with about half of them cultivated as garden shrubs or climbers. The popular *Hydrangea macrophylla* can grow to be a very large shrub, to 3 m high with an equal spread, needing good soil, filtered shade, ample water, and correct pruning in winter. The large bulbs of flowerettes come in every shade of blue, including turquoise, also pink, mauve, purple, crimson and white and make excellent cut flowers. To ensure that they last well in the vase, cut the stems under water and immerse the whole flower and stem in water, overnight if possible, then gently shake off excess water before arranging. Hydrangeas are not scented to any extent but have a delightful cool, dry fragrance that is most refreshing on hot summer days.

CONTINUED

HYDRANGEA

H. macrophylla 'Blue Wave'

H. macrophylla 'Regular'

Hydrangea macrophylla var. **macrophylla**
Japan
Christmas rose, Krismisroos or Hortensie
Deciduous shrub to 3 m, evergreen in warm climates. Glossy, rich green leaves make a dense background to the huge round flower heads that often hide the foliage. Flowers are borne in summer and if left on the plant often fade to attractive purple shades.

H. macrophylla 'Blue Wave' Japan
As above. Showy ornamental shrub to 1,5 m.

H. macrophylla 'Regular' Japan
As above but flowers are pure white.

HYMENOCALLIS

Hymenocallis littoralis

HYMENOCALLIS
Amaryllidaceae

A genus of bulbous plants native to the Americas and grown for their large, fragrant, spider-like flowers at the tips of long stems. Colours are yellow and white. These are warm-climate plants, best suited to frost-free summer rainfall areas where they may be left to form large clumps. Bulbs should be lifted and stored in winter rainfall areas. Spider lilies will grow in both full sun or semi-shade.

Hymenocallis littoralis Tropical America
(*H. americana*)
Spider lily
Leafy clumps to 750 mm; flowers grow to 100 mm across in summer.

HYMENOSPORUM

Hymenosporum flavum

HYMENOSPORUM
Pittosporaceae

An evergreen Australian tree; one species only.

Hymenosporum flavum Australia
Leaves are obovate, entire, to 100 mm in length; flowers, 40 mm long, are borne in terminal umbels and sweetly scented. This is a quick-growing 'open' tree and is becoming very popular in South Africa.

HYOPHORBE

Hyophorbe lagenicaulis

HYOPHORBE
Arecaceae (=Palmae)

Five species, found in Madagascar and the adjacent islands, make up this genus of palms grown as ornamental outdoor plants in warm areas. The trunks are swollen at the base, tapering to a tuft of large, stiffly curving leaves.

Hyophorbe lagenicaulis   Mauritius
(*Mascarena lagenicaulis*)
Bottle palm
Grotesque, solitary palm to 4 m high. Arching fronds 1 to 2 m long.

HYPERICUM

Hypericum calycinum

H. revolutum

HYPERICUM
Hypericaceae

These are annuals, perennials and shrubs native to the temperate regions of the world, making up a genus of about 300 species. Among them are useful plants for the mixed border and rockery, while some species make excellent ground covers. Hypericums are usually easy to grow, most are frost resistant, and several of them will grow in shade or semi-shade. All have most attractive flowers in shades of yellow, with a mass of showy stamens.

Hypericum calycinum   South-eastern Europe, Asia Minor
Rose-of-Sharon, St John's wort or Gold flower
Vigorous ground cover or small shrub, reaching 300 mm in height. Yellow flowers are borne in summer. Leaves often turn bronze in winter. They thrive in full shade.

H. revolutum   Eastern and southern Africa
(*H. lanceolatum*)
Curry bush or Kerriebos
Large spreading shrub to 3 m; flowers are borne in spring and grow to 60 mm across; leaves give off a scent of curry after rain.

HYPOESTES

Hypoestes aristata

HYPOESTES
Acanthaceae

Several species in this genus of perennials and evergreen shrubs are indigenous to South Africa, while others are native to tropical Asia and Madagascar. The latter are most often grown as foliage plants indoors, on stoeps and in greenhouses. The most popular of the indigenous species is *Hypoestes aristata,* which is an easily grown shrub, needing little attention other than trimming back after flowering, or when it becomes woody with age. It will grow in full sun but prefers semi-shade. Like most species in the genus, it seeds itself freely. The common name, Ribbon bush, comes from the way in which the petals coil like florists' ribbon.

Hypoestes aristata   Southern to eastern Cape, Transkei, Natal
Ribbon bush or Seeroogblommetjie
Shrubby perennial to 1,5 m, evergreen but semi-deciduous in cold climates. Small mauve flowers striped darker mauve are borne in winter.

183

HYPOXIS

Hypoxis rooperi

HYPOXIS
Hypoxidaceae

A genus of tuberous plants native mostly to Australia and South Africa, with starry yellow or white flowers. These are tough plants, growing in any well-drained soil and able to withstand drought and frost. A really sunny spot is necessary for good flowering.

Hypoxis rooperi — Eastern Cape, Natal, Transvaal
Star flower
Low growing, to 300 mm, with starry yellow flowers borne in summer.

IBERIS

Iberis sempervirens

I. umbellata

IBERIS
Brassicaceae (=Cruciferae)

The name of this genus comes from Iberia, the old name for Spain, home of several species; others are found elsewhere in the Mediterranean region. They are easily grown garden plants, not fussy about soil, and most useful for bedding, mixed borders and rockeries. The colourful annuals come in shades of crimson, purple, pink, mauve and white, while the taller biennials or perennials have white flowers. Some species are fragrant.

Iberis sempervirens — Southern Europe
Edging candytuft
Evergreen herbaceous shrub to 300 mm; clusters of white flowers in spring.

I. umbellata — Mediterranean region
Candytuft
Annual to about 400 mm. Flowers are all shades of pink and mauve; borne in spring/summer.

IBOZA

Iboza riparia

IBOZA
Lamiaceae (=Labiatae)

The name of this genus is said to come from the Zulu name for these plants, referring to the pleasantly aromatic leaves. This is a genus native to tropical and southern Africa, of which only one, *Iboza riparia*, is commonly grown. This shrub, which grows very easily from cuttings, produces tiny white or mauve flowers in large plumes on bare branches in late winter, covering the bush with feathery, misty bloom. An adaptable plant, it can be grown under a variety of conditions and is most useful as it blooms when little else is in flower. The flowers are good for cutting because they last well in water. Prune well after flowering.

Iboza riparia   Natal, Transvaal
Ginger bush or Vleisalie
Shrub to 2 m, but taller in nature. Flowers are mauve or white and borne in winter/spring. This plant is now known as *Tetradenia riparia*.

ILEX

Ilex aquifolium

I. cornuta

ILEX
Aquifoliaceae

Christmas holly, farmed in orchards in the USA to supply the florist trade, is the best known species in this large genus of mostly evergreen shrubs and trees. Native mainly to the tropical and temperate regions of both Americas and Asia, Northern Europe is actually the home of this species that brightens the snowy winters with glossy dark green leaves and brilliant scarlet berries. Do not be disappointed if Christmas holly does not thrive away from its natural habitat (for one thing, bushes are either male or female and unless both are present, berries will not be produced) as there are numerous other species, including the indigenous *Ilex mitis*, which make useful ornamental shrubs with a good habit, attractive foliage and colourful berries.

Ilex aquifolium   Europe
Evergreen tree to 10 m, much less in South Africa. Shining ovate leaves with spiny teeth along the margins. Scarlet-red berries are borne in winter.

I. wilsonii

I. cornuta   China
Chinese holly
Bushy evergreen shrub; leathery, shining, almost rectangular leaves with spines at the four corners and at the tip. Red berries.

I. wilsonii   Japan/China
Japanese holly
Small evergreen shrub to 3 m, with glossy olive-green leaves to 600 mm and smooth margins. Masses of crimson-red berries are borne in summer.

IMPATIENS

Impatiens aerocoma

I. x *hybridum*

I. balsamina

I. oliveri

I. wallerana 'Red Ripple'

I. wallerana 'Busy Lizzie'

IMPATIENS
Balsaminaceae

Widely distributed in the tropical and subtropical regions of the world, but mainly in Africa and Asia, this is a large genus of annuals, perennials and small shrubs grown for their showy flowers both in the garden and as indoor, stoep or greenhouse plants. Flowers are in all shades of red, purple, pink and yellow-white. Requirements vary depending on the species. The perennial species grow easily from cuttings, the annuals from seed. The name probably comes from the way the seed pods snap open when touched, shooting out seeds, but it could also refer to the speed with which the plants spread.

Impatiens aerocoma   Mauritius
A perennial to 1 m found in tropical climates.

I. balsamina   India, China, Malaya
Balsam or Balseminie
Bushy annual to 750 mm. Flowers are white, yellow and red, found in spring and summer.

I. x **hybridum**
Many new hybrids producing masses of brightly coloured flowers are now available. They make excellent stoep plants.

I. oliveri   Tropical East Africa
Poor man's rhododendron
Shrubby perennial to 2 m with pale lilac or pink flowers, 75 mm across, borne in summer.

I. wallerana 'Busy Lizzie'
Perennial varying in height to 450 mm, can be grown as an indoor or stoep plant, as well as in shade outdoors. It flowers all year round in a variety of colours.

I. wallerana 'Red Ripple'
As above.

INDIGOFERA   IPOMOEA

Indigofera procumbens

Ipomoea acuminata

I. arborescens

I. alba

I. purpurea

INDIGOFERA
Fabaceae (=Leguminosae) Subfam. Faboideae (=Papilionoideae)

This is a large genus distributed worldwide in warmer regions with many of the species indigenous to South Africa. Most species have feathery, acacia-like foliage and all bear small pea-flowers, usually pink or white, in long, dainty sprays. Habit and form vary, depending on the species, as do their requirements. Some species are the source of the dye, indigo; hence the generic name.

Indigofera procumbens　　South-western Cape, Clanwilliom
A prostrate perennial herb with trifoliate leaves. Flowers are dark pink, 7 to 10 mm long and produced in a dense spray in spring.

IPOMOEA
Convolvulaceae

The name of this genus comes from the Greek, *ips,* bindweed, and *homoios,* like, referring to the twining habit of growth of most species. It is a large genus of creepers native to the tropical and warm temperate regions of the world and includes a number of cultivated species, such as the edible sweet potato and the familiar morning glory creeper with its bright blue flowers which fade to mauve by the end of the day. This species will cover large areas, climbing upwards on any support or creeping along the ground, rooting itself as it goes along. Most species are easy to grow, but may be frost tender.

Ipomoea acuminata　　Tropical America
(*Ipomoea learii*)
Morning glory or Purperwinde
Vigorous creeper to any height; blue flowers, 75 mm across, open at dawn and fade to mauve by evening. Summer flowering.

I. alba　　Tropical America
(*Calonyction aculeatum*)
Moonflower or Maanblom
Vigorous creeper with prickly stems cultivated for its large, white, fragrant flowers which open at night. Summer flowering.

I. arborescens　　Tropical Africa
Tree to 4 m, bearing white crinkly flowers 100 mm across in winter.

I. purpurea　　Tropical America
Common morning glory or Gewone purperwinde
Large, funnel-shaped flowers, deep purple-pink with pale yellow throats.

I. quamoclit　　Tropical America
Cypress vine or Cardinal climber
Annual to 6 m, small scarlet flowers 15 mm across. Summer flowering.

CONTINUED

IPOMOEA

I. quamoclit

I. tricolor 'Blue Star'

I. tricolor 'Summer Skies'

I. tricolor 'Blue Star'　　Tropical America
Large creeper, huge leaves to 80 mm across, blue flowers with dark blue stripe. Used by the Aztecs in Mexico as a hallucigen in religious ceremonies and in medicine. Summer flowering.

I. tricolor 'Summer Skies'　Tropical America
Summer flowers of light sky-blue.

IPOMOPSIS

Ipomopsis rubra

IPOMOPSIS
Polemoniaceae

A genus of perennials and biennials, with a few annuals. Native to North America, with the exception of one species found in Argentina, ipomopses are useful in summer borders as they send up tall, stout spikes of flowers in a wide variety of colours. These plants, which make good cut flowers, are easily raised from seed and grow well in most soils and conditions, in full sun.

Ipomopsis rubra　　North-western North
(*Gilia coronopifolia*)　　　　　America

Skyrocket, Gilia or Standing cypress
Biennial to 900 mm. Flowers are scarlet outside and white and dotted red inside, in a long thyrse-like panicle borne in summer.

IRESINE

Iresine herbstii

I. herbstii 'Aureo-reticulata'

IRESINE
Amaranthaceae

This is a genus of quick-growing shrubby perennials, native to the tropical and temperate regions of the world. The cultivated species are grown for their brightly coloured foliage. Easily grown for bedding or in a mixed border, they also make good stoep and indoor plants. Propagate by cuttings and prune or pinch back to keep them in shape. Flowers are insignificant and best removed to improve leaf growth.

Iresine herbstii　　　　South America

Bloodleaf or Bloedblaar
Foliage plant to 2 m in nature, less in cultivation. Leaves are purplish-red or green.

I. herbstii 'Aureo-reticulata'
As above, leaves are red or green with yellow veins.

IRIS

Iris hybrid

Iris hybrid

I. xiphium

IRIS
Iridaceae

The name of this genus comes from the Greek *iris,* meaning rainbow, and in fact red is the only colour missing in this genus. The hybridists have been at work and raised plants with truly gorgeous flower forms in every combination of shades. Irises fall broadly into three types – the bulbous type commonly known as Dutch irises; the rhizomatous bearded iris; and beardless irises which are also rhizomatous and vary greatly in flower form and habitat. 'Dutch' irises are usually treated similarly to other spring bulbs. Bearded irises are tough plants requiring mainly good drainage, but give better results with good feeding and watering, whereas the beardless forms have varied requirements.

Iris hybrids	Garden hybrid
Summer flowering.

I. xiphium	Southern France, Spain, Portugal and North Africa
Dutch iris, Spanish iris or Hollandse iris
Bulb with stems and leaves to 600 mm. Flowers are blue, yellow and white and appear in spring.

IXIA

Ixia campanulata

I. conferta var. *ochroleuca*

IXIA
Iridaceae

A genus of indigenous cormous plants with grassy leaves and dainty clusters of starry flowers, often bi-coloured, carried at the tips of wiry, wind-resistant stems. Most cultivated species are hybrids with a wide range of rich colours including purples, reds, mauves, pinks, green, yellow and white. These are good plants for any sunny corner of the garden and are ideal for well-drained rockery pockets and patio containers. In summer rainfall areas lift the corms after the leaves die down.

Ixia campanulata	South-western Cape
Kalossie
Corm to 300 mm. Purple to crimson flowers in dense, erect spikes in spring.

I. conferta var. **ochroleuca**
	South-western Cape
Bi-coloured flowers borne in profusion in spring. Plant in well-drained soil.

Ixia hybrid	Garden hybrid
Varied, brilliant colours in late spring.

CONTINUED

IXIA

I. hybrids

I. scillaris var. *scillaris*

I. viridiflora

I. scillaris var. **scillaris** — Namaqualand
Cormous plant to 500 mm. Fragrant flowers, 7 to 25 on a slender flower stalk, borne in spring. Flowers 20 mm across, are pink to purple-red.

I. viridiflora — South-western Cape
Greenish flowers with dark purple basal blotches are borne on dense spikes in late spring.

IXORA

Ixora chinensis

I. coccinea 'Fraseri'

IXORA
Rubiaceae

A genus of handsome shrubs and small trees with brightly coloured flowers and attractive foliage, these plants are native mostly to tropical Africa and Asia but are spreading to the Pacific Islands, Australia and America. Grown outdoors in warm, moist climates, these plants do well as stoep or indoor plants in most areas; in cold climates they need greenhouse cultivation. Flowers are borne in dense rounded clusters, mostly in shades of brilliant red, pink and orange, as well as white and yellow. Easily grown from cuttings.

Ixora chinensis — Malaya, China
Shrub to 1 m. Flowers are red to white borne in dense, rounded heads in summer.

I. coccinea 'Fraseri' — Thailand
Flame-of-the-woods, Jungle flame or Jungle geranium
Shrub to 1 m with shiny leaves and brilliant reddish-salmon flowers in summer.

JACARANDA
Bignoniaceae

Only one species in this genus is generally cultivated. This is the lovely huge and familiar *Jacaranda mimosifolia*, widely planted as an ornamental and shade tree along streets and in parks and large gardens. There are about 50 shrubs and trees in this genus, native to tropical America. Most jacarandas bear the well-known misty blue flowers although some have pink or white ones. The jacarandas in Pretoria, now over 100 years old, are a great focal point of the city's spring attractions.

Jacaranda mimosifolia — North-western Argentina
Large trees growing to 16 m, usually less, with a spreading crown. Acacia-like, soft green leaves can themselves make quite a show in autumn when they turn yellow. Lavender-blue hanging flowers, 50 mm long, are borne in 200 to 300 mm erect clusters usually on bare branches, creating a beautiful display in spring. These trees adapt well to varying conditions, although the warmer, summer rainfall areas suit

JACARANDA   JASMINUM

Jacaranda mimosifolia

Jasminum humile 'Revolutum'

J. polyanthum

J. mimosifolia

J. nudiflorum

them best. Young trees need protection from frost, older ones are hardy. Self-seeding and quick growing, these trees are greedy feeders best grown away from flowerbeds. The flowers, borne in spring, can be annoying when they drop.

JASMINUM
Oleaceae

The name of this genus is a Latinized version of the Arabic name, *ysmyn*. The shrubs and climbers in this genus, both evergreen and deciduous, are native to eastern and southern Asia, Malaysia, Australia and Africa, with a number of species indigenous to southern Africa. Although not all species are scented, it is perhaps for their fragrance more than anything else that jasmines are planted, and some species are important in the making of perfume. Flowers are yellow, white and pink. Jasmines will grow in most soils, in semi-shade or full sun. Some species are easily propagated by layering, others can be raised from cuttings.

Jasminum humile 'Revolutum' Himalayas/Garden origin
Italian jasmine or Yellow bush jasmine
Evergreen, tree-like shrub with yellow, fragrant flowers in umbellate clusters.

J. nudiflorum China
Winter jasmine or Winterjasmyn
A semi-deciduous shrub to 2,5 m with glossy green leaves and yellow flowers in winter. It favours colder areas and can be used as a scrambler.

J. polyanthum China
Deciduous or evergreen vigorous scrambling shrub, quick and easy to grow. Very fragrant flowers, white on the inside, pink on the outside, are produced in spring.

JATROPHA

Jatropha podagrica

JOCHROMA

Jochroma cyaneum

JUSTICIA

Justicia brandegeana

J. brandegeana 'Yellow Queen'

JATROPHA
Euphorbiaceae

Widely distributed in the tropics and subtropics, this is a genus of perennials, shrubs and trees grown for their attractive foliage and brilliantly coloured flowers in shades of scarlet, vermillion, purple and yellow. In warm climates these are good shrubs for the rock garden; however, they are better grown indoors, in greenhouses or on warm stoeps in cooler climates. Seed is set freely and plants are easily raised from seed or cuttings. The name is from the Greek *iatros*, a physician, and *trophe*, food, because the plants have medicinal properties.

Jatropha podagrica   Central America

Tartogo or Australian bottle plant
Shrub to about 800 mm with the stem swollen at the base. Flowers are brilliant scarlet and yellow in late winter to summer. It is a good plant for rock gardens.

JOCHROMA
(Iochroma)
Solanaceae

A genus of shrubs and small trees from tropical South America, grown for their clusters of tubular, drooping flowers in shades of purple, blue, white, yellow and scarlet. The most commonly grown species, *Jochroma cyaneum*, is a quick-growing shrub, needing regular pruning to keep it in shape. The name comes from the Greek *ion*, violet and *khroma*, colour, a reference to the striking colour of the flowers of some species.

Jochroma cyaneum   South America

Blue cestrum or Blousestrum
Shrub to 3 m with large leaves 200 mm long. Blue to violet-blue tubular flowers are borne on pendent clusters in summer. They will grow in semi-shade as well as full sun.

JUSTICIA
Acanthaceae

This is a genus of showy perennials and shrubs both evergreen and deciduous. Native to the tropical and subtropical regions of the world, this genus has considerable variation among the plants included in it. All are warm-climate plants; however, in cooler regions they will still thrive in warm, protected positions and many make good container plants for stoeps and sunny patios. Prune or pinch back regularly to keep plants in good shape, particularly those in the shrubbery or border.

Justicia brandegeana   Mexico
(Beleperone guttata)

Shrimp bush
Soft evergreen shrub to 1 m. Flowers are found in graceful drooping spikes hidden inside showy bracts coloured bronze, salmon-pink and brick-red. A most attractive plant in a sunny rockery or in a large patio tub. It will also thrive indoors. Mostly summer flowering, but a few flowers appear throughout most of the year.

J. carnea

Kalanchoe beharensis

K. blossfeldiana

J. brandegeana 'Yellow Queen'
(*Beleperone lutea*)
As above, with yellow-green bracts.

J. carnea — South America
Plume flower
Shrub to 2 m, less in cultivation. Pink to rosy purple flowers in summer; often seen as a pot plant on stoeps or patios.

KALANCHOE
Crassulaceae

Although most of the plants in this genus are native to Africa and Madagascar, the name of the genus is Chinese for one of the species native to Asia. This is a large genus of succulent perennials and small shrubs grown both indoors and out for its bright flowers and often most attractive ornamental foliage. Most species thrive outdoors in frost-free areas; otherwise they are ideal container plants for sunny stoeps and warm, sheltered patios. Most species are easy to grow, and equally easy to propagate from cuttings.

Kalanchoe beharensis — Madagascar
Felt-bush, Velvet bush or Donkey's ear
Foliage plant. Shrub to 1,5 m. Having large, velvety grey leaves with toothed edges, it makes an unusual plant with its striking foliage effect in a sunny outdoor-living area. Flowers are insignificant.

K. blossfeldiana — Madagascar
Small shrub to 300 mm. Leaves are bright, glossy green with masses of small, bright red flowers in winter lasting up to two months. A very useful and popular pot plant.

K. longiflora — Southern Africa
Rooiblaarplakkie
Leaves are deeply serrated, turning a lovely dark red in wintertime.

K. tubiflora — South Africa, Madagascar
Chandelier plant
Quick-growing shrub to 1 m, branching and suckering from the base of the stem. It produces smooth, cylindrical leaves and dense clusters of tubular red-purple flowers. It reproduces rapidly by vegetative offsets at the tips of the leaves and may become a pest plant.

K. waldheimii — Madagascar
Ghost plant
Branching succulent to 800 mm with bluish-green leaves and hanging orange-red flowers 30 mm long.

CONTINUED

KALANCHOE

K. longiflora

K. waldheimii

K. tubiflora

KALMIA

Kalmia angustifolia

KALMIA
Ericaceae

The shrubs in this genus are hardy, evergreen, occasionally deciduous ornamentals native to North America and Cuba with dark, glossy foliage and most attractive, waxy, cup-shaped flowers in shades of white, pink and purple. They need deep, rich, acid soil.

Kalmia angustifolia　　　　North America
Sheep laurel
Slender shrub to 1 m, bearing small purple or crimson flowers in spring.

KENNEDIA

Kennedia rubicunda

KENNEDIA
Fabaceae (=Leguminosae) Subfam. Faboideae (=Papilionoideae)

A genus of about 15 species of showy, scandent shrubs and creepers which are native to Australia. They are grown for their showy pea-flowers in shades of red, including a purple so dark as to be almost black. These plants need a temperate climate and summer rainfall.

Kennedia rubicunda　　　　Australia
Coral pea or Koraalboontjie
Twining creeper to 5 m, bearing red flowers in drooping sprays in spring and summer.

KERRIA

Kerria japonica

KNIPHOFIA

Kniphofia praecox

K. uvaria

K. uvaria var. *maxima*

KERRIA
Rosaceae

There is only one species in this genus, named after William Kerr, one of the earliest English botanists sent to China to collect plants for Kew Gardens; he introduced this plant from the East. The shrub, *Kerria japonica,* has several cultivars, including a double-flowered form. Flowers are bright yellow, borne profusely on long, gracefully arching branches which need regular pruning to keep them in shape. Easily grown in all but the hottest areas, they will thrive in full sun or semi-shade.

Kerria japonica China, Japan

Jew's mallow or Japanese rose
Shrub to nearly 3 m, usually less. Bright yellow flowers are produced in spring and summer.

KNIPHOFIA
Liliaceae

These are stout, rhizomatous perennials native to tropical Africa and Madagascar with many species indigenous to southern Africa. Plants may be deciduous or evergreen, winter or summer flowering, and may need well-drained soil; otherwise they are suitable as waterside plants. Flowers are poker-shaped and carried on tall stout stalks, in shades of red, orange and cream. Some of the spikes are bi-coloured, while some change colour through a range of shades, from top to bottom. Leaves are strap-shaped, somewhat grass-like. Very striking and showy in large waterside clumps, or in the mixed border, these plants should not be moved or divided unless absolutely necessary.

Kniphofia praecox South Africa

Red-hot poker, Torch lily or Vuurpyl
Large, clump-forming perennial to 1,5 m. Orange buds open to yellow flowers in winter. Grow in good, well-drained soil.

K. uvaria South-western Cape

Clumps to 1 m. Red buds open to yellow flowers in summer. Plant in good, well-drained soil.

K. uvaria var. **maxima** South-western Cape

As above, only larger in all respects.

KOCHIA

Kochia scoparia

KOHLERIA

Kohleria eriantha

KOCHIA
Chenopodiaceae

Of this genus of Eurasian sub-shrubs, only one, *Kochia scoparia,* is usually cultivated.

Kochia scoparia   Widespread from southern Europe to Japan
Summer cypress, Belvedere or Somersipres
Foliage plant; quick-growing annual to 1,5 m, forming a densely branched, neat pyramidal or rounded bush, very like a cypress in appearance. Grown for its finely cut foliage and attractive form. It is useful as an accent plant for any sunny part of the garden and is easily grown.

KOHLERIA
Gesneriaceae

A genus of hairy, rhizomatous perennials and shrubs native to tropical America and suitable for indoor and outdoor cultivation. They require compost and rich, well-drained soil.

Kohleria eriantha   Colombia
Shrub to 1,25 m. All parts of the plant are hairy with red-margined leaves; tubular, hairy orange flowers appear in all seasons.

LABURNUM

Laburnum x *watereri* 'Vossii'

LABURNUM
Fabaceae (=Leguminosae) Subfam.
Faboideae (=Papilionoideae)

There are only four species in this genus of deciduous ornamental trees and shrubs native to Europe. They are grown for their golden yellow pea-flowers which hang from the branches in long drooping spikes or chains and, when trained over an arch or a pergola, can be exceptionally lovely, hanging down in a golden mass. Laburnums are poisonous, especially the seeds. Suited to cooler climates, these very hardy plants need good soil and regular watering. Easily propagated by layering, or by seed.

Laburnum x watereri 'Vossii'
🅕 ✤ ✿ ☼   Garden hybrid
Golden chain tree
Tree to 6 m. Very long, pendent sprays of yellow flowers are produced in spring and summer.

LACHENALIA

Lachenalia aloides

LACHENALIA
Liliaceae

Indigenous to South Africa, the plants in this genus are found mainly in the south-western Cape, extending into Namaqualand and the eastern Cape. It is a genus of small bulbous perennials with colourful tubular flowers in a wide range of shades, some being in brilliant purples, reds, oranges and yellows, often variegated, and others in delicate pastel shades including blue, pink and mauve. These rewarding little plants are ideal for sunny rockery pockets and look spectacular in a hollow wall flanking a patio. They are frequently grown as container plants both indoors and out, an excellent method of cultivating lachenalias as they need full sun, particularly good drainage and it is essential that they remain dry when dormant. Propagation is easiest by removing offsets from the bulbs when dormant, then replanting them. Colourful new cultivars are being released by the Department of Agriculture's research unit at Roodeplaat near Pretoria.

L. aloides var. *Ex Hort.*

L. bulbifera

Lachenalia aloides   South-western Cape
🅕 ✤ ✿ ☼
Cape cowslip, Viooltjies or Klipkalossie
Small plant to 300 mm with drooping, brilliantly coloured flowers, red at the base, then yellow, and red at the tip. Flowers are about 25 mm long and very showy, carried on 150 mm spikes. Early to late spring flowering.

L. aloides var. Ex Hort.   Garden origin
🅕 ✤ ✿ ☼
As above. Flowers in shades of light green, flower buds reddish.

L. bulbifera   South-western Cape
🅕 ✤ ✿ ☼
Red lachenalia, Rooiviooltjie or Rooinaëls
Plant to 300 mm, with drooping coral-red flowers, tipped with green and purple, carried on 150 mm spikes and borne in winter and spring.

Lachenalia cvs.   Research origin
🅕 ✤ ✿ ☼
Some of the new cultivars released by the Department of Agriculture's research unit at Roodeplaat near Pretoria.

CONTINUED

LACHENALIA

L. rubida

Lachenalia cvs.

L. rubida   South-western Cape
🌸 ❋ ✿ ☀
Sandkalossie or Rooiviooltjie
Plant to 150 mm. Red flowers, tipped with purple and green, are produced in autumn.

LAGERSTROEMIA

Lagerstroemia indica

L. speciosa

LAGERSTROEMIA
Lythraceae

The showy ornamental shrubs and trees in this genus are native to the warmer parts of Asia and the Pacific Islands. They can be grown as tall flowering trees or even as hedges. Flowering is improved by hard pruning, the new growth being vigorous and bearing large trusses of crinkly, frilly flowers in shades of crimson, pink, purple, mauve and white. Leaves usually turn red before falling. These are warm-climate shrubs, yet frost resistant, and do best in summer rainfall areas. They are easily propagated from suckers or cuttings.

Lagerstroemia indica   China
🌸 ❋ ✿ 🌱 ☀ 💧
Pride of India or Crepe myrtle
Tree to 4 m, or a shrub pruned to required size. Flowers in shades of white, lavender, mauve, pink, purple and crimson are produced in summer.

L. speciosa   India, China
🌸 ❋ ✿ 🌱 ☀
Pride of India or Crepe myrtle
Large tree to 7 m or shrub, as above. Flowers bigger and also borne in summer.

LAGUNARIA

Lagunaria pattersonii

LAGUNARIA
Malvaceae

There is only one species in this genus, *Lagunaria pattersonii*, a tree native to Australia and two small adjacent Pacific Islands.

Lagunaria pattersonii   Australia, Pacific Islands
🌸 ❋ ✿ 🌱 ☀ 💧
This is an excellent coastal tree, usually growing to a symmetrical pyramidal shape regardless of the strongest prevailing winds. It can grow to a huge tree of 25 m, but is usually less in cultivation. The leaves are felted white underneath and the flowers are bell-shaped, pinkish-mauve and borne in profusion. Lagunarias are summer and autumn flowering. Quick growing in warmer areas, they seed themselves freely.

LAMPRANTHUS

Lampranthus aureus

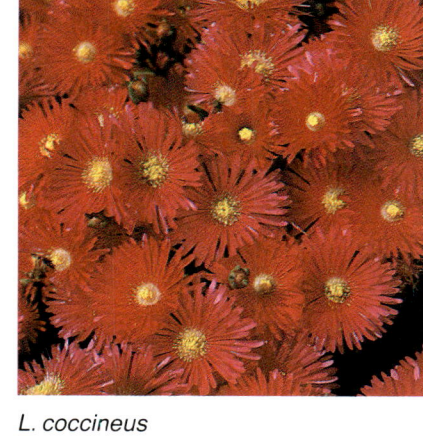

L. coccineus

L. deltoides

L. blandus

L. coralliflorus

L. glaucus

L. roseus

LAMPRANTHUS
Mesembryanthemaceae

A genus of perennial succulents, indigenous to South Africa and familiar as 'vygies'. Lampranthus vary from creeping ground covers to large rounded bushes up to 750 mm high and spreading over 1 m. The flowers have a wide range of brilliant colours in all shades of pink, purple, orange and yellow, enhanced by the silky sheen of the petals. These flowers are produced so freely in spring that the foliage is frequently completely covered by a carpet of dazzling colour. Although mostly native to the winter rainfall area, lampranthus adapt well to summer rainfall areas and will withstand considerable frost. Full sunlight is essential as the flowers only open in the sun, and good drainage is advisable. These are the perfect rockery plants.

Lampranthus aureus South-western Cape
Orange vygie or Golden vygie
Height to 450 mm and spreading more. Orange flowers are borne in spring.

L. blandus South-western Cape
Height to 300 mm. Spreading, pink flowers appear in late spring.

L. coccineus South-western Cape
Red lampranthus
Height to 300 mm, with bright purple-red flowers in spring. Slightly frost tender.

L. coralliflorus South-western Cape
Height to 300 mm, with cyclamen-pink flowers in spring.

L. deltoides South-western Cape
Height to 700 mm, with delicate rose-pink flowers in spring and early summer.

L. glaucus Cape Flats
Height to 150 mm, with solitary yellow or lemon-yellow flowers.

L. roseus South-western Cape
Red vygie
Height to 300 mm, with red, pink or white flowers in spring.

LANTANA

Lantana montevidensis

LAPEIROUSIA

Lapeirousia corymbosa

L. laxa

L. jacquinii

LANTANA
Verbenaceae

A genus of shrubs, sometimes prickly, native to tropical and subtropical America, with a few found in other areas. One species, *Lantana camara*, has been rated one of the ten worst weeds in the world. Unfortunately, it is also one of the most easily grown and colourful garden shrubs. However, these plants set seed which is spread by birds, rodents and monkeys as well as humans and, apart from invading and suppressing natural vegetation, *Lantana camara* is poisonous to stock and humans. Legislation exists proclaiming it a noxious weed. It is possible that some named hybrids and cultivars do not set viable seed and are attractive garden and flower box shrublets. The useful, creeping mauve-flowered *Lantana montevidensis* is not a pest plant and grows easily in most areas.

Lantana montevidensis Uruguay
(L. sellowiana)
A spreading, creeping shrub to 1 m high carrying mauve flowers most of the year.

LAPEIROUSIA
Iridaceae

The cormous plants in this genus are grown for their exquisitely marked flowers, so they are best planted near to paths, or in patio containers so that their delicate beauty can be fully appreciated. Indigenous to South Africa, most species are native to the drier winter rainfall areas and need well-drained, sandy, gritty soil and full sun.

Lapeirousia corymbosa South-western Cape
Grows to 150 mm and the flowers are blue with white purple-lined centres in summer.

L. jacquinii Clanwilliam, Calvinia and south to the Cape Peninsula
Violet painted petals
Cormous perennial to 120 mm. Flowers are violet, marked with cream, and grow 30 to 40 mm long from the base of the tube to the open petals. Found in moist sandy places in nature, it flowers in spring.

L. laxa Widespread in summer rainfall areas of South Africa
Woodland painted petals
This species, growing to 600 mm, is widely distributed in indigenous bush throughout the summer rainfall areas. It needs deep, rich soil and semi-shade. Leaves are long and iris-like; flowers are scarlet with darker spots on the lower petals and borne in summer. *L. laxa* is now known as *Anomatheca grandiflora*.

LATHYRUS

Lathyrus latifolius

LATHYRUS
Fabaceae (=Leguminosae) Subfam. Faboideae (=Papilionoideae)

One of the loveliest cut flowers belongs in this genus – the sweet pea, *Lathyrus odoratus*. A bowl of these flowers is hard to beat for freshness and fragrance. The plants in this genus are native to the temperate regions of the world and are both annual and perennial, some being scandent small shrubs and others climbing by means of tendrils. All are grown for their showy, colourful pea-flowers which come in all shades, although yellow is not included in the colour range of the commonly cultivated species.

Lathyrus latifolius — Europe
Perennial pea or Everlasting pea
This is a light, perennial climber to 3 m, ideal for growing on light fences. Flowers, borne in summer, are large, in shades of purple, pink and white. These plants do well in any soil and will survive in adverse conditions, but best results are obtained when they are well fed and watered. Propagate by seeds freely set, or by root division.

L. odoratus

L. odoratus — Italy
Sweet pea or Pronkertjie
A climbing annual to 2 m, with fragrant pea-flowers in summer growing up to 50 mm across. Sweet peas are crisply frilly in a variety of colours in purple, pink, blue or white, from rich deep colours to exquisite pastels. These plants need deep, rich soil and a good support, preferably wire netting. Modern hybrids are spectacular (but often less fragrant) and there are dwarf bedding varieties as well. These are fairly demanding plants, but they are most rewarding.

LAVANDULA

Lavandula angustifolia subsp. *angustifolia*

LAVANDULA
Lamiaceae (=Labiatae)

The most aromatic of all plants belong in this genus of shrubs and herbs, found in nature from the Atlantic islands through the Mediterranean regions to Somalia and India. Several species yield lavender oil used in perfumery, and lavender flowers, correctly dried, will retain their fresh scent for 20 years and longer. Drying fragrant flowers for household use and making pot-pourri is a most satisfying and therapeutic hobby which adds an extra dimension to the enjoyment of gardening. Apart from the pleasures afforded by its fragrance, lavender is an attractive, easily grown, grey-leafed shrub which will grow in any soil. Although sun-loving, the plants will grow in semi-shade provided drainage is good. Lavender is sufficiently easy to grow from cuttings taken in autumn or spring for any gardener to raise extra plants this way.

Lavandula angustifolia subsp. angustifolia
(L. officinalis) — Mediterranean region
English lavender or Engelse laventel
Shrub to 1 m with grey-green leaves and blue-purple flowers borne in summer.

CONTINUED

LAVANDULA

L. dentata

LAVATERA

Lavatera trimestris

LEBECKIA

Lebeckia cytisoides

L. dentata Mediterranean region
🌱 🌳 ♣ ☀ Ⓦ
French lavender or Franse laventel
Shrub to 1 m with grey leaves and blue-purple flowers borne mainly in summer.

LAVATERA
Malvaceae

This genus includes annuals, perennials and sub-shrubs of widespread distribution, but mostly native to the Mediterranean regions. They are grown for their showy flowers which are shaped like shallow cups and come in all shades of pink, purple and white, with petals often marked or striped in darker shades. The most commonly grown species is the annual, *Lavatera trimestris*, which is raised easily from seed sown in the beds or borders where the plant is to flower.

Lavatera trimestris Mediterranean region
☀ 🌳 ☀ Ⓦ
Mallow
Vigorous annual to 1 m with white or pink flowers in summer.

LEBECKIA

Fabaceae (=Leguminosae) Subfam.
Faboideae (=Papilionoideae)

There are about 45 species in this genus of evergreen shrubs indigenous to South Africa, most of them found in the winter rainfall area. Bright yellow pea-flowers are borne on dense, showy, erect spikes. Like so many plants from the winter rainfall area, lebeckias require good drainage and are best planted on a slope or in a raised rockery.

Lebeckia cytisoides Drier areas of South-western Cape and Namaqualand
🌱 🌳 ♣ ☀ Ⓦ
Wild broom, Wilde besembos or Fluitjies
Sparsely branched shrub to 1 m with bright yellow flowers up to 20 mm long. They are mainly spring flowering, but occasionally flower throughout the year.

LEONOTIS

Leonotis ocymifolia var. *ocymifolia*

L. leonurus var. *albiflora*

L. leonurus var. *leonurus*

LEONOTIS
Lamiaceae (=Labiatae)

The plants in this genus are native to tropical and southern Africa, with those indigenous to South Africa widespread in the summer rainfall areas. The most commonly cultivated species is *Leonotis leonurus*, often referred to as 'Wild dagga'. Although the aromatic leaves of this plant may possess mild narcotic properties, the plant is not related to the true dagga, *Cannabis*. *Leonotis leonurus* has showy orange or cream flowers and is a tough drought and frost-resistant plant. Because it grows so easily, it is often relegated to neglected corners of the garden where it becomes straggly and unattractive, but given good soil, enough water, regular trimming and 'stopping' it can be a very handsome shrub.

Leonotis ocymifolia var. **ocymifolia**
🅕 🌰 🌸 ☼ 🅦　　　　　　Southern Africa
Klipdagga
Very similar to *Leonotis leonurus* var. *leonurus* but leaves are darker green and flowers smaller.

L. leonurus var. **albiflora**　　Southern Africa
🅕 🌰 🌸 ☼ 🅦
As below but with creamy-white flowers.

L. leonurus var. **leonurus**　　Southern Africa
Lion's ear, Lion's tail, Wild dagga, Duiwelstabak or Wilde-dagga
Shrub to 2 m, sending up tall flower spikes in summer. Flowers are arranged in whorls at intervals (at the nodes) up the stem. Strongly aromatic leaves.

LEPTOSPERMUM

Leptospermum scoparium 'Album'

L. scoparium 'Roseum'

LEPTOSPERMUM
Myrtaceae

The plants in this genus of evergreen shrubs and small trees are native mostly to Australia but also to Malaysia and New Zealand. Some species are planted to stabilize and reclaim sandy areas. *Leptospermum laevigata* is a dangerous weed in the south-western Cape but there are several ornamental species which make attractive heath-like shrubs covered in tiny red, pink and white flowers in winter and spring. These plants need an open, airy and sunny position in the garden, which must have excellent drainage. Sandy, coastal soils suit them well, and they withstand coastal winds. The plants are commonly referred to as tea bushes, because, it is said, Captain Cook tried to brew tea from the leaves upon landing in Australia; however, this culinary experiment was apparently not a success.

Leptospermum scoparium 'Album'
🅕 🌰 🌸 ☼ 🅦　　　　　　New Zealand
White tea tree or Wit-teebos
A lovely variety with large white flowers in contrast to the common pink or red ones.

CONTINUED

LEPTOSPERMUM

L. scoparium var. *grandiflorum* 'Flore Pleno'

L. scoparium var. **grandiflorum**
'Flore Pleno' New Zealand
Double red tea bush
As above, but flowers are deep scarlet-red with black centres.

L. scoparium 'Roseum' New Zealand, Tasmania
Tea bush, Manuka or Teebos
Shrub to 2 m with leaves of grey-green, small and almost needle-like. Flowers are rose-pink to red with dark centres, up to 25 mm across. Flowering season is somewhat variable but mainly winter/spring.

LESCHENAULTIA

Leschenaultia biloba

LESCHENAULTIA
Goodeniaceae

A genus of evergreen, heath-like shrubs and herbaceous perennials native to Western Australia, these plants are grown for their brilliant flowers in an unusual range of colours – red, orange, yellow, green and blue. Leschenaultias are not cultivated much, as they prefer their harsh native conditions: perfect drainage, a light soil, not too much water and plenty of sun and air. Like proteas, they appear to resent any cultivation around their roots.

Leschenaultia biloba Western Australia
Bushy shrub to 1 m with striking sky-blue flowers borne in spring/summer.

LEUCADENDRON

Leucadendron argenteum

L. eucalyptifolium

LEUCADENDRON
Proteaceae

This is a genus of evergreen trees and shrubs indigenous to South Africa and found mainly in the southern, south-western and eastern Cape. Plants are either male or female. The male flowers usually have round woolly heads and the female ones small woody cones. The flowers are usually surrounded by large, often colourful bracts in shades of truly sunshine yellow, deep rich reds and pinks, and silvery greys. Many species are excellent for floral decoration, as they are long-lasting in water, while others are most suitable for dried arrangements. In the garden they make colourful splashes in the shrub borders or large rockeries. These shrubs need conditions as near as possible to those of their natural habitat – an airy, open, sunny position, light, well-drained soil, water in winter, and no cultivating around the roots. To control weeds, it is preferable to mulch heavily. The name is from the Greek *leukas*, white, and *dendron*, tree, referring to the best-known species in this genus, *Leucadendron argenteum*, the silver tree.

L. gandogeri

L. macowanii

L. meridianum

Leucadendron argenteum   South-western Cape
🌼🐝🌱☀💧
Silver tree or Silwerboom
Erect, symmetrical tree to 5 m, with silvery grey leaves felted with fine silvery hairs which give the tree a shimmering appearance. They make wonderful accent plants against a background of dark green trees and shrubs. These are trees of the mountains, needing perfect drainage and the constant air movement of the slopes. They often die suddenly and inexplicably in gardens.

L. eucalyptifolium   Montagu to Grahamstown
🌼🐝🌱☀💧
The leaves resemble those of the eucalyptus, hence the name. Bright yellow bracts surround the fragrant flower heads in winter and spring.

L. gandogeri   Southern and south-western Cape
🌼🐝🌱☀💧
Shrub to 1,6 m with very large, bright yellow bracts bearing flushed orange and red flowers in spring.

L. glaberrimum var. *erubescens*

L. glaberrimum var. ***erubescens***
    South-western Cape mountains
🌼🐝🌱☀💧
Erect shrub to 800 mm with spring-borne bracts of deep rosy red. Male and female plants are shown here.

L. macowanii
🌼🐝🌱☀💧
Erect shrub to 3 m. Showy female cones are a deep red-purple in spring.

L. sessile

L. meridianum   Southern Cape
🌼🐝🌱☀💧
Shrub to 2 m. Bright yellow bracts cover the plant in late winter and spring.

L. sessile   Ceres to Cape Peninsula
🌼🐝🌱☀💧
Shrubs to 1,5 m, bracts yellow becoming red at maturity in July and August.

CONTINUED

LEUCADENDRON

L. tinctum

L. strobilinum

L. strobilinum　　　　　　Cape Peninsula
Shrub to 2,6 m, bracts large, ivory white to yellow, very showy.

L. tinctum　　　　　　　　Bredasdorp
Shrubs to 1,3 m, bushy, bracts large, white to pink-red in spring.

LEUCOJUM

Leucojum vernum

LEUCOJUM
Amaryllidaceae

There are nine species in this genus of small bulbous plants native to Europe and the western Mediterranean region. Not particularly showy, they are nevertheless useful in cooler regions, especially under large trees where they can be left undisturbed for many years. Dainty, graceful, bell-shaped flowers are produced in winter and early spring when little else is in bloom. Flowers are white, tipped with yellow, pink or green, according to species. These plants will grow in any soil, but improve with regular watering and feeding. Propagate by offsets or division, but do not disturb unnecessarily.

Leucojum vernum　　　　Central Europe
Snowflake or Sneeuvlokkie
Bulb to 300 mm. It has narrow, lily-like leaves and flowers on short, slightly drooping stems; petals are white tipped with green; flowers in winter and early spring.

LEUCOSPERMUM

Leucospermum cordifolium

L. cordifolium 'Flamespike'

LEUCOSPERMUM
Proteaceae

Perhaps the loveliest of all our indigenous flowering shrubs are to be found in this genus, most species of which are native to the south-western Cape. The form of these evergreen shrubs varies from large erect plants to low-growing, spreading ones. When in flower, these shrubs are immensely showy, and the individual flowers are exceptionally lovely. The delicate-looking flowers are often wiry and durable, making them excellent cut flowers; some species are grown commercially on a large scale. Leucospermums are fairly adaptable and will grow in most areas but, like all Proteaceae, they prefer light, well-drained soil and an airy, open, sunny position. Do not disturb the roots, but mulch heavily around the base of the plant to control weeds. Older plants are frost resistant; younger ones need protection.

Leucospermum cordifolium　　　South-western Cape
Pincushion, Nodding pincushion or Speldekussing
A spreading bush that forms a neat,

L. glabrum

L. oleifolium x *Diastella thymelaeoides*

L. hypophyllocarpodendron

L. reflexum

L. reflexum var. *luteum*

L. mundii

symmetrical mound up to 1,5 m high, spreading slightly more than this. It is covered in crisp, neat, shining 'pins' over a 'cushion' up to 100 mm across, in all shades of apricot, salmon, and flame. The flowering season is somewhat variable, depending on the climate, but usually lasts for several months in winter, spring or early summer. These are important flowers in the floral export trade. Bushes seldom live as long as 10 years.

L. cordifolium 'Flamespike' Garden origin
🅕 ⊕ ♠ ☼ 🅦
Like *Leucospermum cordifolium* but flowers are bright red in spring.

L. glabrum Mountains
🅕 ⊕ ♠ ☼ 🅦 of the southern Cape
Erect, rounded shrub to 1,5 m, bearing large, showy orange-red flower heads in late spring.

L. hypophyllocarpodendron Cape
🅕 ⊕ ♠ ☼ 🅦 Peninsula
A low-growing shrub with trailing branches, bearing bright yellow flower heads from August to January.

L. mundii Swellendam to Riversdale
🅕 ⊕ ♠ ☼ 🅦
Rounded shrub to 1 m, bearing yellow flower heads which gradually turn orange from July to November.

L. oleifolium x Diastella thymelaeoides
🅕 ⊕ ♠ ☼ 🅦 Hybrid origin
A bushy hybrid shrub to 1,5 m. It flowers profusely in spring.

L. reflexum South-western Cape
🅕 ⊕ ♠ ☼ 🅦
Rocket pincushion, Perdekop or Luisies
This is a very large, spreading shrub, growing rapidly to a height of 3 m and spreading over 3 to 4 m. It has most attractive soft grey foliage and crimson flower heads up to 100 mm across, borne in profusion in late winter to mid-summer.

L. reflexum var. luteum South-
🅕 ⊕ ♠ ☼ 🅦 western Cape
Yellow variety of above.

CONTINUED

LEUCOSPERMUM

L. tottum

L. vestitum

L. tottum South-western Cape
Fire-wheel pincushion
Low spreading shrub to 1 m high. Most attractive flowers up to 100 mm across, in shades of pink and scarlet, are borne in summer.

L. vestitum South-western Cape
Similar to *Leucospermum cordifolium* but more upright in habit and growing to 1,5 m; its orange pincushion flowers are produced in late winter and spring.

LIATRIS

Liatris pycnostachya

LIATRIS
Asteraceae (=Compositae)

This genus of herbaceous perennials is native to North America and bears dense spikes of fluffy-looking flowers which open from the top downwards, unlike other plants with similar flower spikes. Flowers are in shades of purple, pink and white. These tall plants are easy to grow in most areas, excepting those with high humidity. They are most striking when grown in large clumps on their own, or in the mixed border. The flower spikes are sturdy and seldom need staking. Do not disturb these plants unnecessarily, although it is possible to divide the large woody rootstocks when the plants are dormant in winter. Propagation is best done by seed.

Liatris pycnostachya United States of America
Gay feather
Perennial to 1,5 m. Flower spikes are dense, cylindrical and about 450 mm long, produced in late summer.

LIGUSTRUM

Ligustrum lucidum 'Tricolor'

L. ovalifolium 'Aureum'

LIGUSTRUM
Oleaceae

Privets are usually thought of as stout hedge plants, and they are excellent for this purpose, but they also make good specimen shrubs and trees, especially the variegated forms. They often seem not to flower, but this is because the flowering shoots are removed by regular trimming. If specimen shrubs are left untrimmed they usually form naturally neat, well-shaped bushes that often produce masses of flowers which are quite showy, and in some species are heavily fragrant. The tiny flowers are white or creamy-yellow and are carried in small, dainty sprays. They are followed by shiny black berries. The most ornamental varieties are the variegated forms. These are best planted in full sun as they tend to become greenish when planted in shade. Plants trained as standards will quickly grow to tree size and make most handsome specimen trees. Ligustrums are native mainly to eastern Asia and Malaysia.

LILIUM

L. lucidum

Lilium cv.

Ligustrum lucidum   Far East
Glossy privet or Wax-leaf privet
A dense, leafy evergreen shrub or tree to 3 m high with glossy, dark green, leathery, ovate leaves 80 to 150 mm long. White flowers are followed by masses of black berries in winter. Often used as a street tree.

L. lucidum 'Tricolor'   Garden origin
Chinese privet
A cultivar with variegated leaves.

L. ovalifolium 'Aureum'   Japan
California privet
Semi-evergreen shrub to 3 m with leaves broadly edged with yellow. If branches bearing green, non-variegated leaves appear, cut these out. A vigorous plant, it is best planted away from flowerbeds. This foliage plant flowers in spring.

LILIUM
Liliaceae

In the civilizations of the East and the West, lilies have a cultural and symbolic significance. This is because they have been cultivated for their loveliness for over 3 000 years. Today, the original genus of 80 to 90 species has been expanded to include hundreds of new hybrids, offering an amazing range of size, colour and form, almost impossible to describe in all their magnificent diversity from the pure white, stately and richly scented Madonna lilies to the exotic, colourful, jaunty Turk's caps, and every possible variation in between. Lily bulbs are delicate and expensive, and the plants have somewhat specialized requirements. It is worth getting specialist advice and following it, for when these richly rewarding plants come into bloom, the gardener, like thousands of generations of gardeners before him, will be amply repaid for his efforts.

Lilium cvs.

Lilium cv.

L. dauricum   Siberia
Candlestick lily
Stems to 1 m with large flowers. Petals are broad, spreading, orange-red and purple-black spotted.

CONTINUED

LILIUM

Lilium cv.

L. lancifolium

L. dauricum

L. longiflorum

L. szovitsianum

L. lancifolium   China, Japan
(*L. tigrinum*)
Tiger lily
Stems to 2 m. Petals of flowers are distinctly spotted.

L. longiflorum   Japan
Trumpet Lily
Stem to 1 m with fragrant, funnel-shaped flowers up to 175 mm long, horizontally borne on stiff, erect flower stalks. It is a species well suited to South African conditions.

L. szovitsianum   Caucasus
Stem to 1,5 m. Flowers are frequent, bell-shaped, pendent, yellow, sometimes spotted, up to 100 mm long.

LIMONIUM

Limonium capense

L. latifolium

LIMONIUM
Plumbaginaceae

Crisp, papery flower heads carried on strong, wiry stems are characteristic of this genus of annuals, perennials and sub-shrubs native to the coastal areas of the world from Siberia to Saldanha Bay. The flowers are actually minute; it is the papery bracts surrounding them that provide the colour, mostly in shades of blues and pinks as well as yellows and white. Long-lasting in water, the flowers can also be dried and used for decoration. The form of these plants varies, and so do the requirements of various species; some are native to salt marshes and will thrive in brackish soil where little else will grow. Most species need sandy, well-drained soil and full sun, and make good rock garden plants. Limoniums are probably familiar to many under their former name, statice.

Limonium capense   Langebaan
Pink flowers but not as showy as *Limonium peregrinum*.

L. peregrinum

Linaria maroccana

LINARIA

LIPARIA

Liparia splendens subsp. *splendens*

L. perezii

L. latifolium Eastern Europe
🌱🌍🌳☀💧
Sea lavender or Papierblom
Perennial to 750 mm, with large showy sprays of many coloured flowers in summer.

L. peregrinum South-western Cape coast
🌱🌍🌳☀💧
Sea lavender, Strandroos or Papierblom
Evergreen shrubby perennial to 600 mm, bearing heads of deep rose-pink to mauve flowers on wiry stems. These plants need sandy, enriched soil with excellent drainage, and must have regular watering away from the coast to compensate for the absence of the humidity of their seaside habitat. They flower mid-winter to mid-summer.

L. perezii Canary Islands
🌱🌍🌳☀💧
Shrubby perennial to 600 mm, with large leaves making dense clumps. Large heads of very showy purple-blue and white flowers, are borne in winter, spring and summer. Limoniums are good for cutting. These plants will thrive in semi-shade in well-drained, airy positions. Freely self-seeding.

LINARIA
Scrophulariaceae

Flowers like miniature snapdragons characterize this genus of useful annuals and perennials, native to the temperate regions of the northern hemisphere. Linarias grow quickly in any soil in full sun, and seed themselves from year to year where conditions suit them. Most commonly grown are the modern cultivars of the annual *Linaria maroccana,* which come in every colour but blue. These are excellent for bedding where their massed colours produce a misty pastel effect.

Linaria maroccana Morocco
🌱🌍☀
Toadflax
Annual to 400 mm although dwarf varieties are available. Original species have purple flowers with a yellow patch but modern cultivars come in all colours in the spring.

LIPARIA
Fabaceae (=Leguminosae) Subfam. Faboideae (=Papilionoideae)

This is a genus of four species of indigenous evergreen shrubs native to the south-western Cape. They bear large round heads of yellow pea-flowers, each covered by a large golden yellow bract. The branches droop at the tips from the weight of the flower heads which resemble dahlias. These are hillside plants, needing very good drainage, good soil, and water in winter. The name is from the Greek *liparos,* meaning brilliant.

Liparia splendens subsp. **splendens**
🌱🌍🌳☀💧 South-western Cape
Mountain dahlia or Geelkoppie
Erect shrub to 1,5 m with golden yellow to deep apricot flower heads borne in summer.

LIRIOPE

Liriope muscari 'Variegata'

LITHOPS

Lithops lesliei

L. turbiniformis

L. otzeniana

L. vanzylii

LIRIOPE
Liliaceae

Very useful little plants are found in this small genus of five species, native to Japan, China and Vietnam. Although they belong to the lily family, their leaves look like grass and their flowers resemble grape hyacinths. The tufted, rhizomatous plants make excellent ground covers both in full shade and sun but need regular watering to look their best. Flowers, carried on erect spikes above the leaves, are in shades of violet, blue and white, and make good cut flowers. As well as being useful outdoors, liriopes make good container plants.

Liriope muscari 'Variegata'   Japan, China
Lily turf
Tufted perennial with thick tubers growing to 450 mm high with leaves to 600 mm long and dark violet flowers carried in a dense spike 450 mm high in summer and autumn. Young leaves are variegated but they become totally green later.

LITHOPS
Mesembryanthemaceae

Fascinating little plants resembling pebbles form this large genus of succulents indigenous mainly to Namaqualand and Namibia but also found in very dry regions elsewhere. Suitable for outdoor cultivation only in arid areas, they make excellent small container plants for stoeps and sunny windowsills. The plants are largely stemless, consisting of a pair of fleshy leaves which are joined to form a symmetrical oval or circular plant, with a small split in the middle from which the relatively big 'vygie' flowers appear. Some species spread slowly, forming dense clumps, while others have beautifully marked leaves. *Lithops* should be grown in soil that comprises half drainage material, such as coarse-grained sand or gravel.

Lithops lesliei   Transvaal, Orange Free State
Solitary or in clumps of three or four, to 40 mm. Leaves are grey to purplish-green, with orange or rust-coloured markings, and yellow flowers grow up to 30 mm across. Flowering season is mainly in summer.

L. otzeniana   Loeriesfontein
Yellow flowers.

L. turbiniformis   Northern Cape
An orange-brown form and a darker brown form; both bear yellow flowers in spring.

L. vanzylii   Northern Cape
Leaves greyish-pink with darker markings.

LITTONIA

LOBELIA

Littonia modesta

Lobelia erinus

L. laxiflora

L. valida

LITTONIA
Liliaceae

This is a genus of plants native to Africa and Arabia with one species indigenous to South Africa, *Littonia modesta*. This is the only species commonly cultivated.

Littonia modesta Widespread in summer rainfall areas
Climbing Bell or Geelklokkie
This is a summer-flowering tuberous climber to 2 m with lax stems and leaves with tendrils at the tips, very similar to *Gloriosa*, to which it is closely related. The showy golden yellow to orange bell-flowers are about 30 mm long. The seed pods are also decorative, splitting open to reveal glossy, bright red seeds. These plants need support, but are easy to grow in most conditions, and in semi-shade or full sun.

LOBELIA
Lobeliaceae

The intensely blue annual lobelia is but one of a large and variable genus of plants native mostly to the tropical and warmly temperate regions of the world; however, a number of species are indigenous to South Africa. One of these is *Lobelia erinus* which has been improved upon to become a most popular annual (and occasionally perennial) for garden cultivation. There are a number of cultivars, of which two of the most popular are the bronze-leafed, royal blue flowered edging lobelia, and the pale green-leafed, sky-blue flowered trailing lobelia which is an exceptionally fine rockery, container or hanging basket plant. Flowers come in related shades of blue, crimson and white. Lobelias seed themselves freely in damp conditions. They will grow well in semi-shade as well as full sun.

Lobelia erinus South-western Cape
Erect and compact or trailing gracefully, bearing masses of flowers in blue (mainly), pink, mauve, burgundy, crimson and white, in spring and summer. Plants seldom grow taller than 200 mm high.

L. laxiflora Arizona, Mexico and Colombia
Herbaceous shrub to 1 m with long-pedicelled, yellowish-red flowers, sub-tended by 150 mm long green bracts, in spring and summer.

L. valida Southern Cape
Galjoenblom
Small herbaceous shrublet to 300 mm high. Summer flowering.

LOBIVIA

Lobivia boliviensis

LOBOSTEMON

Lobostemon fruticosus

LOBULARIA

Lobularia maritima

L. maritima (light blue)

LOBIVIA
Cactaceae

This Peruvian and Bolivian genus contains about 65 species of smallish ribbed cacti. Stem is globose and tubercled. Cultivate like other members of this family.

Lobivia boliviensis Bolivia
Cob cactus
About 20 ribs and needle-shaped brown spines. Flowers are bright pink with yellow centres.

LOBOSTEMON
Boraginaceae

Shrubs, sub-shrubs and perennials are included in this genus of evergreen indigenous plants found mainly in the south-western Cape. Requirements vary, as some species are found on heavy clay soils in nature and others prefer semi-shade, but on the whole well-drained soil and full sun are their basic requirements.

Lobostemon fruticosus South-western Cape
Agtdaegeneesbos
Shrub to 1 m, blue flowers flushed with pink are found in spring. Freely self-seeding in its natural habitat, this shrub was used medicinally by the early settlers; hence the common name.

LOBULARIA
Brassicaceae (=Cruciferae)

This is a small genus of annuals and perennials native to the Mediterranean region, of which only one is cultivated, the familiar sweet alyssum or sweet Alison, *Lobularia maritima*.

Lobularia maritima Southern Europe
(*Alyssum maritinum*)
Sweet Alyssum or Sweet Alison
Perennial, usually grown as an annual, forming a spreading bushy plant to 300 mm, bearing masses of white, delightfully honey-scented flowers for many months of the year, from early spring to autumn. The white variety, which is the tallest, will seed itself profusely in any garden soil, while the named cultivars in shades of purple and pink are lower growing, less scented, and tend to revert to white when self-sown. These are most useful sun-loving plants anywhere in the garden.

LONICERA

Lonicera x *americana*

L. japonica

L. hildebrandiana

L. caprifolium

L. japonica 'Variegata'

L. periclymenum

L. sempervirens

LONICERA
Caprifiliaceae

Widespread in the northern hemisphere, this is a genus of deciduous and evergreen shrubs and creepers grown for their showy flowers, which in many species, although less showy, are worth growing for their unforgettable fragrance alone. Bush honey-suckles make handsome shrubs, and the climbers are tough and quick growing, making useful fence coverings and thriving in semi-shade under large trees.

Lonicera x americana Origin unknown, possibly a hybrid
Honeysuckle or Kanferfoelie
Evergreen to 2 m, which can be grown as a shrub or a creeper. Leaves are slightly blue-green; slender, tubular, orange-yellow fragrant flowers in terminal whorls are produced in spring and early summer. Flower buds are red.

L. caprifolium Europe
Italian woodbine
Evergreen twiner with the top leaves united at the base. Flowers in terminal whorls and sub-tended by a leaf pair.

L. hildebrandiana Burma
Giant honeysuckle, Burmese honeysuckle or Reuse kanferfoelie
Evergreen climber to 10 m with large leaves and large flowers up to 200 mm long. They are yellow, turn orange with age and appear in spring.

L. japonica East Asia
Japanese honeysuckle or Japanse kanferfoelie
Vigorous evergreen climber with white flowers, 36 mm long, borne in pairs in spring.

L. japonica 'Variegata'
As above, but leaves variegated.

L. periclymenum Europe, North Africa and West Asia
Woodbine, English honeysuckle or Engelse kanferfoelie
Deciduous climber becoming bushy, to 3 m. Flowers, in spring, are very fragrant, creamy-yellow and the buds are tinged with purple.

L. sempervirens North America
Evergreen climber to 4 m. Showy, scentless scarlet flowers are borne in summer.

LUCULIA

Luculia gratissima

LUFFA

Luffa aegyptica

LUNARIA

Lunaria annua

L. annua

LUCULIA
Rubiaceae

This is a genus of about five evergreen shrubs native to the Himalayas, which are most useful as they produce masses of fragrant shell-pink or white flowers in winter. The most commonly cultivated species is *Luculia gratissima*.

Luculia gratissima　　　　　Himalayas

An evergreen, winter-flowering shrub or small tree to 5 m with neat, glossy leaves which take on autumn colouring in the colder months. Masses of very fragrant, shell-pink flowers are carried on dense, rounded heads. These shrubs have a reputation for being difficult to grow; like so many mountain plants, drainage must be perfect, humidity high, yet the climate cool, and they will tolerate no disturbance of their roots. However, if you are successful they are most rewarding.

LUFFA
Cucurbitaceae

A small genus of tropical vines which climb by tendrils, with white or yellow flowers and cucumber-like fruits which are very fibrous inside. When the soft flesh rots away, this tough, fibrous interior provides a 'vegetable sponge' or bathroom loofah.

Luffa aegyptica　　　　　Tropical Asia
(*L. cylindrica*)

Sponge gourd or Vadoekplant
Annual creeper bearing cylindrical fruits to 600 mm long. Easily raised from seed.

LUNARIA
Brassicaceae (=Cruciferae)

There are only two or three species in this genus of herbaceous annuals, biennials and perennials native to Europe, which are grown both for their flowers of mauve, pink and white as well as for their seed pods. These take the form of silvery, translucent discs which are most ornamental and very popular for dried arrangements. Lunarias seed themselves freely, and grow best in partial shade. The name of the genus is from the Latin, *luna,* the moon, referring to the flat, round, silvery seed cases.

Lunaria annua　　　　　Southern Europe

Honesty, Money plant, Moonwort or Silver dollar
Biennial to 1 m, large coarse leaves forming a large clump, flowers in white and shades of pink and purple carried in branching spikes above the leaves. Spring flowering.

216

LUPINUS

LYCHNIS

LYSIMACHIA

Lychnis chalcedonica

Lysimachia nummularia

Lupinus polyphyllus

LUPINUS

Fabaceae (=Leguminosae) Subfam. Faboideae (=Papilionoideae)

Hybridization is largely responsible for the spectacular, colourful spikes of flowers which are characteristic of the perennial garden lupins most commonly grown. This large genus also includes annual varieties and herbaceous sub-shrubs of wide distribution, although most numerous in North America. Lupins come in all colours and their tall, stout, densely packed spikes of flowers are ideal for mixed borders. For best results grow in rich, acid soil in full sun.

Lupinus polyphyllus   California
Stout perennial to nearly 2 m with flower heads to 600 mm long in blue and red shades and borne in summer.

LYCHNIS

Caryophyllaceae

A genus of annual or perennial herbaceous plants from temperate and Arctic regions of the northern hemisphere. Flowers are borne in cymes in white, red or pink to mauve. Some species are excellent border plants; others well-suited for a rock garden. Annuals grow easily from seed and perennials can be divided after flowering. Plant in enriched well-drained soil.

Lychnis chalcedonica   Northern Russia
Maltese-cross, Scarlet-lightning or Maltese-kruis
Perennial to 600 mm; each head-like inflorescence bears up to 50 vivid scarlet flowers with two-lobed petals.

LYSIMACHIA

Primulaceae

This is a genus of plants widespread in the temperate and subtropical regions of the world which includes annuals, perennials and a few shrubby species. Some make good border plants, others grow well next to water and others, notably *Lysimachia nummularia*, make good ground covers.

Lysimachia nummularia   Europe
Creeping Jenny or Moneywort
A low-growing ground cover which sends out long stems, rooting as they grow. Leaves are round, pretty and borne in profusion, making a dense mat. Spring-borne flowers are yellow, and fairly showy, although it is best to regard this as a foliage plant. This species is useful as it will grow in full shade as well as part sun and is a pretty plant for hanging baskets. Water well.

MACFADYENA

Macfadyena unguis-cati

MACFADYENA
Bignoniaceae

There are only three or four species of woody vines in this genus of plants native to tropical America, and of these only one is commonly cultivated, *Macfadyena unguis-cati*, the aptly named Cat's claw creeper.

Macfadyena unguis-cati   Tropical America
(*Doxantha unguis-cati*)
Cat's claw creeper
This is a vigorous climber to 5 m, easily recognized by the tiny, three-pronged tendrils, like little claws, with which it climbs. The yellow summer flowers are in the shape of a flattened trumpet up to 100 mm across and borne in profusion, often in adverse conditions, for this is a tough, adaptable plant. It is a fairly light creeper and good as a fence covering.

MACKAYA

Mackaya bella

MACKAYA
Acanthaceae

There is only one species, *Mackaya bella*, which should be grown in warm and temperate gardens.

Mackaya bella   Eastern Transvaal, Natal and Transkei
A shrub or small tree to be planted in semi-shade and preferably near water. Flowers are very pale pink with purple lines, borne in late spring. They are grown easily from cuttings.

MAGNOLIA

Magnolia grandiflora

M. x *soulangiana* 'Amabilis'

MAGNOLIA
Magnoliaceae

Breathtakingly lovely flowers, often heavily fragrant, characterize this genus of evergreen and deciduous shrubs and trees native to Asia and the Americas. The deciduous species often flower on bare branches in spring, making a spectacular display, while the evergreen species bear flowers of a waxen perfection among their glossy green leaves. Magnolias dislike transplanting so buy small plants and be patient. Give them the best possible soil, deep, fertile and slightly acid. Plant them in a spot which is sheltered from the wind and water well.

Magnolia grandiflora South-eastern region of North America
Southern magnolia
This tree can grow to 30 m, given time and the right conditions, but 4 to 6 m is a good average height. The leaves are large, leathery and glossy on top, felted beneath, and the flowers, borne in summer, are magnificent. Although large, up to 300 mm across, they have a delicate beauty which is enhanced by the fragrance that has a lemony tang, just enough to prevent the scent from becoming overpowering. These trees are variable in habit, leaf-size and flower-size.

M. x soulangiana 'Amabilis' Garden hybrid
Chinese magnolia or Tulip magnolia
Small tree to 4 m. Flowers up to 175 mm long are borne on bare branches in spring and are very showy. They are white inside, purplish-pink outside, but somewhat variable. There are numerous named cultivars.

MAHONIA

Mahonia lomariifolia

M. lomariifolia (fruit)

MAHONIA
Berberidaceae

Attractive leaves, like those of Christmas holly, make these plants popular as ground covers, hedges or ornamental specimen shrubs. These evergreens, native to Asia and Central and North America, are grown for their flowers and showy fruits as well as for their foliage, which although evergreen, often colours handsomely in autumn and winter. Flowers are yellow and carried in dainty, drooping or stiffly erect sprays. In many species they are followed by clusters of dark, blue-black berries with a grape-like bloom. Mahonias are frost hardy, not fussy about soil, and will grow in shade as well as full sun.

Mahonia lomariifolia China
An evergreen winter-flowering shrub to 2 m, with sea-green foliage and erect sprays, up to 250 mm long, of densely packed, deep yellow flowers, followed by black berries with a blue bloom. This is another very striking shrub for all but tropical and subtropical areas.

MALCOLMIA

Malcolmia maritima

MALVASTRUM

Malvastrum coromandelianum

MALVAVISCUS

Malvaviscus arboreus

M. arboreus var. *mexicanus*

MALCOLMIA
Brassicaceae (=Cruciferae)

Of this genus of annuals and perennials native to the Mediterranean region, only one, *Malcolmia maritima*, is grown in gardens.

Malcolmia maritima   Mediterranean region
Virginian stock
A bushy, slightly sprawling annual to about 200 mm, with pink, white and mauve flowers profusely borne in spring. These quick-growing plants will grow in any soil and are useful in any sunny part of the garden. Grown from seed sown in spring, these are among the most rewarding annuals, colourful and easy to grow.

MALVASTRUM
Malvaceae

One species of this genus, *Malvastrum coromandelianum*, introduced from America, is a weed in South Africa.

Malvastrum coromandelianum
This weed, with its lovely malvaceous flowers, is commonly found in many ecology-disturbed areas and on dirt heaps.

MALVAVISCUS
Malvaceae

There are only three species in this genus of shrubs from tropical and subtropical America. These quick-growing evergreens, which are semi-deciduous in cold climates, have foliage and flowers resembling those of hibiscus, although the flowers do not open like those of hibiscus. Instead, the bright red petals remain furled, with the stamen column protruding below. This shrub will grow in semi-shade and full sun, and does best in a warm, humid climate.

Malvaviscus arboreus
(*M. mollis*)   Mexico to Peru and Brazil
Fire dart bush
An open, soft-wooded shrub to 2 m, with bright red pendent or erect flowers up to 35 mm long, borne most of the year in warm climates, but in cooler areas appears in summer only.

M. arboreus var. **mexicanus**
Turk's cap
As above, with larger flowers up to 50 mm.

MAMMILLARIA

Mammillaria spinosissima

MANDEVILLA

Mandevilla laxa

M. splendens

MANETTIA

Manettia inflata

MAMMILLARIA
Cactaceae

Many of the species in this large genus of American cacti are most appealing, making them very popular with collectors. Usually low growing, globular or cylindrical, they are sometimes woolly or hairy, but often covered in bristle-like spines, hence the name the pincushion cactus which is applied to many species. The flowers, which are freely produced, come in a wide range of colours and are often fragrant. Grow in well-drained soil and propagate from offsets.

Mammillaria spinosissima Central Mexico
🌱🌼☀️Ⓕ
Simple stem to 300 mm high and 100 mm in diameter, covered with wool and bristles. Flowers are deep pink, arranged terminally in a whorl.

MANDEVILLA
Apocynaceae

The most commonly grown mandevillas are creepers, but this genus includes shrubs as well, all native to tropical America. Mandevillas are grown for their profusion of flowers which are very showy, and often heavily fragrant. They do best in warm climates but given a warm spot, deep, rich soil and plenty of water, they will thrive elsewhere. These are not wall-climbers and are best grown on a fence or pergola.

Mandevilla laxa Bolivia and
Ⓕ🌱🌼☀️ Northern Argentina
Chilean jasmine
A vigorous, woody, twining vine to 6 m or more; deciduous in cold areas. White, fragrant trumpet flowers, good for cut flowers, are borne in profusion in summer.

M. splendens Brazil
(*Dipladenia splendens*)
Ⓕ🌱🌼☀️
Twining creeper to 4 m or more; very showy pink trumpet flowers, up to 80 mm across, are borne in profusion for a long period in summer.

MANETTIA
Rubiaceae

A genus of perennials, shrubs and climbers from the American tropics of which the climbers are most commonly cultivated. These are light, twining evergreens with small, tubular, brightly coloured flowers borne in profusion in spring. Definitely warm-climate plants, they are useful for pillars and to provide filtered shade over patios.

Manettia inflata South America
(*Manettia bicolor*)
Ⓕ🌱🌼☀️
Fire cracker vine
Twining climber to 4 m, with tubular flowers, bright red and tipped with gold, borne in spring.

MARANTA

Maranta leuconeura 'Erythroneura'

MATTHIOLA

Matthiola incana

M. longipetala subsp. *bicornis*

MARANTA
Marantaceae

Beautifully marked foliage is the hallmark of the cultivated species in this genus of tropical American perennials, some of which make popular indoor plants. The most commonly grown species is *Maranta leuconeura* and its varieties.

Maranta leuconeura 'Erythroneura'   Brazil
🌱🌿🍃Ⓕ
Prayer plant or Ten Commandments
Perennial foliage plant to 300 mm. The first of the unusual common names arises from the fact that the leaves have the habit of folding together at night; the second refers to the ten dark splotches on the leaves of most varieties. The oval leaves are usually symmetrically marked with silver, dark green or brown; the flowers are white and insignificant. These plants need a little filtered sun and regular feeding. Although they should be kept perpetually damp, they need perfect drainage.

MATTHIOLA
Brassicaceae (=Cruciferae)

This genus of annuals, perennials and sub-shrubs native to the Mediterranean regions provides gardeners with some of the loveliest scented flower stocks. The popular bedding varieties send up stout spikes crammed with flowers, which are most showy in mixed borders, rockery pockets or bedding schemes. Seed is available in separate colours, mainly in the pink, purple, mauve and white range. Hybridists have produced tall and low-growing strains, as well as fast-growing cultivars, some of which flower within two months of germination. Stocks need enriched soil, ample water and very good drainage, as young plants are liable to 'damp off' and die.

Matthiola incana   Southern Europe
Ⓕ🌿☀
Stock
This species, a biennial or perennial with grey, felty leaves, has single purple or mauve flowers but the cultivars, usually grown as annuals, have flowers in all shades of red, pink, lavender, blue, white and creamy-yellow. Flowers are usually double with a particularly lovely fragrance and are carried in dense spikes with stout stems, making them good cut flowers. Flowering season is late winter and spring.

M. longipetala subsp. **bicornis**
🌿☀   South-eastern Europe
Night-scented stock
This is a rather straggly, grey-leaved species with single, rather insignificant flowers in summer. The flowers are so sweetly scented in the evening that it is worth growing them, especially beneath a window, for the scent alone. They are easily grown, with no special requirements.

MEGASKEPASMA

Megaskepasma erythrochlamys

MELALEUCA

Melaleuca huegelii

M. nesophylla

MELASTOMA

Melastoma sanguineum

MEGASKEPASMA
Acanthaceae

There is only one species in this genus, an evergreen, erect shrub from Venezuela, *Megaskepasma erythrochlamys*.

Megaskepasma erythrochlamys
Venezuela
Brazilian red-cloak
Shrub to 2 m; large leaves to 300 mm long; flower spikes to 300 mm long, with white flowers surrounded by large, showy red bracts, in spring. Easily grown in ordinary garden soil in warm climates. Propagate by cuttings in autumn.

MELALEUCA
Myrtaceae

This genus of evergreen flowering shrubs and small trees is native to Australia and the surrounding areas. The foliage is variable, and often fragrant; the trunks of some species have decorative silvery, peeling bark, and all cultivated species have 'bottle-brush' flowers made up of soft, feathery stamens, mainly in shades of red, yellow and white.

Melaleuca huegelii
Western Australia
Honey myrtle
Evergreen shrub to 3 m, distinguished by whipcord branches and an axis which continues to grow while flowering is in progress. Flower spikes are dense and narrow, to 120 mm long; flowers of white, pink in bud, bloom in summer.

M. nesophylla
Western Australia
Western tea myrtle
Shrub or small tree to 6 m, with thick, spongy bark, peeling in broad strips. Pompom-shaped flowers are lavender to rose-pink and borne in summer.

MELASTOMA
Melastomataceae

A genus of evergreen shrubs and small trees native to South East Asia, with purple, pink or white flowers followed by fleshy, edible, purple-black berries.

Melastoma sanguineum
Malaya to Java
Tropical shrub to 6 m high. Leaves lanceolate with five depressed parallel veins. Showy purple-pink flowers are 50 to 80 mm across.

MELIA

Melia azedarach

M. azedarach (fruit)

MELIA
Meliaceae

One species, *Melia azedarach*, is widely cultivated all over South Africa.

Melia azedarach — Asia
Persian lilac, Bead tree or Sering
A well-shaped deciduous tree to 10 m or more. Leaves are compound and the small, fragrant purplish flowers appear in spring. Mature fruits are yellow and poisonous.

MELIANTHUS

Melianthus minor

M. major (fruit)

M. major

MELIANTHUS
Melianthaceae

There are six species in this genus native to South Africa and India, several of which are grown for their lush-looking ornamental foliage. Flowers are prominent rusty red spikes, followed by inflated seed pods, neither being particularly showy. The foliage of these shrubby perennials usually has a strongly unpleasant smell when bruised, hence the common name, touch-me-not plant or kruidjie-roer-my-nie. These are vigorous, tough, invasive plants; cut down by frost, they will shoot again in the spring, rapidly growing to flowering height.

Melianthus major — Cape Province
Kruidjie-roer-my-nie
Large shrub to 3 m, sending up clumps of thick, bamboo-like stems with large, bluish-green leaves 750 mm or more in length. Rusty red flower spikes appear above the leaves in spring. This is a spreading plant suitable for a large garden; it also makes a good waterside plant.

M. minor — South-western Cape and Namaqualand
Kruidjie-roer-my-nie
Similar to *Melianthus major*, but smaller and forming clumps just over 1 m high. Brick-red flowers are borne among the leaves in spring.

METALASIA

Metalasia muricata

METROSIDEROS

Metrosideros excelsa

MICROLOMA

Microloma sagittatum

METALASIA
Asteraceae (=Compositae)

A genus of about 30 species of indigenous evergreen shrubs, mostly found in the south-western Cape.

Metalasia muricata — Widespread in South Africa
Witsteekbos or Blombos
Shrublets, shrubs and occasionally small trees to 4 m. Green, needle-like foliage but sometimes woolly and greyish. Honey-scented flowers are produced at most times of the year, depending on locality. They are mostly white, or white flushed with pink, red or purple. These plants have been used to stabilize sand dunes.

METROSIDEROS
Myrtaceae

This genus of evergreen shrubs, trees and climbers is native to South Africa, Australia, New Zealand, Malaysia and Polynesia. All have 'bottle-brush' flowers in shades of red, white and occasionally yellow, but only one species is widely cultivated, *Metrosideros excelsa*. The name is from the Latin *metra*, meaning in the heart of the tree, and *sideros*, iron, a reference to the hardness of the wood.

Metrosideros excelsa — New Zealand
New Zealand Christmas tree
This tree grows to 25 m in its native habitat, but is slow growing and seldom exceeds 6 m in cultivation. It is an attractive and useful tree with a neat habit, dark green leaves felted silver on the undersides, and showy red 'bottle-brush' flowers which appear at Christmas time in New Zealand and also in South Africa, hence the common name. These trees are wind and salt resistant at the coast, and also make tidy, trouble-free street trees which can withstand polluted city air. They can also be trimmed to make stout hedges.

MICROLOMA
Ascelepiadaceae

A genus of perennial climbers or much-branched shrublets. Only the one species, *Microloma sagittatum*, is suitable for cultivation at present.

Microloma sagittatum — South-western Cape
Bokhoring
A thin perennial or herbaceous climber. Narrow lanceolate leaves grow opposite and are about 25 mm long. Flowers are tubular, or angular, pink, and about 7 mm long; 3 to 9 flowers per inflorescence appear in spring and summer.

MIMETES

Mimetes cucullatus

M. argenteus

M. hirtus

MIMETES
Proteaceae

The 11 species in this genus are confined to a relatively small area in the south-western and southern Cape; the majority of them are rare, and consequently regarded as being endangered. These handsome evergreen shrubs produce strikingly showy inflorescences, usually in a combination of bright or subtle colours, which are carried at the tips of the branches, often for several months at a time. Mimetes tend to have a highly localized habitat which means that they have very specific requirements in the garden, and it is advisable to ascertain what these requirements are and whether they can be met, before planting.

Mimetes argenteus　　South-western
🅵 🌱 ♣ ☼ 🆆　　Cape mountains
Silver mimetes or Vaalstompie
Evergreen shrub to 1,5 m, with pastel-coloured inflorescences in shades of pink, mauve and silver, in autumn.

M. cucullatus　　South-western
🅵 🌱 ♣ ☼ 🆆　　and southern Cape
Rooistompie
Shrub to 1,5 m with bright red, yellow and white inflorescences appearing mainly from mid-winter to early summer.

M. hirtus　　South-western and
🅵 🌱 ♣ ☼ 🆆　　southern Cape
Shrub to 1,5 m. Yellow, red and white inflorescences in autumn, winter and spring.

MIMOSA

Mimosa pudica

MIMOSA
Fabaceae (=Leguminosae) Subfam. Mimosoideae

This very large genus of perennials, shrubs, trees and creepers with acacia-like foliage and flowers is widespread in the warmer regions of the world. Only one species, *Mimosa pudica*, is commonly cultivated.

Mimosa pudica　　Tropical America
🌱 ☼ 🅵
Sensitive plant, Humble plant, Obedient plant or Touch-me-not
As can be seen from the common names, the most interesting feature of this plant is the unusual sensitivity of the leaves. If they are touched, the leaflets immediately fold together, recovering and unfolding after a few minutes. This is a spiny, shrubby plant to 1 m, with pretty, feathery foliage and pink, fluffy mimosa-like flowers in summer. Easily cultivated in warm regions.

MIMULUS

Mimulus aurantiacus

M. sanguineus

MIMULUS
Scrophulariaceae

This is a genus of annuals, perennials and small shrubs found growing in all regions of the world except Europe, but mainly in North America. The perennial varieties need a damp or even waterside situation, the annuals also need ample water and semi-shade, while the shrubs need a warm, humid climate. All are grown for their flowers which resemble a monkey's face. These come in all colours of the rainbow except green, and are often spotted and blotched in contrasting colours.

Mimulus aurantiacus　　　North America
Monkey flower
An evergreen shrub to 1,5 m. Tubular orange flowers are produced almost all the year round in warmer regions, otherwise summer flowering.

M. sanguineus　　　North America
As above, but flowers are a deep orange and mostly borne in groups of three to four.

MIRABILIS

Mirabilis jalapa

MIRABILIS
Nyctaginaceae

A genus of annuals and perennials native to the warmer regions of America. The perennial species have large tuberous roots, and one of these, *Mirabilis jalapa,* is the species most commonly cultivated.

Mirabilis jalapa　　　Tropical America
Four o'clock or Marvel of Peru
Perennials to 1 m which are usually raised as quick-growing annuals. These plants are unusual in that flowers of different colours often appear on different stems of the same plant. These fragrant, funnel-shaped flowers come in brilliant shades of red, purple, cerise, pink, yellow and white, often striped and mottled. The flowers open in the late afternoon during summer and autumn, and remain open until morning, hence the common name. Easily grown plants in any soil, they are freely self-seeding in favourable conditions.

MISCANTHUS

Miscanthus sinensis 'Variegatus'

MISCANTHUS
Poaceae (=Gramineae)

Several ornamental species are included in this genus of robust perennial grasses native to Asia. The graceful tall grasses make large decorative clumps in the garden, and send up feathery flower heads which make good dried material for arrangements.

Miscanthus sinensis 'Variegatus'　　Eastern Asia
Robust grass forming large clumps up to 3 m high and sending up creamy, silky flower heads, sometimes tinged pink, in summer. Leaves are blue-green, striped white or creamy-yellow. A most attractive accent plant in a windy corner or in a shrub border, they are easily grown with no special requirements.

MOLUCELLA

Molucella laevis

MOLUCELLA
Lamiaceae (=Labiatae)

There are about four species in this genus of annuals found in the Mediterranean region and Asia. The cultivated species are grown for their tall flower spikes which have tiny white flowers surrounded by large, green, cup-shaped calyces which are most ornamental in the garden or in flower arrangements, both fresh and dried. Easily raised from seed, these are not fussy plants but need well-drained soil and full sun.

Molucella laevis   Asia Minor

Bells-of-Ireland, Molucca balm, Shellflower or Ierse klokkies
Annual to 1 m, with tiny white flowers surrounded by green, shell-like calyces in summer.

MONARDA

Monarda didyma

MONARDA
Lamiaceae (=Labiatae)

This is a small genus of annuals and perennials native to North America, with aromatic leaves and fragrant flowers in all shades of red, pink and white. In the damp, shady situations that suit them, the perennial varieties multiply rapidly, forming large clumps which send up tall spikes of flowers in summer and autumn. Easily propagated by seed or division of the clumps, these plants need plenty of water but good drainage, and will grow in full sun as well as semi-shade.

Monarda didyma   North America

Bee balm or Oswego tea
Perennial to 1,2 m, forming clumps of nettle-like leaves and spikes to vivid scarlet-red flowers in summer. The common name, bee balm, refers to the way in which bees, and birds, are attracted to these flowers for their nectar.

MONOPSIS

Monopsis lutea

MONOPSIS
Lobeliaceae

Small annual or perennial herbs which branch profusely. Flowers are solitary. Plant monopsis in well-drained, enriched soil and in full sun.

Monopsis lutea   Southern Africa

MONSTERA

Monstera deliciosa

M. deliciosa var. *borsigiana*

M. deliciosa 'Variegata'

MONSTERA
Araceae

A genus of evergreen climbers native to tropical America, grown for their large, curiously perforated and indented leaves which add an air of tropical luxuriance to the warm-climate garden or greenhouse. However, the most commonly grown species, *Monstera deliciosa,* is more often grown indoors where it makes a smaller ornamental plant.

Monstera deliciosa   Mexico and Central America
Delicious monster, Fruit salad plant or Window plant
In its native habitat this is a large climber to 10 m, with leaves up to 1 m wide and producing arum-like flowers with a creamy spathe up to 300 mm long, and a spadix almost as long which matures into an aromatic and edible fruit. Indoors, this plant needs filtered sun, ample water and feeding, coupled with good drainage.

M. deliciosa var. **borsigiana**
As above, having smaller, less perforated leaves.

M. deliciosa 'Variegata'
Also smaller and less vigorous but with most attractive creamy-white variegations.

MORAEA

Moraea aristata

M. gigandra

MORAEA
Iridaceae

A genus of cormous herbaceous plants from South Africa. Stems may be branched and there are six perianth segments, the outer three spreading and the inner three small. Moraeas make a lovely display when grown grouped together next to a stream or fish pond.

Moraea aristata   South-western Cape
Yellow flowers with a peacock's tail blotch at the base of the petal.

M. gigandra   South-western Cape
Flowers are a pale pink-purple with a dark, multi-coloured basal blotch.

M. loubseri   South-western Cape
Flowers are pale purple with a dark basal blotch.

M. neopavonia   South-western Cape
Peacock flower
Orange flowers with dotted basal parts.

CONTINUED

MORAEA

M. loubseri

M. neopavonia

M. spathulata

M. spathulata George

Yellow flowers resembling a Dutch iris.

MORUS

Morus alba 'Pendula'

MORUS
Moraceae

This is a small genus of useful, quick-growing deciduous trees of worldwide distribution. Most species are grown as ornamentals, although some produce edible purple fruit which is very attractive to birds. One species is a source of food for silkworms which feed on the leaves. These trees are adaptable to a variety of conditions, with attractive bright green foliage that turns a clear pale yellow in autumn when conditions are right. Flowers are insignificant, and the fruit varies from greenish-white to purple-black, depending on the species. Mulberries grow easily from cuttings or seed, and although they will struggle along well enough in adverse conditions, they really thrive in good soil with enough water.

Morus alba 'Pendula' China

White mulberry or Wit moerbei
This species grows to be a large tree of 20 m in its natural habitat, although less than half this in cultivation, where its 'weeping' habit makes it a most ornamental and unusual specimen tree, either on a lawn or next to water.

MUCUNA

Mucuna bennettii

MUCUNA
Fabaceae (=Leguminosae) Subfam. Faboideae (=Papilionoideae)

There are not many ornamental species in this genus of tropical shrubs, herbaceous plants and scrambling climbers of worldwide distribution; however one, *Mucuna bennettii,* is frequently cultivated for its showy flowers.

Mucuna bennettii New Guinea

New Guinea creeper or Scarlet jade vine
A vigorous climber to 10 m, suited best to warm subtropical and tropical conditions, this plant has glossy green leaves and long sprays of showy orange to scarlet flowers up to 75 mm long which flourish during the summer months. This plant needs deep, rich soil, ample water, and regular pruning.

MUSCARI

Muscari botryoides

MUSSAENDA

Mussaenda alicia

M. erythrophylla

M. incana

MUSCARI
Liliaceae

Grape hyacinths are spring-flowering bulbs from the Mediterranean region. The most commonly cultivated species are low-growing ones in shades of blue, although pink, white and yellow-flowered species exist. Several species have a musky fragrance, hence the generic name, from the Greek word *moschos,* meaning musk. Suitable for growing anywhere in the garden, in well-drained, rich soil, muscaris also make good container plants. Propagate from offsets, but do not disturb unnecessarily; they flower best when allowed to form large clumps.

Muscari botryoides   Mediterranean
Grape hyacinth or Druifhiasint
Bulb to 225 mm with spikes of deep violet flowers with white tips, in spring.

MUSSAENDA
Rubiaceae

Mussaenda is the Sinhalese name for the plants in this genus of evergreen shrubs and scrambling climbers native to tropical Africa, Asia and the Pacific, and really only suited to warm-climate gardens. These ornamental shrubs have numerous tiny, insignificant yellow flowers, each of which has one or more – in the case of modern cultivars – greatly enlarged, coloured sepals shining like a flag among the dark green leaves. This makes them unusual and attractive subjects for the shrub border.

Mussaenda alicia   Garden origin
Pink flag bush
Shrub to 1 m or more, with numerous salmon-pink bracts surrounding the tiny flowers.

M. erythrophylla   Tropical West Africa
Red flag bush
Erect or climbing shrub to 10 m in nature, but a smaller erect shrub to 1 m in cultivation, which can be kept pruned to a neat shape. Showy scarlet sepals are profusely borne in summer. They are semi-deciduous in cold areas.

M. incana   East Indies
White flag bush
Erect shrub to 1 m. Each yellow flower is sub-tended by one large ovate, pure white petaloid bract.

MYOPORUM

Myoporum insulare

M. laetum

MYOSOTIS

Myosotis scorpioides

MYRTUS

Myrtus communis

M. communis 'Variegata'

MYOPORUM
Myoporaceae

Native largely to Australia, but also found in New Zealand and Asia, this is a genus of quick-growing evergreen trees and shrubs with glossy foliage, tiny white flowers and small, colourful berries. Most species make good hedge plants or windbreaks, and not fussy about soil. Tender to frost, these are useful plants for coastal gardens.

Myoporum insulare　　　　　　Australia
Manatoka
Shrub or tree reaching 10 m in its native habitat, but in cultivation usually forming a dense, much-branched shrub half this height. The leaves are an attractive, bright, glossy green. Tiny white, purple-spotted flowers are produced in summer, followed by small purplish-blue edible berries.

M. laetum　　　　　　　　　New Zealand
Ngaio
Shrub or small tree to 5 m with light green shiny leaves and tiny white, purple-spotted flowers in summer and reddish-purple berries in autumn.

MYOSOTIS
Boraginaceae

Although forget-me-nots are associated with a particular shade of clear sky-blue, these useful annuals and perennials range in colour through all the blues to pink, white and yellow. Native to the temperate regions of the world, and frequently frost-hardy, myosotis are best planted in damp, rich soil in semi-shade where they often self-seed freely.

Myosotis scorpioides　　　　Europe, Asia
Forget-me-not
Perennial to 450 mm; bright blue spring flowers with a yellow, pink or white 'eye'.

MYRTUS
Myrtaceae

Although most species in this genus are native to the West Indies and neighbouring Florida in the USA, the most commonly grown one, *Myrtus communis*, is native to south-western Europe and the Mediterranean regions. The shrubs and small trees included in this genus are evergreen, with dense, aromatic foliage.

Myrtus communis　　　South-western Europe
　　　　　　　　　　and Mediterranean regions
Myrtle or Greek myrtle
Shrub to 5 m with shiny dense foliage. Leaves are strongly fragrant when crushed and masses of small, fluffy, fragrant white or pinkish flowers are borne in summer, followed by blue-black fruit. This shrub will stand any amount of clipping and pruning and is often used in topiary. Myrtles will grow in any soil, preferably well drained, and in full sun. They make excellent container plants for patios or wherever a neat, attractive accent plant is required.

M. communis 'Variegata'
As above, but leaves margined white.

NANDINA

Nandina domestica

NANDINA
Berberidaceae

There is one species in this genus, *Nandina domestica*.

Nandina domestica — Eastern Africa

Heavenly bamboo or Sacred bamboo
Not a bamboo at all, but an evergreen shrub grown largely for the beauty of its fine, delicate foliage. New growth is pink; older leaves become green, turning a brilliant red in autumn, and remaining red throughout the winter months. Flowers are small and white and are carried in showy spikes up to 300 mm long, followed by red berries in autumn. These neat, erect plants are ideal for small gardens where they blend well with architectural features and make striking accent plants. Grow in good, well-watered soil, preferably in full sun, although the plants will also grow in fairly deep shade.

NARCISSUS

Narcissus cv.

NARCISSUS
Amaryllidaceae

Native to the northern hemisphere, daffodils have been cultivated since classical times, but will not naturalize themselves away from their native habitat. In warm climates new bulbs which have received professional cold-storage treatment have to be planted virtually every year. From the original genus of about 25 species, hybridists have raised thousands of named varieties, of which up to 500 varieties are available commercially. Narcissus, which include jonquils as well as daffodils, are well suited to growing in deep containers where they can receive special attention, although they will do well out of doors in cooler areas. Handle the bulbs with care, as the specialized treatment they receive makes them susceptible to bruising.

Narcissus cvs.

Daffodil
Narcissus can be found in all sizes, shapes and every variation of yellow and white; they bloom from autumn to spring, depending on the variety.

CONTINUED

NARCISSUS

N. jonquilla

N. jonquilla   Southern Europe, North Africa
🅕 ☼ ☀
Long, narrow, rush-like leaves to 750 mm with flowers of bright yellow or white, fragrant and spring flowering. Flowers are much smaller than those of the popular *Narcissus* cvs.

NELUMBO
Nymphaeaceae

Nelumbo nucifera

The sacred lotus flower of the Buddhists is one of the two species of large aquatic plants contained in this genus, which bears the Sinhalese name for the Asian species. The other species is a North American one, with yellow flowers. Both have edible rhizomes that send up blue-green leaves resembling huge nasturtium leaves, carried well above the surface of the water. The large, very fragrant flowers are borne singly above the leaves. Propagate by division and plant in water 300 mm deep.

Nelumbo nucifera
Sacred lotus or Lotus
This is a large aquatic plant with leaves up to 1 m across in their natural environment, and very fragrant summer flowers up to 300 mm across. Pink in the bud, they open to white, with deep pink-tipped petals. There are a number of cultivars, some with double flowers, in various sizes, and in shades of pink, as well as pure white.

NEMESIA

Nemesia strumosa hybrids

N. strumosa hybrid

NEMESIA
Scrophulariaceae

Nemesias are indigenous to South Africa, with a few species extending into tropical Africa. The genus includes annuals, perennials and sub-shrubs, but the species most commonly cultivated is *Nemesia strumosa*. From this and other species have arisen a wonderfully colourful range of hybrids, with cultivars of varying heights. All are large-flowered, and represent a brilliant range of colours, from bronze, through all the reds, orange, yellow, mauve and pinks, white, and even lavender-blue. Flowers are often bi-coloured, marked and spotted. Nemesias make a magnificent display in the spring garden. Best planted in full sun, they will also grow in semi-shade. Sow the seeds in autumn in sandy soil and water regularly during winter. Hybrids come in various colours.

Nemesia ligulata   Namaqualand, Clanwilliam
🅐 ☼ ☀
Kappieblommetjie
Annual, 120 to 300 mm high. The flowers are yellow and white with orange markings and appear in spring.

N. strumosa hybrid

NEOMARICA

Neomarica caerulea

NEOREGELIA

Neoregelia carolinae

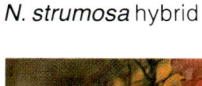

N. strumosa hybrid

N. ligulata

N. strumosa hybrids   South-western Cape
Cape jewels
The original species is an erect, spring-flowering annual with 100 mm spikes of flowers in white, shades of yellow and orange, and purple, sometimes marked and spotted.

NEOMARICA
Iridaceae

A small genus of rhizomatous perennials native to tropical America and the West Indies, with characteristic sword-shaped iris leaves, and short-lived flowers in shades of blue, white or yellow, usually mottled or bi-coloured. These are fairly adaptable plants; although they prefer a tropical climate they will grow elsewhere with winter protection. They also make excellent house plants, if given plenty of light.

Neomarica caerulea   Brazil
Fan iris
Summer flowering, they reach a height of about 600 mm. Leaves are sprawling and up to 1,5 m long. Flowers are up to 100 mm across, light blue or lilac with inner 'petals' marked purple, yellow and brown.

NEOREGELIA
Bromeliaceae

A genus of South American epiphytes, with leaves forming a basal rosette, the inner ones being brightly coloured. These surround the tiny purple, blue or white flowers. Although neoregelias will grow out of doors where conditions are right, they make good container plants for stoeps and light situations indoors.

Neoregelia carolinae   Brazil
Blushing bromeliad
Perennial to 300 mm. The inner leaves are purple to red and flowers violet to lavender.

NEPETA

Nepeta cataria

NEPETA
Lamiaceae (=Labiatae)

A large genus of about 250 species of mostly perennial herbaceous plants native to drier areas of Europe, Asia and North Africa. Catmint is usually grown as a ground cover or in borders and rock gardens. Propagate by seed or division.

Nepeta cataria   Eurasia
Catmint or Kattekruid
Erect growing to almost 1 m; leaves grey-pubescent with a camphor odour when crushed. Flowers are small, whitish and borne in whorls, in summer.

NEPHROLEPIS

Nephrolepis exaltata

NEPHROLEPIS
Polypodiaceae

These are tropical and subtropical ferns of widespread distribution, popular as indoor plants and often useful in the garden as ground covers in deep shade. Some species are tough, drought resistant and invasive, notably *Nephrolepis exaltata*. This species, like most nephrolepis, make useful basket ferns, producing dense, attractive crowns of long, often drooping leaves. Propagate by runners or division of the crowns.

Nephrolepis exaltata   Tropics, Worldwide
Sword fern
Fern to 1 m, although some cultivars have leaves up to 1,75 m long. In the open garden, in shade, this species will spread invasively, sending up dense crowns of bright green fronds. There are numerous cultivars, most of which are more dainty and lacy than the species. These make trouble-free indoor plants, best grown in their own container where they cannot suppress less vigorous plants.

NERINE

Nerine bowdenii

N. filifolia

NERINE
Amaryllidaceae

This is an exclusively South African genus, except for one species found in Zimbabwe, but the bulbs have been widely cultivated for their lovely flowers for many years and one species, *Nerine sarniensis,* naturalized itself so abundantly on Guernsey in the Channel Islands that it is generally known as the Jersey of Guernsey lily. Nerines vary considerably in flowering times, depending largely on whether they are native to the summer or winter rainfall areas, and their requirements vary likewise. General planting rules, however, are to plant the bulbs with the neck of the bulb showing above the ground. They should not be disturbed until the plants become overcrowded.

Nerine bowdenii   Eastern Cape
This is one of the showiest larger species, with 300 mm stems bearing agapanthus-like heads of cyclamen-pink flowers in the autumn. Leaves appear in spring and die away at flowering time; water well throughout the growing season. These bulbs should be planted in semi-shade, or even in deep shade, in hot, dry areas.

NERIUM

N. krigei

Nerium oleander

N. oleander 'Atropurpureum'

N. sarniensis

N. oleander 'Alba'

N. oleander 'Roseum'

N. filifolia   Eastern Cape, Swaziland and Eastern Transvaal
Grass-leaved Nerine
Another autumn-flowering species to 250 mm high with fine, grass-like leaves forming dense clumps, and pale pink flowers, which are borne in masses, together making a sheet of colour. These are good edging plants and are also perfect in rockery pockets.

N. krigei   Transvaal highveld
Curly-leaved nerine
Easily recognized by its spirally twisted leaves, this nerine has pink flowers carried on 400 mm stems in mid-summer. Do not disturb the bulbs unnecessarily and give afternoon shade. Good in frosty areas.

N. sarniensis   South-western Cape
Red nerine or Guernsey lily
This, the most colourful species, has iridescent scarlet flowers with showy stamens carried on stout stems up to 450 mm long. Flowers appear before the leaves in autumn. Plants must be watered when the leaves are growing, but kept dry in the dormant spell.

NERIUM
Apocynaceae

There are two species in this genus of evergreen shrubs native to the Mediterranean, through Asia to Japan, only one of which, *Nerium oleander,* is cultivated.

Nerium oleander   Asia
Oleander, Rosebay or Selousroos
Evergreen shrubs or small trees to 6 m, quick growing, drought and wind resistant, with leathery green leaves. Oleanders are grown for their profuse, showy flowers in every shade of pink, including apricot, crimson, and white. Some varieties, formerly *Nerium odoratum,* are fragrant, and there are double-flowered varieties as well. These spring and summer-flowering shrubs are very showy and will thrive in poor soil but preferably in full sun. There are two warnings: all parts of the oleanders are highly poisonous if eaten and poisoning can occur even when the twigs are used to skewer barbecued meat; secondly, oleanders have become troublesome pest plants in many areas of the world, suppressing other vegetation.

N. oleander 'Variegata'

N. oleander 'Alba'
White-flowered cultivar.

N. oleander 'Atropurpureum'
Deep rose-pink flowers.

N. oleander 'Roseum'
Darker pink than the species.

N. oleander 'Variegata'
Leaves variegated yellow; grows less vigorously.

NICOTIANA

Nicotiana alata 'Grandiflora'

NIEREMBERGIA

Nierembergia hippomanica var. *violacea*

NIGELLA

Nigella damascena

NICOTIANA
Solanaceae

A genus of annuals, perennials and occasionally shrubs, native to tropical and warmly temperate America, Australasia and Polynesia, which includes the plant grown commercially for tobacco. The ornamental species are showy plants as good hybrids, particularly the dwarf varieties, have been raised in shades of white, cream, yellow, pinks and purples. These flowers are worth growing for their scent. Most species are especially fragrant at night, making them worth planting near a window for this alone. Nicotianas need good, rich soil for best results.

Nicotiana alata 'Grandiflora' South America
Tobacco flower
Perennial to 1 m, usually grown as an annual, with flowers in many bright colours up to 50 mm across.

NIEREMBERGIA
Solanaceae

Popular as rockery, border or container plants, nierembergias are a genus of perennials and sub-shrubs found from Mexico to Argentina. Most cultivated species are low-growing perennials, cultivated for their cup-shaped flowers in shades of blue, and occasionally white. Grow in well-drained but moist soil in full sun or semi-shade. Propagate by seed or cuttings.

Nierembergia hippomanica var. violacea Argentina
Perennial to 350 mm, with violet flowers in spring and summer.

NIGELLA
Ranunculaceae

A genus of annuals native to the Mediterranean regions and western Asia of which only one, *Nigella damascena*, is commonly grown.

Nigella damascena North Africa, Southern Europe
Love-in-a-mist or Wild fennel
Annual to 450 mm or more, with very fine, feathery foliage and dainty blue flowers, up to 35 mm across, produced in spring and summer. Pink and white varieties are also available. These are very attractive plants in the mixed border as the fine foliage and misty blue flowers have a softening effect which contrasts well with clumps of bold colour. Nigellas do not transplant well, therefore sow *in situ*. Freely self-seeding, the large purplish seed capsules can be used in flower arrangements, as can the delicate flowers.

NIVENIA

Nivenia stokoei

NIVENIA
Iridaceae

A small genus of eight species indigenous to the mountains of the south-western Cape, of which only two are known in cultivation since the natural conditions of their mountain habitat are not easy to reproduce.

Nivenia stokoei South-western Cape

Evergreen, perennial dwarf shrublet with spikes of dark blue flowers from midsummer to autumn. Plant in a well-drained, partly shaded position and water regularly, and you may be lucky – it just might grow.

NOPALXOCHIA

Nopalxochia ackermannii

NOPALXOCHIA
Cactaceae

The tongue-twisting name of this genus is Aztec for the four species of epiphytic cacti which it comprises. It is native to Mexico. The numerous branches of these plants are flat and often spineless, erect in some species and drooping in others, making these attractive plants for hanging baskets. Flowers are produced in masses along the entire length of the branches in shades of pink, red or purple, depending on the species. These are good container plants, requiring well-drained soil and regular watering.

Nopalxochia ackermannii Mexico
(*Epiphyllum ackermannii*)

Red orchid cactus
The branches of this species are up to 400 mm long, with large red flowers, up to 150 mm across, borne in spring.

NOTOCACTUS

Notocactus concinnus

NOTOCACTUS
Cactaceae

A small genus of South American cacti.

Notocactus concinnus Brazil, Uruguay

Simple stems, nearly globular, ribbed; flowers are bright yellow with scarlet stigmas; petals are almost transparent at the tips.

CONTINUED

NOTOCACTUS

N. vanvlietii

N. werdermannianus

N. vanvlietii   Brazil
As above, but flowers are bigger and petals narrower.

N. werdermannianus   Brazil
As above, but styles are much longer.

NYLANDTIA

Nylandtia spinosa

NYLANDTIA
Polygalaceae

There is one species in this genus, *Nylandtia spinosa*, an evergreen shrub indigenous to South Africa and found in the coastal areas of the Cape from Namaqualand to East London.

Nylandtia spinosa
South-western, southern and eastern Cape coast
Skilpadbessie
Erect, stiffly branched, prickly shrub to 1 m. Masses of pinkish-mauve flowers are borne in spring. It needs sandy soil.

NYMANIA

Nymania capensis

NYMANIA
Aitoniaceae

There is only one species in this genus, the indigenous *Nymania capensis*.

Nymania capensis   Karoo, Namaqualand, Southern Cape and Namibia
Chinese lantern or Klapperbos
Evergreen shrub or small tree to 4 m occurring in the hottest, driest areas of the Cape and Namibia. Although slow growing and usually treated as a shrub, it can make an extremely attractive specimen tree, most valuable in the arid areas where it thrives. The flowers are attractive, in shades of pink, red and dark red, but these are surpassed by the inflated, rose-pink, papery seed pods which really resemble Chinese paper lanterns. Flowers appear from July onwards and the ornamental fruits from October to December. Part of the charm of this tree is its fresh, unexpected loveliness in harsh natural surroundings. It must have well-drained soil, but even so will not last long in a summer rainfall area. Easily grown from seed.

NYMPHAEA

Nymphaea caerulea

N. capensis

NYMPHOIDES

Nymphoides indica

N. caerulea 'Sulfurea'

N. capensis 'Rosea'

NYMPHAEA
Nymphaeaceae

This genus of deciduous, perennial aquatic plants of worldwide distribution is named after the Greek goddess of springs, Nymphe. Water lilies produce large flat leaves that float on water which must be either deep or shallow, depending on the species, and the flowers either float or are carried above the surface on stout stems. The hybridists have been busy on these lovely plants and a wonderful range of colours, shapes and sizes is available. Flowers are often fragrant. Many species are frost resistant; tropical species are not. Special polythene containers are available for water-lily cultivation, allowing for spot-planting of different colours, and the lifting and division of the rhizomes when dormant.

Nymphaea caerulea — North and Central Africa
Egyptian lotus or Blue lotus
Pale blue flowers up to 150 mm across are carried on the surface of the water. White, yellow, pink and red flower forms occur. Leaves are spread over about 1 m.

N. caerulea 'Sulfurea'
As above.

N. capensis
Blue water lily
Sky-blue flowers up to 200 mm across are carried above the water surface. White, cream and pink flower forms occur. Leaves are spread over about 1 m.

N. capensis 'Rosea'
As above, but flowers are pale pink and usually floating.

NYMPHOIDES
Gentianaceae

Often called 'floating hearts' because of the heart-shaped leaves, the plants in this genus are widely distributed aquatic perennials. Not as showy as water lilies, the bright, starry flowers have attractively fringed petals. Both tropical and frost-hardy species are available.

Nymphoides indica — Widespread in South Africa
Geelwateruintjie
Rounded leaves and yellow flowers 20 mm across and borne in summer.

OCHNA

Ochna natalitia

O. pulchra

O. serrulata

ODONTONEMA

Odontonema strictum

OCHNA
Ochnaceae

This is a genus of deciduous and evergreen flowering shrubs and small trees found throughout Africa and tropical Asia. The foliage is attractive with new growth often being reddish-bronze, then turning a shiny pale green, deepening to a lustrous dark green. Flowers are yellow, sometimes fragrant; after they fall the calyces remain. These are usually bright red, and surround the fruit which varies from green to shiny black. They are not fussy about soil.

Ochna natalitia   Ex Hort
Small tree to 4 m in height. A lesser known species, the flowers are bigger than those of *Ochna pulchra*.

O. pulchra   Zimbabwe, Northern Botswana, Namibia, Transvaal
Lekkerbreek
Small deciduous tree from 3 to 7 m in height; leaves fresh light green to yellow-green. The flowers are pale yellow and fragrant, followed by black fruits, with the showy, persistent sepals turning bright pink and then red. Spring flowering, with fruits on display in mid-summer.

O. serrulata   Natal, Northern and north-eastern Transvaal
A very attractive small tree which can also be shrub-like. Leaves are narrow-elliptic, with serrated margins; pale yellow flowers, which appear in spring, are 25 mm across and followed by black fruits with red persistent sepals.

ODONTONEMA
Acanthaceae

A genus of perennials and shrubs native to the tropical regions of America and grown for their tubular flowers in red, yellow or white carried in erect, or in some species, drooping sprays. These are warm-climate plants, needing good soil and regular watering.

Odontonema strictum   Central America
Shrub to 2 m, with large leaves; crimson flowers are carried on showy spikes above the glossy green leaves in summer.

OENOTHERA

Oenothera stricta

O. biennis

OLDENBURGIA

Oldenburgia arbuscula

OLINIA

Olinia ventosa

OENOTHERA
Onagraceae

Annual and perennial herbaceous plants found widespread in the western world. They are easy to grow and the flowers are very showy. Some, such as *Oenothera stricta*, are weeds.

Oenothera biennis Eastern United States
🌼 ❋ ☼ Ⓦ
Evening primrose
It flowers in the evening; leaves form a basal rosette; branched inflorescence up to 1 m high; flowers yellow and trumpet shaped. Plant in any garden soil. It tends to become weedy.

O. stricta Chile
Introduced from Chile, it became a weed widespread in South Africa and known here since the end of the nineteenth century. Flowers are solitary, bright yellow, to 60 mm across, and appear in late spring.

OLDENBURGIA
Asteraceae (=Compositae)

This is a genus of two or three species of South African trees and shrubs, only one of which, *Oldenburgia arbuscula*, is cultivated.

Oldenburgia arbuscula Eastern Cape
🌼 ❋ ❋ ❋ ☼ Ⓦ mountains
Suurberg cushion bush or Suurbergsekussingbos
Shrub or small gnarled tree, usually not more than 3 m in height, occasionally reaching 5 m. Oldenburgias are grown for their satisfying foliage rather than their flowers. The large green leaves are glossy and opulent-looking and make a striking backdrop to the grey-stemmed, decorative and rather appealing buds and purplish-white flowers which appear in spring. Plant in well-drained soil in full sun.

OLINIA
Oliniaceae

An indigenous genus of trees and shrubs, of which *Olinia ventosa* is becoming a popular garden specimen.

Olinia ventosa South-western, southern
☼ ❋ ❋ and eastern Cape coastal forests
Hard pear or Hardepeer
A medium tree with glossy green leaves; insignificant flowers, though sweetly scented are followed by red berry-like fruit in summer.

OPUNTIA

Opuntia ficus-indica

O. ficus-indica

OPUNTIA
Cactaceae

The plants in this genus make striking accent plants, especially in combination with architectural features, but choose your species with care for many of the 300 species of cactus are distinctly unpopular with conservation authorities. Native to the Americas, these drought-resistant, easily propagated succulents come in a variety of shapes and sizes, both spiny and spineless.

Opuntia ficus-indica Origin unknown
Prickly pear
The spiny, so-called 'wild' prickly pear may become a weed, but the spineless variety makes a striking and unusual shrub or small 'tree' to 6 m. Flowers are yellow, followed by edible fruits. These may be greenish-yellow or dark red when ripe.

ORBEOPSIS

Orbeopsis lutea

ORBEOPSIS
Asclepiadaceae

Dwarfs, leafless succulents native to the Mediterranean regions and spreading across to India, with several species indigenous to South Africa. Although these plants will grow well out of doors in a well-drained, sunny, rockery pocket, they are usually grown as container plants on sunny windowsills or patios. Water regularly in the growing season but allow the plants a period of dormancy and relative dryness after flowering.

Orbeopsis lutea Moçambique to
(*Caralluma lutea*) South Africa
Succulent to 120 mm, flowers to 70 mm across are yellow, fringed with purple hairs. These are borne in clusters at the base of the stems with several flowers opening at once. Shown here is the purple-black flowered variety of the species.

ORNITHOGALUM

Ornithogalum dubium

O. flavissimum

ORNITHOGALUM
Liliaceae

Many species in this genus of bulbous perennials are indigenous to South Africa, as well as being found in the rest of Africa, Europe and western Asia. The common name, chincherinchee, is said to come from the sound the stout, shiny flower-stems make when rubbed together by the wind. The best known chincherinchee, or Chink, is perhaps *Ornithogalum thyrsoides,* much used by florists and exported as a cut flower. Like most ornithogalums, this species has creamy-white, starry flowers, but others come in shades of orange, yellow and green. Requirements for cultivation vary slightly according to species, but these are adaptable plants, needing only normal bulb treatment.

Ornithogalum dubium South-
western Cape
Flowers are orange-yellow with dull green centres.

O. saundersiae

O. thyrsoides

OROTHAMNUS

Orothamnus zeyheri

ORPHIUM

Orphium frutescens

O. flavissimum South-western Cape
Snake flower or Orange Chink
Bulb to 300 mm, with orange-yellow, green-centred flowers in spring. Plant in well-drained soil.

O. saundersiae Eastern Transvaal, Swaziland and Natal mountains
Giant Chincherinchee
Height to 2 m; creamy-white flowers with black ovaries in summer. Water well, but plant in well-drained soil.

O. thyrsoides South-western Cape
Chincherinchee or Tjienkerientjee
Height 250 to 600 mm; inflorescence is a many-flowered raceme, its flowers, which appear in late spring, are creamy-white with a buff eye.

OROTHAMNUS
Proteaceae

A genus with one species only, *Orothamnus zeyheri*.

Orothamnus zeyheri South-western Cape
Marsh rose or Vleiroos
A small shrub with exceptionally lovely flowers borne in spring. The innermost bracts are scarlet with long, whitish hairs at the margins. Cultivate this plant like other members of the protea family. Great success is being attained in propagating orothamnus by grafting.

ORPHIUM
Gentianaceae

There is just one species in this genus, a dwarf, evergreen shrub indigenous to the south-western and southern Cape coastal belt, *Orphium frutescens*.

Orphium frutescens South-western and southern Cape
Shrub or shrubby perennial to 600 mm, with glistening pink to mauve flowers up to 50 mm across that are carried at the tips of the branches in summer. This is a useful plant which will grow at the coast and in any soil, provided it is watered regularly in dry areas. It will thrive as a waterside plant, and also fits well into a large rockery.

ORTHOSIPHON

Orthosiphon labiatus

O. serratus var. *Ex Hort*

ORTHOSIPHON
Lamiaceae (=Labiatae)

Herbaceous shrubs to 1,5 m which do well under widespread conditions in South Africa. They prefer morning sun and some shade in the afternoon. Plant in rich, well-drained soil and water regularly.

Orthosiphon labiatus Widespread in summer rainfall areas
Herbaceous branched shrub to 1 m and spreading as much. It produces light purple-pink, two-lipped flowers, typical of the salvia family, that are borne in profusion in spring and summer.

O. serratus var. Ex Hort
As above, but flowers are bright pink.

OSTEOSPERMUM

Osteospermum ecklonis

O. fruticosum

O. jucundum

OSTEOSPERMUM
Asteraceae (=Compositae)

There are annuals, perennials, sub-shrubs and shrubs in this genus, most of them indigenous to South Africa but also found throughout Africa and into Arabia. Of the cultivated species, the three mentioned below are among the most useful, being tough, adaptable and showy plants for rockeries, as ground covers, or almost anywhere in the garden. Frost and drought resistant, they grow in any soil and are freely self-seeding. They start flowering in late winter, burst into a mass of large, showy daisy flowers in spring and continue to bloom for several months.

Osteospermum ecklonis Eastern Cape
Blue-and-white daisy bush
Shrubby evergreen perennial to 600 mm spreading over twice that distance. Large, shining white daisy flowers, up to 75 mm across, with deep blue centres and mauve markings on the reverse of the petals, are borne from early spring to late summer. Freely self-seeding, they will grow in semi-shade but are best in full sun.

O. fruticosum Southern Cape, Natal
Creeping marguerite or Rankmargriet
Perennial; spreading ground cover to 300 mm. Flowers are white with lilac centres, and mauve on the reverse of the petals; self-seeding, and easily raised from rooted cuttings. The picture shows a garden hybrid of this species.

O. jucundum Transvaal, Orange Free State, Natal
Bergbietou
Superb perennial ground cover to 200 mm, growing in full shade or full sun, although producing more flowers in full sun. Flowers come in shades of pink to purple from autumn to late spring. They are easily grown from cuttings, and self-seed freely.

OXALIS

Oxalis flava

O. lanata var. *rosea*

O. purpurea

OXALIS
Oxalidaceae

This is a very large genus with worldwide distribution, although most species are found in South America and South Africa. The genus not only includes the familiar bulbous sorrels but occasionally shrubs and sub-shrubs as well. Some species are quite showy, but when given good garden treatment they spread rapidly, and then having done so, become weedy. In areas where they thrive, most gardeners would welcome eradication hints. The name is from the Greek, *oxis,* acid, referring to the sour-tasting sap of some species.

Oxalis flava South-western Cape
Bulbous perennial to 250 mm; yellow flowers in winter.

O. lanata var. **rosea** South-western Cape
Flowers are pink or white, in spring, with leaves clover-like and slightly hairy.

O. purpurea South-western Cape
Dwarf plant to 75 mm, with deep rose-coloured flowers borne in spring.

OXYPETALUM

Oxypetalum caeruleum

OXYPETALUM
Asclepiadaceae

Perennial, herbaceous sub-shrubs native to Central America, of which only *Oxypetalum caeruleum* is cultivated.

Oxypetalum caeruleum Brazil
(*Tweedia caerulea*) and Uruguay

A few-flowered, somewhat twining, perennial to 1 m or more. Leaves and stems are densely covered with soft, fine, whitish hairs. Flowers 25 mm across with an erect dark blue corona are pale blue at first, becoming darker.

PACHYSTACHYS

Pachystachys lutea

PAEONIA

Paeonia officinalis 'Rubra-Plena'

PACHYSTACHYS
Acanthaceae

A small genus of evergreen perennials and shrubs native to tropical America and grown for their showy flower spikes which consist of large, often very colourful bracts from which the flowers protrude. Easily raised from cuttings and seeds, and easily grown, they need good soil and regular water for best results.

Pachystachys lutea　　　　South America

Shrub to 1 m with dark green leaves and flower spikes of showy golden yellow bracts and white flowers. A good container plant for a semi-shaded patio or a protected spot in the shrub border. They are mainly summer flowering, but produce blooms throughout the year.

PAEONIA
Paeoniaceae

Most garden paeonias or peonies are gorgeous double-flowered hybrids in all shades but blue. They are developed from the wild single-flowered herbaceous species in this genus native to Europe and North America. As well as herbaceous perennials, the genus includes a few shrubby species. Peonies have received much attention from hybridists, resulting in a wide range of forms and colours. Not the easiest plants to grow away from their cool native habitat, they nevertheless are most rewarding in areas where they will thrive. Good soil, partial shade and ample water are among their requirements, but specialist advice is recommended.

Paeonia officinalis 'Rubra-Plena'
　　　　　　　　　　　　　　Southern Europe
Peony
Perennial to 600 mm with red flowers up to 125 mm across in spring.

PANDANUS

Pandanus utilis

PANDANUS
Pandanaceae

This is a large genus of trees and shrubs native to the tropics of Africa and Asia, grown for their handsome foliage. Planted outdoors in warmer areas, they can also make striking container plants. Most species are coastal or waterside plants and need either high humidity or plenty of water, or both. The name is from the Malay name, *Pandang*.

Pandanus utilis — Madagascar
Screw pine
In its natural habitat this is a tree to 20 m with twisted fans of leaves up to 2 m long, but generally smaller in cultivation. It makes a striking accent plant.

PANDOREA

Pandorea jasminoides

PANDOREA
Bignoniaceae

This small genus of evergreen woody vines is native to Malaysia and Australia. The most commonly cultivated species is *Pandorea jasminoides*.

Pandorea jasminoides — Australia
Bower plant
Climber to 4 m with attractive dark green compound leaves which set off the showy flowers. These are up to 50 mm long, white with a deep carmine throat, and borne for most of the year in warm climates. Plant in good soil and water well as this is not an over-vigorous climber.

P. jasminoides 'Rosea'
The pink-flowered cultivar of above.

P. jasminoides 'Rosea'

PAPAVER

Papaver nudicaule

P. orientale

P. nudicaule 'Delicatum'

P. somniferum hybrid

PAPAVER
Papaveraceae

Poppies grow wild from the Arctic across Europe to Asia Minor, and in North America as well. There are about 50 species in the genus, several of which are grown as showy garden annuals and perennials; one is commercially grown, both legally and illegally, as the source of the drug opium. Poppies make a brilliant show in the garden with their shining petals, freshly crinkled from the bud, in all shades of intense red, orange, yellow and pink, and exquisite delicate pastels in the same colour range; some species include shades of lilac and lavender. Sow annual varieties *in situ*; if given a chance and conditions are to their liking, they will self-seed forever. The perennials are usually grown in warmer climates as winter and spring-flowering annuals. Poppies must have full sun.

Papaver nudicaule   Arctic regions, North America, Eurasia
Iceland poppy or Arctic poppy
Perennial, usually grown as a winter and spring-flowering annual to 350 mm with fragrant flowers of white, orange or reddish in the species, but now improved to include a wider range of colours; flowers up to 100 mm across.

P. nudicaule 'Delicatum'   Garden Origin
Cultivar of above.

P. orientale   Mediterranean to Iran
Oriental poppy
A showy perennial with large flowers that are scarlet with a black spot in the base. They appear in spring and summer.

P. somniferum hybrids   South-eastern Europe and West Asia
Opium poppy
Erect, grey-leaved annual to 1,2 m. Flowers grow up to 125 mm across and are often double. Petals are sometimes fringed and come in colours of white, pink, red or purple, often with a dark blotch at the base of the petals.

PAPHIOPEDILUM

Paphiopedilum chamberlainianum

PAPHIOPEDILUM
Orchidaceae

A genus of terrestrial or epiphytic orchids native to tropical Asia, which have been extensively hybridized. Flowers are borne singly in most species, but are very long-lasting, up to three months, making them popular florists' flowers. Numerous hybrids have been raised, some of which are more colourful than the species which have a somewhat muted colour range.

Paphiopedilum chamberlainianum   New Guinea
Slipper orchid or Lady's slipper
Flowers with spiralled petals in shades of green, rose and greenish-purple.

PARKINSONIA

Parkinsonia aculeata

PARTHENOCISSUS

Parthenocissus quinquefolia

P. tricuspidata

PARKINSONIA

Fabaceae (=Leguminosae) Subfam. Caesalpinioideae

There are only two species of spiny shrubs or small trees in this genus; one is native to tropical Africa, the other to tropical America. This latter species is occasionally cultivated as an unusual ornamental.

Parkinsonia aculeata   Tropical America
🅕 ✣ ✿ ✾ ☼ 🅦
Jerusalem thorn
Deciduous shrub or tree to 6 m or more in nature, slightly less in cultivation. Its green branches are similar to Spanish broom, but not as stiffly erect, usually somewhat scandent, with tiny leaves and stout spines, and spikes of yellow flowers. This tree makes an unusual lawn subject.

PARTHENOCISSUS

Vitaceae

The name of this genus is an adaptation of the Greek *parthenos*, meaning virgin, and *kissos*, ivy. There are about 15 species in the genus native to temperate North America and Asia, all of them deciduous creepers, which climb by means of tendrils or tendrils with tiny disc-shaped suckers at the ends of them. The species most commonly grown are those with magnificent autumn colouring because the fruit and flowers are not conspicuous.

Parthenocissus quinquefolia
🅕 ✣ ✿ ☼ 🅦   North America
Virginia creeper, American ivy or Woodbine
High-climbing creeper with disc-tipped tendrils that cling to any surface. Leaves are divided into five leaflets, making a dense, attractive green cover in summer which, when conditions are right, turns a truly breathtaking red in autumn. Ideal for growing on buildings and walls.

P. tricuspidata   Easter
🅕 ✣ ✿ ☼ 🅦
Boston ivy or Japanese ivy
High climbing by means of disc tendr forming a dense covering that clings roughened surfaces despite prevailir winds. Leaves three-lobed and up to 200 mm across on mature growth; tir serrated on new growth, turning to spectacular shades of red and purple in autumn. Fruit is purple, not very showy but popular with birds. A perfect covering for unsightly walls as the winter tracery of bare branches has its own charm.

PASSIFLORA

Passiflora amethystina

P. edulis

P. manicata

P. antioquienensis

P. edulis forma *flavicarpa*

P. mollissima

PASSIFLORA
Passifloraceae

Native to the tropics, but chiefly tropical South America, this is a large genus of vines which climbs by means of tendrils. Several species are grown for their fruit (granadillas) while others are grown as ornamentals with showy flowers in shades of pink, blue, white, purple and red. The name is from the Latin *passus*, suffering, and *flos*, a flower. This is because the early Catholic missionaries to South America saw in these strangely beautiful flowers features which symbolized the Passion of Jesus Christ.

Passiflora amethystina Brazil
A vigorous climber with deeply three-lobed leaves; large showy flowers in summer.

P. antioquienensis South America
Vigorous evergreen creeper to 3 m, or much more in favourable conditions. Flowers are bright red, up to 125 mm across. Best suited to warm areas, it will nevertheless grow in warm, protected spots in colder climates.

P. edulis South America
Granadilla or Passion fruit
Vigorous evergreen climber making a dense cover of shiny leaves, with white and purple flowers and edible, purple fruit. Grow from fresh seed in any soil in a warm spot and water well.

P. edulis forma *flavicarpa*
As above but fruit is yellow.

P. manicata South America
Red passion flower
Evergreen climber to 5 m, grown for its brilliant scarlet flowers.

P. mollissima South America
Bananadilla (Limit it to gardens.)
Vigorous evergreen climber to 5 m, or a lot more in favourable conditions. Rose-pink flowers are followed by long (130 mm) edible yellow fruit.

P. quadrangularis

P. quadrangularis South America
Giant granadilla
A robust climber with winged stems and large oval leaves. Flowers are attractive with dark red petals and purple white-striped curled filaments forming the crown or corona. Fruit is large and edible.

PAVETTA

Pavetta lanceolata

PEDILANTHUS

Pedilanthus tithymaloides subsp. *smallii*

P. tithymaloides subsp. *smallii* 'Variegatus'

PELARGONIUM

Pelargonium bowkeri

P. cucullatum

PAVETTA
Rubiaceae

This is a large genus of shrubs and trees native to the tropical and subtropical regions of Asia and Africa, with several species indigenous to South Africa. Pavettas are grown for their showy clusters of starry white flowers which are often sweetly scented. Although these are fairly tough plants, grow them in good soil for best results and water well in summer.

Pavetta lanceolata   Eastern Cape, Transkei, Natal and Eastern Transvaal
Forest bride's bush or Bosbruidsbos
Shrub or small tree to 7 m with white flowers in summer, followed by dense clusters of black berries in autumn.

PEDILANTHUS
Euphorbiaceae

A genus of deciduous succulent shrubs with milky sap, native to the drier regions of tropical America and grown for their showy inflorescences and, in some species, ornamental foliage. Good warm-climate shrubs, they need a sunny, well-drained position in the rockery or shrub border.

Pedilanthus tithymaloides subsp. **smallii**   Tropical America
Jacob's ladder or Slipper plant
Shrub to 2 m, it has reddish-purple, slipper-shaped bracts and unusual zig-zag stems. A lovely foliage indoor plant.

P. tithymaloides subsp. **smallii** 'Variegatus'
As above but leaves green, variegated white or sometimes red.

PELARGONIUM
Geraniaceae

From the original species in this genus of annuals, perennials and shrubs, mostly indigenous to South Africa, have been raised a wonderful range of useful, free-flowering plants grown for their showy flowers and ornamental, often fragrant, foliage. Pelargoniums are easily grown in any soil and in any position, although most prefer a light soil and full sun. There are few plants as easy to raise from cuttings as these garden hybrids while the indigenous species can be raised from seed.

Pelargonium bowkeri   Transkei and Natal
A geophyte with fine pinnately compound leaves. The outstanding feature is the fringed yellow-green petals of the flowers.

P. cucullatum   South-western Cape
Wilde-malva
Sprawling evergreen shrub to 1 m with large round felted leaves and mauve flowers marked with purple, in spring and

CONTINUED

PELARGONIUM

P. x *domesticum*

P. *echinatum*

P. *peltatum*

P. *fulgidum*

Pelargonium cv.

summer. An important parent plant of the modern garden hybrids, *Pelargonium* x *domesticum*.

P. x domesticum   Garden hybrid
Regal pelargonium or Washington hybrids
Evergreen perennials or small shrubs with spectacularly beautiful, large flowers, often ruffled or frilled, marked and blotched in the full range of purples, reds, pinks and whites, in spring.

P. echinatum   Namaqualand
Perennial with short, thick spiny stems, dormant in summer, with white to red-purple flowers, marked with deeper purple blotches.

P. fulgidum   South-western Cape and Namaqualand, drier regions
Shrubby perennial with bluish-green foliage and tiny scarlet flowers. Spring and summer flowering.

P. x *hortorum*

P. x hortorum   Garden hybrid
Zonal pelargonium
Perennial to 600 mm with leaves often variegated, usually in horseshoe-shaped bands; flowers in shades of red, pink and white. Can bloom for most months of the year.

P. peltatum   Southern and eastern Cape
Ivy-leaved pelargonium
Trailing or climbing evergreen with ivy-shaped leaves and pink, mauve or white flowers streaked with purple in spring and summer. Parent plant of many named cultivars.

Pelargonium cv.
Bontmalva

PELLAEA

Pellaea rotundifolia

P. viridis

PELLAEA
Polypodiaceae

This is a genus of small, rock-loving ferns of wide distribution but found mainly in the temperate and cool tropical regions of the Americas. Several species are indigenous to South Africa. These most attractive little plants grow in rocky, well-drained places in nature and make ideal hanging basket subjects.

Pellaea rotundifolia New Zealand
🌿 ☀ 🌱 🌷
Button fern
Fronds to 300 mm with most attractive, round leaves.

P. viridis Tropical Africa
☀ 🌱 🌷 Ⓕ
Height and spread 600 mm. This species needs warm, humid growing conditions.

PELTOPHORUM

Peltophorum africanum

PELTOPHORUM
Fabaceae (=Leguminosae) Subfam. Caesalpinioideae

A small genus of more or less evergreen, quick-growing trees widespread in the tropics. Peltophorums are grown for shade and their showy yellow flowers.

Peltophorum africanum Tropical Africa, Transvaal, Natal and
🌿 🌱 🌷 🌼 ☀ Ⓦ Namibia
Weeping wattle or Huilboom
Tree to 10 m with a spreading crown and fine, mimosa-like leaves making this an attractive specimen tree. Flowers are bright yellow with attractive crinkled petals carried in dense, showy sprays up to 150 mm long, for several months in the summer. This tree grows easily from seed, transplants well, and is quick growing.

PENNISETUM

Pennisetum setaceum 'Rubrum'

PENNISETUM
Poaceae (=Gramineae)

Some of the loveliest ornamental grasses are found in this genus of annual and perennial grasses native to the tropics, which include grain, millet, and some fodder. These decorative and graceful plants are useful for softening paved and walled areas such as driveways and courtyards, as well as for providing material for flower arranging, particularly dried arrangements. These tough, easily grown, drought-resistant plants are propagated by division of the clumps, or by seed. The name is from the Latin *penna*, a feather, and *seta*, a bristle, referring to the showy inflorescences of some species.

Pennisetum setaceum 'Rubrum'
(*P. rupellii*) Tropical Africa
🌿 🌱 🌷 ☀ Ⓦ
Fountain grass
Graceful perennial to 1 m, sending up arohing flower spikes in summer. The leaves and inflorescences of this cultivar are rose-coloured.

CONTINUED

PENNISETUM

P. villosum

PENSTEMON

Penstemon x *spectabilis*

PENTAS

Pentas lanceolata

P. lanceolata 'Coccinea'

P. villosum — Tropical Africa
Feather grass
Perennial grass to 600 mm with green leaves and creamy, feathery inflorescences, often tinged with purple and borne in summer.

PENSTEMON
Scrophulariaceae

Except for one species found in north-eastern Asia, the shrubs and perennials in this large genus are all native to North America where a great many species are in cultivation. However, the species found elsewhere are usually improved hybrids, both annual and perennial, grown for their tall showy spikes of flowers in the mixed border, or, in the case of the dwarf strains, for their colourful masses of flowers in bedding schemes. Flowers are often bi-coloured and include most shades in the blue, red and white range. Grow in good, deep soil and water well.

Penstemon x spectabilis — Garden hybrid
Densely packed spikes of flowers to over 1 m in summer, in a variety of colours and colour combinations.

PENTAS
Rubiaceae

This is a genus of soft-wooded evergreen shrubs and perennials from tropical Africa and Madagascar, grown for their showy, flat clusters of tiny starry flowers which are profusely borne for many months in spring and summer. Flowers are in all shades of mauve, red, pink and white and last well in water. These colourful shrubs are easily grown from cuttings and do well in any soil.

Pentas lanceolata — Tropical Africa
Shrub to 1,5 m; flowers in all shades of pink, mauve and white.

P. lanceolata 'Coccinea'
As above, with brilliant scarlet flowers.

PENTZIA PEPEROMIA

Pentzia grandiflora

Peperomia argyreia

P. marmorata

P. caperata

PENTZIA
Asteraceae (=Compositae)

A genus of shrublets and herbaceous plants native to Africa with most species indigenous to, and widespread in, South Africa.

Pentzia grandiflora South-western Cape, Namaqualand
Stinkkruid or Knoppies-stinkkruid
Loosely branched annual to 400 mm. Fine, lacy, strongly aromatic leaves and globe-shaped yellow flowers in spring.

PEPEROMIA
Piperaceae

There are about 1 000 species in this large and varied genus of mostly small perennials, which are widely distributed throughout the tropics and subtropics. The foliage of many species is immensely attractive, often marked and variegated, or crinkled and corrugated, making these ideal year-round container plants for stoeps, indoors or greenhouses. The flower spikes, like tiny catkins in some species, add to the decorative value of these plants. As is so often the case when a genus is large and widely distributed, habit and form vary, as do requirements, but these rewarding plants are usually easy to care for and can be propagated from stem or leaf cuttings.

Peperomia argyreia Tropical South America
Watermelon peperomia
Perennial to 300 mm with short stems, and leaves up to 100 mm across, most attractively striped in dark and silvery green. Easily propagated from leaf cuttings.

P. caperata South America
Emerald ripple peperomia
Compact perennial to 150 mm, heart-shaped, deeply crinkled leaves and creamy inflorescences carried on reddish stalks.

P. marmorata Brazil
Perennial to 150 mm. Leaves are glossy and light green. Very showy as hanging basket plants.

PETREA

Petrea volubilis

P. volubilis (bush)

PETREA
Verbenaceae

This genus of trees, shrubs and woody vines, native to tropical America and the West Indies, includes one of the loveliest flowering creepers, *Petrea volubilis*. Petreas are evergreen, deciduous, or semi-deciduous, depending on climate and species, but all flower best in warm, temperate areas.

Petrea volubilis — Tropical America, West Indies
Purple wreath
Scrambling shrub or woody creeper to 5 m with leaves that feel like sandpaper. Its sprays of violet-blue flowers with lavender-mauve calyces cover the plant in spring or summer, depending on the climate. The two tones of the flower sprays give great richness and depth to the colour, making this a truly lovely plant.

PETUNIA

Petunia x hybrida

P. x hybrida

P. x hybrida

PETUNIA
Solanaceae

Petunias are native to South America where about 30 species are found, but most of those grown in gardens are hybrids raised from some of the original species. They are among the most popular annuals, easily grown in bedding schemes, rockeries, window-boxes, hanging baskets or anywhere in the sun. The velvety, fragrant flowers may be double ruffled, frilled or fringed and blotched, striped and veined in every shade of red, pink, purple, mauve, blue, white and yellow. They are easily raised from seed.

Petunia x hybrida — Garden hybrid
Height varies from dwarf varieties 150 mm high to plants 300 mm high, sometimes compact, sometimes trailing. Flowering season is usually spring or summer, but throughout the year in warm climates.

258

PHACELIA

Phacelia campanularia

PHACELIA
Hydrophyllaceae

Perennial, annual or biennial herbaceous plants from the Americas, grown for mass effect in the flower garden. Easily grown from seed or by division.

Phacelia campanularia — California
California bluebell
Quick-growing annual to 500 mm. Leaves are ovate and serrated. Bright blue campanula-like flowers appear in spring/summer.

PHAENOCOMA

Phaenocoma prolifera

PHAENOCOMA
Asteraceae (=Compositae)

There is only one species in this genus, an evergreen shrub, *Phaenocoma prolifera*, indigenous to the south-western Cape.

Phaenocoma prolifera — South-western Cape
Cape everlasting or Rooisewejaartjie
Evergreen shrub to 1 m with stiff, erect branches covered in smaller branches, which in their turn are covered in tiny, knobbly leaves. Flowers appear at the tips of the branches and consist of rows of pointed, shining papery bracts, usually deep pink but sometimes white, which surround the true flower in the centre. This plant needs winter moisture and a dry summer. Grow in full sun in a well-drained rockery.

PHALAENOPSIS

Phalaenopsis x rothschildiana

PHALAENOPSIS
Orchidaceae

The name of this genus comes from the Greek *phalaina*, a moth, and *opsis*, resemblance, referring to the likeness of the flowers to moths or butterflies. It is a genus of epiphytic orchids from tropical Asia, Malaysia and Australia, containing some species with large, showy single flowers and others which produce sprays of smaller, dainty flowers. All need warm, moist greenhouse conditions, and permanent dampness around the roots. The novice orchid grower would be wise to get specialist advice on growing these plants.

Phalaenopsis x rothschildiana — Garden hybrid
Epiphyte with grey-mottled leaves and flowers up to 75 mm across in a pendent spray, glistening white except for their yellow crest.

PHALARIS

Phalaris arundinacea var. *picta*

PHASEOLUS

Phaseolus coccineus

PHILADELPHUS

Philadelphus coronarius

PHALARIS

Poaceae (=Gramineae)

There are about 15 species of annual and perennial grasses in this genus, native to North America, Europe and North Africa, one of which produces the canary seed of commerce; another is grown for forage, and another is cultivated as a vigorously growing ornamental for gardens.

Phalaris arundinacea var. **picta** North America, Eurasia
Ribbon grass or Gardener's garters
Perennial grass to 1,5 m but usually less in cultivation, forming large clumps of graceful green and white striped leaves. Flowering spikes are graceful but colourless. Easily grown anywhere in the garden and propagated by division of the clumps.

PHASEOLUS

Fabaceae (=Leguminosae) Subfam. Faboideae (=Papilionoideae)

A genus of perennial creepers native to the tropical and temperate regions of the Americas, it contains a number of edible beans, including green beans, haricot beans and butterbeans, as well as others widely used in the Far East. These are grown as annual crops.

Phaseolus coccineus Tropical America
Scarlet runner bean
Twining perennial usually grown as an ornamental annual. Flowers are scarlet, up to 25 mm long, appearing over a long period.

PHILADELPHUS

Saxifragaceae

Deciduous shrubs, 2 to 3 m high with dropping branches and well suited for an informal hedge. Flowers are white and saucer-like, sometimes double, and borne late in spring. Pruning, if necessary, should be done after flowering. Easily propagated by hardwood cuttings. The name is an ancient Greek one meaning brotherly love.

Philadelphus coronarius Europe
Mock orange or Boerejasmyn
Fragrant white flowers, 35 mm across, borne in early summer.

260

PHILODENDRON

Philodendron selloum

P. selloum (flower)

P. squamiferum 'Florida'

PHILODENDRON
Araceae

This is a large genus of mostly epiphytic shrubs and creepers from tropical America which make popular foliage plants for indoor decoration, although they can be grown outdoors in favourable climates. There is considerable variation in form and habit among the species, but all need rich, well-drained soil which should be kept permanently damp. The name is from the Greek *phileo,* to love, and *dendron,* tree, referring to the tree-climbing habit of many species.

Philodendron selloum South-western Brazil
Shrubby indoor plant to 5 m with deeply lobed leaves up to 1 m long. It can also be grown on stoeps or shady patios in warmer regions.

P. squamiferum 'Florida' Garden origin
Scandent foliage plant with deeply indented leaves.

PHLOMIS

Phlomis fruticosa

PHLOMIS
Lamiaceae (=Labiatae)

A genus of perennials and shrubs from the Mediterranean region and Asia, with sage-like (but not aromatic) foliage and flowers carried in rounded, ornamental clusters. Most species are easily grown in any soil and are useful in the sunny shrub or mixed border. Easily propagated from cuttings.

Phlomis fruticosa Mediterranean region
Jerusalem sage
Shrub to 1 m or more, velvety silver-green foliage and deep yellow flowers in summer. A tough, wind, frost and drought-resistant shrub.

261

PHLOX

Phlox drummondii

PHLOX
Polemoniaceae

This name is from the Greek *phlego,* to burn, or *phlox,* a flame, referring to the brilliant colours of the flowers of some of the species of annuals, perennials and sub-shrubs, native to North America (with the exception of one species found in Siberia) which belong to this genus. Both annual and perennial varieties are widely cultivated for their colourful, faintly fragrant flowers, in every shade of red, pink, mauve and white. Both annual and perennial phlox need enriched soil, ample moisture and full sun.

Phlox drummondii — North America

Long-flowering annual to 350 mm, with numerous cultivars, including dwarf or compact strains, which make showy bedding plants. Easily grown from seed, phlox are summer flowering in cooler areas, winter flowering in warm climates.

P. paniculata

P. paniculata — North America
Perennial phlox

Perennial to 2 m, usually less in cultivation, with tall, showy, densely packed spikes of flowers in all shades of red, pink, purple, mauve and white, in summer. Plant in good soil, and divide every few years.

PHOENIX

Phoenix reclinata

PHOENIX
Arecaceae (=Palmae)

Handsome ornamentals and economically important trees, particularly the date palm, are included in this genus. Native to the tropical and subtropical regions of Asia and Africa, these are tough, wind and drought-resistant plants, some of which grow to great heights, making them striking features in large gardens. Grown largely for their ornamental foliage, this is sometimes enhanced, when conditions are right, by huge sprays of glossy, colourful, red, orange or yellow fruits.

Phoenix canariensis — Canary Islands

Canary Islands date palm or Palmboom
Stout palm to 15 m or more, trunk up to 1 m in diameter. Arching pinnate leaves to 6 m long form a dense crown. Showy orange fruits, 30 mm long and 10 mm wide, are borne in large clusters.

PHORMIUM

P. canariensis

Phormium tenax

P. tenax 'Atropurpureum Nana'

P. tenax 'Atropurpureum'

P. reclinata   Eastern Transvaal, Natal and Transkei
Wild date palm or Wildedadelpalm
Often several-stemmed; older stems characteristically lean over and curve upwards again near the apex. Sexes are on different trees. Bright orange edible fruit, 20 by 10 mm, are borne in branched heads. The fruit resembles those of the cultivated date palm, but is much smaller and less tasty. Propagation is from seed and seedlings transplant easily.

PHORMIUM
Agavaceae

New Zealand is the home of both species in this genus of strikingly decorative evergreen plants which form clumps of stiff, ornamental leaves. They make dramatic accent plants, especially combined with architectural features, but to reach their full height and spread they should be grown as waterside plants in full sun. Flower spikes are not showy but add to the effectiveness of the plant. Propagate by division. The name is from the Greek *phormos,* meaning basket, as the tough fibrous leaves are much used in basketry.

Phormium tenax   New Zealand
New Zealand flax or Nieu-Seelandse vlas
Perennial to 5 m; leaves to 3 m long and 125 mm wide but usually far less in cultivation. Leaves are margined with a thin orange or red line. Flowers are dull red, not showy.

P. tenax 'Atropurpureum'
As above; leaves reddish-purple.

P. tenax 'Aureum'

P. tenax 'Atropurpureum Nana'
As above; dwarf.

P. tenax 'Aureum'
As above; leaves with broad yellow stripes.

PHOTINIA

Photinia glabra 'Rubens'

PHYGELIUS

Phygelius capensis

PHYLICA

Phylica plumosa

P. pubescens

PHOTINIA
Rosaceae

A genus of deciduous and evergreen trees and shrubs from south and east Asia which are grown for the beauty of their foliage and their sprays of showy white flowers which are followed by red berries. New leaf growth in the spring is usually red, and the glossy green leaves turn brilliant red in autumn, even in the evergreen species. This autumn colour is best where winters are cold. Grow as specimen shrubs, or use to make good, dense hedges.

Photinia glabra 'Rubens'   Japan

Evergreen tree or shrub to 6 m. New growth is bright red. Sprays of white flowers are borne in winter and spring, then followed by red berries which later turn black. This is a good hedge plant as well as a showy single specimen.

PHYGELIUS
Scrophulariaceae

The two species of evergreen, shrubby perennials in this genus are indigenous to the summer rainfall areas of South Africa. They are cultivated for their tall spikes of drooping, tubular red flowers. In nature they are found growing in shady places near perennial water and are best cultivated under similar conditions in the garden, although they will grow in full sun if watered well. Propagate by cuttings or division of the rootstock. The name is from the Greek *phugo,* flee, and *helios,* the sun, meaning that the plants are shade lovers.

Phygelius capensis   Transvaal, Natal, Swaziland, Lesotho and Orange Free State

Cape Fuchsia
Perennial to 1 m or a little more, producing red flowers in summer.

PHYLICA
Rhamnaceae

This is a genus of evergreen shrubs and trees mostly indigenous to the winter rainfall areas of South Africa, but with a few species in Madagascar and Tristan da Cunha. These shrubs are grown for their decorative fluffy flower heads which consist of narrow, densely fringed bracts with silvery hairs giving them the appearance of feathery pompoms. They are useful in flower arrangements.

Phylica plumosa   South-western Cape

Veerkoppie
Winter-flowering evergreen shrublet to 600 mm with large, feathery greenish-yellow flower heads.

P. pubescens   South-western Cape

Small, erect evergreen shrub to 1,2 m with silvery yellow-green flower heads in winter. Best suited to winter rainfall areas, they are wind resistant at the coast.

PHYSALIS

Physalis alkekengi

P. peruviana

PHYSALIS
Solanaceae

These cosmopolitan annual or perennial herbaceous shrublets grown chiefly for their edible fruit are much used in jams, preserves and pickles and also for the ornamental calyces. They prefer full sun and are easily grown from seed. The name is from the Greek, *physa*, a bladder, referring to the inflated calyx.

Physalis alkekengi　　　Europe to Japan
(*P. franchettii*)
Red gooseberry
Fruit is red and globose and the mature red calyx is highly decorative.

P. peruviana　　　Tropical South America
Cape gooseberry or Appelliefie
Contrary to its name, it is not native to the Cape – the name probably comes from 'caped gooseberry', referring to the calyx enclosing the fruit like a cape. This plant is a straggly grower and the ripe fruit is yellow.

PHYSOSTEGIA

Physostegia virginiana

PHYSOSTEGIA
Lamiaceae (=Labiatae)

A small genus of herbaceous perennials native to North America grown for their showy spikes of flowers in all shades of pink and mauve. Most commonly cultivated species is *Physostegia virginiana*.

Physostegia virginiana　　　North America
False dragonhead or Obedience plant
Perennial to over 1 m, with tall spikes of pinky mauve flowers in autumn. A number of cultivars, found in various allied shades, make good cut flowers. These are stout, vigorous-growing plants which create a colourful display in a mixed border or planted in clumps in full sun or semi-shade. Propagate by division, or by allowing the plants to seed themselves.

PHYTOLACCA

Phytolacca dioica

PHYTOLACCA
Phytolaccaceae

A genus of perennials, shrubs and trees, native to the tropical and subtropical regions of the world. Some are edible, others poisonous in parts, and still others are grown for their ornamental flowers and fruit. Some species have unpleasant-smelling foliage but all are easily cultivated in ordinary garden conditions.

Phytolacca dioica　　　South America
Belhambra
Quick-growing evergreen tree to 20 m or more forming a thick trunk and a large root system, making it unsuitable for planting near buildings. Insignificant flowers and fruit are borne. Freely self-seeding.

PILEA

Pilea cadierei

P. microphylla

P. spruceana

P. spruceana 'Norfolk'

PILEA
Urticaceae

Widespread in the tropical and warmly temperate regions of the world, the herbaceous annuals and perennials in this genus are widely grown for their ornamental foliage. They make ideal container plants for indoors, stoeps or greenhouses, and the trailing kinds are particularly suited to hanging baskets. Grow in good soil and water well. Easily propagated by cuttings.

Pilea cadierei South East Asia

Aluminium plant or Watermelon pilea
Perennial to 300 mm with equal spread and grown for its showily variegated foliage. The leaves are marked with silver, giving a metallic effect.

P. microphylla Tropical America

Artillery plant
Annual or short-lived perennial to 300 mm with equal spread and bearing small, pale green leaves. The anthers forcefully shoot out the pollen, hence the common name.

P. spruceana South America, Peru

Trailing or erect perennial bearing heavily textured bronze-green leaves.

P. spruceana 'Norfolk' Garden origin

Angel wings
Small ornamental plant; this is an English cultivar. Leaves are deeply quilted, bronze above and reddish underneath.

PIMELEA

Pimelea ferruginea

PIMELEA
Thymelaeaceae

This genus of evergreen flowering shrubs and herbaceous perennials is native to Australia, New Zealand and the surrounding islands. Pimeleas are cultivated for their showy fragrant, pompon-like flowers in all shades of pink, and are very similar to the flowers of *Dais cotinifolia*. Grow in light, well-drained soil and full sun for a long-lasting display in spring and summer. A good rockery plant.

Pimelea ferruginea Western Australia
(*P. rosea*)

Evergreen shrub to 1 m with small, shiny leaves and rounded heads of rose-pink flowers, in spring and summer.

PISONIA

Pisonia umbellifera 'Variegata'

PISONIA
Nyctaginaceae

A genus of trees and shrubs native to the tropical and subtropical regions of the world.

Pisonia umbellifera 'Variegata'   Tropical Asia, Australia
(*Heimerliodendron brunonianum*)
Small tree to 6 m with large leaves to 400 mm long, blotched with cream; usually grown as a greenhouse plant.

PISTIA

Pistia stratiotes

PISTIA
Araceae

There is one species of this genus widespread in the tropics and subtropics where it is sometimes a serious pest plant. The name is from the Greek *pistos,* watery, referring to the plant's aquatic habitat.

Pistia stratiotes   Tropics, worldwide
Water lettuce
This is a dangerous weed and shown here for you to identify. An aquatic plant grown for its attractive rosettes of velvety leaves up to 150 mm across which resemble young lettuces, hence the common name. These plants are free floating and rarely anchored by their roots.

PITTOSPORUM

Pittosporum crassifolium

PITTOSPORUM
Pittosporaceae

This is a genus of evergreen trees and shrubs widespread in Asia, Africa and especially Australia and New Zealand, grown for its attractive foliage, small, not very showy but often very fragrant flowers and, in some species, decorative fruits. The plants can be grown in the shrub border, or pruned when young to make most attractive specimen trees, or clipped to form dense hedges. Most species are wind resistant and withstand a fair amount of frost. They self-seed freely when conditions suit them and are not fussy about soil.

Pittosporum crassifolium   New Zealand
Karo
Shrub or small tree to 10 m with dark green, leathery leaves felted white underneath; dark red to purple flowers, not very showy, are borne in summer. This species makes a good hedge or windbreak at the coast.

CONTINUED

PITTOSPORUM

P. eugenioides

P. eugenioides — New Zealand
Tarata
Shrub or tree to 12 m; dark shining green leaves with sprays of creamy-yellow, fragrant flowers in summer. Makes a good hedge or specimen tree.

PLATANUS

Platanus x *acerifolia*

PLATANUS
Platanaceae

Large trees which are widespread in the northern hemisphere, where they are much used as street or park trees. They grow fairly quickly in rich, moist soil.

Platanus x acerifolia — Origin unknown
London plane tree, Sycamore or Plataan
An excellent, deciduous specimen tree with three to five-lobed leaves. Globular fruit heads are borne in pairs.

PLATYCERIUM

Platycerium bifurcatum

PLATYCERIUM
Polypodiaceae

This is a genus of large, spreading or drooping epiphytic ferns from the tropical and subtropical regions of Asia, Africa and Australia. They are grown for their striking appearance which lends an exotic touch to a shady patio or stoep garden. In warm areas they will grow outdoors in the fork of a tree. Indoors, grow the plant in a basket or attached to a slab of wood. The name is from the Greek *platys*, broad, and *keras*, a horn, referring to the broad, horn-shaped fronds which give the plant its common name, staghorn fern.

Platycerium bifurcatum — Australia, Polynesia
Staghorn fern
An unusual and dramatic-looking epiphytic fern with grey-green leaves to 1 m long and forked.

PLATYCODON

Platycodon grandiflorus

PLECTRANTHUS

Plectranthus barbatus

P. ambiguus

P. barbatus 'Variegata'

PLATYCODON
Campanulaceae

A genus of a single herbaceous perennial, *Platycodon grandiflorus,* with bell-shaped flowers. Flower buds are inflated and balloon-like before they open in summer. Grow them in rich, well-drained soil in full sun and propagate by seeds. The name is from the Greek *platys,* broad, and *kadon,* a bell, from the shape of the flower.

Platycodon grandiflorus East Asia
Erect plant to 600 mm; flowers are solitary and terminal, deep blue, lilac or white. Rich soil and full sun will secure successful cultivation.

PLECTRANTHUS
Lamiaceae (= Labiatae)

A genus of softwood, evergreen perennials and shrubs native to Asia, Australia and Africa, with a number of species indigenous to South Africa. They are grown for their plumes of dainty flowers in shades of pink, mauve, purple, blue and white. These are useful plants as they will grow in deep shade, most of them being best in semi-shade, although a few species will grow in full sun. For best results and a long-lasting display of showy flowers, grow plectranthus in good soil and water well. If cut down by severe frost they will shoot again in spring. Easily propagated by cuttings, many species make excellent ground covers.

Plectranthus ambiguus Natal and Eastern Cape
A soft, spreading herb with heads of long, narrow purple flowers. Very showy as a ground cover for shady areas.

P. barbatus East Africa
An aromatic shrub 2 to 3 m tall with spikes of dark purple flowers. It comes from East Africa.

P. barbatus 'Variegata'
As above, but leaves variegated.

P. ecklonii Eastern Cape, Natal, Zululand, Eastern Transvaal
Spreading shrub to 1,25 m with masses of purple flower spikes carried above the foliage in autumn. This species will tolerate a sunnier position than most, especially near the coast.

P. ecklonii 'Medley-Wood'
As above, but leaves larger and spikes shorter.

P. fruticosus Eastern Cape, Natal, Transvaal
Erect shrub to 1,25 m with a mass of showy purple flowers, in late summer. Best planted in full shade.

P. hilliardiae Southern Natal
A low-growing shrublet suitable for planting in pots and growing indoors.

CONTINUED

PLECTRANTHUS

P. ecklonii

P. ecklonii 'Medley-Wood'

P. fruticosus

P. hilliardiae

P. praetermissus

P. madagascariensis var. *madagascariensis*

Pleiospilos bolusii

Plumbago auriculata

P. saccatus

P. prismaticus

P. auriculata 'Alba'

P. madagascariensis var. **madagascariensis** Eastern Cape, Natal
A common sprawling garden plant which produces spikes of white flowers. Suitable as a ground cover.

P. praetermissus Coastal forests, Transkei
Dense spikes of purple flowers appear in autumn. Suitable for growing in pots.

P. saccatus Eastern Cape, Natal, Zululand
Stoep jacaranda
Dwarf shrub to 300 mm, making an excellent ground cover in the shade, with small, light green leaves. Sprays of purple flowers (largest in the genus) are borne in mid-summer.

PLEIOSPILOS
Mesembryanthemaceae

This is a genus of stemless, usually clump-forming succulents indigenous to South Africa. The leaves, which are very fleshy and covered in tiny, translucent dots, grow in pairs and often resemble pebbles. Flowers, in shades of yellow and white, are large and vygie-like. If grown in containers, pleiospilos must be planted in deep soil as most species have long roots. Plant in well-drained soil in full sun and only water during the growing season.

Pleiospilos bolusii Graaff-Reinet and Aberdeen

P. prismaticus North-western Cape

PLUMBAGO
Plumbaginaceae

Although there are about 20 species in this genus, only one is widely cultivated, the indigenous *Plumbago auriculata*. Other species include climbing and scandent shrubs and perennials of worldwide distribution, mostly in the tropics.

Plumbago auriculata Eastern Cape, Natal
Spreading, scrambling shrub to 3 m, producing masses of powder-blue flowers in summer. Plumbago makes a good informal hedge; if clipped too severely flowering may be impaired. Although these tough plants will survive in poor soil and withstand drought and wind, they are worth feeding and watering well as the long-lasting display of flowers can be truly spectacular.

P. auriculata 'Alba'
As above, but with white flowers.

PLUMERIA

Plumeria obtusa

P. rubra

P. rubra forma *lutea*

P. rubra forma *rubra*

PLUMERIA
Apocynaceae

One of the most exotically fragrant of all plants, the frangipani is included in this small genus of deciduous trees and shrubs native to tropical America. These rather strange-looking plants have bare, stubby branches with most of the large, leathery leaves carried near the tips. The large waxy flowers are borne in profuse, showy clusters during the warmer months. These last well in water. Grow in good, deep soil and water well.

Plumeria obtusa — Singapore
Singapore plumeria or Temple tree
Small evergreen tree to 8 m high. Leaves grow up to 180 mm long; flowers are large, white and waxy with spreading petals, and very fragrant.

P. rubra — Central America
Frangipani
Tree to 8 m, usually less in cultivation, with leaves to 450 mm in length. The flowers, to 70 mm across, are white with yellow centres and intensely fragrant. This tree has become naturalized in India where it is used extensively in temples.

P. rubra forma lutea
As above; flowers yellow, flushed pink on the outside.

P. rubra forma rubra
As above; flowers rose-pink with yellow centres.

PODALYRIA

Podalyria calyptrata

PODALYRIA
Fabaceae (= Leguminosae) Subfam. Faboideae (= Papilionoideae)

This is a genus of evergreen indigenous trees and shrubs which include several very decorative species. The greyish-green leaves of most cultivated species make these plants most useful additions to the shrub border and are a perfect foil for the pink, often fragrant pea-flowers. Most species are native to the winter rainfall area, need well-drained soil and are best grown in full sun, although they will also grow in semi-shade. Podalyrias are usually raised from seed.

Podalyria calyptrata — Southern and south-western Cape
Sweet pea bush, Keur or Ertjiebos
This very attractive species usually forms a bushy shrub to 2 m but may be pruned to form a tree to about 4 m. Foliage is grey-green and the showy, pink to mauve, fragrant pea-flowers are up to 25 mm across. These cover the plants in late winter and spring.

PODOCARPUS

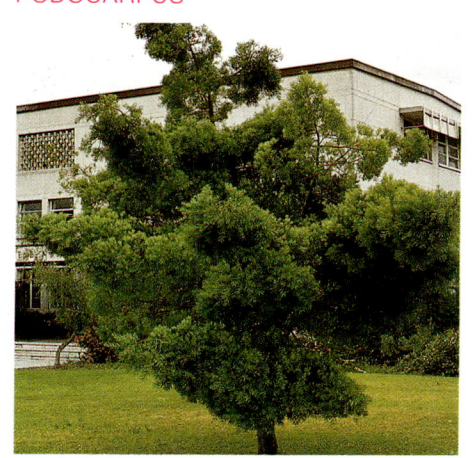

Podocarpus falcatus

P. henkelii

PODOCARPUS
Podocarpaceae

Of widespread distribution, largely in the southern hemisphere, several species in this genus of evergreen trees and shrubs are indigenous to South Africa where one species is an important timber tree. In nature, these trees grow in deep, rich soil in heavy rainfall areas and reach enormous proportions. Young trees are slow growing into a most attractive pyramidal form which, with their ornamental leaves, makes them good garden specimens.

Podocarpus falcatus   Coastal forests from Southern Cape to Eastern Transvaal
Outeniqua yellowwood, Outeniekwageelhout or Kalander
Medium to large tree reaching 20 m or more in the garden. Leaves are often sickle-shaped.

P. henkelii   Eastern Cape, Natal, Transvaal
Natal yellowwood or Henkelgeelhout
Large tree to 20 m in nature, but in cultivation is usually much less and slower growing, with long, narrow, curved and drooping leaves.

PODRANEA

Podranea brycei

P. ricasoliana

PODRANEA
Bignoniaceae

There are two species in this genus, one native to Zimbabwe, the other to Pondoland in the Transkei. Both are evergreen showy climbers bearing clusters of trumpet-shaped pink flowers. It is easy to confuse the two species, but the Zimbabwean species, *Podranea brycei*, has slightly smaller, darker flowers. These showy creepers need support and will climb rapidly to 6 m. Flowers are carried above the leaves, completely covering the plant in a mass of blooms. Easily grown in any soil and propagated by cuttings or layering.

Podranea brycei   Zimbabwe
Zimbabwe creeper or Zimbabweranker
Creeper requiring a hot situation.

P. ricasoliana   Transkei
Port St John's creeper or Port St Johnranker
Evergreen creeper to 6 m, with pinky mauve flowers striped with red in the throat, profusely borne in summer.

POLIANTHES

Polianthes tuberosa

POLIANTHES
Amaryllidaceae

Mexico is the home of this small genus of rhizomatous plants with grass-like leaves and spikes of red and white flowers, only one of which, *Polianthes tuberosa*, is commonly cultivated. This plant has been in cultivation for so long and is so widespread in the tropics that its original habitat is not known. Tuberoses are widely grown commercially as cut flowers and as a source of perfume as they have a powerful fragrance.

Polianthes tuberosa   Origin unknown, presumably Mexico
Tuberose
Summer-flowering bulb to 1 m with waxy white, very fragrant flowers up to 60 mm long, in both double and single forms.

POLYGALA

Polygala myrtifolia

P. virgata

POLYGALA
Polygalaceae

This is a large genus of cosmopolitan distribution, containing trees, shrubs, perennials and annuals, a number of which are indigenous to South Africa. Of the shrubby species, *Polygala myrtifolia* is one of the most commonly cultivated.

Polygala myrtifolia — Eastern Province and Natal
Bloukappie
Quick-growing evergreen shrub to 3 m, bearing bright reddish-purple flowers for most months of the year except for a few months in summer. These are tough plants that will survive in most soils but for best results plant in enriched soil and water regularly.

P. virgata — South-western and eastern Cape
Most attractive species up to 2 m in height. Leaves reach 10 to 40 mm in length and are narrow lanceolate. Pea-shaped flowers, 10 mm across and enclosed by two purple wing-like bracts, are borne terminally in inflorescences 200 to 250 mm long.

POLYGONUM

Polygonum capitatum

POLYGONUM
Polygonaceae

Annuals, perennials, ground covers, climbers and aquatics are included in this genus of cosmopolitan plants, several of which are cultivated for their profusion of small red, pink, white or greenish flowers which are often carried in showy, feathery sprays, or for their attractive foliage. Most species are quick growing in good soil, self-seed freely and are easily propagated by cuttings or division.

Polygonum capitatum — Himalayas
Knotweed
Vigorous evergreen ground cover to 150 mm with foliage variegated in bands of green and dark green or showy shades of red, bronze and bronzy pink. Masses of tiny, round pink flower heads are borne in spring, summer and autumn. This is an invasive, spreading ground cover, good for covering large areas in both sun and semi-shade. In shade, the leaf colouring is green; in sun, reddish.

POLYPODIUM

Polypodium aureum

POLYPODIUM
Polypodiaceae

A genus of about 75 species of evergreen cosmopolitan ferns with leathery fronds, usually epiphytic with creeping rhizomes. Propagation by division of clumps.

Polypodium aureum — Florida, USA to Argentina
Rabbit's-foot fern or Haaspootvaring
Leaves to 1 m long and 600 mm wide.

PONTEDERIA

Pontederia cordata

P. cordata forma *angustifolia*

PONTEDERIA
Pontederiaceae

A few species of aquatic perennials native to the Americas are contained in this genus, of which one, *Pontederia cordata,* is the most commonly cultivated for its intensely blue flowers.

Pontederia cordata   North America
Pickerel weed
Aquatic to 600 mm, with heart-shaped, olive-green leaves and long spikes of densely packed blue flowers in summer. This attractive plant should be grown in water from 150 to 300 mm deep. Propagate by root division.

P. cordata forma **angustifolia**
As above, but with sword-shaped leaves.

POPULUS

Populus deltoides

POPULUS
Salicaceae

Dioecious trees with soft, white wood belong to this genus. Leaves are usually broad with long petioles and flowers are borne in hanging catkins. The poplars are very easy to cultivate but should be planted away from drains, buildings or pathways because their roots can badly affect foundations. Propagate by hardwood cuttings.

Populus deltoides   North America
Cotton wood or Populier
A fast-growing tree to 10 m or more.

PORTULACA

Portulaca grandiflora

PORTULACA
Portulacaceae

Many of the species in this cosmopolitan genus are considered to be weeds, one of which, common purslane, is occasionally used as a herb for flavouring salads. Both annual and perennial species occur, all having small, fleshy leaves and one, *Portulaca grandiflora,* has large, dazzlingly brilliant flowers.

Portulaca grandiflora   South America
Moss Rose
Prostrate annual, sometimes reaching 350 mm high with large, brilliantly coloured flowers in all shades except blue, in both single and double forms. These are excellent plants for the rockery, the front of a mixed border, or for window-boxes; in fact anywhere in full sun. Soil need not be too rich, but should be well drained. Easily raised from seed.

PORTULACARIA

Portulacaria afra

POTENTILLA

Potentilla fruticosa 'Gold Finger'

PRIMULA

Primula malacoides

PORTULACARIA
Portulacaceae

The one species in this genus is South African, *Portulacaria afra,* found growing in the hot dry areas of the eastern Cape and up the Transkei coast, into Natal, Moçambique and northern Transvaal.

Portulacaria afra — Eastern Cape, Transkei, Natal, Northern Transvaal
Elephant's food, Jade plant or Spekboom
In nature, a large, spreading evergreen shrub, or tree to 4 m, making a good hedge plant in dry regions, where it is also a valuable fodder plant. In cultivation it often remains a decorative small shrub, ideal for rockeries or containers, both indoors and out, with small round fleshy leaves carried on red stems. Tiny pink flowers appear in summer. These are followed by pinkish fruits. Easily propagated from cuttings.

POTENTILLA
Rosaceae

A large genus of annuals, perennials and a few shrubs, native largely to the northern hemisphere including the Arctic regions. Many make useful perennials for cooler climates where numerous species are cultivated and a number of cultivars have been developed. Flowers are in all shades of red, pink, yellow and white. Soil needs to be enriched and well drained.

Potentilla fruticosa 'Gold Finger' — North America, Europe, Asia
Deciduous, densely leafy shrub to 1 m, with graceful ferny foliage and bright yellow flowers freely borne in summer. Good for rock gardens, mixed borders or shrubberies.

PRIMULA
Primulaceae

This is a large genus of annuals and perennials widely distributed in the temperate regions of the northern hemisphere, with a few species found in the southern hemisphere. The name is from the Latin *primus,* referring to the early flowering of some species, such as the English primrose. Primulas are grown for their fragrant, colourful flowers which are carried above neat rosettes of crinkled green leaves. They are cool-climate plants, needing rich, well-drained soil, ample water and semi-shade. Propagate from seed or by division in autumn.

Primula malacoides — China
Fairy primula
Annual to 450 mm, bearing masses of small, dainty lavender to pink flowers in winter and spring. There are numerous cultivars in a variety of shades from white to deep rosy pink, and double-flowered strains as well. These delicate flowers make a striking display when massed, and also combine well with spring bulbs.

PROTEA

P. x polyantha

Protea aristata

P. caffra

P. aurea subsp. *aurea*

P. compacta

P. x polyantha — Garden hybrid
Polyanthus primrose
A hybrid group with a range of brilliant flowers in virtually every colour. They are very showy and well worth cultivating in a shady spot. Flowers, usually carried about 300 mm above the leaves, are borne in winter and spring.

PROTEA
Proteaceae

This genus, which includes South Africa's national flower, needs little introduction to South African gardeners. Widespread in South Africa, proteas are found in tropical Africa as well. The genus is named after the Greek god Proteus, who was able to change his shape at will, an indication of the diversity and variety to be found within the genus. Some proteas grow readily in gardens and are freely available, while others are rare, strictly protected and confined to very small natural habitats. There are several superb books available on proteas, some of them very recently published, that provide the protea enthusiast with a great deal of information as well as pleasure. The species depicted here give an indication of the fascinating diversity of these plants and, it is hoped, will inspire further interest in cultivating them.

Protea aristata — Swartberg
Needle-like leaves.

P. cynaroides

P. aurea subsp. *aurea* — Langeberg and Outeniqua mountains
P. caffra — Eastern Cape, Suikerbos, Natal and Transvaal
P. compacta — Kleinmond to Bredasdorp
Bot river protea or Botrivierprotea
P. cynaroides — South-western Cape to Grahamstown
Giant protea or Reuseprotea
Our national flower

CONTINUED

PROTEA

P. eximia

P. magnifica

P. nana

P. grandiceps

P. neriifolia

P. repens

P. longifolia

P. speciosa

P. stokoei

PRUNUS

P. scolymocephala

Prunus cerasifera 'Atropurpurea'

P. persica 'Carnation Striped'

P. persica 'Alboplena'

P. persica 'Clara Meyer'

P. persica 'Rubroplena'

P. eximia	Mountains from Worcester to Port Elizabeth
P. grandiceps	Cape Peninsula to Uitenhage
P. longifolia	Sir Lowry's Pass to Cape Agulhas
P. magnifica	Cedarberg to Houwhoek
P. nana	Tulbagh to Wemmershoek
Mountain rose, Bergrosie, Skaamrosie	
P. neriifolia	Southern coastal mountains
P. repens	Widespread in the Cape Province
Sugarbush, Suikerbos or Suikerkan	
P. scolymocephala	Cape Peninsula to Somerset West and Cedarberg
P. speciosa	Mountains in the South-western Cape
P. stokoei	Hottentots Holland mountains

PRUNUS
Rosaceae

A large genus of deciduous and evergreen trees and shrubs native to the temperate regions of the world, mainly those of the northern hemisphere. The genus includes such fruits as plums, apricots, almonds, peaches, cherries, nectarines etc. as well as their ornamental varieties which are grown frequently for their foliage, but chiefly for their spectacular displays of spring blossom. Plant in enriched soil and water regularly.

Prunus cerasifera 'Atropurpurea'   Western Asia
Flowering plum, Purple-leaf plum or Blompruim
Deciduous shrub or small tree to 6 m bearing white or pink flowers in spring before the leaves appear. Leaves are dark purple in summer.

P. persica 'Alboplena'   Garden origin
Flowering peach or Blomperske

P. persica 'Carnation Striped'   Garden origin
Flowering peach or Blomperske

P. persica 'Clara Meyer'   China
Flowering peach or Blomperske
Tree to 3 m bearing double pink flowers in spring.

P. persica 'Rubroplena'   China
Flowering peach or Blomperske
Tree to 3 m with double red flowers in spring.

279

PSEUDERANTHEMUM

Pseuderanthemum alatum

PSEUDERANTHEMUM
Acanthaceae

These are glabrous herbs and shrubs, mostly grown in greenhouses or in warm climates. There are about 60 species in this tropical genus. Propagation is mostly by cuttings.

Pseuderanthemum alatum   Mexico and Central America
Chocolate plant
A low-growing small shrublet with broad ovate leaves that are copper-brown above and silver blotched along the midrib. A lovely foliage plant which needs rich, well-drained soil.

PSIDIUM

Psidium littorale var. *longipes*

PSIDIUM
Myrtaceae

A genus of evergreen trees and shrubs native to tropical America, of which the best known is *Psidium guajava*, the commercial fruit tree, also an attractive garden tree. Psidiums grow easily without special attention and in all frost-free areas. The name is from the Greek *psidion*, meaning pomegranate, a reference to the 'pippy' fruits.

Psidium littorale var. **longipes**   South America
Strawberry guava
Small dense tree or shrub with showy purplish-red edible fruits borne in summer.

PTERONIA

Pteronia camphorata

PTERONIA
Asteraceae (=Compositae)

Shrublets or shrubs with opposite fine leaves. The only species, *Pteronia camphorata*, is in cultivation.

Pteronia camphorata   South-western Cape
Terminal flower heads appear in early summer. This plant must have rich, well-drained soil in a sunny spot.

PTERYGODIUM　　　　　PUNICA

Pterygodium catholicum

Punica granatum

P. granatum 'Flore Pleno'

P. granatum 'Legrellei'

P. granatum 'Nana'

PTERYGODIUM
Orchidaceae

This is a genus of indigenous orchids. Most species are found in Namaqualand, the south-western and southern Cape. These are tuberous plants which flower in spring.

Pterygodium catholicum　　South-western Cape
Moederkappie
Several flowers are produced simultaneously. These are greenish-yellow, about 15 mm across, and appear in August.

PUNICA
Punicaceae

There are two species in this genus, one native to the island of Socotra in the Indian Ocean, and the other, *Punica granatum*, found from the eastern Mediterranean region extending to India. It is this species and its cultivars which are commonly cultivated for their edible fruit, the pomegranate, or as ornamentals. Although these are tough, drought-resistant plants, good soil and regular watering will give better results.

Punica granatum　　Mediterranean region, Western Asia
Pomegranate or Granaat
Shrub or small tree to 6 m, sometimes spiny, bearing crinkled, orange-red flowers in spring, followed by fruits up to 125 mm across that are decorative as well as edible.

P. granatum 'Flore Pleno'
Flowering pomegranate
As above with double red flowers in spring and summer. This makes an excellent symmetrical shrub with its neat, glossy foliage that is red-bronze in spring and turns a clear yellow in autumn before falling, making it delightfully showy for many months of the year.

P. granatum 'Legrellei'
As above, but the double orange-red flowers are streaked with white-yellow.

P. granatum 'Nana'
Dwarf pomegranate
Shrub to 2 m, usually less, making an ideal outdoor container plant with neat, glossy foliage, red flowers and dwarf fruit.

281

PYCNOSTACHYS

PYRACANTHA

Pycnostachys urticifolia

Pyracantha coccinea

P. coccinea 'Keessenii'

P. angustifolia

PYCNOSTACHYS
Lamiaceae (=Labiatae)

Erect herbaceous perennials from Madagascar and South Africa. Flowers are carried in dense terminal spikes.

Pycnostachys urticifolia   Tropical and South Africa
A much-branched shrublet with bright blue flowers.

PYRACANTHA
Rosaceae

There are only six species in this genus of popular evergreen shrubs, but numerous cultivars have been raised from the most ornamental of these. Native to south-eastern Europe and Asia, pyracanthas are usually thorny, making excellent long-lived stout hedges. They are also among the most showy ornamentals for autumn display when the insignificant white flowers turn into masses of brilliant orange or orange-red berries. These are carried in dense clusters on gracefully arching branches for many weeks and are most useful in flower arrangements. The name is from the Greek *pyros*, fire, and *akanthos*, thorn, referring to the brilliantly coloured berries and the thorny branches.

Pyracantha angustifolia   China
Fire thorn
Erect shrub to 3 m bearing orange-red berries in autumn.

P. coccinea   Eurasia
Fire thorn
Shrub to 5 m with scarlet fruit in autumn. There are many named cultivars of this species.

P. coccinea 'Keessenii'
As above, but fruit is orange-red.

PYROSTEGIA

Pyrostegia venusta

QUERCUS

Quercus suber

PYROSTEGIA
Bignoniaceae

This is a small genus of evergreen climbing shrubs, native to South America, of which one, *Pyrostegia venusta,* the familiar golden shower, is commonly cultivated.

Pyrostegia venusta　　　South America
Golden shower
Creeper to great height making a dense cover and needing a fairly strong support. It is grown chiefly for its brilliant display of orange-gold flowers that are borne in various seasons, depending on the climate. This is a vigorous plant in warm climates, thriving in ordinary soil, but best if watered regularly. It will only flower well in full sun, where it makes a spectacular show.

QUERCUS
Fagaceae

These are popular deciduous trees known as oaks, mostly from the northern hemisphere, and grown both as ornamentals and for the wood which makes fine furniture. The fruit is called an acorn and is largely used as pig food. Oaks need rich, moist soil. Of the many species grown in South Africa, the evergreen cork oak, *Quercus suber,* above, was selected.

Quercus suber　　　Southern Europe and
　　　　　　　　　　　Northern Africa
Cork oak or Kurkeik
Large evergreen tree and the bark is the source of commercial cork.

Q. suber (bark)

283

QUISQUALIS

Quisqualis indica

RANUNCULUS

Ranunculus asiaticus

R. asiaticus

QUISQUALIS
Combretaceae

There are four species in this genus of climbing shrubs native to the tropics of Asia and Africa, but only one is cultivated, *Quisqualis indica*.

Quisqualis indica South East Asia
Rangoon creeper
Creeper to 10 m or more. The flowers are fragrant, especially at night, opening white and deepening to pink and then red, in summer. A warm-climate plant requiring regular water, it also needs good soil and a sturdy support. Prune after flowering.

RANUNCULUS
Ranunculaceae

Of this large genus of about 250 species of worldwide distribution, one, *Ranunculus asiaticus*, is familiar to most gardeners as a showy, colourful, spring-flowering bulb which also makes a long-lasting cut flower. This species has been extensively hybridized to include single, double and frilled flower forms in a wide range of reds, yellows, oranges, pinks and white. Plant the forked tubers with the 'fingers' pointing down, in deep, enriched soil, and water well. The name is from the Latin *rana*, a frog, as some species are aquatics or waterside plants.

Ranunculus asiaticus South-eastern Europe and South-eastern Asia
Spring-flowering annual to 600 mm.

RAPHIOLEPIS

Raphiolepis x delacourii

RAVENALA

Ravenala madagascariensis

REINWARDTIA

Reinwardtia indica

R. indica

RAPHIOLEPIS
Rosaceae

A small genus of evergreen shrubs native to Asia, with leathery, shiny, dark green leaves and sprays of pink or white flowers which are followed by small purple or black fruits. These are tough wind-resistant shrubs which will grow in any soil. Propagate from cuttings, or watch for self-sown seedlings.

Raphiolepis x delacourii Garden hybrid
Shrub to 1,5 m; leaves obovate and flowers rosy pink in early spring.

R. indica China
Indian hawthorn
Evergreen shrub to 1,5 m; flowers white to pinkish, and black berries, often borne simultaneously with flowers, are carried for many months in spring and into summer.

RAVENALA
Strelitziaceae

There is only one species in this genus, *Ravenala madagascariensis*, commonly known as the Traveller's tree because rain water is collected in the leaf bases, making it useful for emergency drinking. Ravenala is the name used by the inhabitants of Madagascar.

Ravenala madagascariensis Madagascar
Traveller's tree
A strikingly dramatic evergreen accent plant to 20 m or more in its natural habitat with a number of trunks, each crowned with a fan of huge, banana-like leaves up to 3 m long. Spikes of greenish-white flowers appear in summer. Suited only to tropical and warm subtropical climates. Propagate from suckers.

REINWARDTIA
Linaceae

There is one species, or possibly two, in this genus from the mountains of northern India and China, named after K.G.K. Reinwardt, 1773-1822, Director of the Leyden Botanic Garden.

Reinwardtia indica India, China
Yellow flax
Small, herbaceous shrub to 1 m with bright yellow flowers up to 50 mm across profusely borne from autumn to spring. This is a most useful shrub as it will flower under large trees at a time of year when little else flowers in the shade. It will also grow in full sun. Grow in enriched soil, particularly if it is to compete with tree roots, and water well.

RHIGOZUM

Rhigozum obovatum

RHIPSALIDOPSIS

Rhipsalidopsis gaertneri

R. rosea

RHODODENDRON

Rhododendron hybrid

Rhododendron hybrid

RHIGOZUM
Bignoniaceae

Rhigozum is a small genus of twiggy, spiny, small-leafed evergreen shrubs native to Africa, with several species indigenous to the hot, arid central regions of South Africa. The most commonly cultivated species is *Rhigozum obovatum*.

Rhigozum obovatum Karoo and southern Orange Free State
Karoo Gold, Yellow pomegranate, Geelgranaat or Berggranaat
Shrub to 3 m, with sparse, tiny, blue-green leaves and covered with golden yellow flowers in spring and early summer, making a striking display, especially when seen in its dry natural surroundings. Grow in very well-drained soil in summer rainfall areas and water in winter; in winter rainfall areas grow in ordinary well-drained soil. This is a drought and frost-resistant shrub that needs full sun. Propagate from seed.

RHIPSALIDOPSIS
Cactaceae

This genus consists of two species of epiphytic much-branched cacti native to Brazil. The branches may be erect or pendent, with showy flowers carried at the tips, making them effective plants for hanging baskets. Usually grown indoors, they will grow outdoors in humid, frost-free areas in semi-shade, if kept permanently moist. Propagate from stem cuttings which should be dried for several days and then placed on sand until roots form.

Rhipsalidopsis gaertneri Brazil
Easter cactus
Cactus with flattened, pendulous stems and large, showy red flowers up to 80 mm across in spring.

R. rosea
As above, but flowers purplish-pink.

RHODODENDRON
Ericaceae

Botanically, this very large genus of 800 species includes azaleas, although these are usually considered by gardeners to be distinct from rhododendrons. The plants in this genus are native chiefly to the temperate regions of the northern hemisphere, particularly the Himalayas and the mountains of South East Asia. Although the genus includes plants ranging in size from ground covers to large trees, it is the shrubby species that are most commonly cultivated for their magnificent, showy, and often fragrant flowers. Most species are best in semi-shade, needing deep, well-composted acid soil, ample water and supplementary feeding. The name is from the Greek *rhodon*, rose, and *dendron*, tree.

Rhododendron hybrids Garden hybrid
Most rhododendrons are not suited to South African conditions.

R. indicum Japan
(*Azalea indica*)
Azalea

RHOEO

R. indicum

Rhoeo spathacea

Rhododendron hybrid

R. pulchrum var. *phoenicium*

Rhododendron hybrid

Evergreen shrub to 2 m, flowers in shades of red and pink, in spring.

R. pulchrum var. phoenicium China
(*Azalea phoenicea*)
Azalea
Evergreen shrub to 2 m, magenta flowers in spring.

R. indicum

RHOEO
Commelinaceae

There is one species in this genus, *Rhoeo spathacea*, a succulent evergreen perennial native to Mexico, Guatemala and the West Indies, which is usually grown as a greenhouse plant for its ornamental foliage, but which is also suitable as a house or stoep plant in humid, warm areas.

Rhoeo spathacea Mexico, Gautemala, West Indies
Boat lily
Perennial to 600 mm; leaves green, purple underneath; flowers insignificant, white, carried in boat-shaped bracts giving rise to a host of common names such as 'Three-men-in-a-boat'.

RHOICISSUS

Rhoicissus tomentosa

RHOICISSUS
Vitaceae

This is a small genus of evergreen climbers native to tropical and southern Africa of which one, *Rhoicissus tomentosa*, is commonly cultivated for its attractive foliage.

Rhoicissus tomentosa   Cape, Natal, Transvaal
Wild grape or Bosdruif
Climber to 3 m (more in nature); large grape-like leaves often turning red in winter, and clusters of reddish-purple, grape-like berries in autumn and winter. To succeed, this plant needs compost-enriched soil and ample water when young. Propagate from seed.

RHUS

Rhus pendulina

RHUS
Anacardiaceae

There are about 150 species in this genus of widespread distribution, found mainly in North America, Africa, the Mediterranean regions and the Far East. The genus includes evergreen and deciduous shrubs, trees and vines, with about 70 species indigenous to South Africa. The exotic species are grown for their brilliant autumn foliage; the indigenous species make tough wind and drought-resistant evergreen shrubs and attractive specimen trees. The leaves are usually three-foliolate with the petiole sometimes winged.

Rhus pendulina   Northern Cape
(*R. viminalis*)
White karee or Wit karee
Quick-growing tree to 5 m or more with willow-like habit and attractive light green foliage. A very attractive and tough specimen tree.

R. pyroides

R. pyroides   Widespread in South Africa, except in the Western Cape
Common wild currant
An extremely variable, dense shrub up to 5 m, often thorny, frequently found near watercourses in nature.

RHYNCHELYTRUM

Rhynchelytrum repens

RHYNCHELYTRUM
Poaceae (=Gramineae)

A genus of annual and perennial grasses native to Africa, with a number found in South Africa. One indigenous species, *Rhynchelytrum repens*, has colourful, feathery flower spikes, making it a useful ornamental for a sunny rockery pocket.

Rhynchelytrum repens   Natal, Transvaal
(*R. roseum*)
Natal red-top, Bergrooigras or Rooihaargras
Short-lived perennial or annual grass with stalks to 1 m; flower spike to 150 mm long, rosy purple fading to pink and finally silver, making it most attractive and useful in both fresh and dried flower arrangements.

RICINUS

Ricinus communis

RICINUS
Euphorbiaceae

There are numerous cultivars of the only species in this genus, a strikingly ornamental foliage plant thought to be of African origin but found widespread in the tropical and temperate regions of the world. The poisonous seeds are extensively used in the manufacture of soap, paint and lubricants, as well as medicinally. These plants thrive under any conditions in warm climates, and are easily raised from the large, tick-like seeds which give the genus its name, *ricinus* being the Latin for a tick.

Ricinus communis   Tropical Africa
Castor oil plant, Castor bean or Kasterolie
Annual growing rapidly to 5 m, or in the tropics to 10 m, with dramatic foliage often a deep green to purplish-red, with insignificant flowers and showy, prickly, bright red seed capsules.

ROBINIA

Robinia hispida

R. pseudoacacia

ROBINIA
Fabaceae (=Leguminosae) Subfam. Faboideae (=Papilionoideae)

North America is the home of this genus of deciduous flowering trees and shrubs widely grown as ornamentals for their attractive foliage and especially their masses of pea-flowers, often fragrant, carried in dainty, drooping sprays in the spring. Flowers vary in colour from white, through pink to purple. Robinias are frost resistant and will grow in all but tropical or subtropical areas. Plant in good soil and full sun.

Robinia hispida   North America
Rose acacia
Small tree to 3 m bearing masses of rose-pink flowers in spring and summer.

R. pseudoacacia   Europe and Central America
False acacia or Valsakasia
A deciduous tree to 6 m in cultivation Branches with spines and white fragrant flowers are borne on dense racemes in late spring.

ROELLA

Roella ciliata

ROMULEA

Romulea rosea var. *rosea*

RONDELETIA

Rondeletia amoena

ROELLA
Campanulaceae

This is a genus of indigenous evergreen small shrubs and perennials found mostly in the south-western Cape with a few extending to Natal. The most attractive species is *Roella ciliata*.

Roella ciliata — South-western Cape

Evergreen perennial to 400 mm high with exquisitely marked lilac-blue flowers up to 50 mm across in summer. In its natural habitat this plant grows in full sun in poor, gravelly, well-drained soil, near enough to the sea to benefit from coastal humidity, and is not easy to cultivate in other climatic regions.

ROMULEA
Iridaceae

This is a genus of cormous plants native to the Mediterranean regions and Africa with a number of species indigenous to South Africa. These dwarf plants with grass-like foliage bear satiny, brightly coloured flowers in a variety of shades including pale blue, cream, yellow, and a wide range of pinks. Romuleas will grow in the sandy soil of its natural habitat, and in heavy clay as well. Most species need copious water in the growing season and a very dry dormant period. Full sun is essential, otherwise the plants will not flower. Freely self-seeding, romuleas can be raised from seed or by lifting and dividing the clumps of pea-sized corms.

Romulea rosea var. **rosea** — South-western Cape
Froetang

Dwarf corm to 150 mm with rose-pink flowers up to 50 mm or more across, borne in spring. This species grows in a wet clay soil similar to its natural habitat.

RONDELETIA
Rubiaceae

A genus of evergreen shrubs from tropical America of which *Rondeletia amoena* is the one mostly cultivated in South Africa. Named after a sixteenth-century French physician, Rondelet.

Rondeletia amoena — Southern Mexico to Panama

Shrub to about 1,2 m with pink flowers in terminal panicles borne in spring. Propagate from cuttings.

ROSA ROSMARINUS ROTHMANNIA

Rosa canina

Rosmarinus officinalis

Rothmannia capensis

Rosa 'Dorothy Perkins'

R. capensis (fruit)

ROSA
Rosaceae

From the temperate regions of the northern hemisphere come these universal favourites, loved and cultivated for centuries for the beauty and fragrance of their flowers. Most modern roses (and new varieties are produced each year) resent competition from the roots of trees and nearby shrubs, require good soil, full sun, and ample water. They also need regular pruning and spraying against insect pests and fungus when necessary. Conversely, some of the old-fashioned rambling roses (which bear clusters of small flowers instead of large single flowers) will thrive for years in a state of apparent neglect, covering themselves with blossom in their flowering season. There are many books available for the rose enthusiast.

Hybrid roses

Rosa canina
❶ ✿ ❀ ☼
Dog rose

Rosa 'Dorothy Perkins'
❶ ✿ ❀ ☼
A climber.

ROSMARINUS
Lamiaceae (= Labiatae)

There are not more than three or four species in this genus of evergreen shrubs from the Mediterranean regions. One species, the strongly aromatic *Rosmarinus officinalis,* has been cultivated for thousands of years, often for its real or imagined medicinal properties, among them the belief that it stimulates the mind; hence the saying, 'Rosemary for remembrance'. More prosaically, this shrub is extensively used in perfumery and medicine, as well as being a popular culinary herb. The name has an attractive origin from the Latin *ros,* dew, and *marinus,* the sea, a reference to its seaside habitat.

Rosmarinus officinalis   Mediterranean
❶ ✿ ❀ ☼ ⓕ ⓦ   region, Spain, Portugal
Rosemary
Evergreen shrub to 1,25 m, occasionally to 2 m; flowers not very showy, pale blue, rarely pink or white. This is a tough, wind and drought-resistant plant, easily grown in any soil, requiring only adequate drainage and full sun. It makes a good rockery plant, or a container plant near a pathway where the aromatic leaves may be picked and crushed by passers-by.

ROTHMANNIA
Rubiaceae

Shrubs or trees with showy, solitary flowers, bell-shaped and borne in late spring. Only one species, *Rothmannia capensis,* is grown in cultivation.

Rothmannia capensis   Widespread in
                 South and eastern Transvaal, Natal
❶ ✿ ❀ ☼ ⓦ   and eastern coastal areas
Wildekatjiepiering
Attractive small tree with leathery, elliptic, glossy, dark green leaves. Flowers are cream and yellow, solitary, widely bell-shaped with maroon stripes in the throat.

ROYSTONEA

RUDBECKIA

Roystonea regia

Rudbeckia fulgida

R. hirta 'Double Gloria Daisy'

R. hirta 'Gloria Daisy'

ROYSTONEA
Arecaceae (= Palmae)

From the Caribbean and surrounding areas comes this small genus of neat, slender and most ornamental palms. The single trunks are tall and smooth, sometimes swollen in places, and carry large, arching fronds which are most decorative. These quick-growing palms make excellent lawn specimens and are resistant to sea winds. Plant in rich, well-drained soil and water well. Only suited to warm, coastal areas.

Roystonea regia   Cuba
Royal palm
Tree to 15 m, feathery fronds to 3 m long. A handsome ornamental which has considerable economic importance in its native habitat where all parts are used; the young leaf shoots are edible, the older leaves are used for thatch, the trunk yields a form of sago, and oil is obtained from the fruit.

RUDBECKIA
Asteraceae (= Compositae)

This is a genus of herbaceous annuals, biennials and perennials from North America, with showy, daisy-like flowers in a range of warm, glowing colours. These are useful plants for mixed borders and remain in flower until well into autumn. Easily grown from seed in any soil, they flower best in full sun. The genus is named after Olaf Rudbeck, 1660 – 1740, a Swedish botanist and Counsellor of Linnaeus. The common name, cone flower, refers to the dark, conical centres.

Rudbeckia fulgida   North America
Cone flower
Perennial to 1 m; orange-yellow flowers in summer.

R. hirta 'Double Gloria Daisy'   North America
Annual, more often perennial to 1 m with double flower heads up to 150 mm across in summer.

R. hirta 'Gloria Daisy'
As above.

R. hirta var. *pulcherrima*

R. hirta var. **pulcherrima**
As above except flowers banded in maroon.

RUELLIA

Ruellia macrantha

R. makoyana

RUMEX

Rumex usambarensis

RUMOHRA

Rumohra adiantiformis

RUELLIA
Acanthaceae

A genus of evergreen perennials and shrubs, mainly from the tropical regions of the world, grown either indoors or out for their showy, trumpet-shaped, deeply veined flowers. Given ample water, enriched and well-drained soil, these plants will grow outdoors in warm subtropical areas; in other climates, treat as greenhouse plants. Propagate from cuttings.

Ruellia macrantha — Brazil
Shrub to 2 m with large, showy, rose-purple flowers in winter and spring.

R. makoyana — Brazil
Perennial to 600 mm; leaves marked with white above, purple beneath; flowers red-purple.

RUMEX
Polygonaceae

A genus of weedy perennials widespread in the temperate regions of the world.

Rumex usambarensis — Northern temperate regions
A spreading, peculiar shrub-like plant reaching 2 m. The leaves are simple and masses of small red flowers, borne in racemes, appear in early summer. Flowers are peculiar because petals are absent.

RUMOHRA
Polypodiaceae

Only one species of terrestrial ferns, *Rumohra adiantiformis*, from tropical and subtropical parts in Africa.

Rumohra adiantiformis — Widespread
Seweweeksvaring
Leaves are leathery and broadly pyramidal.

RUSCUS

Ruscus aculeatus

RUSPOLIA

Ruspolia hypccrateriformis var. *australis*

RUSSELIA

Russelia equisetiformis

RUSCUS
Liliaceae

This is a genus of three species of evergreen rhizomatous shrubs native to western Europe and the Mediterranean regions, whose chief merit lies in the fact that they will thrive most successfully as ground covers in dense shade under large trees. In addition the stiff, leathery 'leaves' (in actual fact, flattened stems) are totally wind resistant. Showy red or yellow berries are borne on the female plants when both male and female plants are present, although seldom abundantly even in their natural habitat. Plant in any soil in full shade and propagate by division, or seed if you can get it.

Ruscus aculeatus   Europe, Mediterranean region
Box holly or Butcher's broom
Shrub to 1 m; stiff, spiny, pointed 'leaves' and red or yellow fruit.

RUSPOLIA
Acanthaceae

There are four species in this genus of evergreen shrubs native to Africa and Madagascar, with one species, *Ruspolia hypocrateriformis* var. *australis,* spreading from tropical Africa into the northern Transvaal. These somewhat straggling shrubs bear showy, rounded heads of flowers in shades of red and pink at the tips of the branches. Propagate from cuttings.

Ruspolia hypocrateriformis var. **australis**   Tropical Africa
Small straggling shrub with showy heads of crimson flowers in summer.

RUSSELIA
Scrophulariaceae

This is a genus of shrubs and sub-shrubs from Cuba and Central America, which form large, straggly clumps of rush-like, drooping stems, with tiny leaves and long, pendent sprays of vivid red tubular flowers. Unusual and showy, russelias look striking when grown in large, white-painted containers which set off the cascading red flowers. Easily grown in ordinary garden soil, they are also good for rockeries or hanging baskets. Propagate from cuttings.

Russelia equisetiformis   Mexico
(*R. juncea*)
Coral bush
Much-branched shrub to 1,25 m; branches pendent, bearing coral-red flowers almost continuously.

Ruttya fruticosa

x Ruttyruspolia 'Phyllis van Heerden'

RUTTYA
Acanthaceae

Three species of evergreen shrubs are contained in this genus, one of which is indigenous to South Africa. However, the most commonly cultivated species, *Ruttya fruticosa*, is native to East Africa.

Ruttya fruticosa East Africa
Jammy mouth
Evergreen shrub to 4 m, less in cultivation, with showy red or yellow flowers with a shiny dark blotch in the centre, giving rise to the highly memorable common name. Flowers are borne for a long period in summer. Propagate from cuttings and prune hard after flowering.

X RUTTYRUSPOLIA
Acanthaceae

This is a bi-generic hybrid between the two genera *Ruttya* and *Ruspolia*, the original specimen of which was found in the wild by a South African plant collector, Mrs. Phyllis van Heerden. Subsequent experiments confirmed that this unusual plant was indeed a new hybrid. This shrub has something in common with both parent plants and has striking pinky mauve flowers freely borne in summer.

x Ruttyruspolia 'Phyllis van Heerden'
(*Ruttya ovata* x *Ruspolia hypocrateriformis*) South Africa

A small shrub with showy heads of dark pink flowers in summer. Propagate from cuttings.

SAINTPAULIA

Saintpaulia ionantha cv.

SAINTPAULIA
Gesneriaceae

Possibly the most popular house plant of all are saintpaulias, or African violets, native to tropical East Africa. With their rosettes of thick, heart-shaped leaves and showy heads of flowers which appear at regular intervals throughout the year, this dainty plant is much loved. Saintpaulias have a reputation for being somewhat touchy – if conditions are not right they will not flower. Warmth and humidity are essential, and plenty of light but not direct sun. Good professional advice is a must for the novice who is keen to grow these attractive plants successfully.

Saintpaulia ionantha cvs.   Coastal East Africa
African violet
Perennial to 100 mm with showy heads of flowers in a wide range of colours including every shade of pink, purple, violet, mauve and white. These appear at regular intervals throughout the year.

SALIX

Salix babylonica

S. discolor

SALIX
Salicaceae

A genus including some attractive specimen trees native to the colder climates of the northern hemisphere. Flowers are insignificant, arranged in catkins and precede the new foliage in spring. They prefer a moist habitat and one species, *Salix babylonica*, is a common sight along streams in all four provinces. They grow rapidly from mature wood cuttings – the best and quickest way to propagate them.

Salix babylonica   China
Weeping willow, Treurwilg or Wilgerboom
A deciduous tree to 5 m.

S. discolor   North America
Pussy willow
A small tree or bushy deciduous shrub bearing silky catkins in spring.

SALPIGLOSSUS

Salpiglossus sinuata

SALPIGLOSSUS
Solanaceae

A genus of about five species of erect annual, biennial and perennial herbaceous plants native to Chile. Most popular for the flower garden is the *Salpiglossus sinuata*; grown in enriched, well-drained soil it flowers abundantly. The name is from the Greek *salpin*, a tube, and *glossa*, a tongue, referring to the tongue-like style in the corolla tube.

Salpiglossus sinuata   Chile
Painted tongue or Trumpet flower
A showy annual bearing large 60 mm funnel-shaped flowers brilliantly coloured yellow or orange or dark purple to scarlet or nearly blue, but all are prominently veined in contrasting colours in summer.

SALVIA

Salvia africana-lutea

S. dolomitica

S. involucrata

S. chamelaeagnea

S. farinacea

S. leucantha

S. greggii 'Rosea'

SALVIA
Lamiaceae (=Labiatae)

This is a very large genus of annuals, perennials, biennials and shrubs with worldwide distribution; a number of species are indigenous to South Africa. Many species have aromatic leaves and a number make showy garden plants. Almost all species are easily grown in full sun and ordinary garden soil. The name is from the Latin *salveo*, meaning to save, or heal, as some species have medicinal properties. The well-known flavouring herb, sage, *Salvia officinalis*, belongs in this genus.

Salvia africana-lutea South-western Cape
(*S. aurea*)
Beach salvia, Golden salvia, Strandsalie or Geelblomsalie
Evergreen shrub to 2 m with grey leaves and yellow flowers which soon fade to brick-red and then reddish-brown. After the petals fall the calyx, which is purplish-yellow, remains. Spring and early summer is flowering time. Water in winter.

S. chamelaeagnea Southern Cape
Much-branched shrublet to 1 m; leaves are leathery; light blue flowers are borne in summer.

S. dolomitica Transvaal
Perennial to 1 m with greyish-green woolly leaves and pink flowers borne in spring.

S. farinacea North America
Perennial to 1 m. Spikes of intense violet-blue flowers appear in summer. Excellent in mixed borders or rockeries. Propagate by division, or seed.

S. greggii 'Rosea' North America
Sub-shrub to 1 m; red flowers in autumn.

S. involucrata Mexico
Perennial to 1,2 m; pink or red flowers up to 50 mm long are produced in late summer and autumn.

S. leucantha Mexico
Shrub or woody perennial to 600 mm with greyish-green leaves, woolly purple calyces and white, nectar-filled flowers. Easily grown in any soil. Cut back hard after flowering.

S. microphylla Mexico
(*S. grahamii*)
Shrub to 1 m; spikes of red tubular flowers.

CONTINUED

SALVIA

S. splendens

S. microphylla

S. splendens   South America
Scarlet salvia or Rooi-salie
Perennial or sub-shrub to nearly 3 m in its natural habitat. Usually grown as a garden annual to 400 mm for its brilliant display in bedding schemes or the mixed border. Flowers are bright scarlet and the plants bloom for many months of the year in warm climates.

SAMBUCUS

Sambucus canadensis

S. nigra 'Albo-variegata'

SAMBUCUS
Caprifoliaceae

A genus of perennials, shrubs and small trees. Some are grown for their foliage and others for their large showy heads of white or creamy-white flowers that are followed by shiny black or red berries. Some berries are edible in certain species but poisonous in others. Elders are best grown in rich, moist soil and propagated from seeds, cuttings or suckers.

Sambucus canadensis   North America
American elder or Kanadese vlier
Shrub to 3 m with white flowers in large, flattened, showy clusters up to 250 mm across, borne in early summer and followed by purple-black edible fruits.

S. nigra 'Albo-variegata'   Europe, North Africa, Western Asia
European elder or Europese vlier
Shrub or tree to 10 m. Leaves are variegated with white; the foliage is disagreeably pungent when bruised. Flowers, produced in late spring, are creamy-white, in large flattened heads up to 200 mm across and heavily fragrant. Edible black berries follow the flowers.

SANCHEZIA

Sanchezia nobilis

SANCHEZIA
Acanthaceae

Named after Josef Sanchez, an early professor of botany at Cadiz, this genus of shrubs, climbers and perennials is native to Central and South America. One species only is cultivated, *Sanchezia nobilis*, a handsome foliage plant.

Sanchezia nobilis   South America
Evergreen to 1,5 m and grown for its large, leathery, glossy leaves which are veined yellow or white. Flowers are yellow and appear in summer but are not particularly showy. An outdoor plant in really warm temperate to subtropical areas, this shrub also makes a good indoor or stoep plant, needing plenty of sun in cooler areas. Propagate from cuttings.

SANDERSONIA

Sandersonia aurantiaca

SANDERSONIA
Liliaceae

Only one tuberous-rooted perennial, native to South Africa, in this genus.

Sandersonia aurantiaca   South Africa
Chinese lantern flower, Christmas bells or Geelklokkie
Climbing plant to 600 mm with lanceolate leaves, often tipped with a tendril, and producing beautiful urn-shaped, globose orange flowers at Christmas time. It prefers semi-shade and enjoys a soil high in organic content as well as regular watering. It is to be hoped that nurserymen will commercialize this relative of *Gloriosa* in a big way.

SANSEVIERIA

Sansevieria pearsonii

S. trifasciata

SANSEVIERIA
Liliaceae

Although most often grown as house plants for their ornamental foliage, sansevierias will grow out of doors in most warm areas. The plants in this genus are grown commercially in a small way for their strong, white leaf fibres, known as bowstring hemp. Indoors, do not over water, and plant in well-drained soil; outdoors they grow easily in any soil. Propagate by division or leaf cuttings, which produce roots if placed upright in sand.

Sansevieria pearsonii   Tropical Africa
Evergreen perennial; short stemmed or without a stem; leaves stiff, erect, cylindrical, up to 1,5 m long with dark green vertical stripes. Flowers are white or tinged pink, produced in a spray up to 1 m long.

S. trifasciata   Angola
Snake plant, Mother-in-law's tongue or Skoonma-se-tong
Evergreen perennial. Stemless, with stiff, erect leaves to over 1 m long in length, silvery or creamy-green with black or dark green horizontal stripes.

SANTOLINA

Santolina chamaecyparissus

SANTOLINA
Asteraceae (=Compositae)

A genus of hardy dwarf evergreen shrubs, native to the Mediterranean areas and grown mainly for their finely divided and aromatic foliage. Santolinas are useful for front of shrub borders or as ground covers on sloping ground. The name is from the Latin *sanctum*, holy, and *linum*, flax.

Santolina chamaecyparissus   Mediterranean
Lavender cotton or Sipreskruid
Much-branched shrub to 500 mm with silky, grey-white, fern-like foliage and daisy-like yellow summer flowers.

SAPONARIA

Saponaria officinalis

SARACA

Saraca thaipingensis

SARITAEA

Saritaea magnifica

SAPONARIA
Caryophyllaceae

This is a genus of annuals, biennials and perennials from the Mediterranean region, easily cultivated in any soil for their pink, red or white flowers. Some species are woody, others very invasive, but grown in good soil and kept under control, they make a most rewarding show in early summer. They are particularly good where less tough plants do not thrive.

Saponaria officinalis Europe and Asia

Bouncing Betty or Soapwort
Stout, rhizomatous perennial to 1 m, forming spreading clumps. They are drought, frost, and wind resistant. Rounded heads of fragrant pink and white flowers appear in early summer. Propagate by division. The juice of the crushed leaves forms a lather in water and has been used as a soap substitute, hence the common name, as well as the generic name which is from the Latin *sapo,* meaning soap.

SARACA
Fabaceae (=Leguminosae) Subfam. Caesalpinioideae

A genus of small trees from the tropical forests of South East Asia, grown as ornamentals in warm, damp climates for their masses of flowers produced in shades of yellow and red. These trees grow beneath taller trees in their natural habitat and therefore require shade, preferably that of taller trees. Soil should be rich, moist and well drained.

Saraca thaipingensis Malay Peninsula

Tree to 10 m; yellow flowers are flushed with red.

SARITAEA
Bignoniaceae

There are two species of climbers in this genus native to South America of which one, *Saritaea magnifica,* is cultivated for its showy clusters of flowers.

Saritaea magnifica South America

Creeper to 3 m with attractive, glossy, leathery leaves and large, showy rose to mauve trumpet-shaped flowers up to 75 mm long.

SATYRIUM

Satyrium acuminatum

S. coriifolium

S. carneum

S. erectum

SATYRIUM
Orchidaceae

This is a genus of deciduous, tuberous, terrestrial orchids, native to Asia and Africa with a number of species indigenous to South Africa. From a small rosette of sometimes only two leaves, a stout stem appears bearing a dense spike of flowers in spring and summer. Requirements vary according to whether the plant is native to the winter or summer rainfall area but most require full sun, adequate moisture and good, well-drained soil.

Satyrium acuminatum — South-western Cape
Height to 450 mm with flower spikes to 300 mm long and densely packed with white flowers produced in spring.

S. carneum — South-western Cape
Rooikappie
Height to 450 mm with flower spikes to 150 mm long and densely packed with deep pinky red flowers in spring and summer. Strictly protected.

S. coriifolium — South-western Cape
Ewwatrewwa or Oumatrewwa
Height 300 to 450 mm; orange flowers are borne in spring.

S. erectum — South-western Cape and Namaqualand
Height to 350 mm with red-pink flowers.

SAXIFRAGA

Saxifraga stolonifera

SAXIFRAGA
Saxifragaceae

A large and varied genus of annuals, biennials and perennials native to the mountains and rocky places in the temperate, sub-Arctic and alpine regions of the world. A number are cultivated as garden plants, and numerous hybrids have been raised as these are most attractive little plants. The name is from the Latin *saxum,* rock or stone, and *frango,* to break, either referring to an ancient medicinal treatment for bladder stones or because of the ability of the roots of these plants to penetrate rock in many of their natural habitats.

Saxifraga stolonifera — East Asia
Mother-of-thousands or Jodebaard
Dwarf perennial to 200 mm. Suitable for indoor culture, with tufts of rounded green leaves veined in white, with reddish undersides, and spikes of dainty white, cream or red flowers borne in spring. Easily propagated by the numerous runners it produces, this habit also makes the plant ideal for basket culture.

301

SCABIOSA

Scabiosa africana

S. atropurpurea

S. atropurpurea 'Grandiflora'

S. columbaria

SCABIOSA
Dipsacaceae

A genus of annuals and perennials of widespread distribution in the temperate regions. Some species make colourful additions to the mixed border and a number of cultivars of both annual and perennial species exist. Colours are in the mauve-pink range, varying from white to a deep velvety purple; the blooms last well in water. Grow from seed or propagate by division. Scabiosas will grow in any soil, preferably enriched, and in full sun.

Scabiosa africana South-western Cape
A shrubby, evergreen perennial to 1 m with blue-mauve or white flowers on long stems, borne in spring, and suitable for cutting. Cut back after flowering to prevent the plants getting straggly.

S. atropurpurea Southern Europe
Pincushions or Sweet scabiosa
Erect annual to 600 mm with flowers in all shades of pink from almost white to crimson and purple.

S. atropurpurea 'Grandiflora'
Southern Europe
As above, but flower heads large.

S. columbaria Europe, Asia, Africa, including South Africa
Perennial to 600 mm; flowers mauve, pink and white, up to 50 mm across.

SCADOXUS

Scadoxus membranaceus

S. multiflorus subsp. *multiflorus*

SCADOXUS
Amaryllidaceae

All species in this genus were formerly classified under the genus *Haemanthus*, from which they differ in not having a true bulb but a rhizome or a globose bulb with definite rhizomatous parts. Also their leaves are not distinctly distichous and they are thin-textured with a definite middle nerve. Their diploid chromosome number is 18 compared to 16 in the case of the *Haemanthus*. *Scadoxus* need compost-rich, well-drained soil and a moist, warm climate. Grown for their summer and autumn blooms.

Scadoxus membranaceus Eastern coastal areas from Zululand to Stilbaai, Southern Cape
Flowers are in a dense umbellate head resembling a powder puff, and have bright coloured involucre bracts.

S. multiflorus subsp. *katharinae*

Sceletium concavum

Schefflera arboricola

S. puniceus

S. arboricola 'Variegatum'

S. multiflorus subsp. **katharinae** Natal
Catherine wheel
Bulbous plant to 300 mm; leaves thin, up to 360 mm long and 150 mm wide; flower heads to 250 mm across; flowers bright red, lobes spreading. The most beautiful of all scadoxus and a superb cut flower.

S. multiflorus subsp. **multiflorus**
Widespread in northern and eastern Transvaal and Swaziland
Blood lily or Bloedlelie
To 450 mm high; blood-red flowers to 25 mm long with involucre bracts reflexed.

S. puniceus Eastern parts of Africa, from Eastern Cape to Ethiopia
Paintbrush
To 500 mm high and pale scarlet flowers. Floral head is 100 mm across.

SCELETIUM
Mesembryanthemaceae

A genus of 22 succulent species distributed in the dry areas of the Cape Province. The desiccated leaf becomes a dried skeleton; hence the botanical name. The plant is a short-stemmed sub-shrub which develops spreading branches. Terminal white flowers appear in spring.

Sceletium concavum Cape Province
Flowers are 40 mm across with fine petals that are white at the tips, becoming yellow in the centre.

SCHEFFLERA
Araliaceae

From the tropical and subtropical regions come the shrubs and small trees in this genus. Some of these are grown for their foliage and are useful either indoors or outdoors if planted in warm areas. Flowers are profusely borne in long spikes that on the whole are insignificant in colour and form.

Schefflera arboricola Subtropical regions
Hawaiian elf
When young this resembles a miniature *Brassaia*. Palmate foliage is glossy green, 150 mm across, with seven to eight leaflets arranged in a circle. An attractive, successful indoor plant.

S. arboricola 'Variegatum'
As above, but with variegated foliage.

SCHINUS

Schinus molle

S. terebinthifolius

SCHINUS
Anacardiaceae

This is a genus of evergreen trees, mainly from South America. Some make lovely ornamental specimens but equally useful as drought and wind-resistant shade trees.

Schinus molle　　　　　　　　Peru
🌸🐝🦋🌱☼Ⓦ
Pepper tree or Peperboom
Evergreen tree to 20 m; the willowy, finely cut foliage is extremely graceful, and leaves have a delightfully peppery fragrance. This tree is dense enough to give deep shade in the hot, dry areas where it thrives. The rose-red berries are decorative in summer and give off a spicy scent when crushed.

S. terebinthifolius　　　　　　Brazil
🌸🐝🦋🌱☼Ⓦ
Brazilian pepper tree or Brasiliaanse peperboom
Shrub or tree to 6 m, not willowy like *Schinus molle* but with attractive foliage and red berries in late summer. Not as well suited to hot dry climates as *Schinus molle*, this tree makes an excellent coastal windbreak. Freely self-seeding.

SCHIZANTHUS

Schizanthus pinnatus

SCHIZANTHUS
Solanaceae

A small genus of annuals and biennials from Chile. Schizanthus are grown for their showy, colourful flowers borne in profusion in greenhouses, indoors, or in temperate climates in a summer border. The lovely, exotic flowers fully deserve their common names; the ferny foliage is attractive too. Flowers are in every shade of pink and mauve with yellow blotched centres. Good, well-drained soil is required, with ample water and semi-shade or full sun.

Schizanthus pinnatus　　　　Chile
🦋☼
Poor man's orchid, Butterfly flower, Skoenlapperblom or Armmansorgidee
Annual to 1,2 m, with showy flowers often blotched or bi-coloured. Modern cultivars are more compact than the species. Flowering season is variable – winter in warmer regions or spring and early summer where it is cooler.

SCHIZOSTYLIS

Schizostylis coccinea

SCHIZOSTYLIS
Iridaceae

There are two species in this South African genus, of which only one, *Schizostylis coccinea,* and its cultivars, is grown.

Schizostylis coccinea　Mountains of North-eastern Cape, Orange Free State,
🌸🦋🌢☼　　　Natal and Transvaal
River lily or Rivierlelie
Rhizomatous perennial with very showy, starry crimson flowers up to 50 mm across carried on spikes 750 mm high in summer. In its natural habitat this plant grows near water and needs similar conditions in the garden, with good soil and shade for part of the day. It also makes an attractive pot plant. Propagate by division but only when the clumps become large as this plant takes some time to recover from being disturbed.

SCHLUMBERGERA

Schlumbergera bridgesii

S. truncata

SCHLUMBERGERA
Cactaceae

From Brazil come the three species of epiphytic cacti in this genus, all of which are grown for their abundance of flowers in autumn, winter and spring. Usually grown indoors or on stoeps as they make good plants for hanging baskets. Grow in rich, porous soil, and feed and water regularly. Easily propagated from stem cuttings.

Schlumbergera bridgesii Brazil
Christmas cactus or Kersfeeskaktus
Low-growing cactus with flattened, arching stems and large, cerise, nearly regular flowers in winter. The drooping habit makes it ideal for hanging baskets.

S. truncata Brazil
(*Zygocactus truncatus*)
Crab cactus or Krapkaktus
Similar to above but margins of the stem joints are sharply 2 to 4 serrated with showy pink, irregular flowers in autumn.

SCHOTIA

Schotia afra var. *afra*

S. brachypetala

SCHOTIA
Fabaceae (=Leguminosae) Subfam. Caesalpinioideae

A genus of shrubs and trees native to tropical and southern Africa, with feathery foliage and large clusters of red or cerise flowers. They withstand frost but grow faster in warmer areas. Propagate by sowing the large, bean-like seeds; transplant carefully.

Schotia afra var. afra Eastern Cape, Karoo
Boerboon
Spreading shrub or small tree to 5 m, often very gnarled and twisted in its natural arid habitat, with large dense clusters of very showy red or pinky red flowers and protruding red stamens borne in spring.

S. brachypetala Transkei, Natal, Transvaal
Tree fuschia, Weeping Boer-bean or Huilboerboon
Tree to 15 m in its natural habitat, but a small tree in cultivation with showy, drooping clusters of crimson flowers borne in spring. These produce copious nectar which drips from the flowers, giving rise to the tree's common name.

SCILLA

Scilla natalensis

S. peruviana

SCILLA
Liliaceae

A genus of bulbous perennials native to Europe, Africa and Asia with a few species in South Africa, notably *Scilla natalensis*, which is widespread in the summer rainfall regions.

Scilla natalensis Eastern Cape, Natal, Orange Free State and Transvaal
Blue squill or Blouberglelie
Bulb with a short tuft of broad leaves from which arise flower stems to 1 m high, carrying numerous small blue flowers in spring. Plant in full sun or semi-shade with the top half of the bulb above the ground. Soil should be rich and well drained.

S. peruviana Mediterranean region
Peruvian lily or Peru-lelie
Bulb to 450 mm or more with stout spikes of densely packed, intense blue-purple flowers. Not from Peru, despite the universally used common name.

SECHIUM

Sechium edule

SEDUM

Sedum morganianum

S. pachyphyllum

S. x rubrotinctum

S. spectabile 'Rubrum'

SECHIUM
Cucurbitaceae

There is only one species, *Sechium edule*, in this genus from the West Indies.

Sechium edule West Indies
Chayote or Soe-soe
A tendril-bearing, herbaceous vine to 6 m; yellow pumpkin-like flowers in late spring, followed by large, somewhat pear-shaped, creamy-white furrowed fruit, which is often cooked as a vegetable.

SEDUM
Crassulaceae

This is a very large genus of succulent annuals, perennials and sub-shrubs native to the northern temperate regions and the mountains of the tropics. Many species are cultivated for their bright starry flowers, attractive ornamental foliage and often neat, compact, pleasing habit.

Sedum morganianum Mexico
Lamb's tail or Lamstert
Perennial with trailing or hanging branches up to 3 m long, covered in thick succulent leaves up to 25 mm long and rosy purple flowers in spring. A handsome basket plant which is easily propagated by detaching and rooting the leaves.

S. pachyphyllum Mexico
Many fingers or Jelly beans
A sub-shrub to 250 mm, with curved, club-shaped leaves 20 to 40 mm long, 10 mm thick, greyish-green and red-tipped.

S. x rubrotinctum Garden hybrid
Jelly bean plant
Succulent to 150 mm, with stubby succulent leaves like jelly beans, which often turn bright red. Clusters of tiny, starry yellow flowers appear in winter. A very attractive rockery or edging plant.

S. spectabile 'Rubrum' China, Korea
Perennial to 450 mm with flat-topped heads of tiny, deep red flowers borne in late summer and autumn. They make useful plants in the rockery or mixed border.

SELAGINELLA

Selaginella sp.

SEMNANTHE

Semnanthe lacera

SENECIO

Senecio cineraria

S. echinata

SELAGINELLA
Selaginellaceae

This is not a flowering plant but a primitive fern. The genus has many species, some of which make excellent ground covers in hot, humid areas like Tzaneen in the north-eastern Transvaal. They favour well-drained soil and such light shadow localities as the floor of rain forests where they form delicate green mossy cushions. The stem is usually a dichotomously branched creeper bearing minute sessile leaves. Propagate by sub-division of the creeping stem.

Selaginella sp.   Widespread in forests and kloofs
Away from hot, humid areas this ground cover must be grown in a glass house.

SEMNANTHE
Mesembryanthemaceae

One species only in this genus.

Semnanthe lacera   Stellenbosch and Paarl Mountains
An erect succulent shrub to 1 m; branches are two-angled; leaves incurved; and solitary 'vygie' flowers of mauve-pink are borne in late spring.

SENECIO
Asteraceae (=Compositae)

This is one of the largest genera of flowering plants, possibly containing as many as 3 000 species, most of which are found all over the world. It includes annuals, perennials, succulents, shrubs, climbers and trees. Flowers are usually daisy-like and yellow, although most other colours occur. They are grown for their flowers and ornamental foliage (often succulent) and are easily raised from seed, division or cuttings. A large number of weeds are included, some poisonous to stock, and some species are poisonous to humans.

Senecio cineraria   Mediterranean region
Dusty Miller
Perennial to 750 mm with silvery grey to almost white foliage. Most ornamental in the sunny rockery or beneath red or bronze-leaved shrubs. Yellow flowers are borne in rounded clusters in summer.

CONTINUED

SENECIO

S. elegans

S. x hybridus

S. grandifolius

S. radicans

S. scaposus

S. echinata — Southern to eastern Cape
Erect, shrub-like perennial to 1 m with scrub-like foliage and terminal dark pink flower heads with yellow centres in spring.

S. elegans — South Africa
Wild cineraria or Wilde cineraria
Annual to 600 mm; showy purple flowers with yellow centres in spring.

S. grandifolius — Mexico
Large, evergreen, semi-woody shrub, 2 to 4 m high, with erect, purplish stems and large ovate leaves to 450 mm long, coarsely toothed. It flowers with large clusters of yellow heads in winter.

S. x hybridus — Originated as hybrids in England
Florist's cineraria
Mostly showy, herbaceous annuals to 300 mm. Widely cultivated for their single or double heads of spring flowers that range from white to shades of pink to red, purple and blue. *Senecio cruentus* is one of the supposed parents of this hybrid complex.

S. radicans — South Africa
Low-growing succulent forming mats of fleshy, pointed leaves, grey-green in colour, sometimes tinged with red and with a vertical stripe down each leaf. Flowers are white and sweetly scented.

S. scaposus — South Africa
Low-growing succulent with cylindrical grey-green leaves rising from a short stem; it bears yellow flowers. A very attractive container or rockery plant. Grow in full sun in well-drained soil.

S. tamoides — Eastern Cape, Natal
Canary creeper or Kanarieklimop
Vigorous evergreen to semi-evergreen climber which needs the support of a fence or other plants and dies back in severe winters. In autumn it is covered with large, showy heads of yellow daisy flowers. In nature this plant grows in the shade of trees and scrambles up them to flower in the sun, conditions which also suit it well in gardens. It can be pruned to make a spreading shrub suitable for a large rockery pocket.

S. tamoides

SERRURIA

Serruria florida

S. vallaris

SERRURIA
Proteaceae

There are between 40 and 50 species in this genus, all native to the south-western Cape, the best known of which is *Serruria florida*, the famous blushing bride, or pride of Franschhoek. This is one of the few species in which the fluffy or silky flower heads are surrounded by coloured bracts that greatly enhance the beauty of the flowers. These are usually in exquisitely delicate shades of pink and mauve, often silvery or creamy, with a few yellow-flowered species. Serrurias and their requirements need careful study before being planted.

Serruria florida South-western Cape mountains
Blushing bride, Trots-van-Franschhoek or Bergbruidjie
Evergreen shrub to 1,6 m; short-lived in cultivation with showy pale to dark pink flowers which appear in winter and spring. These are long-lasting cut flowers.

S. vallaris Cape Peninsula
Evergreen shrub to 500 mm; yellow inflorescences in spring.

SESBANIA

Sesbania punicea

SESBANIA
Fabaceae (=Leguminosae) Subfam. Fabiodeae (=Papilionoideae)

A genus of perennials and shrubs widespread in the warmer regions of the world. One species, *Sesbania punicea*, is commonly grown in gardens and has escaped to become a serious pest plant. Not only does this shrub invade and suppress natural vegetation but its seeds, leaves and flowers are extremely poisonous to small stock and birds, including domestic fowl.

Sesbania punicea South America
Rooikeurtjie
Shrub or small tree to 3 m with brilliant orange-red pea-flowers borne in showy sprays. It is illegal to grow this plant and gardeners are advised to replace any specimens they have with other plants.

SETCREASEA

Setcreasea pallida 'Purple Heart'

SETCREASEA
Commelinaceae

A small genus of low-growing, spreading perennials native to Mexico and southern Texas which are grown for their attractive, colourful foliage as indoor plants or as ground covers, rockery plants or bedding plants. Flowers are in shades of mauve and pink, sometimes quite showy. Setcreaseas are easily propagated by division or cuttings.

Setcreasea pallida 'Purple Heart'
(*S. purpurea*) Garden origin
Perennial to 400 mm high, usually less, and sprawling; leaves are green to intense violet-purple, up to 150 mm long, with violet-purple flowers. This can be a spectacular plant in a sunny rockery pocket.

SINNINGIA

Sinningia cardinalis

S. speciosa

SINNINGIA
Gesneriaceae

The perennials and shrubs in this genus are found from Mexico to Argentina and grown as greenhouse, indoor or stoep plants for their velvety, trumpet-shaped flowers carried in showy clusters above the dark green leaves, which are sometimes flushed with red. Flowers are usually in the red, purple, pink and white range. Grow in light, well-drained soil and water well (but not on the leaves) in the growing season. Propagate from seed or leaf cuttings.

Sinningia cardinalis   Tropical America
(*Gesneria cardinalis*)
Cardinal flower or Kardinaalblom
A tuberous plant with velvety leaves and bright scarlet tubular flowers in spring/summer.

S. speciosa   Brazil
Gloxinia or Brazilian gesneria
Perennial to less than 300 mm in the species. Violet-red or white flowers but has now been much hybridized, giving a wide range of colours and many showy cultivars.

SMODINGIUM

Smodingium argutum

SMODINGIUM
Anacardiaceae

A genus with only one species, *Smodingium argutum*.

Smodingium argutum   South Africa
A shrub or tree to 5 m, leaves digitately three-foliate; leaflets lanceolate and coarsely toothed. Flowers are insignificant. This is an excellent shade tree resembling species of the genus *Rhus*. Plant in enriched, well-drained soil. Once established it will grow fairly quickly in ordinary garden conditions. The leaves of this plant can cause great irritation if you are allergic to it.

SOLANDRA

Solandra maxima

SOLANDRA
Solanaceae

A small genus of climbing or sprawling, woody evergreen shrubs or vines from tropical America with huge creamy-gold flowers. These are large, sprawling, vigorous plants, requiring plenty of space and a sturdy support if grown as climbers. Wind and drought resistant, once established they are best in warmer areas and need protection from frost in cold climates. Propagate from cuttings and suckers.

Solandra maxima   Mexico
Cup-of-gold or Goldcup
Sprawling woody scrambler with large shiny leaves and golden flowers up to 250 mm across with a neat purple-brown stripe down the centre of each petal. Flowering season is variable depending on climate.

SOLANUM

Solanum capsicastrum

S. melongena var. *esculentum* cv.

S. pseudocapsicum 'Pattersonii'

S. jasminoides

S. muricatum

S. seaforthianium

S. wendlandii

SOLANUM
Solanaceae

A very large and cosmopolitan genus which includes potatoes, aubergines and other food plants as well as a few medicinal and poisonous plants and a number of ornamentals. The name is from the Latin, *solamen*, quieting, referring to the narcotic properties of some species.

Solanum capsicastrum — Brazil
False Jerusalem cherry
Spreading dwarf herbaceous shrub to 600 mm bearing ovoid, pointed scarlet to orange-red and even purple fruit, 12 mm across and up to 30 mm long.

S. jasminoides — Brazil
Potato creeper
Quick-growing climber to 5 m with trusses of bluish-white flowers up to 25 mm across in summer.

S. melongena var. esculentum cv. — Africa, Asia
Eggplant
This cultivar of the eggplant is a small annual ornamental shrub to 350 mm grown especially for its strange egg-like fruits up to 70 mm long.

S. muricatum — Andes
Pepino, Melon shrub, Pear melon or Spanspekboompie
Perennial sprawling sub-shrub to 600 mm high bearing violet-purple, ovoid fruit 90 mm long and 60 mm across. The fruit has firm, edible flesh resembling that of a sweet melon in taste and appearance — hence the common name. Easy to grow from cuttings in summer.

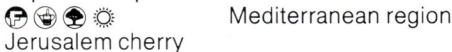

S. pseudocapsicum 'Pattersonii' — Mediterranean region
Jerusalem cherry
Spreading dwarf shrub bearing small green to yellow, or scarlet globose fruits which persist for many months. An ideal pot plant or rockery specimen. The fruits are poisonous.

S. seaforthianum — Tropical America
Slender woody vine to 3 m with delicate foliage and bearing large clusters of dainty violet-blue fragrant flowers in summer, followed by small, shiny red berries. A most attractive creeper where space is limited; it survives under adverse conditions and is very rewarding when well treated.

S. wendlandii — Tropical America
Potato creeper or Aartappelranker
Vigorous, bushy climber to 5 m with large showy clusters of bluish-mauve flowers up to 65 mm across, in summer.

SOLEIROLIA

Soleirolia soleirolii

SOLIDAGO

Solidago virgaurea

SPARAXIS

Sparaxis aartiloba

S. grandiflora subsp. *acutiloba*

SOLEIROLIA
Urticaceae

Only one species in this genus native to the Mediterranean.

Soleirolia soleirolii Mediterranean
◉◉◉Ⓕ
Peace-in-the-home or Baby's tears
A creeping herbaceous ground cover normally raised in greenhouses; suitable for hanging baskets. Leaves small, nearly orbicular and almost sessile.

SOLIDAGO
Asteraceae (=Compositae)

Goldenrods are a genus of rhizomatous perennials native largely to North America, with a few species found in Europe, Asia and South America. Most of them are tough, adaptable plants, growing in semi-shade or full sun and inclined to be invasive and weedy but there are a number of good garden cultivars which bring vivid colour to the mixed border in summer and especially autumn. Propagate by division of the clumps; many species self-seed.

Solidago virgaurea Europe, Asia,
Ⓕ◉◉☼ North Africa
European goldenrod or Goudroede
Perennial to 1 m with erect stems bearing dense spikes of tiny golden flowers in summer and autumn.

SPARAXIS
Iridaceae

A small genus of cormous perennials indigenous to South Africa and grown for their brilliantly coloured, showily marked flowers carried at the tips of slender, wiry stems. They make excellent plants for rockery pockets or outdoor containers and often thrive in a bed at the base of a sunny wall where they may self-seed freely. Soil should be well drained. Propagate from seed or offsets but do not disturb unnecessarily.

Sparaxis aartiloba South-western Cape
Ⓕ◉☼◉Ⓦ
Ferweeltjie
Corm to 200 mm with flowers 40 mm across; petals are pink-orange with a dark purple blotch at the base.

Sparaxis elegans South-western Cape
Ⓕ◉☼◉Ⓦ
A perennial erect corm to 450 mm. Flowers, yellow with black spots at the base of the petals, bloom in spring.

Sparaxis hybrid

S. hybrids

Sparaxis hybrids   Garden hybrid
Corm to 450 mm high; flowers up to 50 mm across are borne on wiry stems in colours ranging from a dark purple jewel-like brilliance to clear pastels, often blotched or marked in contrasting colours around a bright yellow centre.

SPARMANNIA

Sparmannia africana

SPARMANNIA
Tiliaceae

Named after Dr Anders Sparmann (1748-1820) Swedish naturalist and early traveller in South Africa, this genus contains seven species found in Africa and Madagascar, with two species in South Africa. Of these only one, *Sparmannia africana,* is cultivated.

Sparmannia africana   Eastern Cape

Wild hollyhock or Kaapse-stokroos
Large, evergreen, soft-wooded shrub or small tree up to 7 m high, grown for the showy flowers which appear from mid-winter to the end of spring. These most attractive flowers are white with a showy, colourful cluster of stamens. The foliage is also ornamental, the leaves large and bright green. Planted in good soil and watered regularly, sparmannias will grow quickly and easily in full sun or semi-shade. Propagate from cuttings.

SPARTIUM

Spartium junceum

SPARTIUM
Fabaceae (=Leguminosae) Subfam. Faboideae (=Papilionoideae)

A genus with only one species, the well-known Spanish broom, *Spartium junceum.*

Spartium junceum   Mediterranean region

Spanish broom
Shrub to 4 m with a mass of rush-like branches having tiny insignificant leaves and masses of sweetly scented yellow pea-flowers in spring. It is a wonderfully useful shrub, wind and drought resistant, and not fussy about soil. Pinch back or prune while young to form a rounded bush; heavy pruning after the plants have become leggy often kills them off.

SPATHIPHYLLUM

Spathiphyllum x hybridum

SPATHIPHYLLUM
Araceae

A genus of tropical perennials grown indoors for its ornamental foliage and striking, fragrant, anthurium-like flowers in shades of creamy-green and white. Grow in rich soil, water abundantly and avoid full sun, and the flowers will last for months.

Spathiphyllum x hybridum Garden hybrid
This is one of the many recent hybrids.

SPATHODEA

Spathodea campanulata

SPATHODEA
Bignoniaceae

A genus of two or three handsome evergreen trees native to tropical Africa and grown for the showy orange to scarlet tulip or bell-shaped flowers which appear in summer. Best suited to the warmer regions, these trees need deep, rich soil and protection from wind.

Spathodea campanulata Tropical Africa
Flame tree or Vlamboom
Tree to 20 m with rich scarlet flowers that are carried above the leaves in summer.

SPILOXENE

Spiloxene capensis

SPILOXENE
Hypoxidaceae

A genus of indigenous cormous plants with bright, starry flowers, some of which are attractively marked and blotched. White, yellow and pale pink flower forms occur. Found growing in damp, marshy places in their natural habitat, these flowers should be planted where they can be kept dry after they have blossomed in spring.

Spiloxene capensis South-western Cape
Sterretjies
Corm to 300 mm high, starry white flowers with showily marked centres, in spring.

SPIRAEA

Spiraea x *arguta*

S. x *bumalda* 'Atrorosea'

S. cantoniensis

SPIRAEA
Rosaceae

A genus of adaptable deciduous and evergreen shrubs native to the northern hemisphere and grown for their masses of white and pink flowers which are often fragrant. If left unpruned, the plants form large dense bushes with gracefully arching branches, making them most attractive when in bloom. These are tough, drought, frost and wind-resistant plants, but the garden cultivars need good feeding and watering for best results. Grow in full sun or semi-shade.

Spiraea x arguta Garden hybrid
Garland May
Shrub to 2 m with posies of tiny white flowers, 8 mm across, carried the length of the branches in spring.

S. x bumalda 'Atrorosea' Garden hybrid
Shrub to 400 mm; leaves coarsely serrated, and deep rose flowers in racemes, 50 mm long, are borne in summer.

S. cantoniensis China
Cape May
Shrub to 2,5 m; leaves serrated and arranged in umbels 25 to 35 mm across; white flowers are borne in spring.

SPREKELIA

Sprekelia formosissima

SPREKELIA
Amaryllidaceae

There is only one species in this genus, a bulb native to Mexico, *Sprekelia formosissima*.

Sprekelia formosissima Mexico
Maltese cross, Jacobean lily, Maltese kruis or Jakobslelie
Bulb to 400 mm grown for its bright crimson flowers up to 100 mm long, which usually appear before or with the leaves in late spring and summer. Plant in patio containers or in the rock garden and do not disturb the bulbs unless they become overcrowded. Soil should be enriched with compost, and water given regularly in the growing season. Propagate from seed or offsets.

315

STACHYS

Stachys rugosa var. *linearis*

STAPELIA

Stapelia coegaensis

S. peculiaris

S. rufa

STACHYS
Lamiaceae (=Labiatae)

A large genus of annuals, perennials and small shrubs with worldwide distribution. Most species are regarded as weeds, although one species has edible tubers and a few species are raised as ornamentals for their foliage and flowers. Easily grown, frost and drought resistant, and not at all fussy about soil, these plants will nevertheless give better results if grown in good soil and watered well.

Stachys rugosa var. **linearis**　　Eastern Cape
Boesmantee or Boesmankruie
Herbaceous shrub to 450 mm, densely white-tomentose in all parts. Leaves are slightly recurved with pink to lilac flowers arranged in small whorls in summer.

STAPELIA
Asclepiadaceae

A genus of low-growing succulents native to the arid regions of tropical and southern Africa. The star-shaped flowers are borne on the stubby leafless stems and come in rather dingy shades of purple and yellow, often fascinatingly marked or fringed, making them more interesting than attractive. Many species have a putrid smell which attracts insects and flies for pollination. Propagate from seed, or cuttings as they root easily.

Stapelia coegaensis　　Namaqualand
Small compound succulent to 120 mm high. Flowers are reddish-brown, 20 to 30 mm across, borne in late spring.

S. peculiaris　　Namaqualand
Succulent with erect stems to 100 mm. Flowers are yellowish-green mottled with pale purplish-brown. This plant is now known as *Tridentea peculiaris*.

S. rufa　　Karoo
Stems 100 to 220 mm high; late spring flowers, 30 to 50 mm across, whose reddish petals with yellow centres narrow to a point.

STENOCARPUS

Stenocarpus sinuatus

STICTOCARDIA

Stictocardia beraviensis

STIGMAPHYLLON

Stigmaphyllon ciliatum

STENOCARPUS
Proteaceae

A genus of about 20 species of evergreen trees and shrubs native to Australia and the Malay Archipelago, of which only one, *Stenocarpus sinuatus,* is commonly grown in South Africa.

Stenocarpus sinuatus　　　　　Australia
Firewheel tree or Vuurwielboom
A slow-growing tree 6 to 9 m high. Leaves are lucid green, up to 300 mm long and partly cut. Flowers are bright red, 25 mm long, arranged in umbels and appear in autumn.

STICTOCARDIA
Convolvulaceae

A genus of herbaceous climbers native to tropical Africa, Madagascar and Asia. Only one species, *Stictocardia beraviensis,* is grown in warmer parts.

Stictocardia beraviensis　　　Madagascar
Madagascar convolvulus
A fast-growing woody twiner, 6 to 9 m high, related to *Convolvulus* and bearing trumpet-shaped, bright crimson-yellow flowers. Plant in enriched, well-drained soil.

STIGMAPHYLLON
Malpighiaceae

Twining, woody vines of which only *Stigmaphyllon ciliatum* is grown generally in South Africa.

Stigmaphyllon ciliatum　　Tropical America
Brazilian golden vine, Orchid vine, Golden vine or Amasone-klimop
Slender, twining evergreen vine limited to hot, humid areas. Leaves bear hairs on the margin. Moth-like yellow flowers are borne in summer and autumn.

STRELITZIA

Strelitzia juncea

S. nicolai

S. reginae

S. reginae var. *lutea*

STRELITZIA
Strelitziaceae

A small genus of shrubby evergreen perennials indigenous to South Africa and grown for their striking foliage and, in some species, spectacularly showy flowers which resemble exotic birds poised for flight. Strelitzias resent disturbance and really only flower well when established. Plant in good, enriched soil and water regularly. Propagation is best from suckers, although the plants can be divided when the clumps become too large.

Strelitzia juncea Port Elizabeth area
This curious strelitzia has no leaves at all, just a dense cluster, 1 to 1,5 m high, of cylindrical, reed-like stalks. Flowers have bright orange sepals and a blue tongue.

S. nicolai Coastal districts of eastern Cape and Natal
Wild banana or Wilde-piesang
Tree-like plant to 6 m with large arching leaves. A lush, tropical-looking plant needing plenty of space and a warm climate, its flowers are the typical bird-of-paradise blooms but in muted shades of purple, blue and creamy-white. Spring and early summer blooming, these are definitely warm-climate plants.

S. reginae Eastern Cape
Crane flower, Bird-of-paradise or Kraanvoëlblom
Perennial to 1 m with large, greyish-green or green banana-like leaves, and striking flowers. They are familiar to most gardeners as the floral emblem of Natal (and also, strangely enough, of Los Angeles). These showy flowers, carried above the foliage, are wind resistant, making them most useful for coastal gardens. Grow in full sun or partial shade, in good soil, and water well. Flowering season is autumn, winter, and mainly spring.

S. reginae var. *lutea*
As above, but petals yellow.

318

STREPTOCARPUS

Streptocarpus cyaneus

S. dunnii

S. x hybridus

S. rexii

STREPTOCARPUS
Gesneriaceae

A genus of annuals, perennials and sub-shrubs native to Africa, Madagascar and Asia with a number of species indigenous to South Africa. Prized for their trumpet-shaped, showy flowers in shades of mauve, purple, pink, red and white, they sometimes have deeper shades streaking the throat. Usually found in greenhouses or as indoor plants, they can also be grown out of doors in cool, moist climates if kept watered and planted in well-drained, rich soil, and in semi-shade. Propagate by division, leaf cuttings or from seed, which is very fine. The name is from the Greek *streptos,* twisted, and *karpos,* fruit, referring to the twisted seed capsules.

Streptocarpus cyaneus Natal, Eastern Transvaal
Cape primrose
Smaller, less showy flowers than the *Streptocarpus rexii* cultivars. Flowers are deep violet, bright pink, rarely white with yellow, and all have purple streaks in the throat.

S. dunnii Eastern Transvaal
One or several leaves up to 300 mm long and 200 mm wide. Flowers are pink to reddish and the bottom lobe is striped.

S. x hybridus Garden hybrid
Cape primrose
A hybrid with the habit of *Streptocarpus rexii;* reddish/pink flowers, each with a darker throat.

S. rexii cvs. Garden origin
Cape primrose
Large showy flowers in a wide range of colours, all with purple streaks in the throat. Flowering time is varied.

STREPTOSOLEN

Streptosolen jamesonii

S. jamesonii

STREPTOSOLEN
Solanaceae

A genus of one species, an evergreen shrub, *Streptosolen jamesonii,* which is native to the Andes of Colombia and Ecuador.

Streptosolen jamesonii South America
Marmalade bush or Marmeladebos
Shrub to 2 m with orange and yellow trumpet-shaped flowers profusely borne in the summer months but in warm climates produced most of the year. This is a graceful spreading shrub with arching branches that can be trimmed to make a small hedge. It is wind resistant at the coast. Plant in normal garden soil in full sun. Propagate from cuttings.

STROBILANTHES

Strobilanthes anisophyllus

S. dyeranus

STROBILANTHES
Acanthaceae

A large and variable genus, including herbaceous perennials and shrubs, native to tropical Asia and grown both indoors and out for its attractive foliage and flowers. If outdoors, plant in a warm, semi-shaded spot and protect from wind and frost. Propagate from cuttings.

Strobilanthes anisophyllus Assam
☼ 🌡 🌱 Ⓕ
Shrub to 1 m with handsome, metallic, silvery purple leaves and blue, pink or white flowers. Prune regularly as the new growth has the best colouring.

S. dyeranus Burma
☼ 🌡 🌱 Ⓕ
Shrub to 600 mm with iridescent purple leaves that make this a most attractive foliage plant for indoors or stoeps and even in full sun if near the coast. Flowers are violet.

STRONGYLODON

Strongylodon macrobotrys

STRONGYLODON
Fabaceae (=Leguminosae) Subfam. Faboideae (=Papilionoideae)

A genus of shrubs and climbers of which one only, *Strongylodon macrobotrys*, is normally cultivated. Flowers are carried in long peduncled clusters. Plant in good, well-drained soil in a protected area.

Strongylodon macrobotrys Philippines
☼ 🌡 🌱 Ⓕ
Jade vine or Jaspisklimop
The spectacular jade vine favours frost-free, warmly temperate to subtropical areas; it bears a tremendous number of blue-green flowers in racemes almost a metre long throughout summer. This vine should be grown over a large pergola so that the long racemes of flowers may hang free and clear.

SUTERA

Sutera grandiflora

SUTERA
Scrophulariaceae

A genus of annuals, perennials and small shrubs native mostly to South Africa, with a few species found in tropical Africa. Several species are grown in gardens, the most popular of these being *Sutera grandiflora*.

Sutera grandiflora Eastern Transvaal,
🌱 🌡 🌱 ☼ Swaziland
Wild phlox or Wilde floks
Woody perennial or sub-shrub to 1,25 m with grey-green aromatic leaves; clusters of lavender-coloured flowers borne near the tips of the branches are produced in summer and autumn. Grow in ordinary garden soil and water well in the growing season. Easily grown from seed.

TECOMANTHE　　　TECOMARIA

Tecomanthe venusta

Tecomaria capensis

T. capensis (orange-yellow cv.)

T. capensis 'Aurea'

T. capensis (pink cv.)

T. capensis (scarlet cv.)

TECOMANTHE
Bignoniaceae

A genus of tropical, woody climbers with attractive tubular flowers.

Tecomanthe venusta　　　New Guinea

This is the only species normally grown in South Africa. A beautiful, rare, evergreen woody climber to 3 m with compound leaves and pendent, tubular, waxy reddish flowers that are cream inside and borne in clusters along the twining stems in spring. Plant in rich, well-drained soil in tropical climates.

TECOMARIA
Bignoniaceae

This is a small genus of evergreen, sometimes scandent shrubs native to Africa, with one species, *Tecomaria capensis*, indigenous to the summer rainfall areas of South Africa. Commonly grown as a flowering shrub or climber, it also makes a quick-growing, dense and wind-resistant hedge.

Tecomaria capensis　　Natal, Transvaal and Eastern Cape
Cape honeysuckle or Kaapse kanferfoelie
Rambling, scandent and scrambling shrub with fiery orange-red flowers borne in autumn and winter. It is easily grown in any soil in full sun or semi-shade.

T. capensis, orange-yellow cv.
T. capensis, pink cv.
T. capensis, scarlet cv.
T. capensis 'Aurea'　　　Garden origin
As above, but yellow flowers.

TELOPEA

Telopea speciosissima

TELOPEA
Proteaceae

An Australian genus containing four species of evergreen shrubs or small trees with large brilliant scarlet flowers that are sometimes surrounded by showy red bracts. Carried above the foliage, these flowers are most eye-catching and their common name, waratah, comes from the Aborigine word meaning see-from-afar, while the generic name comes from the Greek word, *telopas,* with the same meaning. Not easily cultivated, waratahs have similar requirements to proteas.

Telopea speciosissima　　　　　　Australia
Waratah
Shrub to 1,5 m with brilliant scarlet flowers up to 100 mm across that appear in spring.

TETRAGONIA

Tetragonia rosea

TETRAGONIA
Aizoaceae

A family closely related to the Mesembryanthemaceae (vygies). Annual or perennial herbaceous sub-shrubs; nearly 40 species are widespread in South Africa. They need well-drained soil and full sun.

Tetragonia rosea　　　　　　Clanwilliam
Flowers are purplish-red in spring and most attractive when planted in a rock garden.

TETRAPANAX

Tetrapanax papyriferus

TETRAPANAX
Araliaceae

There is one species in this genus, *Tetrapanax papyriferus,* native to southern China and Taiwan.

Tetrapanax papyriferus　　China and Taiwan
Rice-paper plant, Chinese paper plant or Ryspapierplant
Shrub or small tree to 6 m with large felty leaves up to 400 mm across and bearing sprays of fluffy white or creamy-green globular flowers carried above the foliage in autumn. The white pith of the stems was once used to make paper in China. Easily grown in any soil, including sandy coastal areas, these shrubs are propagated by suckers.

THALICTRUM

Thalictrum dipterocarpum

THEVETIA

Thevetia peruviana

THORNCROFTIA

Thorncroftia succulenta

THALICTRUM
Ranunculaceae

Perennial herbaceous plants with fern-like foliage and small flowers that are borne in panicles, racemes or corymbs. For the best display, plant them in a mass in moist, well-drained soil.

Thalictrum dipterocarpum Western China
Meadow rue
Masses of small mauve flowers are borne in summer. Plant in a sunny spot and water regularly.

THEVETIA
Apocynaceae

A small genus of evergreen trees and shrubs native to tropical America, all of which are poisonous to some extent. Grown for their showy flowers, these plants need rich, well-drained soil. Propagate from cuttings and seeds and plant in full sun.

Thevetia peruviana Tropical America
Yellow oleander or Geeloleander
Quick-growing tree to 10 m with glossy, narrow dark green leaves to 150 mm long. Fragrant orange or yellow trumpet-shaped flowers up to 50 mm across appear at intervals all year round in warm climates. In spite of the similarity and the common name, this tree is not related to the oleanders.

THORNCROFTIA
Lamiaceae (= Labiatae)

The three species in this genus are endemic to the Transvaal. Herbaceous, erect plants to 1 m, their many-flowered whorls turn into panicled racemes. They are easy to grow from seed in well-drained soil.

Thorncroftia succulenta Nylstroom, Northern Transvaal
Excellent large bedding plants; purplish-pink salvia-like flowers are borne in profusion in terminal clusters in autumn.

THRYPTOMENE

THUNBERGIA

Thryptomene sp.

Thunbergia alata

T. grandiflora

T. gregorii

THRYPTOMENE
Myrtaceae

A genus of heath-like evergreen shrubs in Australia, with small white flowers. Thryptomenes are drought and wind resistant.

Thryptomene sp.　　　　　　Australia
Leaves are small and dark green. Pure white flowers are borne in winter.

THUNBERGIA
Acanthaceae

A genus of shrubs and perennials, some of which are climbers, and native to central Africa, South Africa, Madagascar and Asia. The well-known black-eyed Susan, *Thunbergia alata,* is probably the species most familiar to gardeners. The name of this genus commemorates Carl Peter Thunberg (1743 – 1822), sometimes referred to as the 'father of South African botany' and author of *Flora capensis,* an account of the flora of the Cape. Thunbergias are grown easily from seed.

Thunbergia alata　　　　Tropical Africa
Black-eyed Susan or Swartoognooi
Quick-growing twining perennial to 3 m or more and often treated as an annual. Flowers are trumpet-shaped and usually orange, occasionally creamy-yellow, with a black throat. This is a light dainty climber, ideal for growing on a fence, on pillars, or in hanging baskets. It will grow in semi-shade or full sun and flowers for most of the warmer months of the year. It self-seeds easily.

T. grandiflora　　　　　　　　India
Clock vine, Sky vine, Sky flower or Bloutrompetter
Quick-growing vigorous twiner to 5 m which produces rich blue trumpet flowers in summer and autumn.

T. gregorii　　　　　Tropical Africa
(*T. gibsonii*)
Golden glory vine
Twining perennial bearing solitary orange flowers on long, hairy peduncles in spring.

TIBOUCHINA

Tibouchina urvilleana

T. granulosa

TIBOUCHINA
Melastomataceae

This is a genus of evergreen shrubs and small trees from tropical America, grown for their large vivid flowers which cover the plants in the flowering season in warm, humid climates. Plant in rich, deep, well-drained soil and water regularly. The generic name is Guianese for the plant.

Tibouchina elegans   Brazil
Shrub to 2 m; purple-pink flowers with purple stamens are borne in summer.

T. granulosa   Brazil
Handsome small trees to 6 m; absolutely spectacular when covered in a solid mass of pink or purple flowers that are borne in spring, and in warm areas are often produced again in autumn.

T. elegans

T. urvilleana   Brazil
(*T. semidecandra*)
Brazilian glory bush or Lasiandra
Shrub to 5 m, with showy violet-purple flowers. This species is particularly susceptible to wind and needs regular pruning to keep it shapely.

TIGRIDIA

Tigridia pavonia

TIGRIDIA
Iridaceae

Bulbous perennial herbaceous plants native to temperate areas of the Americas. Bulbs should be planted 50 to 70 mm deep. They are easily grown from seeds.

Tigrida pavonia   Mexico, Guatemala
Tiger flower or Tierblom
Flowers are 100 mm across, red spotted with yellow, and purple in the cup-like centres. Borne on tall stems surrounded by stiff leaves, they appear in summer.

TILLANDSIA

Tillandsia cyanea

T. usneoides

T. tenuifolia

TILLANDSIA
Bromeliaceae

A large genus of epiphytic plants native to tropical and subtropical America that are suitable for growing indoors or in greenhouses, or even outdoors in warm climates. The spiky leaves usually form loose rosettes and the flowers usually appear in spikes, sometimes with colourful bracts. Indoors, these plants need strong light; outdoors, plenty of morning sun and regular watering by wetting the leaves. Propagate from suckers.

Tillandsia cyanea Ecuador
Pink quill
Linear leaves that form a rosette. Inflorescences are produced on a short spike with broad flattened pink bracts and large violet-blue flowers.

T. tenuifolia Tropical America
Lugplant
An epiphyte with small succulent grey-green leaves forming a rosette. Pretty arching inflorescences produce flowers with pink bracts and spreading purple petals in spring.

T. usneoides Tropical America
Spanish moss, Greybeard or Spaansmos
Stems are slender and leafy and hang to 1 m or more in cultivation. Flowers are very small and blue.

TIPUANA

Tipuana tipu

TIPUANA
Fabaceae (= Leguminosae) Subfam. Faboideae (= Papilionoideae)

There is one tree in this genus, *Tipuana tipu,* native to South America.

Tipuana tipu Bolivia
Tipu, Pride of Bolivia, Trots van Bolivië or Tipuana
Large, deciduous tree to 10 m or more with a spreading crown. Quick-growing in warm climates but slower in cooler areas, the tipuana has finely cut foliage and large sprays of golden yellow flowers that are borne in late spring and summer. Freely self-seeding, the seedlings must be transplanted while very young as they resent disturbance once established. The branches of older trees are brittle and break easily in the wind but if these are removed the stump will shoot again.

TORENIA

Torenia fournieri

TRACHELOSPERMUM

Trachelospermum jasminoides

TRADESCANTIA

Tradescantia blossfeldiana

T. fluminensis 'Variegata'

TORENIA
Scrophulariaceae

A genus of attractive annual or perennial herbaceous plants of tropical and subtropical Asia and Africa. They require no special cultivation but prefer some shade and regular watering. They are easily propagated from seeds sown in spring, or cuttings.

Torenia fournieri Vietnam
Bluewings
An attractive pot plant if supported with a stake. Flowers have a corolla tube of pale violet with yellow on the back and lips of pale blue; middle lower lip lobe has a yellow blotch at the base. Flowers are borne over a long period.

TRACHELOSPERMUM
Apocynaceae

A genus of twining shrubs with jasmine-like flowers in thick clusters which will enjoy some shelter in inland gardens. These attractive evergreens will flourish once established. Grow them in soil enriched with organic matter in some shade. Propagate from cuttings in summer.

Trachelospermum jasminoides China
Star jasmine or Sterjasmyn
A small woody evergreen climber to 1,5 m with very fragrant star-like white flowers 20 mm across and borne in summer. Prune regularly. It can also be used as a ground cover.

TRADESCANTIA
Commelinaceae

A genus of perennials native to the Americas that grow either upright or trailing. Some species are raised for their showy flowers, others for their attractive foliage. They make good hanging basket plants or, ground covers or rockery plants if placed either in full sun or semi-shade.

Tradescantia blossfeldiana South America
Flowering inch plant
Trailing perennial with leaves which are green above and purple beneath; small pink flowers are borne at irregular intervals.

T. fluminensis 'Variegata' South America
Wandering Jew
A useful, versatile perennial that makes a good outdoor ground cover in semi-shade but is best grown indoors in a hanging basket. Leaves are green on top, striped with yellow and white and deep purple underneath, with tiny insignificant white flowers. This plant is easily propagated from cuttings.

CONTINUED

TRADESCANTIA

T. sillamontana

T. virginiana

T. sillamontana — Mexico
White velvet or White gossamer
Rhizomatous trailing perennial covered in white velvety hairs; rosy magenta flowers.

T. virginiana — Northern America
Widow's tears or Weduweestrane
A good herbaceous perennial for damp soil. Flowers are violet-purple.

TRICHOCAULON

Trichocaulon cactiforme

T. grande

TRICHOCAULON
Asclepiadaceae

A genus of succulent perennials of which there are about 12 species in Madagascar and Africa, mostly from Namibia as well as the northern Cape. Commonly known as ghaap, the stems of many species are generally edible in the raw state or can be preserved in sugar or pickled in vinegar like cucumbers.

Trichocaulon cactiforme — Namaqualand and Namibia
Ghaap
Stems are club-shaped to 100 mm tall and crowded with rounded tubercles. Flowers are small with granulose corollas, yellow and stippled in red.

T. grande — Laingsburg
Ghaap
A robust, tall-stemmed plant to 600 mm high. Flowers are greenish-yellow, 20 mm across, and borne in late spring.

TRICHOCEREUS

Trichocereus spachianus

TRICHOCEREUS
Cactaceae

A genus of ribbed, cylindrical cacti native to South America with white funnel-shaped nocturnal flowers. Cultivate as for other cacti.

Trichocereus spachianus — South America
Torch cactus
Stems are erect to 2 m in height and branching from the base, with white flowers up to 200 mm long.

TRIFOLIUM

Trifolium repens 'Atropurpureum'

TRISTELLATEIA

Tristellateia australasiae

TRITONIA

Tritonia crocata

Tritonia hybrids

TRIFOLIUM
Fabaceae (=Leguminosae) Subfam. **Faboideae** (=Papilionoideae)

All species in this genus have trifoliate leaves. Annual or herbaceous perennials, they are widely distributed over the temperate and subtropical parts of the northern hemisphere. Trifolium is especially suited to places with hot dry summers for clover will always remain a green and showy ground cover. The name is from the Latin *tres*, three, and *folium*, leaf.

Trifolium repens 'Atropurpureum'   Europe
(*T. repens* 'Purpurascens')
Clover or Klawer
An ornamental dwarf cultivar bearing leaflets of deep bronzy red with green margins.

TRISTELLATEIA
Malpighiaceae

Woody vines that are native to tropical Africa, Madagascar, South East Asia and the Pacific Islands. Flowers are yellow and borne in terminal clusters.

Tristellateia australasiae   South East Asia
Galphimia vine
Climbing shrub with dull green ovate leaves, 80 mm long; flowers bright yellow with red stamens. It likes enriched, well-drained soil and regular watering.

TRITONIA
Iridaceae

Brilliantly coloured flowers on graceful wiry stems have made these indigenous flowers popular all over the world. Found in both the winter and summer rainfall areas, they are both spring and summer-flowering species. Spring-flowering tritonias are excellent for rockeries and outdoor containers if kept in full sun, while the summer-flowering species are best suited to the herbaceous border and will grow in semi-shade as well as full sun. All species multiply rapidly and are best propagated by offsets.

Tritonia crocata   Southern Cape
Blazing star, Rooikalossie or Rooikalkoentjie
Corm to 250 mm; flowers are reddish-orange and yellow at the base, borne in late spring. Grow in light sandy soil with plenty of water during the growing season.

CONTINUED

TRITONIA

T. disticha subsp. *rubrolucens*

Tritonia hybrids Garden hybrids
Blazing star or Kalkoentjies
Large, showy flowers which come in a wide range of both bright and pastel colours.

T. disticha subsp. **rubrolucens**
South-western Cape
As above. Flowers are rose-pink and borne on a branched spike.

TROPAEOLUM

Tropaeolum majus

TROPAEOLUM
Tropaeolaceae

Native to the cool highlands of Central and South America, nasturtiums are spreading and climbing annuals and perennials with showy flowers ranging from cream through to yellow, orange, pink and red, even a deep mahogany red. Easily grown from seed and freely self-seeding, nasturtiums will grow in full sun or semi-shade.

Tropaeolum majus Andean South America
Nasturtium or Kappertjie
Summer-flowering annual, usually climbing or spreading. Dwarf and compact cultivars are available and suitable for bedding. Flowers are single or double and come in a wide range of colours, often striped and spotted. Leaves are occasionally used in salads and the flower buds and seeds for seasoning.
Nasturtiums have naturalized themselves in many parts of South Africa and are often found in shady places. It is worth allowing a few plants to take over a wild corner of the garden as they provide fresh-scented, intensely bright flowers for informal flower arrangements.

TULBAGHIA

Tulbaghia simmleri

TULBAGHIA
Liliaceae

A genus of tuberous or cormous perennials native to tropical and southern Africa with a few species grown for their purple or white flowers. Unfortunately, most species have a powerful garlic smell but nevertheless they make useful garden plants as they are frost and drought resistant and can be grown in full sun or semi-shade.

Tulbaghia simmleri Widespread
Sweet garlic or Soetknoffel
Bulb to 450 mm; 5 to 7 leaves of 125 mm long and 10 mm wide; umbel with 30 to 40 lilac-coloured flowers borne in summer.

TULIPA   TUPIDANTHUS

T. simmleri

Tulipa hybrids

Tupidanthus calyptratus

T. violacea

T. violacea   Eastern Cape, Natal, Transvaal
Wild garlic or Wildeknoffel
Bulb to 450 mm forming tufts of grey-green leaves. The plant should be left undisturbed as long as possible. The dainty lilac-coloured flowers in umbels are borne in summer.

TULIPA
Liliaceae

Seldom flowering more than once under South African conditions, tulips have been extensively hybridized since the first species were introduced to Europe from the Near East in the sixteenth century. The colour range of the flowers is almost complete; there is even a so-called 'black' tulip and the richly coloured Rembrandts, with blotched petals, streaked in different colours. Flower shapes vary, too, from the traditional 'tulip' shape to the exotic 'bizarre-flowered' varieties, with spreading uneven petals. Native to the temperate regions of Europe and Asia; Central Asia, however, is the home of most species. Tulips have specialized requirements under South African conditions and specialist advice is recommended.

Tulipa hybrids   Garden hybrid
Tulip
Plant the bulbs in deep, fertile, well-drained soil in autumn. They flower in spring.

TUPIDANTHUS
Araliaceae

There is one species in this genus, which is native to tropical Asia, the *Tupidanthus calyptratus*.

Tupidanthus calyptratus   Tropical Asia
In nature this is a high-climbing, scandent creeper; in cultivation it is a shrub, from 1 to 4 m high, with large, palmately divided, somewhat pendent leaves and reddish petioles. Leaflets are obovate to 180 mm long. It resembles *Brassaia* but grows denser and the leaves are more leathery tough. It is often incorrectly referred to as *Schefflera*.

335

TURRAEA

Turraea obtusifolia

TURRAEA
Meliaceae

A genus of tropical and subtropical shrubs and small trees, one of which, *Turraea obtusifolia*, is indigenous to South Africa.

Turraea obtusifolia — Widespread in South Africa
Wild honeysuckle, Kleinkanferfoelieboom or Wilde kanferfoelie
Deciduous shrub or small bushy tree to 3 m with fragrant, showy white flowers in spring, which are then followed by red berries. Plant in well-drained soil.

TYLECODON

Tylecodon cacalioides

T. grandiflorus

TYLECODON
Crassulaceae

The name is an anagram of *Cotyledon*. *Tylecodon* species are distinguished from those of *Cotyledon* by their spirally arranged, soft, herbaceous, non-waxy leaves which are deciduous. They vary from shrubs to small plants and are limited to the drier parts of the Cape Province and Namibia.

Tylecodon cacalioides — Little Karoo
(*Cotyledon cacaliodes*)
Showy inflorescence to 600 mm tall with yellow flower buds in summer.

T. grandiflorus — South-western Cape
(*Cotyledon grandiflora*)
Leaves are linear to 70 mm long and 10 mm wide. Inflorescences up to 500 mm tall; corolla tubes are orange-red and slightly curved; borne in summer.

TYPHA

Typha capensis

TYPHA
Typhaceae

Bullrushes make striking accent plants for the water garden with their large leafy clumps and velvety brown cylindrical inflorescences. There are about 15 species in the genus, all of which grow in marshy places throughout the world.

Typha capensis — Widespread
Bullrush or Papkuil
Leaves to 2 m, 25 mm across; spikes are dark brown and most useful in floral arrangements.

ULEX

Ulex europeus

URSINIA

Ursinia cakilifolia

U. calenduliflora

ULEX

Fabaceae (=Leguminosae) Subfam. **Faboideae (=Papilionoideae)**

A genus of very spiny shrubs native to Europe and North Africa and grown for their masses of golden yellow pea-flowers. These are tough, wind and frost-resistant shrubs which will grow in poor, dry soils. Easily propagated by seed.

Ulex europeus Western Europe
🇫 ⊛ ☼ ⊕ 🇼
Gorse, Furze or Whin
Spiny shrub to 2 m with fragrant yellow pea-flowers borne in spring.

URSINIA

Asteraceae (=Compositae)

A genus of annuals, perennials, sub-shrubs and shrubs indigenous to South Africa and grown for their bright daisy-like flowers. Easily grown in full sun and light, well-drained soil, ursinias are useful for rockeries and bedding areas and should be planted close together for maximum effect. In the wild, the annual species make great sheets of colour in the spring.

Ursinia cakilifolia South-western Cape
🇫 ⊛ ☼
Annual to 250 mm with deep yellow or orange flowers with purple-black centres produced in spring; flowers measure up to 35 mm across.

U. calenduliflora South-western Cape
🇫 ⊛ ☼
Spring-flowering annual to 350 mm; orange flowers with a purple ring at the base of the petals.

CONTINUED

URSINIA

U. geyeri

U. sericea

U. geyeri   South-western Cape
Delicate plants with bright red flowers in late spring.

U. sericea   South-western Cape
Shrubby perennial to 450 mm with silver-grey foliage and yellow flowers borne in mid-summer.

VALERIANA

Valeriana officinalis

VALERIANA
Valerianaceae

A large genus of perennials, sub-shrubs and shrubs found on every continent except Australia. Grown in borders or rock gardens for their spikes of red, pink, white or yellow flowers, these plants have no particular soil requirements and are easily propagated by seeds or division. The species mentioned below yields the drug valerian and the name of the genus is possibly derived from the Latin word, *valeo*, meaning to be healthy, referring to the plant's medicinal uses.

Valeriana officinalis   Widespread
Perennial to 1,5 m with fragrant white, pink or lavender flowers in summer.

VANDA

VELTHEIMIA

Vanda x *rothschildiana*

Veltheimia bracteata

V. capensis

V. teres

VANDA
Orchidaceae

A genus of epiphytic orchids native to tropical Asia, grown for their fragrant, exotic flowers which come in a wide range of shades including blues and are fascinatingly marked, dotted or streaked. These orchids require high humidity, constant warmth and plenty of light. Novice orchid growers should get advice from an expert as requirements vary according to local conditions.

Vanda x rothschildiana　　Garden hybrid
Stems to 1 m long; flowers blue to purple-pink, chequered with darker blue, growing up to 125 mm across.

V. teres　　South East Asia
Stems to 1 m; colourful, sculptured flowers to 100 mm across, seen from spring to autumn.

VELTHEIMIA
Liliaceae

A small genus of bulbs indigenous to South Africa, with clumps of shiny, broad and wavy-edged leaves and spikes of tubular, drooping flowers. Suitable for growing in the shade under large trees in frost-free areas, veltheimias also make good pot plants. Grow in enriched, well-drained soil and propagate from offsets.

Veltheimia bracteata　　Eastern Cape
Boslelie
Bulb to 450 mm with dusty pink flowers tipped with green that are borne in early spring.

V. bracteata 'Lemon Flame'　　Garden origin
As above, but flowers are pale yellow.

V. capensis　　South-western Cape
Sandlelie
Bulb growing to 400 mm with attractive bluish-green, wavy-edged leaves and green-tipped, purplish-pink flowers borne in spring and followed by interesting inflated seed pods.

V. bracteata 'Lemon Flame'

VERBASCUM

Verbascum x hybridum

V. thapsus

VERBENA

Verbena canadensis 'Rosea'

V. x hybrida

VERBASCUM
Scrophulariaceae

A large genus of biennials, with a few annuals and perennials, native to Asia and Europe and grown for their velvety grey foliage as well as for their spikes of mostly yellow flowers. Grow in full sun in well-drained soil. Propagate from seeds (many species self-seed freely) or from root cuttings in the case of hybrids which do not set viable seed. The name is possibly from the Latin *barba,* a beard, as many species have a hairy or downy look.

Verbascum x hybridum Garden origin
Lamb's tail or Lamstert
Perennial with velvety, silvery leaves and long spikes of yellow flowers in summer.

V. thapsus Europe and Asia
Mullein, Velvet plant, Aaron's rod or Aaronstaf
Biennial to 2 m with velvety leaves up to 300 mm long and dense, woolly spikes of yellow flowers in summer.

VERBENA
Verbenaceae

A genus of annuals, perennials and sub-shrubs native mostly to the American tropical and suptropical regions and widely cultivated for their long-lasting, faintly fragrant flowers. The perennial species make excellent ground covers and rockery plants while the annual species tend to be more compact and suitable for bedding. Both carry masses of rounded heads of small flowers in all shades of red, pink, lavender-blue, purple and mauve, and white. Grow in full sun in ordinary garden soil and remove dead flower heads to prolong the flowering season. The perennial varieties are easily propagated by division and are occasionally self-seeding, while the annual varieties are easily raised from seed.

Verbena canadensis 'Rosea'
  North America
Rose verbena or Roosverbena
Spreading perennial to 450 mm with rose-purple, fragrant flowers for most months of the year.

V. peruviana

VERNONIA

Vernonia mespilifolia

VERONICA

Veronica scutellata

V. x hybrida   Garden hybrid
Garden verbena or Tuinverbena
Perennial, grown mostly as a summer-flowering annual, spreading and creeping up to 600 mm high. Flowers are in the full range of colours, often with a white 'eye'. A number of cultivars exist, often in dwarf, compact forms.

V. peruviana   South America
Rooiverbena
Spreading perennial, grown as an annual, with scarlet or crimson flowers in summer.

VERNONIA
Asteraceae (= Compositae)

A very large genus of worldwide distribution containing perennials, shrubs and small trees, a number of which are indigenous to South Africa.

Vernonia mesphilifolia South-western Cape

VERONICA
Scrophulariaceae

A genus of annuals and perennials native to the northern temperate regions and grown for their spikes of blue, mauve, pink or white flowers. Veronicas are easily grown from seed or by division. The taller varieties are best planted in the mixed border while the more compact varieties are ideally suited to rockery pockets. Although they will grow in a wide range of conditions, they do best in enriched, well-drained soil.

Veronica scutellata Europe, North America
Marsh speedwell
Creeping perennial with pale blue, pink or white flowers in summer.

341

VIBURNUM

Viburnum odoratissimum

V. opulus

V. tinus 'Lucidum'

V. opulus 'Sterile'

VIBURNUM
Caprifoliaceae

In a climate that suits them, viburnums are possibly the most ornamental of all shrubs. Grown for their showy, often heavily fragrant flowers, richly coloured autumn foliage and huge clusters of bright berries which persist into winter, they consequently also make good bird trees. Native to Europe, Asia and America, most species do best in cool temperate climates and the deciduous species are hardy to severe frost. Prune viburnum as little as possible; most species are best left to assume their own characteristic and very pleasing shape.

Viburnum odoratissimum Himalayas to Japan
Sweet viburnum or Geurviburnum
Evergreen shrub with leathery leaves and white, very fragrant spring flowers borne in panicles.

V. opulus Europe, Northern Africa, Northern Asia
Guelder rose or Gelderroos
Deciduous shrub; leaves have 3 to 5 lobes; and white spring flowers are borne in peduncled cymes 100 mm across.

V. opulus 'Sterile' Garden origin
Snowball tree or Witbalroos
Deciduous shrub to 4 m with colourful autumn foliage; large rounded clusters of densely packed, very showy white flowers are profusely borne in spring but, being sterile, do not produce berries.

V. tinus 'Lucidum' Mediterranean region
Evergreen shrub to 3 m with large glossy, dark green leaves and flattish heads up to 75 mm across, of white or pinkish flowers borne in early spring, followed by blue-black berries in autumn.

VINCA

Vinca major

V. minor 'Variegata'

VINCA
Apocynaceae

Widespread in Europe and the Near East, vincas are a small genus of trailing evergreen sub-shrubs which spread rapidly by means of rooting stems. The leaves are a glossy, bright green and the flowers are clear shades of blue, violet and white. Most commonly used as ground covers in semi-shade, these are immensely tough plants. Their long, slightly arching, graceful stems make these ideal container or hanging basket plants, particularly the variegated cultivars. Periwinkle flowers, if correctly dried, turn a deep violet colour.

Vinca major Europe
Periwinkle
Ground cover or trailing plant with blue flowers up to 50 mm across in the spring.

V. minor 'Variegata' Europe
Periwinkle
Smaller, lilac-blue flowers up to 20 mm across and leaves variegated with yellow; needs good soil and regular water.

VIOLA

Viola odorata

V. tricolor subsp. *subalpina*

V. x wittrockiana

VIOLA
Violaceae

Three well-loved garden plants are contained in this large genus of widespread distribution in the temperate regions. Firstly, there are the fragrant violets, perfect for small posies, then the colourful, profusely flowering violas and finally the velvety, richly coloured pansies. Ideal for bedding, rockeries or outdoor containers, pansies and violas respond to the best possible treatment although too much loving care may cause violets to produce leaf growth at the expense of flowers. They make lovely delicate cut flower arrangements.

Viola odorata Europe, Africa, Asia

Sweet violet, English violet or Viooltjie
Spreading perennial, best grown where it can receive afternoon shade. The flowers are richly fragrant, and usually deep violet although occasionally white and rarely, rose-pink. They are commercially important as a source of perfume and, to a lesser extent, to the florist trade. Violets make good ground covers in semi-shade. They seed themselves freely and are easily propagated by division.

V. tricolor subsp. **subalpina** Europe

Wild pansy
Perennial or biennial to 300 mm with yellow, or yellow and purple flowers in winter and spring.

V. x wittrockiana Garden hybrid
(*V. tricolor*)

Pansy or Gesiggie
Annual to 180 mm with winter and spring flowers up to 80 mm across in a wide range of colours. There are deep rich shades enhanced by the velvety texture of the petals, usually bi-coloured, marked, blotched and streaked in contrasting as well as pastel colours, usually blues or yellows. This is a hybrid between *Viola tricolor* and apparently *Viola lutea* together with *Viola altaica*.

VIRGILIA

Virgilia divaricata

VIRGILIA
Fabaceae (= Leguminosae) Subfam. Faboideae (=Papilionoideae)

Keurbooms are the perfect trees for new gardens as they are quick growing and attractive from an early age with soft, feathery foliage and sprays of deep to pale pink flowers. However, few trees blow over as easily as keurbooms; it is advisable to plant them in sheltered spots or near to a stout fence post or pillars to be unobtrusively tied and supported against the wind. There are only two species in this indigenous genus, both equally easy to grow and needing only protection from severe frost when young. Keurbooms seed themselves freely and can be raised easily from seed sown in the spring.

Virgilia divaricata South-western and southern Cape

Keurboom
Tree to 6 m; quick growing but short-lived in gardens, with luxuriant dark green leaves and fragrant purplish-pink flowers which are produced in masses in spring and early summer, sometimes almost covering the trees. This tree has a low-branching, spreading habit, making it less

CONTINUED

VIRGILIA

V. oroboides

VITEX

Vitex trifolia 'Variegata'

VRIESEA

Vriesea carinata

susceptible to wind but it will eventually require plenty of space.

V. oroboides — South-western and southern Cape
Keurboom
Tree to 10 m or more, quick growing and short-lived in gardens, with silvery pale green leaves and fragrant pale to rose-pink flowers produced intermittently throughout spring and early summer. This tree tends to have a more upright habit than *Virgilia divaricata* and is more susceptible to wind damage when grown as a garden specimen. In choice spots in their natural habitat, such as in deep, damp, shady mountain kloofs, these keurbooms can reach a height of 20 m with trunks up to 1 m in diameter.

VITEX
Verbenaceae

This is a large genus of deciduous and evergreen trees and shrubs, widespread in the tropical and temperate regions with attractive, occasionally aromatic foliage and clusters or spikes of white, yellow, red or blue to purple flowers, sometimes followed by berries. They have no special requirements in the garden and can be propagated most easily by layering.

Vitex trifolia 'Variegata' — Asia to Australia
Shrub or shrubby, partly deciduous tree to 6 m with variegated leaves and sprays of purple to blue fragrant flowers up to 275 mm long that are produced in late summer.

VRIESEA
Bromeliaceae

Handsome leaves and showy inflorescences characterize the large, attractive and mostly epiphytic perennials in this genus from tropical America. The stiff leaves, which are arranged in large decorative rosettes, are often attractively marked and variegated. The long-lasting flower spikes often have brilliantly coloured shiny bracts which are prettier than the inconspicuous yellow, green or rarely white flowers. Cultivate as for other bromeliads and propagate from the suckers which appear round the base of the adult plant that dies after flowering.

Vriesea carinata — South-eastern Brazil
Lobster claws
Dainty plant bearing a striking flattened spike with bracts of yellow and crimson and yellow flowers.

V. incurvata — South-eastern Brazil
Sidewinder vriesea
Fleshy red bracts edged with yellow; flowers are yellow.

V. incurvata

V. x mariae

V. psittacina

V. x mariae South-eastern Brazil
(*V. barilletii* x *V. carinata*)
⊜⊛⊛⑤
Painted feather

V. psittacina Brazil
⊜⊛⊛⑤
Perennial to 450 mm, sword-shaped leaves to 400 mm long; flower bracts are green to red, or red and yellow.

WACHENDORFIA
Haemodoraceae

This genus is a small one containing five species of tuberous-rooted perennials that are found in the Cape from the south-western districts to the Eastern Province. Wachendorfias can be recognized by their clumps of pleated, strap-shaped leaves and starry flowers with delicate, spidery stamens in shades of warm, muted yellow. The rootstock is always red or orange in colour, hence the common names. Wachendorfias are best propagated by division of the roots.

Wachendorfia paniculata South-western
⊕⊛☼ southern and eastern Cape
Blood root or Rooiknol
Tuberous perennial, with branched flowering stems to 300 mm high bearing pale yellow flowers faintly striped in a darker orange-yellow down the centre of the petals. The flowering season is from spring to mid-summer.

W. thyrsiflora South-western,
⊕⊛☼ southern and eastern Cape
Blood root or Rooiknol

WACHENDORFIA

Wachendorfia paniculata

W. thyrsiflora

Perennial to 2 m, with tall, stout, showy spikes of golden yellow starry flowers in spring. This plant grows in damp places in its natural environment, thriving in moist peaty soil and wet heavy clay, making it a very useful waterside plant in the garden.

WARSZEWICZIA

Warszewiczia coccinea

WASHINGTONIA

Washingtonia robusta

WATSONIA

Watsonia angusta

W. beatricis

WARSZEWICZIA
Rubiaceae

A small genus of trees and shrubs native to the American tropics, of which only one species is usually cultivated, *Warszewiczia coccinea*.

Warszewiczia coccinea Central and South America
Tree to 6 m or more with small yellow or orange funnel-shaped flowers; each with one enlarged bright red calyx lobe up to 45 mm long, the most showy part of the inflorescence.

WASHINGTONIA
Arecaceae (=Palmae)

This genus contains two species of massive palms native to the arid regions of Mexico and adjacent North America. The tall trunks bear rounded crowns of large, fan-shaped fronds which are deeply slit around the edges. Dead leaves remain attached to the tree in a dense, shaggy, but usually fairly symmetrically tapered mass called a 'shag'. They make effective accent plants and grow best in poor, sandy soils. Propagation is from seed.

Washingtonia robusta Mexico
Tall, slender, quick-growing palm to 30 m in its natural habitat, but much shorter in cultivation, with a trunk that tapers from a stout base. This is a good palm for coastal planting and is not suited to areas of severe frost.

WATSONIA
Iridaceae

With the exception of one species found in Madagascar, this is an entirely South African genus containing about 70 species of cormous plants. Watsonias often form spectacular sheets of colour in their natural environment, usually damp, and make showy garden plants with their flowers found in all shades of red, pink, orange, mauve and white. Both deciduous and evergreen species occur and the height of the plants, their flowering season and cultivation requirements all vary considerably. These cormous plants self-seed and multiply freely in nature and are easily propagated in the garden by these methods.

Watsonia angusta South-western Cape
Corm to 1,5 m and long spikes of tubular orange-pink flowers in spring.

W. beatricis Southern Cape
Evergreen to 1 m, growing in full sun or semi-shade, forming large leafy clumps. Apricot-coloured flowers bloom in mid-

WEDELIA

W. fulgens

Watsonia hybrid

Wedelia trilobata

W. meriana

W. pyramidata

W. pyramidata 'Ardernei'

summer. A number of hybrids have been developed with flowers in a wide range of colours.

W. fulgens　　　Southern Cape
Rooi watsonia
Flowers are scarlet, anthers purple and the branched style is yellow-red.

W. meriana　　　South-western Cape
Waspypie
Deciduous species, dormant in the summer months, growing to 450 mm high with magenta-pink flowers borne in spring and early summer. This is one of the many species of watsonia which, in its natural habitat, flowers best after a veld fire.

W. pyramidata　　　South-western Cape
Suurknol
Deciduous plant with graceful spikes to 1,75 m high and carrying large, showy, pinkish-mauve flowers in spring; the plants then die down and remain dormant for the summer months.

W. pyramidata 'Ardernei'　　　Garden origin
As above, but flowers are white.

Watsonia hybrid　　　Garden origin
As above, with magenta flowers in spring.

WEDELIA
Asteraceae (= Compositae)

One garden plant, *Wedelia trilobata*, is contained in this varied genus of cosmopolitan distribution in the tropics and subtropics.

Wedelia trilobata　　　Tropical America
Perennial ground cover to 300 mm high with creeping and rooting stems to 2 m long; rough, dark green glossy leaves and golden yellow daisy flowers to 30 mm across which bloom for most of the year in warm climates. The long, trailing stems make this a good plant for a hanging basket. Propagate from cuttings.

347

WEIGELA

Weigela florida

WEIGELA
Caprifoliaceae

Masses of rosy pink and white blossoms in spring characterize the most commonly grown species in this genus of deciduous shrubs from temperate eastern Asia. Weigelas are frost hardy and will grow in any reasonably good soil with regular watering. As flowers are borne on the preceding year's growth the shrubs should not be trimmed until after flowering. Propagate by cuttings in late summer.

Weigela florida　　　Northern China, Korea

Deciduous shrub to 3 m with slightly drooping trusses of rose-coloured, trumpet-shaped flowers in spring. This is an extremely variable species with numerous cultivars, the flowers ranging in colour from white to rosy purple. The attractiveness of the blossom is often enhanced by several shades of pink usually found in each flower.

WIDDRINGTONIA

Widdringtonia nodiflora

WIDDRINGTONIA
Cupressaceae

A genus with three indigenous cypress-like evergreen shrubs or trees with fragrant wood. Adult leaves are scale-like, forming tightly against the branches. Both male and female cones are on the same tree; female cones are almost globular.

Widdringtonia nodiflora　　　Widespread in mountains
Mountain cedar or Bergsipres
A scrubby bush or small tree to 6 m. This is a good specimen tree for planting in a large lawn.

WIGANDIA

Wigandia urens

WIGANDIA
Hydrophyllaceae

A genus of sub-shrubs or small trees native to tropical America and grown chiefly as foliage plants in subtropical conditions.

Wigandia urens　　　Peru

Leaves are large, rough and cordate at the base. Flowers are violet.

WILLDENOWIA

Willdenowia argentea

WISTERIA

Wisteria sinensis

WILLDENOWIA
Restionaceae

Fifteen species of rhizomatous erect reed-like plants of the fynbos, found mainly in the south-western Cape. Members of this family supply the reeds used in thatched roofs.

Willdenowia argentea South-western Cape
Reed or Riet
Robust tufts of minutely grooved stems up to 2 m tall. They grow especially well in sandy soil and are very showy when the tan bracts reflect sunlight. These bracts are showiest in autumn.

WISTERIA
Fabaceae (=Leguminosae) Subfam. Faboideae (=Papilionoideae)

Grown for their large drooping sprays of violet-blue flowers in spring, the fragrant species of wisteria will fill the whole garden with their scent in spring. These deciduous, woody climbers are native to temperate eastern Asia and eastern North America and, although they take some time to establish themselves after transplanting, become large vigorous plants, ideal for patios and pergolas. The soft luxuriant foliage is a particularly attractive shade of green. Blue is by far the most common colour of the flower; however, they also come in shades of white, purple and a variety of pinks. Grow wisterias in good, deep soil and full sun; perhaps the best method of propagation for the garden is by layering.

Wisteria sinensis China
Bloureën
Creeper to 30 m; deciduous, with flower sprays up to 300 mm long appearing in spring on bare branches before the leaves. The violet-blue flowers of this species are slightly fragrant.

XEROPHYTA

Xerophyta viscosa

YUCCA

Yucca filamentosa

Y. gloriosa

XEROPHYTA
Velloziaceae

Fibrous perennials with dwarf and tufted stems up to 4 m tall, usually less, protected characteristically by dense non-inflammable persistent leaf bases. Leaves are thin and slender with flowers solitary on each peduncle. These plants are not easy to cultivate and therefore should not be disturbed. They grow wild, particularly on the 'rantjies' in and around Johannesburg, the West Rand and Pretoria, and if you are lucky enough to find them on your property, they should be treasured.

Xerophyta viscosa   Transvaal
Bobbejaanstert
Showy, lily-like flowers borne in spring.

YUCCA
Agavaceae

Striking, bayonet-leaved foliage plants, ideal for complementing architectural features. Yuccas are native to Mexico and North America but found also in our arid regions where they grow well in poor, sandy soil and withstand drought and wind, making them useful, trouble-free plants for seaside gardens. In addition to their year-round value as accent plants, yuccas have tall, showy spikes of waxy, night-scented flowers, usually creamy-white but occasionally violet. Propagate from suckers, offsets and by division. Several species are hardy to frost.

Yucca filamentosa   North America
Adam's needle, Needle palm, Palmlelie or Adam-se-naald
Frost hardy evergreen, usually stemless, forming a large rosette of sharply pointed leaves up to 1 m long with coarse curly threads forming along the margins of the leaves. The flower spikes reach 5 m in their natural environment and in summer carry a mass of white bell-shaped flowers up to 50 mm long.

Y. gloriosa   North America
Spanish dagger or Palmlelie
This species usually has a short, stout trunk. The whole plant reaches a height of 2,5 m; leaves, up to 750 mm long, have sharply pointed reddish tips. Flowers are large, drooping, greenish-white to reddish and carried on spikes to 1 m high in summer.

ZALUZIANSKYA

Zaluzianskya villosa

ZANTEDESCHIA

Zantedeschia aethiopica

Z. pentlandii

Z. rehmannii

ZALUZIANSKYA
Scrophulariaceae

Unusual among South African flowers since they only open in the late afternoon and evening; this is an indigenous genus of widespread distribution throughout the country. The small, usually very fragrant flowers are in shades of white, yellow and lilac, often with a dark yellow or orange 'eye', with petals of purple and crimson on the outside. Requirements and flowering seasons vary according to where the different species are native.

Zaluzianskya villosa South-western Cape
Annual to 300 mm high with very fragrant white to mauve flowers which have a yellow or orange 'eye'. Flowering time lasts for many months through winter and spring.

ZANTEDESCHIA
Araceae

The familiar arum lily, with its opulent and sophisticated pure white spathes which light up marshes and watercourses throughout the country in spring and summer, belongs to an indigenous genus of six species. Flower colours besides white are deep yellow, lemon yellow, and some species are blotched with black at the base of the spathe while others come in a wide range of pink shades. The large, rich green leaves are flecked with white in some species. Excellent and long-lasting as cut flowers, all arums are moisture-loving to a greater or lesser extent, depending on the species. Propagate by division or from seed.

Zantedeschia aethiopica Cape, Natal, Transvaal
Arum lily or Aronskelk
Perennial to 1,5 m with large white flower spathes to 100 mm long, with a bright yellow spadix. Flowering season varies from winter/spring in winter rainfall areas to spring/summer in summer rainfall areas.

Z. pentlandii Eastern Transvaal
Golden arum or Geelaronskelk
Deciduous perennial to 600 mm. The deep golden yellow flowers, which appear in summer, have a black patch at the base of the spathe. This is the flower emblem of the Transvaal.

Z. rehmannii Eastern Transvaal, Swaziland and Natal
Pink arum or Rooiaronskelk
Perennial to 450 mm; flowers vary from white flushed with pink, to a deep purplish-pink.

ZEBRINA

Zebrina pendula

ZEPHYRANTHES

Zephyranthes grandiflora

ZINNIA

Zinnia elegans

Z. elegans 'Thumbelina'

ZEBRINA
Commelinaceae

There are two species of trailing perennials in this genus from Central America. One, *Zebrina pendula*, is often grown for its variegated leaves as a ground cover or as a stoep or indoor plant. The generic name refers to the zebra-like stripes on the leaves.

Zebrina pendula   Mexico

Wandering Jew, Inch plant or Wandelende-Jood
Trailing, creeping perennial; white-striped green leaves, occasionally variegated with dark red, have purple undersides. Flowers, which appear at irregular intervals, are rose-pink, but not showy.

ZEPHYRANTHES
Amaryllidaceae

From the warmer regions of America and the West Indies come the romantically named 'Flowers of the West Wind' (*Zephyr*, Greek for the west wind, *anthos*, a flower). This is a genus of small bulbous plants with grass-like leaves and white, yellow, pink and red flowers. Low growing, they make useful edging plants and fit well into small rockery pockets. Grow in well-drained, enriched soil in full sun and propagate from offsets.

Zephyranthes grandiflora   Central America

Flower of the West Wind, Zephyr lily, Rain lily or Stormlelie
Bulb to 300 mm, with pink flowers up to 170 mm across borne in spring and summer.

ZINNIA
Asteraceae (=Compositae)

For a blaze of colour in the hottest, sunniest parts of the garden, zinnias are ideal, and thanks to the hybridists, come in almost every shade except the blues, and in a range of sizes from tiny dwarf plants with charming miniature flowers, to large, erect varieties, with exotically ruffled, quilted and curly petals. Zinnias belong in a genus of annuals, perennials and small shrubs from the warmer regions of the Americas, chiefly Mexico, and will grow in any soil in full sun. Propagate from seed.

Zinnia elegans   Mexico

Jakobregop
Annual to 1 m. The summer flowers are usually red in this species but the numerous cultivars occur in a wide range of shades, and are sometimes bi-coloured.

Z. elegans 'Thumbelina'   Garden origin
Dwarf cultivar of the above.

BOTANICAL TERMS AND THEIR MEANINGS

Abaxial: The lower surface of a leaf is the abaxial surface
Acicular: Needle-like
Acuminate: Drawn out, tapering point
Acute: Sharply pointed, abrupt
Adaxial: The upper surface of a leaf is the adaxial surface
Adventitious: Growing from an unexpected place, e.g. roots growing from a stem or a leaf
Alternate: (leaves) Growing at different levels
Annual: A plant that completes its life cycle within one year and then dies
Anther: Pollen-bearing portion of a stamen
Apex: The tip or distal end
Arborescent: A tree-like habit
Areole: Confined to cacti; cushion-like structure from which branches, flowers and spines may rise
Aril: An accessory seed covering formed by an outgrowth at the base of the ovule
Articulate: With prominent nodes and internodes
Asexual: Reproduction without seeds
Asymmetrical flower: Having some parts different in form and size from others of the same whorl, e.g. petals. Such a flower cannot be divided into two equal halves
Auriculate: Having basal ears (auricles)

Auricles on monocotyledon leaf

Autotrophic: A plant that manufactures its own food
Axil: Angle of junction between leaf and stem
Bark: The external group of tissues of a woody stem or root
Biennial: A plant that requires two years to complete its life cycle. Flowering is normally delayed until the second year.
Bilabiate: Two-lipped as in the flower of *Salvia*
Bipinnate: Twice pinnate
Bisexual: Hermaphrodite; stamens and pistil in same flower
Blade: The expanded part of a leaf
Bract: Modified leaf, from the axil of which arises a flower or an inflorescence
Bud: An undeveloped shoot, e.g. overwintering buds
Bulb: A short underground stem with many fleshy scale-leaves filled with stored food

Buds *Bulbs*

Bulbil: A small bulb or bulb-like structure borne in leaf axils or on an inflorescence
Calyx: Outer whorl of floral parts (sepals), usually green
Campanulate: Bell-shaped flower, broadly based
Capsule: A dry dehiscent fruit with pores or valves through which the seeds are set free

Capsule (poppy) *Carpels*

Carpel: A floral leaf, part of the ovary, bearing ovules along the margins
Caruncle: A spongy outgrowth of the seed coat, prominent in castor bean seed
Catkin: A spike or spike-like inflorescence typical of *Salix* and *Populus*
Ciliate: Fringed with fine hairs
Cladophyll: A flattened branch having the form and function of a leaf as in prickly-pear
Coalescence: The union of separate parts of any one whorl of flower parts: sepals, petals, stamens and pistil (carpels)

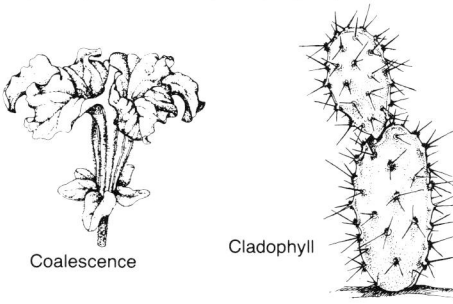

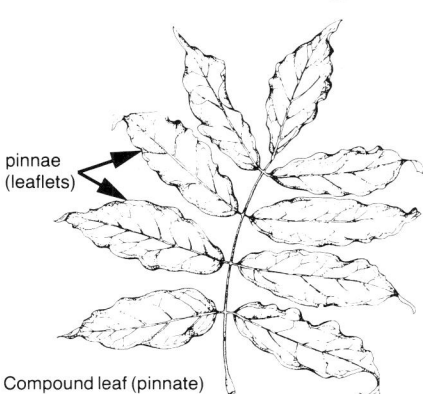

Coalescence *Cladophyll*

pinnae (leaflets)

Compound leaf (pinnate)

Compound leaf: A leaf whose blade is divided into several distinct leaflets
Cone: A fruiting structure composed of modified leaves or branches, which bear pollen sacs or naked ovules, e.g. a pine cone
Cordate: Heart-shaped
Corm: Similar to a bulb, but solid fleshed, e.g. gladiolus
Corolla: Inner circle of petals usually coloured (see drawing of the complete flower)

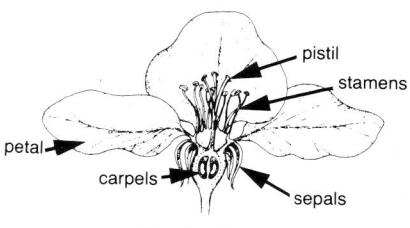

Complete flower (petal, pistil, stamens, carpels, sepals)

Corm *Seed of bean (split open)* (cotyledons)

Corona: A circular outgrowth of the perianth as in *Narcissus*
Corymb: A flat-headed inflorescence, opening from outside first
Cotyledon: A seed leaf, generally two in dicotyledons and one in monocotyledons
Culm: The hollow stem of grasses
Cultivar: See chapter on How to use the book
Cuneate: Triangular
Cyme: Usually a flat-topped inflorescence, but opening first from inside
Deciduous: Leaves falling off; not evergreen
Dentate: Toothed; teeth directed outwards
Dichotomous: Forking regularly with the two branches (forks) usually equal
Dioecious: Unisexual; male and female organs on different individuals
Distal: At or toward the apex
Distichous: Arranged in two vertical rows
Drupe: A stone fruit, as in apricot

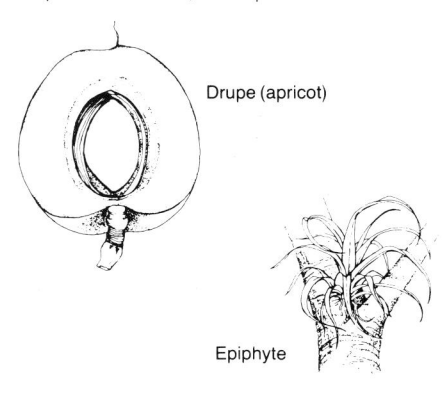

Drupe (apricot)

Epiphyte

Ecology: The study of life in relation to its environment
Elliptical: Longer than wide; widest point at centre
Elongate: Long, drawn out
Endemic: Confined to a particular area or region
Endosperm: The nutritive tissue in many seeds
Entire: Leaf margin smooth, without indentation
Epiphyte: A plant which uses another for support, but takes no food from it. An aerial plant not attached to the ground

353

Follicle (*Grevillea robusta*)

Nodes (n) and internode (i)

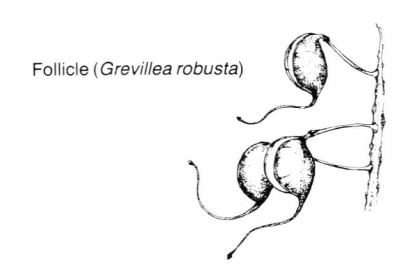

Filament: Fine stalk of an anther
Follicle: A fruit of one carpel, containing more than one seed, dehiscing or splitting on the ventral side
Frond: A synonym for a large divided leaf, especially for a fern leaf
Fruit: A matured ovary
Geophyte: A plant with a modified underground stem, e.g. a bulb, corm or rhizome
Glabrous: Smooth, not hairy
Glaucous: Bluish-grey, sometimes with a waxy bloom
Glutinous: Sticky
Head: A short, flattened, dense cluster of flowers
Herbaceous: Non-woody
Hirsute: Coarsely haired
Hybrid: The offspring produced by mating two plants that differ genetically
Imcomplete flower: A flower lacking one or more of the four kinds of flower parts
Indigenous: Native
Inferior ovary: An ovary more or less (sometimes completely) attached to the calyx and corolla
Inflorescence: The arrangement of the flowering portion of a plant; a flower cluster, e.g. raceme, umbel
Insectivorous: Plants which derive nourishment from insect life
Internode: The section of a stem between successive nodes or joints
Involucre: Ring or rings of bracts surrounding numbers of flowers

Involucre

Irregular flower: An asymmetrical flower
Lamina: The blade of a leaf
Lanceolate: Lance-shaped, tapering
Lateral: From the sides
Legume: A simple, dry dehiscent fruit with one carpel, splitting along two sutures
Linear: Narrow, sides parallel
Lobed: Leaf cut or deeply indented, nearly to the midrib or base
Metabolism: Overall set of chemical reactions in the living plant
Midrib: The main rib or vein of a leaf
Monoecious: Male and female organs in separate flowers but on the same plant
Mutation: A sudden, heritable change appearing in an individual as the result of a change in genes or chromosomes
Node: Slightly enlarged portion of the stem where leaves and buds arise and where branches originate
Oblanceolate: Broad-ended, tapering towards base
Obovate: Ovate but with the broader end uppermost

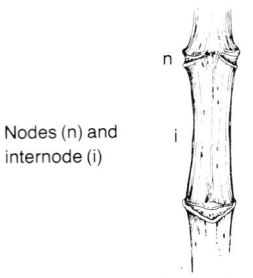

Obtuse: Blunt, rounded at the end
Opposite: On opposite sides of an axis, e.g. opposite leaves
Organic: Referring to compounds that contain both carbon and hydrogen; the material products of living organisms
Ovary: Basal part of pistil, which becomes the fruit and contains the seed

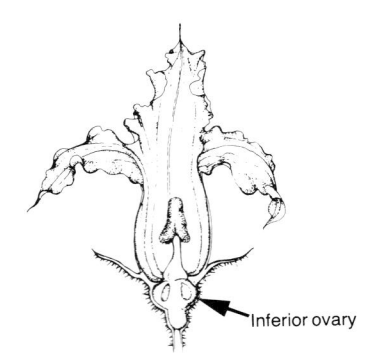

Inferior ovary

Ovate: Leaf broad-based, egg-shaped
Ovule: Very young seed; rudimentary seed
Palmate: Leaflets radiating from the apex of the petiole
Panicle: An open, branched inflorescence
Pedicel: The stalk of a single flower in an inflorescence
Peduncle: The stalk of a flower that is borne singly or the main stem of an inflorescence
Peltate: Shield-shaped
Perennial: A plant that lives from year to year
Perfect flower: A flower having both stamens and pistil(s)
Perianth: Calyx, corolla or both
Petal: A unit of the corolla, usually coloured
Petiole: Stalk of a leaf
Pinna: Leaflet or division of a compound leaf
Pinnate: Having leaflets arranged on either side of the leaf stalk
Pistil: Central organ (female) of the flower including ovary, style and stigma

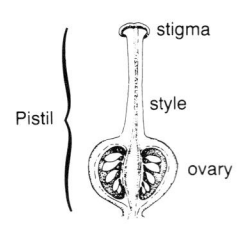

Pistil { stigma, style, ovary }

Pollination: The transfer of pollen from the anther of a plant to a stigma of the same species
Prostrate: Growing or lying flat on the ground

Pubescent: Downy with short, soft hairs
Raceme: Inflorescence in which stalked flowers are arranged along an elongated stem

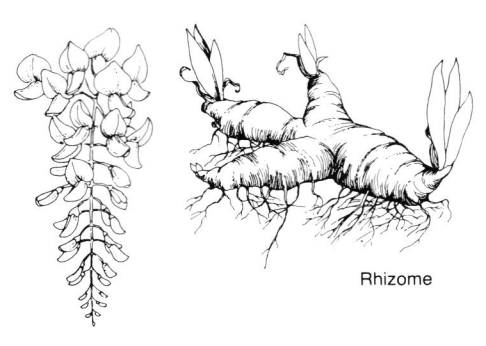

Raceme

Rhizome

Ray-floret: The strap-shaped floret of a flower head, e.g. daisy flower (see drawing of flower head)
Regular flower: A flower in which the corolla is made up of similarly shaped petals equally spaced and radiating from the centre of the flower
Rhizome: A creeping rootstock (stem), usually swollen and underground, capable of sending up shoots
Rosette: A circular cluster of leaves, usually close to the ground
Runner: A stem that grows horizontally along the ground surface
Sagittate: Arrow-shaped
Scabrous: Rough to touch
Scandent: More scrambling than climbing
Scape: A leafless peduncle rising from the ground
Seed: A matured ovule containing the embryo
Sepal: Segment of a calyx, normally green
Serrate: Saw-toothed
Sessile: Stalkless, close to stem
Simple leaf: Not divided into leaflets
Sinuate: Curved, deep wavy margin
Solitary: Borne singly
Sorus: A group of sporangia in ferns
Spadix: A fleshy spike, usually bearing large numbers of small flowers

Spadix and spathe

Spike

Spathe: A bract-like structure partly surrounding an inflorescence; often showy, e.g. arum lily
Spike: Unstalked flowers on an elongated stem
Stamen: Pollen-bearing male organ made up of an anther and filament
Stigma: That portion of the pistil which receives the pollen

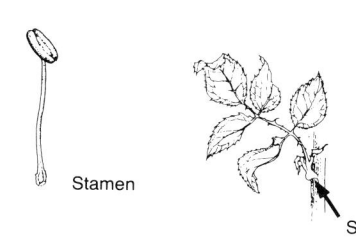

Stipule: A leaf-like structure at base of petiole; may also be thorns
Stolon: A shoot which hugs the ground, taking root and so creating new plants
Style: Connecting stalk between the ovary and the stigma (see drawing of a pistil)
Succulent: A plant with fleshy, water-storing parts
Superior ovary: An ovary completely separate and free from the calyx
Synonym: See chapter on How to use the book
Tendril: A curled thread-like outgrowth by which a plant clings to a support
Terrestrial: A plant growing in the ground
Trichome: A cellular outgrowth or a short filament of cells
Trifoliate: Three-leafed
Trifoliolate: A compound leaf having three leaflets, e.g. *Trifolium*
Tuber: An underground swollen stem with eyes, e.g. potato tuber
Umbel: A stalked inflorescence with flowers arising from a single point
Undulate: Wavy margined
Venation: Arrangement of veins in a leaf blade
Viviparous: Having the facility to produce young that are attached to a living plant
Whorl: Arrangement of organs in a circle, e.g. leaves, petals, etc.
Whorled: Leaves in whorl around stem
Xerophytic: Capable of living with minimal moisture

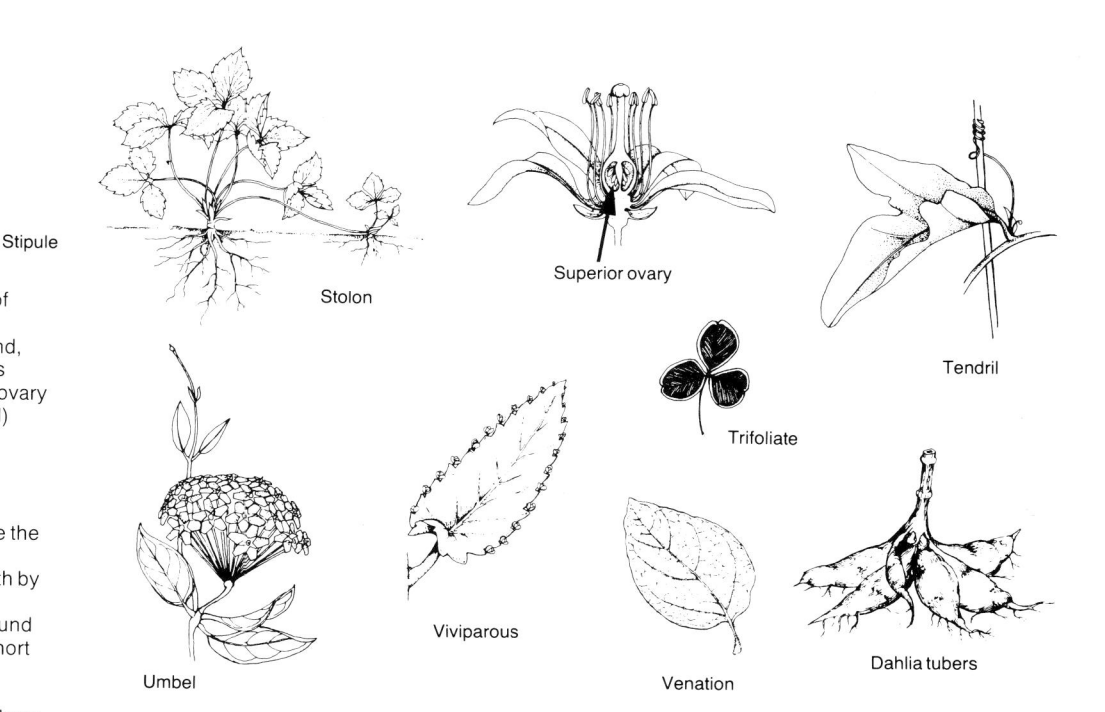

INDEX

Aarbeiboom: see Arbutus unedo
Aarbeikaktus: see Ferocactus setispinus
Aaron's rod: see Verbascum thapsus
Aaronstaf: see Verbascum thapsus
Aartappelranker: see Solanum wendlandii
Abelia
 floribunda 16
 floribunda 'Francis Mason' 16
 x grandiflora 16
Abutilon
 x hybridum 17
 megapotamicum 'Variegata' 17
 pictum 17
 pictum 'Thompsonii' 17
Abyssinian banana: see Ensete ventricosum (Tropical Africa)
Acacia
 False: see Robinia pseudoacacia
 Rose: see Robinia hispida
Acacia
 ataxacantha 17
 baileyana 17
 caffra 18
 cultriformis 18
 cyclops 18
 elata: see A. terminalis
 karroo 18
 podalyriifolia 18
 robusta 18
 saligna 18-19
 schweinfurthii 19
 terminalis 19
 xanthophloea 19
Acalypha
 hispida 19
 wilkesiana 'Godseffiana' 20
 wilkesiana 'Macrophylla' 20
 wilkesiana 'Marginata' 20
 wilkesiana 'Obovata' 20
 wilkesiana 'Tricolor' 20
Acanthus mollis 20

Achillea millefolium 'Rosea' 21
Achimenes grandiflora 21
Acokanthera oblongifolia 21
Acridocarpus natalitius 22
Adam-se-naald: see Yucca filamentosa
Adam's needle: see Yucca filamentosa
Adenandra
 fragrans 22
 uniflora 22
Adenium
 boehmianum 22
 multiflorum 22, 23
 obesum 23
 obesum var. *multiflorum*: see A. multiflorum
Adiantum
 capillus-veneris 23
 raddianum 23
Aechmea
 fasciata 23
 fulgens var. discolor 23
Aeonium
 arboreum 24
 arboreum 'Atropurpureum' 24
African marigold: see Tagetes erecta
African milk-bush: see Synadenium grantii 'Rubra'
African violet: see Saintpaulia
African winter sweet: see Acokanthera oblongifolia
Afrikaners: see Tagetes erecta
Agapanthus spp. 24-5
Agathosma ovata 25
Agave
 americana 25
 americana 'Marginata' 25
 attenuata 26
 parryi 26
Ageratum houstonianum 26
Aglaonema
 commutatum 'Pseudobracteatum' 26
 crispum 'Malay Beauty' 26
 crispum 'Parrot Jungle' 26-7

crispum 'Silver King' 27
Agrimony, Hemp: see Eupatorium cannabinum var. plenum
Agtdaegeneesbos: see Lobostemon fruticosus
Air potato: see Dioscorea bulbifera
Ajuga
 reptans 27
 reptans 'Atropurpurea' 26
Albanybroodboom: see Encephalartos latrifrons
Albany cycad: see Encephalartos latrifrons
Alberta magna 27
Albertinia heath: see Erica bauera
Albertiniaheide: see Erica bauera
Albuca sp. 28
 altissima 28
 cooperi 28
Alcea rosea 28
Alder, Red: see Cunonia capensis
Aleurites fordii 29
Algerian ivy: Hedera canariensis 'Gloire de Marengo'
Allamanda
 cathartica 'Hendersonii' 29
 neriifolia 29
Allium christophii 29
Alocasia
 cuprea 30
 macrorhiza 30
 sanderana 30
Aloe
 arborescens 30, 31
 ciliaris 30, 31
 distans 31
 ferox 31
 hybrid 31
 plicatilis 31
 reynoldsii 31
 striata 32
 thorncroftii 32
 variegata 32

 wickensii 32
Aloysia triphylla 32
Alpinia
 purpurata 33
 zerumbet 33
Alsophila dregei 33
Alstroemeria
 aurantiaca 34
 psittacina 34
Alternanthera ficoidea 'Bettsickiana' 34
Althea rosea see Alcea rosea
Aluminium plant: see Pilea cadierei
Alyssum maritimum see Lobularia maritima
Alyssums, Sweet: see Lobularia maritima
Amaranth, Globe: see Gomphrena globosa
Amaranthus
 caudatus 34
 tricolor 'Splendens' 34
Amaryllis belladonna 35
Amasone-klimop: see Stigmaphyllon ciliatum
Amatungulu: see Carissa macrocarpa
Amazon Lily: see Eucharis grandiflora
American elder: see Sambucus canadensis
American ivy: see Parthenocissus quinquefolia
Amethyst flower: see Browallia speciosa
Ammi majus 35
Anchor plant: see Colletia cruciata
Anchusa capensis 35
Anemone
 coronaria 36
 x hybrida 36
Angel-wing begonia: see Begonia coccinea
Angel wings: see Pilea spruceana 'Norfolk'
Angel's trumpet: see Brugmansia x candida

355

Anigozanthos flavidus 36
Anisodontea scabrosa 36
Annatto tree: see Bixa orellana
Annual poinsettia: see Euphorbia heterophylla
Anomalesia cunonia 37
Anomatheca grandiflora: see Lapeirousia laxa
Ansellia gigantea var. nilotica 37
  cupaniana 37
  tinctoria 37
Antholysa
  plicata 38
  ringens 38
Anthurium
  andraeanum 38
  andraeanum 'Album' 38
  crystallinum 38
  scherzeranum 38
Antigonon leptopus 39
Antirrhinum majus 39
Anysboegoe: see Adenandra fragrans
Aphelandra squarrosa 39
Aponogeton
  distachyos 40
  junceus 40
Apelliefie: see Physalis peruviana
April fool: see Haemanthus coccineus
Aquilegia caerulea 40
Arabian coffee: see Coffea arabica
Aralia, False: see Dizygotheca elegantissima
Arbutus unedo 40
Archontophoenix cunninghamiana 41
Arctic poppy: see Papaver nudicaule
Arctotheca calendula 41
Arctotis
  breviscapa 41
  fastuosa 41
  hirsuta 42
  stoechadifolia 42
Ardisia crispa 42
Argemone mexicana 42
Argentinian trumpet vine: see Clytostoma callistegioides
Aristea
  major 43
  thyrsiflora: see A. major
Aristolochia
  durior 43
  elegans 43
  gigantea 43
Armeria maritima 44
Armmansorgidee: see Schizanthus pinnatus
Aronskelk: see Zantedeschia aethiopica
Artichoke, Globe: see Cynara scolymus
Artichoke, Jerusalem: see Helianthus tuberosus
Artillery plant: see Pilea microphylla
Artisjok: see Cynara scolymus
Artist's acanthus: see Acanthus mollis
Arum palaestinum 44
Arums: see Zantedeschia spp.
Aruncus
  dioicus 44
  sylvester: see A. dioicus
Arundunaria
  disticha 45
  variegata 45
Arundo
  donax var. *variegata*: see A. donax var. versicolor
  donax var. versicolor 45
Asarina barclaiana 45
Asclepias
  fruticosa 46
  physocarpa 46
Ash, Cape: see Ekebergia capensis
Asparagus
  aethiopicus 46
  densiflorus 46
  densiflorus 'Myers' 46
  densiflorus 'Sprengeri' 46
Asparagus fern: see Asparagus densiflorus 'Myers'
Aspidistra elatior 47
Asplenium nidus 47

Aster
  novi-belgii 47
  tradescantii 47
Asters, China/Chinese: see Callistephus chinensis
Astilbe japonica 48
Astrophytum myriostigma 48
Athanasia
  crithmifolia 48
  parviflora 48
Aubrieta deltoidea 49
Aucuba japonica 'Variegata' 49
Australian bottle plant: see Jatropha podagrica
Australian lilac: see Hardenbergia comptoniana
Australian umbrella tree: see Brassaia actinophylla
Azalea indica: see Rhododendron spp.

Baakhoute: see Greyia spp.
Babiana
  disticha 50
  rubrocyanea 50
  stricta var. stricta 50
  villosa 50
Baby orchid: see Epidendrum x obrienianum
Baby toes: see Fenestraria rhopalophylla
Baby's tears: see Soleirolia soleirolii
Bachelor's button: see Bellis perennis
Baeometra uniflora 50
Bailey's wattle: see Acacia baileyana
Balm, Bee: see Monardia didyma
Balm, Molucca: see Molucella laevis
Balsam: see Impatiens spp.
Balseminie: see Impatiens balsamina
Bamboes: see Bambusa glaucescens
Bamboo
  Common: see Bambusa vulgaris
  Dwarf-fern-leaf: see Arundinaria disticha
  Dwarf white-striped: see Arundinaria variegata
  Heavenly: see Nandina domestica
  Hedge: see Bambusa glaucescens
  Sacred: see Nandina domestica
Bambusa
  glaucescens 51
  multiplex: see B. glaucescens
  vulgaris 51
Banana
  Abyssinian: see Ensete ventricosum (Tropical Africa)
  Wild: see Ensete ventricosum (South Africa); Strelitzia nicolai
Bananadilla: Passiflora mollissima
Banksia
  ericifolia 51
  integrifolia 51, 52
  serrata 51, 52
Bar room plant: see Aspidistra elatior
Barberry: see Berberis thunbergii 'Atropurpurea'
Barbeton daisy: see Gerbera jamesonii
Barleria
  obtusa 52
  repens 'Rosea' 52
Basket asparagus: see Asparagus densiflorus 'Sprengeri'
Bastard cobas: see Cyphostemma currorii
Basterkobas: see Cyphostemma juttae
Bauhinia
  blakeana 52
  galpinii 52, 53
  purpurea 53
  variegata 53
  variegata 'Candida' 53
Beach salvia: see Salvia africana-lutea
Bead tree: see Melia azedarach
Bear's breeches: see Acanthus mollis
Beaumontia grandiflora 53
Beauty berry: see Callicarpa dichotoma
Bedding begonia: see Begonia x semperflorens-cultorum
Bee balm: see Monarda didyma

Beech, Copper: see Fagus sylvatica 'Atropunicea'
Beefsteak heliconia: see Heliconia mariae
Beefsteak plant: see Acalypha wilkesiana
Beestebul: see Crassula ovata
Begonia
  caffra 54
  coccinea 54
  dregei 54
  x elatior 54
  masoniana 54
  rex-cultorum 54
  x semperflorens-cultorum 55
  x tuberhybrida 55
  x tuberhybrida 'Pendula' 55
Beloperone
  guttata: see Justicia brandegeana
  lutea: see Justicia brandegeana 'Yellow Queen'
Belhambra: see Phytolacca dioica
Belladonna lily: see Amaryllis belladonna
Bellflower: see Campanula spp.
Bellis perennis 55
Bells-of-Ireland: see Molucella laevis
Belvedere: see Kochia scoparia
Berberis thunbergii 'Atropurpurea' 55
Berg lily: see Galtonia candicans
Bergaalwyn: see Aloe spp.
Bergbietou: see Osteospermum jucundum
Bergbruidjie: see Serruria florida
Bergenia cordifolia 56
Berggranaat: see Rhigozum obovatum
Berglelie: see Galtonia candicans
Bergpypie: see Gladiolus carneus
Bergriet: see Brachycarpaea juncea
Bergrooigras: see Rhynchelytrum repens
Berpspires: see Widdringtonia nodiflora
Bergtree: see Geranium incanum
Berzelia lanuginosa 56
Beschorneria yuccoides 56
Besembos, Wilde: see Lebeckia cytisoides
Betsie: see Adenandra uniflora
Betula pendula 57
Bidens
  formosa 57
  sulphureus 57
Bietou: see Chrysanthemoides monilifera
Bignonia
  capreolata 57
  cherere: see Distictis buccinatoria
Billbergia
  nutans 58
  pyramidalis 58
Birch, Silver: see Betula pendula
Bird flower: see Crotalaria agatiflora
Bird of paradise: see Caesalpinia gilliesii; Strelitzia reginae
Bird's nest fern: see Asplenium nidus
Bishop's cap: see Astrophytum myriostigma
Bitter aloe: see Aloe ferox
Bitter gousblom: see Arctotis fastuosa
Bitteraalwyn: see Aloe ferox
Bitterblaar: see Brachylaena discolor subsp. transvaalensis
Bitterbos: see Chironia baccifera
Bitterghaap: see Hoodia bainii
Bixa orellana 58
Black calla: see Arum palaestinum
Black-eyed Susan: see Thunbergia alata
Blanket flower: see Gaillardia spp.
Blazing star: see Tritonia spp.
Bleeding heart vine: see Clerodendrum thomsoniae
Bleeding hearts: see Dicentra spectabilis
Bloedblaar: see Iresine herbstii
Bloedlelie: Scadoxus multiflorus subsp. multiflorus
Blombos: see Metalasia muricata
Blomperske: see Prunus persica cultivars

Blompruim: see Prunus cerasifera 'Atropurpurea'
Blood lily: see Scadoxus multiflorus subsp. multiflorus
Blood root: see Wachendorfia spp.
Bloodleaf: see Iresine herbstii
Blousuurknol: see Aristea major
Blouberglelie: see Scilla natalensis
Blougif: see Albuca cooperi
Bloukappie: see Polygala myrtifolia
Bloumargriet: see Felicia amelloides
Bloureën: see Wistaria sinensis
Blousestrum: see Jochroma cyaneum
Bloutrompetter: see Thunbergia grandiflora
Blue-and-white daisy bush: see Osteospermum ecklonis
Blue butterfly: see Delphinium grandiflorum
Blue cestrum: see Jochroma cyaneum
Blue daisy: see Felicia amelloides
Blue lotus: see Nymphaea caerulea
Blue marguerite: see Felicia amelloides
Blue spiraea: see Caryopteris incana
Blue squill: see Scilla natalensis
Blue water lily: see Nymphaea capensis
Bluebell, California: see Phacelia campanularia
Bluebell, Spanish: see Endymion hispanicus
Bluewings: see Torenia fournieri
Blushing bride: see Serruria florida
Blushing bromeliad: see Neoregelia carolinae
Boat lily: see Rhoeo spathacea
Bobbejaanstert: see Xerophyta viscosa
Bobbejaantjie: see Babiana spp.
Boegoe: see Agathosma ovata
Boerboon: see Schotia spp.
Boerejasmyn: see Philadelphus coronarius
Boesmankruie: see Stachys rugosa var. linearis
Boesmantee: see Stachys rugosa var. linearis
Boetabessie: see Chrysanthemoides monilifera
Bokbaaivygie: see Dorotheanthus bellidiformis
Bokhoring: see Microloma sagittatum
Bolusanthus speciosus 58
Bontaalwyn: see Aloe variegata
Bontblaargaringboom: see Agave americana 'Marginata'
Bontblaarwasplant: see Hoya carnosa 'Variegata'
Bontmalva: see Pelargonium cv.
Boomatamie: see Cyphomandra betacea
Boomvaring: see Alsophila dregei
Boophane disticha 59
Bosbruidsbos: see Pavetta lanceolata
Bosdruif: see Rhoicissus tomentosa
Boslelie: see Clivia miniata var. miniata; Crinum moorei; Veltheimia bracteata
Boston ivy: see Parthenocissus tricuspidata
Bosviooltjie: see Barleria obtusa; Browallia spp.
Bot River protea: see Protea compacta
Botterblom: see Dimorphotheca sinuata Gazania krebsiana
Bottlebrush: see Callistemon citrinus 'Splendens'
Bottlebrush, Weeping: see Callistemon viminalis
Bottle palm: see Hyophorbe lagenicaulis
Bottle plant, Australian: see Jatropha podagrica
Bottlebrush, Natal: see Greyia sutherlandii
Bottlebrush, Transvaal: see Greyia radlkoferi
Bougainvillea 59
Bouncing Betty: see Saponaria officinalis
Box holly: see Ruscus aculeatus

Brachycarpaea juncea 30
Brachychiton
    acerifolium 60
    discolor 60
    populneus 60
Brachylaena discolor subsp.
    transvaalensis 61
Brasiliaanse peperboom: see Schinus
    terebinthifolius
Brassaia actinophylla 61
Brassica oleracea 61
Brazilian gesneria: see Sinningia
    speciosa
Brazilian glory bush: see Tibouchina
    urvilleana
Brazilian golden vine: see Stigmaphyllon
    ciliatum
Brazilian pepper tree: see Schinus molle
Brazilian red-cloak: see Megaskepasma
    erythrochlamys
Breath of heaven: see Diosma ericoides
Breeblaarkoraalboom: see Erythrina
    latissima
Breekhout: see Alberta magna
Breynia disticha 'Roseo-picta' 62
Bridal broom: see Cytisus x praecox
    'Albus'
Bridal heath: see Erica bauera
Bridal wreath: see Deutzia scabra 'Plena'
Broad-leaved coral tree: see Erythrina
    latissima
Bromeliad, Blushing: see Neoregelia
    carolinae
Broodbome: see Encephalartos spp.
Broom, Spanish: see Spartium junceum
Broom, Wild: see Lebeckia cytisoides
Browallia
    americana 62
    speciosa 62
    speciosa 'Major' 62
Brownea coccinea 63
Brugmansia x candida 63
Bruidbesem: see Cytisus x praecox
    'Albus'
Brunfelsia
    pauciflora 'Eximia' 63
    pauciflora 'Magnifica' 63
Brunia
    neglecta 64
    nodiflora 64
    stokoei 64
Brunsvigia orientalis 64
Brush cherry: see Syzygium
    paniculatum
Buchu: see Agathosma ovata
Buchu, Klip: see Coleonema album
Buck Bay vygie: see Dorotheanthus
    bellidiformis
Buddleia: see Buddleja
Buddleja
    davidii 65
    madagascariensis 65
    salviifolia 65
Bulbine frutescens 65
Bulbinella floribunda 66
Bullrush: see Typha capensis
Burchellia bubalina 66
Burmese honeysuckle: see Lonicera
    hildebrandiana
Burning bush: see Combretum
    microphyllum
Bush felicia: see Felicia amelloides
Bush lily: see Clivia miniata var. miniata
Bush tea: see Cyclopia genistoides
Bush-tick berry: see Chrysanthemoides
    monilifera
Bush violet: see Barleria obtusa;
    Browallia spp.
Bushman poison tree: see Acokanthera
    oblongifolia
Busy lizzie: see Impatiens walleriana
Butcher's broom: see Ruscus aculeatus
Butterfly bush: see Buddleja davidii
Butterfly delphinium: see Delphinium
    grandiflorum
Butterfly flower: see Schizanthus
    pinnatus
Butterfly lily: see Hedychium coronarium

Butterfly orchid: see Epidendrum x
    obrienianum
Butterfly tree: see Bauhinia purpurea
Button fern: see Pellaea rotundifolia

Cabbage tree: see Cordyline australis;
    Cussonia spicata
Cactus
    Christmas: see Schlumbergera
        bridgesii
    Cob: see Lobivia boliviensis
    Crab: see Schlumbergera truncata
    Easter: see Rhipsalidopsis gaertneri
    Easter lily: see Echinopsis multiplex
    Golden barrel: see Echinocactus
        grusonii
    Hedgehog: see Echinopsis multiplex
    Peanut: see Chamaecereus sylvestri
    Rainbow: see Echinocactus pectinatus
        var. neomexicanus
    Red orchid: see Nopalxochia
        ackermannii
    Sea urchin: see Echinopsis multiplex
    Strawberry: see Ferocactus setispinus
    Torch: see Trichocereus spachianus
Caesalpinia
    gilliesii 67
    pulcherrima 67
Caladium x hortulanum 67
Caladiums, Giant: see Alocasia cuprea
Calathea
    insignis 67
    ornata 'Roseo-lineata' 67
Calceolaria crenatiflora 68
Calendula officinalis 68
Calico plant: see Alternanthera ficoidea
    'Bettsickiana'; Aristolochia elegans
California bluebell: see Phacelia
    campanularia
California privet: see Ligustrum
    ovalifolium 'Aureum'
Californian poppy: see Eschscholzia
    californica
Calla, Black: see Arum palaestinum
Calliandra
    brevipes 68
    selloi: see C. brevipes
    tweedii 68
Callicarpa dichotoma 69
Callisia elegans 'Nana' 69
Callistemon
    citrinus 'Splendens' 69
    coccineus: see C. macropunctatus
    macropunctatus 69
    viminalis 70
Callistephus chinensis 70
Calodendrum capense 70
Calonyction aculeatum: see Ipomoea
    alba
Calpurnia aurea 71
Camellia japonica cv. 71
Camomile: see Anthemis cupaniana
Camomile, Golden: see Anthemis
    tinctoria
Campanula
    carpatica 71
    glomerata 71
    medium 72
    trachelium 72
Campsis grandiflora 72
Canary bird bush: see Crotalaria
    agatiflora
Canary creeper: see Senecio tamoides
Canary Islands date palm: see Phoenix
    canariensis
Canary ivy: see Hedera canariensis
    'Gloire de Marengo'
Cancer bush: see Sutherlandia
    frutescens
Candelabra flower: see Brunsvigia
    orientalis
Candelabra tree: see Euphorbia spp.
Candelstick lily: see Lilium dauricum
Candytuft: see Iberis spp.
Canna
    x generalis 'Confetti' 72
    indica 72
Canterbury bells: see Campanula
    medium

Canterburyklokkies: see Campanula
    medium
Cantua buxifolia 73
Cape ash: see Ekebergia capensis
Cape candelabra tree: see Euphorbia
    curvirama
Cape chestnut: see Calodendrum
    capense
Cape coast lily: see Crinum moorei
Cape cowslip: see Lachenalia aloides
Cape daisy: see Dimorphotheca
    pluvialis
Cape dandelion: see Arctotheca
    calendula
Cape everlasting: see Helipterum
    eximium: Phaenocoma prolifera
Cape forget-me-not: see Anchusa
    capensis
Cape fuchsia: see Phygelius capensis
Cape gooseberry: see Physalis
    peruviana
Cape honeysuckle: see Tecomaria
    capensis
Cape hyacinth: see Galtonia candicans
Cape jewels: see Nemesia strumosa
    hybrids
Cape laburnum: see Crotalaria capensis
Cape may: see Coleonema album;
    Spiraea cantoniensis
Cape pondweed: see Aponogeton
    distachyos
Cape primrose: see Streptocarpus spp.
Cape rattle pod: see Crotalaria agatiflora
Cape weed: see Arctotheca calendula
Capsicum annuum 73
Caralluma lutea: see Orbeopsis lutea
Cardinal climber: see Ipomoea
    quamoclit
Cardinal flower: see Sinningia cardinalis
Carissa
    bispinosa 73
    edulis 73
    macrocarpa 74
Carnation: see Dianthus caryophyllus
Carob: see Ceratonia siliqua
Carolina jasmine: see Gelsemium
    sempervirens
Carpanthea pomeridiana 74
Carpet bugle: see Ajuga spp.
Carpet geranium: see Geranium
    incanum
Carpobrotus
    deliciosus 74
    edulis 74
    muirii 74, 75
    quadrifidus 75
    sauerae 75
Caryopteris incana 75
Caryota mitis 75
Cassia
    artemisiodes 76
    corymbosa 76
    didymobotrya 76
    multijuga 76
    nodosa 76
Cassine crocea 77
Cast-iron plant: see Aspidistra elatior
Castalis nudicaulis 77
Castanea sativa 77
Castor bean: see Ricinus communis
Castor oil plant: see Ricinus communis
Catharanthus
    roseus 78
    roseus 'Albus' 78
Catherine wheel: see Scadoxus
    multiflorus subsp. Katharinae
Catmint: see Nepeta cataria
Cat's claw creeper: see Macfadyena
    unguis-cati
Cat's tail: see Bulbinella floribunda
Cattleya x hybridum
Ceanothus
    x delilianus 'Gloire de Versailles' 78
    papillosus 'Roweanus' 78
Cedar, Mountain: see Widdringtonia
    nodiflora
Cedar wattle: see Acacia terminalis
Celosia
    argentea 'Pyramidalis' 79

cristata 79
Celtis africana 79
Centaurea
    cineraria 79
    cyanus 79
Centipede plant: see Homaloocladium
    platycladum
Centradenia
    grandiflora 80
    rosea 80
Century plant: Agave spp.
Cephalophyllum
    alstonii 80
    procumbems 80
Cerastium tomentosum 80
Ceratonia siliqua 81
Ceratostigma willmottianum 81
Ceratotheca triloba 81
Cercis siliquastrum 82
Cereus
    hildmannianus 82
    peruviana 'Monstrosa' 82
Ceropegia woodii 82
Cestrum
    elegans 'Smithii' 83
    nocturnum 83
Cestrums, Blue: see Jochroma cyaneum
Chaenomeles
    lagenaria: see C. speciosa
    speciosa 83
    speciosa 'Umbilicata Nana' 83
Chamaecereus sylvestri 84
Chamaecyparis obtusa 'Crippsii' 84
Chamaedorea
    cataractarum 84
    elegans 84
    geonomiformis 85
    seifrizii 85
Chamelaucium uncinatum 85
Chandelier plant: see Kalanchoe
    tubiflora
Chasmanthe
    floribunda 85
    floribunda var. duckittii 85
Chayote: see Sechium edule
Cheiranthus cheiri 86
Cheiridopsis
    herrei 86
    serrulata 86
Chenille plant: see Acalypha hispida
Cherry, Brush: see Syzygium
    paniculatum
Cherry, False Jerusalem: see Solanum
    capsicastrum
Cherry pie: see Heliotropium
    arborescens
Chestnut, Cape: see Calodendrum
    capense
Chestnut, European, see Castanea sativa
Chestnut, Spanish: see Castanea sativa
Chilean jasmine: see Mandevilla laxa
Chilean lily: see Alstroemeria aurantiaca
Chili, Ornamental: see Capsicum
    annuum
China aster: see Callistephus chinensis
China flower: see Adenandra uniflora
Chincherinchees: see Ornithogalum
    spp.
Chinese holly: see Ilex cornuta
Chinese hat plant: see Holmskioldia
    sanguinea
Chinese lantern: see Abutilon spp.;
    Nymania capensis
Chinese lantern flower: see Sandersonia
    aurantiaca
Chinese magnolia: see Magnolia x
    soulangiana 'Amabilis'
Chinese paper plant: see Tetrapanax
    papyriferus
Chinese plumbago: see Ceratostigma
    willmottianum
Chinese privet: see Ligustrum lucidum
    'Tricolor'
Chinese trumpet creeper: see Campsis
    grandiflora
Chironia baccifera 86
Chlorophytum
    capense 87
    comosum 'Picturatum' 87

comosum 'Variegatum' 87
comosum 'Vittatum' 87
Chocolate plant: Pseuderanthemum alatum
Chondropetalum tectorum 87
Chonemorpha fragrans 88
Christ thorn: see Euphorbia milii var. splendens
Christmas bells: see Sandersonia aurantiaca
Christmas berry: see Chironia baccifera
Christmas cactus: see Schlumbergera bridgesii
Christmas rose: see Hydrangea macrophylla var. macrophylla
Christusdoring: see Euphorbia milii var. splendens
Chrysanthemoides monilifera 88
Chrysanthemum
 coronarium 88
 frutescens hybrids 88, 89
 maximum 88, 89
 morifolium hybrids 88, 89
Cigar flower: see Cuphea ignea
Cigarette bush: see Cuphea ignea
Cineraria: see Senecio spp.
Cissus rhombifolia 'Ellen Danica' 89
Cistus
 crispus 90
 incanus 90
 purpureus 90
 vaginatus 90
Citharexylum quadrangulare 90
Clanwiliam marguerite: see Euryops speciosissimus
Clarkia
 amoena subsp. whitneyi 91
 unguiculata 91
Clematis
 brachiata 91
 x jackmanii 'Rubra' 91
Cleome spinosa 91
Clerodendrum
 glabrum 92
 splendens 92
 thomsoniae 92
 ugandense 92
Climbing aloe: see Aloe ciliaris
Climbing bell: see Littonia modesta
Clivia
 miniata var. miniata 92
 miniata var. citrina 92
 nobilis 93
Clock vine: see Thunbergia grandiflora
Clock pink: see Dianthus caryophyllus
Clover: see Trifolium repens 'Atropurpureum'
Clustered bellflower: see Campanula glomerata
Clustered fishtail palm: see Caryota mitis
Clytostoma callistegioides 93
Coast erythrina: see Erythrina caffra
Cob cactus: see Lobivia boliviensis
Cobas: see Cyphostemma currorii
Cockscomb: see Celosia cristata
Codiaeum variegatum var. pictum 93-4
Coffea arabica 94
Coffee: see Coffea arabica
Coleonema
 album 94
 aspalathoides 94
 pulchellum 95
 pulchrum 95
Coleus x hybridus 95
Colletia cruciata 95
Colocasia esculenta 'Euchlora' 96
Columbine: see Aquilegia caerulea
Columnea
 x banksii 96
 microphylla 96
Combretum
 bracteosum 96
 microphyllum 96
Common bamboo: see Bambusa vulgaris
Common camellia: see Camellia japonica

Common coffee: see Coffea arabica
Common coral tree: see Erythrina lysistemon
Common gardenia: see Gardenia jasminoides
Common hook-thorn: see Acacia caffra
Common lilac: see Syringa vulgaris
Common morning glory: see Ipomoea purpurea
Common tree fern: see Alsophila dregei
Common wild currant: see Rhus pyroides
Common wild fig: see Ficus natalensis
Cone flower: see Rudbeckia fulgida
Confetti bush: see Coleonema pulchrum
Conicosia pugioniformis 97
Conophytum spp. 97
Consolida ambigua 98
Convolvulus
 cneorum 98
 mauritanicus 98
Convolvulus, Madagascar: see Stictocardia beraviensis
Copper beech: see Fagus sylvatica 'Atropunicea'
Copperleaf: see Acalypha wilkesiana
Coprosma
 x kirkii 98
 repens 98
 repens 'Marble Chips' 98, 99
 repens 'Variegata' 99
 robusta 99
Coral berry: see Aechmea fulgens var. discolor; Ardisia crispa
Coral bush: see Russelia equisetiformis
Coral creeper: see Antigonon leptopus
Coral pea: see Kennedia rubicunda
Coral trees: see Erythrina spp.
Cordyline
 australis 99
 terminalis 99
Coreopsis grandiflora 99
Cork oak: see Quercus suber
Cornflower: see Centaurea cyanus
Cortaderia selloana 100
Cosmos: see Bidens formosa
Cosmos bipinnatus: see Bidens formosa
Cotoneaster
 amoenus 100
 conspicuus 100
 franchetii 100
 frigidus 100, 101
 horizontalis 100, 101
 hupehensis 101
 x watereri 'Cornubia' 101
Cotton wood: see Populus deltoides
Cotula turbinata 101
Cotyledon
 cacalioides: see Tylecodon cacalioides
 grandiflora: see Tylecodon cacalioides
 orbiculata 101
 tomentosa 101
Coulter bush: see Athanasia spp.
Cow's horn: see Euphorbia grandicornis
Cowslip, Cape: see Lachenalia aloides
Crab cactus: see Schlumbergera truncata
Crane flower: see Strelitzia reginae
Crane's bill: see Geranium sanguineum
Crassula
 argentea: see C. ovata
 capitella subsp. thyrsiflora 102
 coccinea 102
 multicava 102
 ovata 102
 perfoliata 102
 portulacea: see C. ovata
 rubricaulis 102
 rupestris 102, 103
 subulata 103
Crataegus
 x grignonensis 103
 laevigata 103
 oxyacantha: see C. laevigata
 phaenopyrum 103
 prunifolia 103
 pubescens forma stipulacea 103

Creeping fig: see Ficus pumila
Creeping Jenny: see Lysimachia nummularia
Creeping marguerite: see Osteospermum fruticosum
Crepe myrtle: see Lagerstroemia spp.
Crimson babiana: see Babiana villosa
Crinum
 bulbispermum 104
 campanulatum 104
 macowanii 104
 moorei 104
 paniculata 105
Crocosmia
 masonorum 104
 paniculata 105
Cross-berry: see Grewia occidentalis
Cross vine: see Bignonia capreolata
Crossandra infundibuliformis 105
Crotalaria
 agatiflora 105
 capensis 105
Cryptanthus bromelioides 106
Cryptostegia grandiflora 106
Crystal anthurium: see Anthurium andraeanum
Cunonia capensis 106
Cup-of-gold: see Solandra maxima
Cuphea
 hyssopifolia 107
 ignea 107
 micropetala 107
Curiosity plant: see Cereus peruviana 'Monstrosa'
Curly kale: see Brassica oleracea
Curly-leaved nerine: see Nerine krigei
Currant, Common wild: see Rhus pyroides
Curry bush: see Hypericum revolutum
Cushion bush, Suurberg: see Oldenburgia arbuscula
Cussonia spicata 107
Cyathea dregei: see Alsophila dregei
Cycads: see Encephalartos spp.
Cycas circinalis 108
 revoluta 108
Cyclamen persicum cv. 108
Cyclopia genistoides 108
Cymbidium cvs. 109
Cynara scolymus 109
Cyperus
 alternifolius 110
 papyrus 110
Cyphomandra betacea 110
Cyphostemma
 currorii 110
 juttae 110
Cypress
 Golden: see Chamaecyparis obtusa 'Crippsii'
 Hinoki: see Chamaecyparis obtusa 'Crippsii'
 Summer: see Kochia scoparia
 Vine: see Ipomoea quamoclit
Cyrtanthus
 brachyscyphus 111
 elatus 111
 falcatus 111
 mackenii var. mackenii 111
Cyrtomium falcatum 111
Cyrtostachys lakka 112
Cytisus x praecox 'Albus' 112

Daffodil: see Narcissus cvs
Dagga: see Leonotis spp.
Dahlia
 imperialis 112, 113
 pinnata cvs 113
 pinnata 'Pompon' 113
Dais cotinifolia 113
Dakriet: see Chondropetalum tectorum
Date palm: see Phoenix spp.
Datura cornigera: see Brugmansia x candida
Day lilies: see Hemerocallis spp.
Delicious monster: see Monstera deliciosa
Delonix regia 114

Delphinium
 ajacis: see Consolida ambigua
 x elatum 114
 grandiflorum 114
Dendrobium phalaenopsis 115
Deutzia
 gracilis 115
 scabra 'Plena' 115
Dianthus
 x allwoodii 115
 barbatus 115, 116
 caryophyllus 116
 chinensis 'Heddewiggii' 116
Diascia integerrima 116
Dicentra spectabilis 116
Dichondra
 micrantha 117
 repens: see D. micrantha
Dichorisandra thyrsiflora 117
Dichrostachys cinerea subsp. africana 117
Dicliptera suberecta 118
Dicoma zeyheri 118
Didelta
 carnosa var. carnosa 118
 spinosa 118
Dieffenbachia
 amoena 119
 maculata 119
 maculata 'Rudolph Roehrs' 119
Dierama pendulum 119
Dietes
 bicolor 120
 grandiflora 120
Digitalis purpurea 120
Dilatris pillansii 120
Dimorphotheca
 pluvialis 121
 sinuata 121
Dionaea muscipula 121
Dioscorea bulbifera 121
Diosma ericoides 122
Diospyros kaki 122
Dipladenia splendens: see Mandevilla splendens
Disa
 uniflora 122
 uniflora x cardinalis: see Disa uniflora 'Kirstenbosch Pride'
 uniflora 'Kirstenbosch Pride' 122
Dissotis canescens 123
Distictis
 buccinatoria 123
 buccinatoria x D. laxiflora: see D. x riversii
 laxiflora 123
 x riversii 123
Divine flower or Angelier: see Dianthus caryophyllus
Dizygotheca elegantissima 124
Dodonaea
 angustifolia 124
 angustifolia 'Purpurea' 124
Dog fennel: see Anthemis cupaniana
Dog rose: see Rosa canina
Dombeya
 burgessiae 124
 rotundifolia var. rotundifolia 124, 125
 x tiliacea 125
 wallichii 125
Donkey's ear: see Kalanchoe beharensis
Dorotheanthus bellidiformis 125
Doryanthes excelsa 125
Doxantha unguis-cati: see Macfadyena unguis-cati
Draaklelie: see Dracunculus vulgaris
Dracaena
 deremensis 'Warneckii' 126
 hookerana 126
 marginata 'Tricolor' 126
Dracophilus dealbatis 126
Dracunculus vulgaris 127
Dragon lily: see Dracunculus vulgaris
Drolpeer: see Dombeya rotundifolia var rotundifolia
Drosanthemum
 bicolor 127

speciosum 127
Druifhiasint: see Muscari botryoides
Dubbelkarlienblom: see Euphorbia pulcherrima 'Plenissima'
Duchesnea indica 127
Duinegousblom: see Didelta carnosa var. carnosa
Duiwelstabak: see Leonotis leonurus var. leonurus
Dumb cane: see Dieffenbachia amoena
Duranta
  repens 128
  repens 'Variegata' 128
Dusty miller: see Senecio cineraria
Dutch iris: see Iris xiphium
Dutchman's breeches: see Dicentra spectabilis
Dutchman's pipe: see Aristolochia spp.
Duvernoia adhatodoides 128
Dwarf erythrina: see Erythrina humeana
Dwarf-fern-leaf bamboo: see Arundinaria disticha
Dwarf glory bush: see Dissotis canescens
Dwarf pomegranate: see Punica granatum 'Nana'
Dwarf-striped inch plant: see Callisia elegans 'Nana'
Dwarf white-striped bamboo: see Arundinaria variegata
Dwergkarlienblom: see Euphorbia pulcherrima cv.
Dymondia margaretae 128

Easter cactus: see Rhipsalidopsis gaertneri
Easter lily cactus: see Echinopsis multiplex
Eastern Cape cycad: see Encephalartos altensteinii
Echeveria
  elegans 129
  x hybrida 129
Echinocactus grusonii 129
Echinocereus
  melanocentrus 130
  pectinatus var. neomexicanus 130
Echinopsis multiplex 130
Echium fastuosum 130
Edging candytuft: see Iberis sempervirens
Eggplant: see Solanum melongena var. esculentum cv.
Egyptian lotus: see Nymphaea caerulea
Egyptian reed: see Cyperus papyrus
Eichhornia crassipes 131
Ekebergia capensis 131
Elaeagnus pungens 'Aurea-variegata' 131
Elandsvy: see Carpobrotus sauerae
Elder, Yellow: see Tecoma alata
Elders: see Sambucus spp.
Elegia capensis 132
Elephant's ear: see Alocasia macrorrhiza; Colocasia esculenta 'Euchlora'
Elephant's food: see Portulacaria afra
Elephant's wood: see Bolusanthus speciosus
Emerald feather: see Asparagus densiflorus 'Sprengeri'
Emerald fern: see Asparagus densiflorus 'Sprengeri'
Emerald ripple peperomia: see Peperomia caperata
Encephalartos
  altensteinii 132
  frederici-guilielmi 132
  horridus 132
  latifrons 132
  transvenosus 133
Endymion hispanicus 133
Engelse kanferfoelie: see Lonicera periclymenum
Engelse madeliefie: see Bellis perennis
Engelselaventel: see Lavandula angustifolia subsp. angustifolia
English daisy: see Bellis perennis

English hawthorn: see Crataegus laevigata
English honeysuckle: see Lonicera periclymenum
English ivy: see Hedera helix 'Aureovariegata'
English lavender: see Lavandula angustifolia subsp. angustifolia
English marigold: see Calendula officinalis
English violet: see Viola odorata
English wallflower: see Cheiranthus cheiri
Enkeldoring: see Acacia robusta
Ensete ventricosum 133
Epidendrum x obrienianum 134
Epiphyllum
  ackermannii: see Nopalxochia ackermannii
  chrysocardium 134
Epipremnum aureum 134
Episcia cupreata 135
Erica
  bauera 135
  blenna 135
  cerinthoides 135
  conspicua 135
  fastigiata 135, 136
  patersonia 135, 136
  regia 136
  speciosa 136
  versicolor 136
  vestita 136
Erigeron karvinskianus 136
Eriocephalus africanus 137
Eroeda capensis 137
Ertjiebos: see Podalyria calyptrata
Erythrina
  caffra 137
  crista-galli 137
  humeana 138
  latissima 138
  lysistemon 138
  variegata var. orientalis 138
  zeyheri 138
Escallonia
  x langleyensis 139
  rubra var. macrantha 139
Eschscholzia californica 139
Essenhout: see Ekebergia capensis
Eucalyptus
  calophylla 139
  erythrocorys 139
  ficifolia 140
Eucharis grandiflora 140
Eucomis
  autumnalis subsp. autumnalis 140
  autumnalis subsp. clavata 140, 141
  clavata: see Eucomis autumnalis subsp. clavata
  comosa var. comosa 140, 141
  undulata: see Eucomis atumnalis subsp. autumnalis
Eugenia myrtifolia: see Syzygium paniculatum
Eulophia speciosa 141
Euonymus
  japonica 141
  japonica 'Aureo-marginata' 141
  japonica 'Aureo-variegata' 142
Eupatorium
  cannabinum var. plenum 142
  sordidum 142
Euphorbia
  caput-medusae 142
  cooperi 142, 143
  curvirama 143
  grandicornis 143
  heterophylla 143
  ingens 143
  marginata 143
  mauritanica 143
  milii var. splendens 143, 144
  pulcherrima 144
  pulcherrima cv. 144
  pulcherrima 'Plenissima' 144
  splendens: see E. milii var. splendens

European chestnut: see Castanea sativa
European elder: see Sambucus nigra 'Albo-variegata'
European goldenrod: see Solidago virgaurea
Europese kastaiing: see Castanea sativa
Europese vlier: see Sambucus nigra 'Albo-variegata'
Euryops
  pectinatus 144
  spathaceus 144
  speciosissimus 144, 145
  tenuissimus 145
  virgineus 145
Everlasting: see Helichrysum bracteatum
Everlasting, Cape: see Helipterum eximium; Phaenocoma prolifera
Everlasting pea: see Lathyrus latifolius
Ewwatrewwa: see Satyrium coriifolium
Exacum affine 145

Fabiana imbricata 146
Fagus
  sylvatica 'Atropunicea' 146
  sylvatica 'Cuprea': see Fagus sylvatica 'Atropunicea'
Fairy bells: see Dierama pendulum
Fairy duster: see Calliandra brevipes
Fairy elephant's feet: see Frithia pulchra
Fairy primula: see Primula malacoides
Falling stars: see Crocosmia paniculata
False acacia: see Robinia pseudoacacia
False aralia: see Dizygotheca elegantissima
False dragonhead: see Physostegia virginiana
False heath: see Fabiana imbricata
False heather: see Cuphea hyssopifolia
False jasmine: see Gelsemium sempervirens
False Jerusalem cherry: see Solanum capsicastrum
Fan aloe: see Aloe plicatilis
Fan iris: see Neomarica caerulea
Fan-leaved boophane: see Boophane disticha
x Fatshedera lizei 146
  lizei 'Variegata' 146
Fatsia japonica 147
Faucaria sp. 147
  felina 147
Feather climber: see Acridocarpus natalitius
Feather grass: see Pennisetum villosum
Feathery cassia: see Cassia artemisioides
Feijoa sellowiana 147
Felicia
  amelloides 148
  fruticosa subsp. fruticosa 148
  heterophylla 148
Felt bush: see Kalanchoe beharensis
Fenestraria
  aurantiaca 148
  rhopalophylla 148
Fennel: see Foeniculum vulgare
Fennel, Dog: see Anthemis cupaniana
Fennel, Wild: see Nigella damascena
Fern
  Birds' nest: see Asplenium nidus
  Button: see Pellaea rotundifolia
  Holly: see Cyrtomium falcatum
  Rabbit's foot: see Polypodium aureum
  Staghorn: see Platycerium bifurcatum
  Sword: see Nephrolepis exaltata
Fern palm: see Cycas spp.
Ferocactus setispinus 149
Ferraria crispa var. crispa 149
Ferweeltjie: see Sparaxis elegans
Fever tree: see Acacia xanthoploea
Feverfew chrysanthemums 88
Ficus
  capensis: see F. sur
  elastica 149
  elastica 'Variegata' 149

lyrata 150
natalensis 150
nitida 150
pumila 150
sur 150
Fiddle leaf: see Ficus lyrata
Fiddle leaf fig: see Ficus lyrata
Fiddlewood: see Citharexylum quadrangulare
Figs: see Ficus spp.
Fijian firebush: see Acalypha wilkesiana
Fire dart bush: see Malvaviscus arboreus
Fire lily: see Clivia miniata var. miniata
Fire plant, Mexican: see Euphorbia heterophylla
Fire thorn: see Pyracantha spp.
Firebush: see Hamelia chrysantha
Firebush, Fijian: see Acalypha wilkesiana
Firecracker flower: Crossandra infundibuliformis
Firecracker plant: see Cuphea hyssopifolia
Firecracker vine: see Manettia inflata
Firewheel pincushion: see Leucospermum tottum
Firewheel tree: see Stenocarpus sinuatus
Fishtail palm: see Caryota mitis
Fittonia verschaffeltii 150
Flag bush: see Mussaenda spp.
Flamboyant: see Delonix regia
Flame acacia: see Acacia ataxacantha
Flame bush, Mexican: see Calliandra tweedii
Flame lily: see Gloriosa superba
Flame nettle: Coleus x hybridus
Flame-of-the-woods: see Ixora coccinea 'Fraseri'
Flame tree: see Brachychiton acerifolium; Spathodea campanulata
Flame tree, Natal: see Alberta magna
Flame violet: see Episcia cupreata
Flaming creeper: see Combretum microphyllum
Flaming sphere: see Euphorbia pulcherrima 'Plenissima'
Flamingo lily: see Anthurium andreaanum
Flax, New Zealand: see Phormium tenax
Flax, Yellow: see Reinwardtia indica
Floks, Wilde: see Sutera grandiflora
Florist's chrysanthemum: see C. morifolium cvs.
Florist's cineraria: see Senecio x hybridus
Florist's cyclamen: see Cyclamen persicum cv.
Florist's spiraea: see Astilbe japonica
Floss flower: see Ageratum houstonianum
Flower of the west wind: see Zephyranthes grandiflora
Flowering inch plant: see Tradescantia blossfeldiana
Flowering maple: see Abutilon pictum
Flowering peach: see Prunus persica cultivars
Flowering plum: see Prunus cerasifera 'Atropurpurea'
Flowering pomegranate: see Punica granatum 'Flore Pleno'
Flowering quince, Japanese: see Chaenomeles speciosa
Fluitjies: see Lebeckia cytisoides
Foeniculum vulgare 151
Foliage flower: see Breynia disticha 'Roseo-picta'
Fonteinbossie: see Brunia nodiflora
Forest bride's bush: see Pavetta lanceolata
Forget-me-not: see Myosotis scorpioides
Forget-me-not, Cape: see Anchusa capensis
Forget-me-not tree: see Duranta repens
Forsythia x intermedia 'Spectabilis' 151
Fortunella margarita 151

Fountain grass: see Pennisetum setaceum
Four o'clock: see Mirabilis jalapa
Foxglove: see Digitalis purpurea
Foxglove, Wild: see Ceratotheca triloba
Foxtail fern: see Asparagus densiflorus 'Myers'
Fragaria indica: see Duchesnea indica
Frangipani: see Plumeria rubra
Franse lavender: see Lavandula dentata
Freesia x hybrida 152
French lavender: see Lavandula dentata
French marigold: see Tagetes patula 'Naughty Marietta'
Freylinia
 lanceolata 152
 visseri 152
Friendship plant: see Billbergia nutans
Frithia pulchra 153
Froetang: see Romulea rosea var. rosea
Frost flower: see Aster novi-belgii
Fruit salad plant: see Monstera deliciosa
Fuchsia, Cape: see Phygelius capensis
Fuchsia, Wild: see Halleria elliptica
Fuchsia
 x hybrida 153
 magellanica 153
 triphylla 153
Furcraea foetida
Furze: see Ulex europeus
Fuschia, tree: see Schotia brachypetala

Gaillardia
 aristata 154
 x grandiflora 154
 pulchella 'Lorenziana' 154
Galjoenblom: see Lobelia valida
Galphimia vine: see Tristellateia australasiae
Galtonia candicans 155
Gansies: see Asclepias fruticosa
Ganskos: see Cotula turbinata
Gansvoet: see Syngonium podophyllum
Garden verbena: see Verbena x hybrida
Gardener's garters: see Phalaris arundinacea var. picta
Gardenia
 cornuta 155
 jasminoides 'Veitchii' 155
 thunbergia 155
Garingboom: see Agave americana
Garland flower: see Hedychium coronarium
Garland may: see Spiraea x arguta
Garlic, Sweet: see Tulbaghia fragrans
Garlic, Wild: see Tulbaghia violacea
Gasteria
 acinacifolia 156
 batesiana 156
 excelsa 156
 transvaalensis 156
Gaura lindheimeri 157
Gay feather: see Liatris pycnostachya
Gazania
 hybrid 157
 krebsiana 157
 lichtensteinii 157, 158
 rigens var. rigens 157, 158
 rigens var. uniflora 157, 158
Geelaronskelk: see Zantedeschia pentlandii
Geelblomsalie: see Salvia africana-lutea
Geeldaglelie: see Hemerocallis lilioasphodelus
Geelgemmerlelie: see Hedychium gardneranum
Geelgranaat: see Rhigozum obovatum
Geelklokkie: see Littonia modesta; Sandersonia aurantiaca
Geelkoppie: see Liparia splendens subsp. splendens
Geeloleander: see Thevetia peruviana
Geelwateruintjie: see Nymphoides indica
Geissorhiza
 radians 158
 tulbaghensis 158
Geldbeursie: see Albuca cooperi

Gelderroos: see Viburnum opulus
Gelsemium sempervirens 158
Gemmerlelies: see Hedychium spp.
Gentian, Wild: see Chironia baccifera
Geraldton-wasplant: see Chamelaucium uncinatum
Geraldton wax plant: see Chamelaucium uncinatum
Geranium
 anemonifolium: see G. palmatum
 incanum 159
 palmatum 159
 sanguineum 159
Gerbera
 jamesonii 159
 jamesonii hybrid 159
German violet: see Exacum affine
Gesiggie: see Viola x wittrockiana
Gesneria cardinalis: see Sinningia cardinalis
Gethyllis ciliaris 160
Geurviburnum: see Viburnum odoratissimum
Gewone koraalboom: see Erythrina lysistemon
Gewone purperwinde: see Ipomoea purpurea
Gewone sering: see Syringa vulgaris
Gewone wildevy: see Ficus natalensis
Ghaap: see Trichocaulon spp.
Ghostweed: see Euphorbia marginata
Giant alocasia: see Alocasia cuprea
Giant caladium: see Alocasia cuprea
Giant chincherinchee: see Ornithogalum saundersiae
Giant Dutchman's pipe: see Aristolochia gigantea
Giant granadilla: see Passiflora quadrangularis
Giant honeysuckle: see Lonicera hildebrandiana
Giant lily: see Doryanthes excelsa
Giant reed: see Arundo donax var. versicolor
Gifbol: see Boophane disticha
Gifboom: see Acokanthera oblongifolia
Gifmelkbos: see Euphorbia mauritanica
Gilia: see Ipomopsis rubra
Gilia coronopifolia: see Ipomopsis rubra
Ginger: see Alpinia spp.
Ginger bush: see Iboza riparia
Ginger lilies: see Hedychium spp.
Ginkgo biloba 160
Gladiolus alatus 160
 cardinalis x G. carmineus 161
 carneus 161
 dalenii 161
 x hortulanus 161
 watsonius: see Homoglossum watsonium
Gleditsia triacanthos 161
Globe amaranth: see Gomphrena globosa
Globe artichoke: see Cynara scolymus
Gloriosa
 rothschildiana 162
 simplex 162
 superba 162
 virescens: see G. simplex
Glory bush: see Tibouchina spp.
Glossy abelia: see Abelia x grandiflora
Glossy privet: see Ligustrum lucidum
Glottiphyllum parviflorum 162
Gloxinia: see Sinningia speciosa
Goat's beard: see Astilbe japonica
Godetia grandiflora: see Clarkia amoena subsp. whitneyi
Gold-dust tree: see Aucuba japonica 'Variegata'
Gold flower: see Hypericum calycinum
Goldcup: see Solandra maxima
Golden arum: see Zantedeschia pentlandii
Golden barrel cactus: see Echinocactus grusonii
Golden camomile: see Anthemis tinctoria
Golden Ceylon creeper: see Epipremnum aureum

Golden chain tree: see Laburnum x watereri 'Vossii'
Golden cypress: see Chamaecyparis obtusa 'Crippsii'
Golden dewdrop: see Duranta repens
Golden glory vine: see Thunbergia gregorii
Golden guinea everlasting: see Helichrysum argyrophyllum
Golden guinea plant: see Hibbertia scandens
Golden salvia: see Salvia africana-lutea
Golden shower: see Pyrostegia venusta
Golden swans: see Crocosmia masonorum
Golden tassel tree: see Calpurnia aurea
Golden trumpet bush: see Allamanda neriifolia
Golden trumpet vine: see Allamanda cathartica 'Hendersonii'
Golden vine: see Stigmaphyllon ciliatum
Golden vygie: see Lampranthus aureus
Goldenrod, European: see Solidago virgaurea
Gomphrena globosa 163
Good-luck palm: see Chamaedorea elegans
Good luck plant: see Cordyline terminalis
Goose foot plant: see Syngonium podophyllum
Gooseberries: see Physalis spp.
Gorse: see Ulex europeus
Goudroede: see Solidago virgaurea
Goue sipres: see Chamaecyparis obtusa 'Crippsii'
Gouna: see Carpobrotus edulis
Gousblom: see Arctotis spp.; Calendula officinalis; Gazania krebsiana
Granaat: see Punica granatum
Granadilla: see Passiflora spp.
Grape, Wild: see Rhoicissus tomentosa
Grape hyacinth: see Muscari botryoides
Grasklokkie: see Dierama pendulum
Grass-leaved nerine: see Nerine filifolia
Grass palm: see Cordyline australis
Greek myrtle: see Myrtus communis
Green aloe: see Furcraea foetida
Grevillea
 banksii 'Forsteri' 163
 glabrata 163
 juniperina 'Rubra' 163
 punicea 163
 robusta 164
 rosmarinifolia 164
Grewia occidentalis 164
Grey-leaved euryops: see Euryops pectinatus
Greybeard: see Tillandsia usneoides
Greyia
 radlkoferi 164
 sutherlandii 164
Grielum humifusum 165
Grondboontjiebotterkassia: see Cassia didymobotrya
Grondboontjiekaktus: see Chamaecereus sylvestri
Grootharpuisbos: see Euryops tenuissimus
Grootnoemnoem: see Carissa macrocarpa
Guava, Strawberry: see Psidium littorale var. longipes
Guelder rose: see Viburnum opulus
Guernsey lily: see Nerine sarniensis
Guinea gold vine: see Hibbertia scandens
Gums: see Eucalyptus spp.
Gunnera manicata 165
Guzmania
 lingulata var. major 165
 lingulata var. minor 165
Gymea lily: see Doryanthes excelsa
Gymnocalycium
 gibbosum 'Nigrum' 166
 mihanovichii 166
Gypsophila
 elegans 166
 elegans 'Grandiflora Alba' 166

Haakdoring: see Acacia caffra
Haaspootvaring: see Polypodium aureum
Haemanthus
 coccineus 167
 humilis 167
Halleria elliptica 167
Halssnoer-ranker: see Ceropegia woodii
Hamelia chrysantha 167
Hanekam: see Antholyza ringens
Hanekom: see Celosia cristata
Hanging lobster claws: see Heliconia rostrata
Hard pear: see Olinia ventosa
Hardenbergia comptoniana 168
Hardepeer: see Olinia ventosa
Harebell, Zuurberg: see Dierama pendulum
Harpuisbos: see Euryops speciosissimus
Hawaiian elf: see Schefflera arboricola
Hawaiian hibiscus: see Hibiscus rosa-sinensis
Haworthia
 comptoniana 168
 cooperi var. leightonii 168
 cymbiformis 168
 herbacea 168
 reinwardtii 168, 169
 venosa subsp. recurva 168, 169
Hawthorn, Indian: see Raphiolepis indica
Heath, False: see Fabiana imbricata
Heather, False: see Cuphea hyssopifolia
Heaths: see Erica spp.
Heavenly bamboo: see Nandina domestica
Hebe
 x andersonii 'Variegata' 169
 salicifolia 169
 speciosa 169
 speciosa cv. 169
Hedera
 canariensis 'Gloire de Marengo' 170
 helix 'Aureo-variegata' 170
 helix 'Bulgaria' 170
 helix 'Marmorata' 170
 helix 'Minima Luzi' 170
 helix 'Star' 170
Hedge bamboo: see Bambusa glaucescens
Hedgehog cactus: see Echinopsis multiplex
Hedychium
 coccineum 171
 coronarium 171
 gardneranum 171
Heimerliodendron brunonianum: see Pisonia umbellifera 'Variegata'
Helianthus
 annuus 171
 debilis 171
 decapetalus 'Multiflorus' 172
 tuberosus 172
Helichrysum
 argyrophyllum 172
 bracteatum 172
 petiolare 172
 pinifolium 172
 retortum 173
 splendidum 173
Heliconia
 humilis 173
 mariae 173
 psittacorum 173
 rostrata 173
Heliophila coronopifolia 174
Heliotrope: see Heliotropium arborescens
Heliotropium arborescens 174
Helipterum eximium 174
Hemerocallis
 aurantiaca 175
 flava: see H. lilioasphodelus
 lilioasphodelus 175
Hemizygia transvaalensis 175
Hemp, Mauritius: see Furcraea foetida
Hemp agrimony: see Eupatorium cannabinum var. plenum

Hen-and-chickens: see Chlorophytum comosum 'Picturatum'
Hen-en-kuikens: see Chlorophytum comosum 'Picturatum'
Henkelgeelhout: see Podocarpus henkelii
Herald's trumpet: see Beaumontia grandiflora
Herreanthus meyeri 175
Herringbone cotoneaster: see Cotoneaster horizontalis
Heuningklokkiesbos: see Freylinia lanceolata
Heuningmargriet: see Euryops virgineus
Heuningtree: see Cyclopia genistoides
Hiasint: see Hyacinthus orientalis cv.
Hibbertia scandens 176
Hibiscus
  rosa-sinensis 176, 177
  schizopetalus 176, 177
  syriacus 176, 177
  tiliaceus 177
  vitifolius 177
Hibiskus: see Hibiscus rosa-sinensis
Hiccough creeper: see Combretum bracteosum
Hiccup nut: see Combretum bracteosum
Hikranker: see Combretum bracteosum
Hinoki cypress: see Chamaecyparis obtusa 'Crippsii'
Hippeastrum x hybrida 178
Hoffmannia
  giesbreghtii 178
  refulgens 178
Hollandse iris: see Iris xiphium
Holly: see Ilex spp.
Holly fern: see Cyrtomium falcatum
Hollyhock: see Alcea rosea
Hollyhock, Wild: see Sparmannia africana
Holmskioldia
  sanguinea 178
  tettensis 178
Homocladium platycladum 179
Homeria
  comptonii 179
  elegans 179
Homoglossum watsonium 179
Honesty: see Lunaria annua
Honey locust: see Gleditsia triacanthos
Honey myrtle: see Melaleuca huegelii
Honey plant: see Hoya carnosa
Honey tea: see Cyclopia genistoides
Honeysuckle: see Lonicera spp.
  Cape: see Tecomaria capensis
  Wild: see Turraea obtusifolia
Honeysuckle fuchsia: see Fuchsia triphylla
Hoodia
  bainii 180
  triebneri 180
Hook-thorn, Common: see Acacia caffra
Hop bush: see Dodonaea angustifolia
Hop bush, Purple: see Dodonaea angustifolia 'Purpurea'
Hortensie: see Hydrangea macrophylla var. macrophylla
Hosta crispula 180
Hot water plant: see Achimenes grandiflora
Hotnotsvy: see Carpobrotus edulis
Hottentot fig: see Carpobrotus edulis
Hoya
  carnosa 180
  carnosa 'Variegata' 180
Huilboerboon: see Schotia brachypetala
Huilboom: see Peltophorum africanum
Humble plant: see Mimosa pudica
Hunnemannia fumariifolia 181
Hyacinth: see Hyacinthus orientalis cv.
  Cape: see Galtonia candicans
  Grape: see Muscari botryoides
  Water: see Eichhornia crassipes
Hyacinthus orientalis cv. 181
Hydrangea
  macrophylla 'Blue Wave' 182
  macrophylla var. macrophylla 181, 182
  macrophylla 'Regular' 182

Hymenocallis
  americana: see H. littoralis
  littoralis 182
Hymenosporum flavum 182
Hyophorbe lagenicaulis 183
Hypericum
  calycinum 183
  lanceolatum: see H. revolutum
  revolutum 183
Hypoestes aristata 183
Hypoxis rooperi 184

Iberis
  sempervirens 184
  umbellata 184
Iboza riparia 185
Icecream bush: see Breynia disticha 'Roseo-picta'
Iceland poppy: see Papaver nudicaule
Ierse klokkies: see Molucella laevis
Ifafa lily: see Cyrtanthus mackenii var. mackenii
Ifafalelie: see Cyrtanthus mackenii var. mackenii
Ilex
  aquifolium 185
  cornuta 185
  wilsonii 185
Immortelle: see Helichrysum bracteatum
Impala lily: see Adenium spp.
Impatiens
  aerocoma 186
  balsamina 186
  x hybridum 186
  oliveri 186
  wallerana 186
  wallerana 'Red Ripple' 186
Inch plant: see Zebrina pendula
  Dwarf-striped: see Callisia elegans 'Nana'
  Flowering: see Tradescantia blossfeldiana
Indian hawthorn: see Raphiolepis indica
Indian rubber tree: see Ficus elastica
Indian shot: see Canna indica
Indian strawberry: see Duchesnea indica
Indigofera procumbens 187
Iochroma see Jochroma
Ipomoea
  acuminata 187
  alba 187
  arborescens 187
  learii: see I. acuminata
  purpurea 187
  quamoclit 187, 188
  tricolor 'Blue Star' 188
  tricolor 'Summer Skies' 188
Ipomopsis rubra 188
Iresine
  herbstii 188
  herbstii 'Aureo-reticulata' 188
Iris
  Fan: see Neomarica caerulea
  Wild: see Dietes grandiflora
  Yellow wild: see Dietes bicolor
Iris hybrids 189
Iris xiphium 189
Iron cross plant: see Begonia masoniana
Italian jasmine: see Jasminum humile 'Revolutum'
Italian woodbine: see Lonicera caprifolium
Ivy: see Hedera spp.; Parthenocissus spp.
Ivy, Tree: see x Fatshedera lizei
Ivy-leaved pelargonium: see Pelargonium peltatum
Ixia
  campanulata 189
  conferta var. ochroleuca 189
  hybrids 189, 190
  scillaris var. scillaris 190
  viridiflora 190
Ixora
  chinensis 190
  coccinea 'Fraseri' 190
Jacaranda mimosifolia 190, 191

Jacobean lily: see Sprekelia formosissima
Jacobinia suberecta: see Dicliptera suberecta
Jacob's ladder: see Pedilanthus tithymaloides subsp. smallii
Jade plant: see Portulacaria afra
Jade vine: see Strongylodon macrobotrys
  Scarlet: see Mucuna bennettii
Jakkalsblom: see Dimorphotheca sinuata
Jakkalbos: see Dicoma zeyheri
Jakkalskos: see Euphorbia mauritanica
Jakobregop: see Zinnia elegans
Jakobs-lelie: see Sprekelia formosissima
Jammy mouth: see Ruttya fruticosa
Japanese barberry: see Berberis thunbergii 'Atropurpurea'
Japanese fern palm: see Cycas revoluta
Japanese flowering quince: see Chaenomeles speciosa
Japanese holly: see Ilex wilsonii
Japanese honeysuckle: see Lonicera japonica
Japanese ivy: see Parthenocissus tricuspidata
Japanese lantern: see Hibiscus schizopetalus
Japanese persimmon: see Diospyros kaki
Japanese pinks: see Dianthus chinensis 'Heddewiggii'
Japanese rose: see Kerria japonica
Japanese sago palm: see Cycas revoluta
Japanse blomkweper: see Chaenomeles speciosa
Japanse grasangelier: see Dianthus chinensis 'Heddewiggii'
Japanse kanferfoelie: see Lonicera japonica
Japanse varingpalm: see Cycas revoluta
Japonika: see Camellia japonica cv.
Jasmine
  Carolina: see Gelsemium sempervirens
  Chilean: see Mandevilla laxa
  False: see Gelsemium sempervirens
  Italian: see Jasminum humile 'Revolutum'
  Malayan: see Chonemorpha fragrans
  Star: see Trachelospermum jasminoides
  Winter: see Jasminum nudiflorum
  Yellow bush: see Jasminum humile 'Revolutum'
Jasmine heath: see Erica fastigiata
Jasminum
  humile 'Revolutum' 191
  nudiflorum 191
  polyanthum 191
Jasmyn, Maleisiese: see Chonemorpha fragrans
Jaspisklimop: see Strongylodon macrobotrys
Jatropha podagrica 192
Jelly bean plant: see Sedum x rubrotinctum
Jelly beans: see Sedum pachyphyllum
Jerusalem artichoke: see Helianthus tuberosus
Jerusalem cherry: see Solanum spp.
Jerusalem lily: see Arum palaestinum
Jerusalem sage: see Phlomis fruticosa
Jerusalem thorn: see Parkinsonia aculeata
Jerusalemmartisjok: see Helianthus tuberosus
Jessamine, Yellow: see Gelsemium sempervirens
Jewelled aloe: see Aloe distans
Jew's mallow: see Kerria japonica
Jochroma cyaneum 192
Jodebaard: see Saxifraga stolonifera
Josefsleed: see Coleus x hybridus
Joseph's coat: see Alternanthera ficoidea 'Bettsickiana'

Joseph's coat: see Amaranthus tricolor 'Splendens'
Joyweed: see Alternanthera ficoidea 'Bettsickiana'
Judas tree: see Cercis siliquastrum
Judas tree: see Cercis siliquastrum
Jungle flame: see Ixora coccinea 'Fraseri'
Jungle geranium: see Ixora coccinea 'Fraseri'
Justicia
  brandegeana 192
  brandegeana 'Yellow Queen' 192, 193
  carnea 193

Kaapse kandelaarnaboom: see Euphorbia curvirama
Kaapse kanferfoelie: see Tecomaria capensis
Kaapse kastaiing: see Calodendrum capense
Kaapse klapperpeul: see Crotalaria capensis
Kaapse stokroos: see Sparmannia africana
Kahili ginger: see Hedychium gardneranum
Kalanchoe
  beharensis 193
  blossfeldiana 193
  longiflora 193, 194
  tubiflora 193, 194
  waldheimii 193, 194
Kale, Curly: see Brassica oleracea
Kale, Ornamental: see Brassica oleracea
Kaliforniese-papawer: see Eschscholzia californica
Kalkoentjie: see Gladiolus alatus
Kalkoentjies: see Tritonia hybrids
Kalmia angustifolia 194
Kalossie: see Ixia campanulata
Kalwebossie: see Dissotis canescens
Kamiemie: see Albuca altissima
Kammetjies: see Freesia x hybrida
Kanadese vlier: see Sambucus canadensis
Kanarieklimop: see Senecio tamoides
Kandelaarblom: see Brunsvigia orientalis
Kandelaarnaboom: see Euphorbia spp.
Kanferfoelie: see Lonicera spp.
Kanferfoelie, Wilde: see Turraea obtusifolia
Kanferfoeliefuchsia: see Fuchsia triphylla
Kangaroo paw: see Anigozanthos flavidus
Kankerbossie: see Sutherlandia frutescens
Kanna: see Canna indica
Kannabas: see Dais cotinifolia
Kanniedood: see Aloe variegata; Catharanthus roseus
Kapokbossie: see Eriocephalus africanus
Kappertjie: see Tropaeolum majus
Kappieblommetjies: see Nemesia ligulata
Kardinaalblom: see Sinningia cardinalis
Karee, White/Wit: see Rhus viminalis
Karlienblom: see Euphorbia pulcherrima
Karo: see Pittosporum crassifolium
Karob: see Ceratonia siliqua
Karoo gold: see Rhigozum obovatum
Kastaiing, Europese: see Castanea sativa
Kastaiing, Kaapse: see Calodendrum capense
Kasterolie: see Ricinus communis
Katjiepiering: see Gardenia jasminoides 'Veitchii'
Katstert: see Asparagus densiflorus 'Myers'
Katstert: see Bulbine frutescens; Bulbinella floribunda
Kattekruid: see Nepeta cataria
Kelkiewyn: see Babiana rubrocyanea; Geissorhiza radians
Kennedia rubicunda 104

Kerria japonica 195
Kerriebos: see Hypericum revolutum
Kersfeeskaktus: see Schlumbergera bridgesii
Keur: see Podalyria calyptrata
Keurboom: see Virgilia spp.
Kiepersol: see Cussonia spicata
King palm: see Archontophoenix cunninghamiana
Klaaslouwbossie: see Athanasia crithmifolia
Klapperbos: see Nymania capensis
Klawer: see Trifolium repens 'Atropurpureum'
Kleinkanferfoeliebom: see Turraea obtusifolia
Kleinkoraalboom: see Erythrina humeana
Kleinrooipypie: see Cyrtanthus brachyscyphus
Klimaalwyn: see Aloe ciliaris
Klimop: see Clematis brachiata
Klip buchu: see Coleonema album
Klipblom: see Crassula coccinea
Klipboegoe: see Coleonema album
Klipdagga: see Leonotis ocymifolia var. ocymifolia
Klipkalossie: see Lachenalia aloides
Kliproos: see Cistus spp.
Klokblom: see Campanula carpatica
Knife-leaf wattle: see Acacia cultriformis
Kniphofia
  praecox 195
  uvaria 195
  uvaria var. maxima 195
Knolbegonia: see Begonia x tuberhybrida
Knoppies-stinkkruid: see Pentzia grandiflora
Knotweed: see Polygonum capitatum
Kobas: see Cyphostemma currorii
Kochia scoparia 196
Koekemakranka: see Gethyllis ciliaris
Koemkwat: see Fortunella margarita
Koffieboom: see Coffea arabica
Kohleria eriantha 196
Kolkol: see Berzelia lanuginosa
Konfettibos: see Coleonema pulchrum
Koningbegonia: see Begonia rex-cultorum
Koningspalm: see Archontophoenix cunninghamiana
Kooigoed: see Helichrysum petiolare
Koorsboom: see Acacia xanthophloea
Koperbeuk: see Fagus sylvatica 'Atropunicea'
Koraalbessie: see Ardisia crispa
Koraalbome: see Erythrina spp.
Koraalboontjie: see Kennedia rubicunda
Koraalranker: see Antigonon leptopus
Kosmos: see Bidens formosa
Kouterbossie: see Athanasia crithmifolia
Kraanvoëlblom: see Strelitzia reginae
Krapkaktus: see Schlumbergera truncata
Kreefklou: see Heliconia humilis
Krisant: see Chrysanthemum morifolium cvs.
Krismisroos: see Hydrangea macrophylla var. macrophylla
Kruidjie-roer-my-nie: see Melianthus spp.
Kruisbessie: see Grewia occidentalis
Kukumakranka: see Gethyllis ciliaris
Kumquats: see Fortunella margarita
Kurkeik: see Quercus suber
Kurrajong: see Brachychiton populneus
Kuskoraalboom: see Erythrina caffra

Laburnum, Cape: see Crotalaria capensis
Laburnum, Wild: see Calpurnia aurea
Laburnum x watereri 'Vossii' 197
Lace-bark tree: see Brachychiton discolor
Lace plant: see Ammi majus
Lachenalia
  aloides 197
  aloides var. Ex Hort 197
  bulbifera 197
  cultivars: 197, 198
  rubida 198
Ladies purses: see Calceolaria crenatiflora
Lady's locket: see Dicentra spectabilis
Lady's slipper: see Paphiopedilum chamberlainianum
Lagerstroemia
  indica 198
  speciosa 198
Lagunaria pattersonii 198
Lamb's tail: see Sedum morganianum; Verbascum x hybridum
Lampranthus
  aureus 199
  blandus 199
  coccineus 199
  coralliflorus 199
  deltoides 199
  glaucus 199
  roseus 199
Lamstert: see Sedum morganianum; Verbascum x hybridum
Lantana
  montevidensis 200
  sellowiana: see L. montevidensis
Lantern heath: see Erica blenna
Lanternheide: see Erica blenna
Lapeirousia
  corymbosa 200
  jacquinii 200
  laxa 200
Larkspur: see Consolida ambigua
Lasiandra: see Tibouchina urvilleana
Lathyrus
  latifolius 201
  odoratus 201
Lavandula
  angustifolia subsp. angustifolia 201
  dentata 202
  officinalis: see L. angustifolia subsp. angustifolia
Lavatera trimestris 202
Lavender: see Lavandula spp.
Lavender cotton: see Santolina chamaecyparissus
Laventel: see Lavandula spp.
Leaf plant: see Breynia disticha 'Roseo-picta'
Lebeckia cytisoides 202
Leeubekkie: see Antirrhinum majus
Lekkerbreek: see Ochna pulchra
Lemon verbena: see Aloysia triphylla
Leonotis
  ocymifolia var. ocymifolia 203
  leonurus var. albiflora 203
  leonurus var. leonurus 203
Leptospermum
  scoparium 'Album' 203
  scoparium var. grandiflorum 'Flore Pleno' 204
  scoparium 'Roseum' 203, 204
Leschenaultia biloba 204
Lesser candelabra tree: see Euphorbia cooperi
Leucadendron
  argenteum 204, 205
  eucalyptifolium 204, 205
  gandogeri 295
  glaberrimum var. erubescens 205
  macowanii 205
  meridianum 205
  sessile 295
  strobilinum 206
  tinctum 206
Leucojum vernum 296
Leucospermum
  cordifolium 206-7
  cordifolium 'Flamespike' 206, 207
  glabrum 207
  hypophyllocarpodendron 207
  mundii 207
  oleifolium x Diastella thymelaeoides reflexum 207
  reflexum var. luteum 207
  tottum 208
  vestitum 208
Liatris pycnostachya 208
Licorice plant: see Helichrysum petiolare
Ligustrum
  lucidum 209
  lucidum 'Tricolor' 208, 209
  ovalifolium 'Aureum' 208, 209
Lilac
  Australian: see Hardenbergia comptoniana
  Common: see Syringa vulgaris
  Persian: see Melia azedarach
  Summer: see Buddleja davidii
Lilium
  cvs. 209, 210
  dauricum 209, 210
  lancifolium 210
  longiflorum 210
  szovitsianum 210
  tigrum: see L. lancifolium
Lily turf: see Liriope muscari 'Variegata'
Limonium
  capense 210
  latifolium 210, 211
  peregrinum 211
  perezii 211
Linaria maroccana 211
Lintwurmplant: see Homalocladium platycladum
Lion's ear: see Leonotis leonurus var. leonurus
Lion's tail: see Leonotis leonurus var. leonurus
Liparia splendens subsp. splendens 211
Lipstick palm: see Cyrtostachys lakka
Lipstick plant: see Bixa orellana
Liriope muscari 'Variegata' 212
Lithops
  lesliei 212
  otzeniana 212
  turbiniformis 212
  vanzylii 212
Littonia modesta 213
Livingstone daisy: see Dorotheanthus bellidiformis
Lobelia
  erinus 213
  laxiflora 213
  valida 213
Lobivia boliviensis 214
Lobostemon fruticosus 214
Lobster claws: see Vriesea carinata
  Hanging: see Heliconia rostrata
Lobster's claw: see Heliconia humilis
Lobularia maritima 124
Locust bean: see Ceratonia siliqua
London plane tree: see Platanus x acerifolia
Lonicera
  x americana 215
  caprifolium 215
  hildebrandiana 215
  japonica 215
  japonica 'Variegata' 215
  periclymenum 215
  sempervirens 215
Looking-glass plant: see Coprosma repens
Lotus: see Nelumbo nucifera
  Blue: see Nymphaea caerulea
  Egyptian: see Nymphaea caerulea
Love-in-the-mist: see Nigella damascena
Love-lies-bleeding: see Amaranthus caudatus
Luculia gratissima 216
Luffa
  aegyptica 216
  cylindrica: see L. aegyptica
Lugplant: see Tillandsia tenuifolia
Luisies: see Leucospermum reflexum
Lunaria annua 216
Lupinus polyphyllus 217
Lychnis chalcedonica 217
Lyre plant: see Dicentra spectabilis
Lysimachia nummularia 217

Maagwortel: see Dicoma zeyheri
Maanblom: see Brugmansia x candida;
Ipomoea alba
Maartblom: see Haemanthus coccineus
Macfadyena unguis-cati 218
Mackaya bella 218
Madagascar convolvulus: see Stichtocardia beraviensis
Madagascar periwinkle: see Catharanthus roseus
Madeira ivy: see Hedera canariensis 'Gloire de Marengo'
Madonna lily: see Eucharis grandiflora
Magic flower: see Cantua buxifolia
Magnolia
  grandiflora 219
  x soulangiana 'Amabilis' 219
Mahoe coast hibiscus: see Hibiscus tiliaceus
Mahonia lomariifolia 219
Maidenhair: see Adiantum capillus-veneris
Maidenhair fern: see Adiantum raddianum
Maidenhair tree: see Ginkgo biloba
Malay apple: see Syzygium malaccense
Malayan jasmine: see Chonemorpha fragrans
Malcolmia maritima 220
Maleisiese jasmyn: see Chonemorpha fragrans
Mallow: see Anisodontea scabrosa; Lavatera trimestris
Mallow, Jew's: see Kerria japonica
Maltese-cross: see Lychnis chalcedonica; Sprekelia formosissima
Maltese-kruis: see Lychnis chalcedonica; Sprekelia formosissima
Malvastrum coromandelianum 220
Malvaviscus
  arboreus 220
  arboreus var. mexicanus 220
  mollis: see M. arboreus
Mammillaria spinosissima 221
Manatoka: see Myoporum insulare
Mandevilla
  laxa 221
  splendens 221
Manettia
  bicolor: see M. inflata
  inflata 221
Manuka: see Leptospermum scoparium 'Roseum'
Many fingers: see Sedum pachyphyllum
Maple, Flowering: see Abutilon pictum
Maranta leuconeura 'Erythroneura' 222
March lily: see Amaryllis belladonna
Marguerite: see Chrysanthemum frutescens
  Blue: see Felicia amelloides
  Clanwilliam: see Euryops speciossimus
  Creeping: see Osteospermum fruticosum
Marigold: see Tagetes spp.
  English: see Calendula officinalis
  Pot: see Calendula officinalis
Marmalade bush: see Streptosolen jamesonii
Marmeladebos: see Streptosolen jamesonii
Marsh rose: see Orothamnus zeyheri
Marsh speedwell: see Veronica scutellata
Marvel of Peru: see Mirabilis jalapa
Mascarena lagenicaulis: see Hyophorbe lagenicaulis
Matthiola
  incana 222
  longipetala subsp. bicornis 222
Maurandia barclaiana: see Asarina barclaiana
Mauritius hemp: see Furcraea foetida
Mauritiusvlas: see Furcraea foetida
May, Cape: see Coleonema album; Spiraea cantoniensis
May, Garland: see Spiraea x arguta
Meadow rue: see Thalictrum dipterocarpum
Mealie heath: see Erica patersonia

Medusa's head: see Euphorbia caput-medusae
Megaskepasma erythrochlamys 223
Meksikaanse vlambos: see Calliandra tweedii
Melaleuca
　huegelii 223
　nesophylla 223
Melastoma sanguineum 223
Melia azedarach 224
Melianthus
　major 224
　minor 224
Melon, Pear: see Solanum muricatum
Melon shrub: see Solanum muricatum
Metalasia muricata 225
Metrosideros excelsa 225
Mexican abelia: see Abelia floribunda
Mexican blood-trumpet: see Distictis buccinatoria
Mexican fire plant: see Euphorbia heterophylla
Mexican flame bush: see Calliandra tweedii
Mexican poppy: see Argemone mexicana
Mexican snowball: see Echeveria elegans
Mexican tulip poppy: see Hunnemannia fumariifolia
Michaelmas daisy: see Aster novi-belgii
Microloma sagittatum 225
Mielieheide: see Erica patersonia
Milfoil: see Achillea millefolium 'Rosea'
Milk bush, Yellow: see Euphorbia mauritanica
Milkweed: see Asclepias spp.
Mimetes
　argenteus 226
　cucullatus 226
　hirtus 226
Mimosa pudica 226
Mimulus
　aurantiacus 227
　sanguineus 227
Mirabilis jalapa 227
Mirror plant: see Coprosma repens
Miscanthus sinensis 'Variegatus' 227
Mock orange: see Philadelphus coronarius
Mock strawberry: see Duchesnea indica
Modjadji-broodboom: see Encephalartos transvenous
Modjadji cycad: see Encephalartos transvenosus
Moederkappie: see Pterygodium catholicum
Moerbei, Wit: see Morus alba 'Pendula'
Molucca balm: see Molucella laevis
Molucella laevis 228
Monarda didyma 228
Money plant: see Lunaria annua
Moneywort: see Lysimachia nummularia
Monkey flower: see Mimulus aurantiacus
Monkshood: see Molucella laevis
Monopsis lutea 228
Monstera
　deliciosa 229
　deliciosa var. borsigiana 229
　deliciosa 'Variegata'
Monbretia: see Crocosmia
Moonflower: see Brugmansia x candida; Ipomoea alba
Moonwort: see Lunaria annua
Moore's crinum: see Crinum moorei
Moraea
　aristata 229
　gigandra 229
　loubseri 229, 230
　neopavonia 229, 230
　spathulata 230
Morning glory: see Ipomoea spp.
Morus alba 'Pendula' 230
Mosaic plant: see Fittonia verschaffeltii
Mosaïekplant: see Fittonia verschaffeltii
Moss rose: see Portulaca grandiflora
Moth fruit: see Acridocarpus natalitius

Mother-in-law's chair: see Echinocactus grusonii
Mother-in-law's tongue: see Sansevieria trifasciata
Mother-of-thousands: see Saxifraga stolonifera
Mountain cedar: see Widdringtonia nodiflora
Mountain dahlia: see Liparia splendens subsp. splendens
Mucuna bennettii 230
Mulberry, White: see Morus alba 'Pendula'
Mullein: see Verbascum thapsus
Muscari botryoides 231
Mussaenda
　alicia 231
　erythrophylla 231
　incana 231
Muurblom: see Cheiranthus cheiri
Myoporum
　insulare 232
　laetum 232
Myosotis scorpioides 232
Myrtle: see Myrtus communis
Myrtle, Honey: see Melaleuca huegelii
Myrtle, Western tea: see Melaleuca nesophylla
Myrtus
　communis 232
　communis 'Variegata' 232

Naboom: see Euphorbia ingens
Namakwaland gousblom: see Arctotis fastuosa
Namaqualand daisy: see Dimorphotheca sinuata
Nandina domestica 233
Narcissus
　cvs. 233
　jonquilla 234
Nasturtium: see Tropaeolum majus
Natal bottlebrush: see Greyia sutherlandii
Natal flame tree: see Alberta magna
Natal gardenia: see Gardenia cornuta
Natal plum: see Carissa macrocarpa
Natal red-top: see Rhynchelytrum repens
Natal yellowwood: see Podocarpus henkelii
Natalkatjiepiering: see Gardenia cornuta
Natalpruim: see Carissa macrocarpa
Natalse baakhout: see Greyia sutherlandii
Natalvlamboom: see Alberta magna
Necklace vine: see Ceropegia woodii
Needle palm: see Yucca filamentosa
Nelumbo nucifera 234
Nemesia
　ligulata 235
　strumosa hybrids 234-5
Neomarica caerulea 235
Neoregelia carolinae 235
Nepal trumpet flower: see Beaumontia grandiflora
Nepeta cataria 236
Nephrolepis exaltata 236
Nerine
　bowdenii 236
　filifolia 236, 237
　krigei 237
　sarniensis 237
Nerium oleander and cultivars 237
Nettle-leaved bellflower: see Campanula trachelium
New Guinea creeper: see Mucuna bennettii
New Zealand Christmas tree: see Metrosideros excelsa
New Zealand flax: see Phormium tenax
Ngaio: see Myoporum laetum
Ngami kumquat: see Fortunella margarita
Nicotiana alata 'Grandiflora' 238
Nierembergia hippomanica var. violacea 238

Nieu-Seelandse vlas: see Phormium tenax
Nigella damascena 238
Night cestrum: see Cestrum nocturnum
Nivenia stokoei 239
Nodding pincushion: see Leucospermum cordifolium
Noem-noem: see Carissa spp.
Nooienshaarboom: see Ginkgo biloba
Nopalxochia ackermannii 239
Notocactus
　concinnus 239
　vanvlietii 240
　werdermannianus 240
Num-num: see Carissa spp.
Nylandtia spinosa 240
Nymania capensis 240
Nymphaea
　caerulea 241
　caerulea 'Sulfurea' 241
　capensis 241
　capensis 'Rosea' 241
Nymphoides indica 241

Oak, Cork: see Quercus suber
Oak, Silky: see Grevillea robusta
Oak, Silver: see Grevillea robusta
Obedience plant: see Physostegia virginiana
Obedient plant: see Mimosa pudica
Ochna
　natalitia 242
　pulchra 242
　serrulata 242
Odontonema strictum 242
Oenothera
　biennis 243
　stricta 243
Oilcloth flower: Anthurium andraeanum
Oldenburgia arbuscula 243
Oleander: see Nerium oleander
Oleander, Yellow: see Thevetia peruviana
Olifantsoor: see Alocasia macrorhiza; Colocasia esculenta 'Euchlora'
Olifantsriet: see Chondropetalum tectorum
Olinia ventosa 243
Olive, Sand: see Dodonaea viscosa
Oos-Kaapse broodboom: see Encephalartos altensteinii
Opium poppy: see Papaver somniferum hybrids
Opuntia ficus-indica 244
Orange chink: see Ornithogalum flavissimum
Orange star: see Guzmania lingulata var. minor
Orange vygie: see Lampranthus aureus
Orbeopsis lutea 244
Orchid
　Baby: see Epidendrum x obrienianum
　Butterfly: see Epidendrum x obrienianum
　Scarlet: see Epidendrum x obrienianum
　Slipper: see Paphiopedilum chamberlainianum
Orchid tree: see Bauhinia spp.
Orchid vine: see Stigmaphyllon ciliatum
Orgideeboom: see Bauhinia purpurea
Oriental hedge: see Bambusa glaucescens
Oriental poppy: see Papaver orientale
Ornamental chili: see Capsicum annuum
Ornamental kale: see Brassica oleracea
Ornithogalum
　dubium 244
　flavissimum 244, 245
　saundersiae 245
　thyrsoides 245
Orothamnus zeyheri 245
Orphium frutescens 245
Orthosiphon
　labiatus 246
　serratus var. Ex Hort 246
Osteospermum
　ecklonis 246

　fruticosum 246
　jucundum 246
Oswego tea: see Monarda didyma
Oumatrewwa: see Satyrium coriifolium
Oupa-se-pyp: see Aristolochia spp.
Outeniqua yellowwood: see Podocarpus falcatus
Oval kumquat: see Fortunella margarita
Ox-eye daisy: see Castalis nudicaulis
Oxalis
　flava 247
　lanata var. rosea 247
　purpurea 247
Oxford and Cambridge bush: see Clerodendrum ugandense
Oxypetalum caeruleum 247

Pachystachys lutea 248
Paeonia officinalis 'Rubra-Plena' 248
Paintbrush: see Scadoxus puniceus
Painted drop-tongue: see Aglaonema crispum 'Malay Beauty'
Painted feather: see Vriesea x mariae
Painted homeria: see Homeria elegans
Painted lady: see Gladiolus natalensis
Painted nettle: see Coleus x hybridus
Painted petals: see Lapeirousia spp.
Painted tongue: see Salpiglossus sinuata
Palm
　Bottle: see Hyophorbe lagenicaulis
　Fern: see Cycas spp.
　Fish-tail: see Caryota mitis
　Good-luck: see Chamaedorea elegans
　King: see Archontophoenix cunninghamiana
　Lipstick: see Cyrtostachys lakka
　Parlour: see Chamaedorea elegans
　Piccabeen: see Archontophoenix cunninghamiana
　Royal: see Roystonea regia
　Sago: see Cycas spp.
　Sealing wax: see Cyrtostachys lakka
Palm lily: see Cordyline australis
Palmboom: see Phoenix canariensis
Palmlelie: see Cordyline australis; Yucca spp.
Pampas grass: see Cortaderia selloana
Pampasgras: see Cortaderia selloana
Pandanus utilis 249
Pandorea
　jasminoides 249
　jasminoides 'Rosea' 249
Pansies: see Diascia integerrima
Pansy: see Viola x wittrockiana
Pansy, Wild: see Viola tricolor subsp. subalpina
Pantoffelblom: see Calceolaria crenatiflora
Papaver
　nudicaule 250
　nudicaule 'Delicatum' 250
　orientale 250
　somniferum hybrids 250
Papawer, Kaliforniese: see Eschscholzia californica
Paphiopedilum chamberlainianum 250
Papierblom: see Limonium spp.
Papierriet: see Cyperus papyrus
Papirus: see Cyperus papyrus
Papkuil: see Typha capensis
Papyrus: see Cyperus papyrus
Paradysblom: see Caesalpinia gilliesii
Parasol flower: see Holmskioldia sanguinea
Parkinsonia aculeata 251
Parlour palm: see Aspidistra elatior; Chamaedorea elegans
Parrot flower: see Heliconia psittacorum
Parrot gladiolus: see Gladiolus dalenii
Parthenocissus
　quinquefolia 251
　tricuspidata 251
Partridge aloe: see Aloe variegata
Passiflora
　amethystina 252
　antioquienensis 252
　edulis 252

edulis forma flavicarpa 252
manicata 252
mollissima 252
quadrangularis 252
Passion flower/fruit: see Passiflora spp.
Pavetta lanceolata 253
Pea, Everlasting: see Lathyrus latifolius
Pea, Perennial: see Lathyrus latifolius
Peace-in-the-home: see Soleirolia soleirolii
Peach, Flowering: see Prunus persica 'Alboplena'
Peacock flower: see Dietes bicolor
Peanut butter cassia: see Cassia didymobotrya
Peanut cactus: see Chamaecereus sylvestri
Pear, Hard: see Olinia ventosa
Pear, Wild: see Dombeya rotundifolia var. rotundifolia
Pear melon: see Solanum muricatum
Pearl acacia: see Acacia podalyriifolia
Pedilanthus
tithymaloides subsp. smallii 253
tithymaloides subsp. smallii 'Variegatus' 253
Pelargonium
cv. 254
bowkeri 253
cucullatum 253-4
x domesticum 254
echinatum 254
fulgidum 254
x hortorum 254
peltatum 254
Pellaea
rotundifolia 255
viridis 255
Peltophorum africanum 255
Pennisetum
rupellii: see P. setaceum 'Rubrum'
setaceum 'Rubrum' 255
villosum 256
Penstemon x spectabilis 256
Pentas
lanceolata 256
lanceolata 'Coccinea' 256
Pentzia grandiflora 257
Peony: see Paeonia officinalis 'Rubraplena'
Paperboom: see Schinus spp.
Peperomia
argyreia 257
caperata 257
marmorata 257
Pepino: see Solanum muricatum
Pepper, Red: see Capsicum annuum
Pepper trees: see Schinus spp.
Perdeblom: see Didelta carnosa var. carnosa
Perdekop: see Leucospermum reflexum
Perdevy: see Carpobrotus edulis
Pêrebos: see Didelta spinosa
Perennial pea: see Lathyrus latifolius
Perennial phlox: see Phlox paniculata
Periwinkle: see Catharanthus roseus; Vinca spp.
Persian lilac: see Melia azedarach
Persian violet: see Exacum affine
Persimmon: see Diospyros kaki
Perssandolien: see Dodonaea angustifolia 'Purpurea'
Peru-lelie: see Scilla peruviana
Peruvian lily: see Alstroemeria aurantiaca; Scilla peruviana
Petrea volubilis 258
Petunia x hybrida 258
Phacelia campanularia 259
Phaedranthus buccinatorius: see Distictis buccinatoria
Phaenocoma prolifera 259
Phalaenopsis x rothschildiana 259
Phalaris arundinacea var. picta 260
Phaseolus coccineus 260
Philadelphus coronarius 260
Philodendron
selloum 261
squamiferum 'Florida' 261
Phlomis fruticosa 261

Phlox, Wild: see Sutera grandiflora
Phlox
drummondii 262
paniculata 262
Phoenix
canariensis 262, 263
reclinata 262, 263
Phormium
tenax 263
tenax 'Atropurpureum' 263
tenax 'Atropurpureum Nana' 263
tenax 'Aureum' 263
Photinia glabra 'Rubens' 264
Phygelius capensis 264
Phylica
plumosa 264
pubescens 264
Phyllanthus nivosus: see Breynia disticha 'Roseo-picta'
Physalis
alkekengi 265
franchettii: see P. alkekengi peruviana 265
Physostegia virginiana 265
Phytolacca dioica 265
Piccabeen palm: see Archontophoenix cunninghamiana
Pickerel weed: see Pontederia cordata
Piempiempie: see Chasmanthe floribunda
Pigeon berry: see Duranta repens
Pig's ear: see Cotyledon orbiculata
Pigtail plant: see Anthurium scherzeranum
Pilea
cadierei 266
microphylla 266
spruceana 266
spruceana 'Norfolk' 266
Pimelea
ferruginea 266
rosea: see P. ferruginea
Pincushions: see Leucospermum spp.; Scabiosa atropurpurea
Pine, Screw: see Pandanus utilis
Pineapple flower: see Eucomis autumnalis subsp. autumnalis
Pineapple guava: see Feijoa sellowiana
Pink-and-white-shower: see Cassia nodosa
Pink arum: see Zantedeschia rehmannii
Pink cryptanthus: see Cryptanthus bromelioides
Pink dombeya: see Dombeya burgessiae
Pink flag bush: see Mussaenda alicia
Pink joy: see Crassula ovata
Pink porcelain lily: see Alpinia zerumbet
Pink quill: see Tillandsia cyanea
Pinks: see Dianthus spp.
Pisonia umbellifera 'Variegata' 267
Pistia stratiotes 267
Pistol bush: see Duvernoia adhatodoides
Pittosporum
crassifolium 267
eugenioides 268
Plakkies: see Crassula ovata
Plane tree, London: see Platanus x acerifolia
Plataan: see Platanus x acerifolia
Platanus x acerifolia 268
Platycerium bifurcatum 268
Platycodon grandiflorus 269
Plectranthus
ambiguus 269
barbatus 269
barbatus 'Variegata' 269
ecklonii 269, 270
ecklonii 'Medley-Wood' 269, 270
fruticosus 269, 270
hilliardiae 269, 270
madagascariensis var. madagascariensis 271
praetermissus 270, 271
saccatus 271
Pleiospilos
bolusii 271
prismaticus 271
Ploegbreker: see Erythrina zeyheri

Plum, Flowering: see Prunus cerasifera
Plum, Purple-leaf: see Prunus cerasifera 'Atropurpurea'
Plumbago, Chinese: see Ceratostigma willmottianum
Plumbago
auriculata 271
auriculata 'Alba' 271
Plume asparagus: see Asparagus densiflorus 'Myers'
Plume flower: see Justicia carnea
Plumeria
obtusa 272
rubra 272
rubra forma lutea 272
rubra forma rubra 272
Podalyria calyptrata 272
Podocarpus
falcatus 273
henkelii 273
Podranea
brycei 273
ricasoliana 273
Poeierkwas: see Calliandra brevipes
Poinciana: see Delonix regia
Poinsettia: see Euphorbia pulcherrima
Poinsettia, Annual: see Euphorbia heterophylla
Polianthes tuberosa 273
Polyanthus primrose: see Primula x polyantha
Polygala
myrtifolia 274
virgata 274
Polygonum capitatum 274
Polypodium aureum 274
Pomegranate: see Punica spp.
Pomegranate, Wild: see Burchellia bubalina
Pomegranate, Yellow: see Rhigozum obovatum
Pompon tree: see Dais cotinifolia
Pondweed, Cape: see Aponogeton distachyos
Pontederia
cordata 275
cordata forma angustifolia 275
Poor man's orchid: see Schizanthus pinnatus
Poor man's rhododendron: see Impatiens oliveri
Poppy: see Papaver spp.
Californian: see Eschscholzia californica
Mexican: see Argemone mexicana
Mexican tulip: see Hunnemannia fumariifolia
Poppy anemone: see Anemone coronaria
Populier: see Populus deltoides
Populus deltoides 275
Port Jackson willow: see Acacia saligna
Port St Johnsranker: see Podranea ricasoliana
Port St John's creeper: see Podranea ricasoliana
Portulaca grandiflora 275
Portulacaria afra 276
Pot marigold: see Calendula officinalis
Potato, Air: see Dioscorea bulbifera
Potato creeper: see Solanum spp.
Potentilla fruticosa Gold Finger 276
Poublom: see Dietes bicolor; Homeria elegans
Powder puff tree: see Calliandra brevipes
Prayer plant: see Maranta leuconeura 'Erythroneura'
Prickly pear: see Opuntia ficus-indica
Pride of Barbados: see Caesalpinia pulcherrima
Pride of Bolivia: see Tipuana tipu
Pride-of-De-Kaap: see Bauhinia galpinii
Pride of India: see Lagerstroemia spp.
Pride of Maderia: see Echium fastuosum
Pride of Table Mountain: see Disa uniflora
Primrose, Cape: see Streptocarpus spp.

Primula
malacoides 276
x polyantha 277
Privet: see Ligustrum spp.
Pronkertjie: see Lathyrus odoratus
Protea
aristata 277
aurea subsp. aurea 277
caffra 277
compacta 277
cynaroides 277
eximia 278, 279
grandiceps 278, 279
longifolia 278, 279
magnifica 278, 279
nana 278, 279
neriifolia 278, 279
repens 278, 279
scolymocephala 279
speciosa 278, 279
stokoei 278, 279
Prunus
cerasifera 'Atropurpurea' 279
persica 'Alboplena' 279
persica 'Carnation Striped' 279
persica 'Clara Meyer' 279
persica 'Rubroplena' 279
Pseuderanthemum alatum 280
Psidium littorale var. longipes 280
Pteronia camphorata 280
Pterygodium catholicum 281
Punica granatum 281
'Flore Pleno' 281
'Legrellei' 281
'Nana' 281
Purperwinde: see Ipomoea spp.
Purple hop bush: see Dodonaea viscosa 'Purpurea'
Purple-leaf plum: see Prunus cerasifera 'Atropurpurea'
Purple rock cress: see Aubrieta deltoidea
Purple wreath: see Petrea volubilis
Purse flower: see Calceolaria crenatiflora
Pussy willow: see Salix discolor
Pussyfoot: see Ageratum houstonianum
Pycnostachys urticifolia 282
Pynappelkoejawel: see Feijoa sellowiana
Pyrancantha
angustifolia 282
coccinea 282
coccinea 'Keessen' 282
Pyrethrum chrysanthemums 88
Pyrostegia venusta 283

Queen Anne's lace: see Ammi majus
Queen's tears: see Billbergia nutans
Queensland lace-bark: see Brachychiton discolor
Quercus suber 283
Quince, Japanese flowering: see Chaenomeles speciosa
Quisqualis indica 284

Rabbit's foot fern: see Polypodium aureum
Rain daisy: see Dimorphotheca pluvialis
Rain lily: see Zephyranthes grandiflora
Rainbow cactus: see Echinocereus pectinatus var. neomexicanus
Rainbow pink: see Dianthus chinensis 'Heddewiggii'
Rangoon creeper: see Quisqualis indica
Rankbotterblom: see Gazania rigens var. rigens
Rankmargriet: see Osteospermum fruticosum
Ranktrompet: see Campsis grandiflora
Ranunculus asiaticus 284
Raphiolepis
x delacourii 285
indica 285
Rat's tail: see Antholyza ringens
Ravenala madagascariensis 285
Red Afrikaner: see Homoglossum watsonium
Red alder: see Cunonia capensis

Red crassula: see **Crassula coccinea**
Red disa: se **Disa uniflora**
Red flag bush: see **Mussaenda erythrophylla**
Red flowering gum: se **Eucalyptus ficifolia**
Red ginger: see **Alpinia purpurata**
Red ginger lily: see **Hedychium coccineum**
Red gooseberry: see **Physalis alkekengi**
Red helmet: see **Eucalyptus erythrocorys**
Red-hot cat's tail: see **Acalypha hispida**
Red-hot poker: see **Kniphofia praecox**
Red lachenalia: see **Lachenalia bulbifera**
Red lampranthus: see **Lampranthus coccineus**
Red nerine: see **Nerine sarniensis**
Red orchid cactus: see **Nopalxochia ackermanii**
Red passion flower: see **Passiflora manicata**
Red pepper: see **Capsicum annuum**
Red posy: see **Boophane disticha**
Red spider flower: see **Grevillea punicea**
Red vygie: see **Lampranthus roseus**
Reed: see **Willdenowia argentea**
Reënboogkaktus: see **Echinocereus pectinatus** var. **neomexicanus**
Regal pelargonium: see **Pelargonium x domesticum**
Reinwardtia indica 285
Reuse kanferfoelie: see **Lonicera hildebrandiana**
Reuse oupa-se-pyp: see **Aristolochia gigantea**
Rex begonia: see **Begonia rex-cultorum**
Rhigozum obovatum 286
Rhipsalidopsis
  gaertneri 286
  rosea 286
Rhododendron
  hybrids 286, 287
  indicum 286, 287
  pulchrum var. phoenicium 287
Rhoeo spathacea 287
Rhoicissus tomentosa 288
Rhubarb, Wild: see **Acanthus mollis**
Rhus
  pendulina 288
  pyroides 288
Rhynchelytrum
  repens 289
  roseum: see **R. repens**
Ribbon bush: see **Homalocladium platycladum; Hypoestes aristata**
Ribbon grass: see **Phalaris arundinacea** var. **picta**
Rice-paper plant: see **Tetrapanax papyriferus**
Ricinus communis 289
Ridderspoor: see **Brachycarpaea juncea; Consolida ambigua**
Riet: see **Wildenowia argentea**
River climbing acacia: see **Acacia schweinfurthii**
River lily: see **Schizostylis coccinea**
Rivierlelie: see **Schizostylis coccinea**
Rivierrankdoring: see **Acacia schweinfurthii**
Robinia
  hispida 289
  pseudoacacia 289
Rock rose: see **Cistus** spp.
Rocket pincushion: see **Leucospermum reflexum**
Roella ciliata 290
Romulea rosea var. rosea 290
Rondeletia amoena 290
Rooi-afrikaner: see **Chasmanthe floribunda; Homoglossum watsonium**
Rooi-salie: see **Salvia splendens**
Rooi watsonia: see **Watsonia fulgens**
Rooiaronskelk: see **Zantedeschia rehmannii**
Rooiblaarplakkie: see **Kalanchoe longiflora**

Rooibloekom: see **Eucalyptus ficifolia**
Rooibobbejaantjie: see **Babiana villosa**
Rooidisa: see **Disa uniflora**
Rooiels: see **Cunonia capensis**
Rooigemmer: see **Alpinia purpurata**
Rooigemmerlelie: see **Hedychium coccineum**
Rooihaargras: see **Rhynchelytrum repens**
Rooihaartjie: see **Erica cerinthoides**
Rooikalkoentjie: see **Gladiolus alatus; Tritonia crocata**
Rooikalossie: see **Tritonia crocata**
Rooikappie: see **Satyrium carneum**
Rooikeurtjie: see **Sesbania punicea**
Rooiknol: see **Wachendorfia** spp.
Rooikrans: see **Acacia cyclops**
Rooinaëls: see **Lachenalia bulbifera**
Rooirissie: see **Capsicum annuum**
Rooisewejaartjie: see **Helipterum eximium; Phaenocoma prolifera**
Rooistompie: see **Brunia stokoei; Mimetes cucullatus**
Rooiverbena: see **Verbena peruviana**
Rooivioolties: see **Lachenalia** spp.
Rooivlamboontjie: see **Brownea coccinea**
Rooiwortel: see **Dilatris pillansii**
Roomysbossie: see **Breynia disticha** 'Roseo-picta'
Roosverbena: see **Verbena canadensis** 'Rosea'
Rosa canina 291
Rosa 'Dorothy Perkins' 291
Rosary vine: see **Ceropegia woodii**
Rose acacia: see **Robinia h spida**
Rose apple: see **Syzygium malaccense**
Rose of China: see **Hibiscus rosa-sinensis**
Rose-of-Sharon: see **Hibiscus syriacus; Hypericum calycinum**
Rose verbena: see **Verbena canadensis** 'Rosea'
Rosebay: see **Nerium oleander**
Rosemary: see **Rosmarinus officinalis**
Rosemary, Wild: see **Eriocephalus africanus**
Rosmarinus officinalis 291
Rothmannia capensis 291
Rotstert: see **Antholyza ringens**
Royal palm: see **Roystonea regia**
Roystonea regia 292
Rubber plant: see **Ficus elastica**
Rubber tree, Indian: see **Ficus elastica**
Rubber vine: see **Cryptostegia grandiflora**
Rubberklimop: see **Cryptostegia grandiflora**
Ruby ball: see **Gymnocalycium mihanovichii**
Rudbeckia
  fulgida 292
  hirta 'Double Gloria Daisy' 292
  hirta 'Gloria Daisy' 292
  hirta var. pulcherrima 292
Rue, Meadow: see **Thalictrum dipterocarpum**
Ruellia
  macrantha 293
  makoyana 293
Rumex usambarensis 293
Rumohra adiantiformis 293
Runner bean, Scarlet: see **Phaseolus coccineus**
Ruscus aculeatus 294
Ruspolia hypocrateriformis var. australis 294
Russelia
  equisetiformis 294
  juncea: see **R. equisetiformis**
Ruttya
  fruticosa 295
  ovata x **Ruspolia hypocrateriformis**: see x **Ruttyruspolia** 'Phyllis van Heerden'
x Ruttyruspolia 'Phyllis van Heerden' 295
Ryspapierplant: see **Tetrapanax papyriferus**

Sabie crinum: see **Crinum macowanii**

Sabie star: see **Adenium multiflorum**
Sabielelie: see **Crinum macowanii**
Sacred bamboo: see **Nandina domestica**
Sacred flower of the Incas: see **Cantua buxifolia**
Sacred lotus: see **Nelumbo nucifera**
Saffierblom: see **Browallia americana**
Saffraan: see **Cassine crocea**
Saffron spike: see **Aphelandra squarrosa**
Sage, Jerusalem: see **Phlomis fruticosa**
Sage wood: see **Buddleja salviifolia**
Sago palm: see **Cycas** spp.
Saintpaulia ionantha cvs. 296
Salie: see **Salvia** spp.
Salix
  babylonica 296
  discolor 296
Salpiglossus sinuata 296
Salvia
  africana-lutea 297
  aurea: see **S. africana-lutea**
  chamelaeagnea 297
  dolomitica 297
  farinacea 297
  grahamii: see **S. microphylla**
  greggii 'Rosea' 297
  involucrata 297
  leucantha 297
  microphylla 297, 298
  splendens 298
Sambreelbiesie: see **Cyperus alternifolius**
Sambreelblom: see **Holmskioldia sanguinea**
Sambreelboom: see **Brassaia actinophylla**
Sambucus
  canadensis 298
  nigra 'Albo-variegata' 298
Sanchezia nobilis 298
Sand olive: see **Dodonaea angustifolia**
Sandersonia aurantiaca 299
Sandkalossie: see **Lachenalia rubida**
Sandlelie: see **Veltheimia capensis**
Sandolien: see **Dodonaea angustifolia**
Sansevieria
  pearsonii 299
  trifasciata 299
Santolina chamaecyparissus 299
Saponaria officinalis 300
Sapphire flower: see **Browallia speciosa**
Saraca thaipingensis 300
Saritaea magnifica 300
Sarsaparilla vine: see **Hardenbergia comptoniana**
Satin flower: see **Clarkia** spp.
Satynblom: see **Clarkia** spp.
Satyrium
  acuminatum 301
  carneum 301
  coriifolium 301
  erectum 301
Saxifraga stolonifera 301
Scabiosa
  africana 302
  atropurpurea 302
  atropurpurea 'Grandiflora' 302
  columbaria 302
Scadoxus
  membranaceus 302
  multiflorus subsp. multiflorus 302, 303
  multiflorus subsp. 'Katharinae' 303
  puniceus 303
Scarlet flame bean: see **Brownea coccinea**
Scarlet ginger lily: see **Hedychium coccineum**
Scarlet jade vine: see **Mucuna bennettii**
Scarlet-lightning: see **Lychnis chalcedonica**
Scarlet orchid: see **Epidendrum x obrienianum**
Scarlet runner bean: see **Phaseolus coccineus**
Scarlet salvia: see **Salvia splendens**
Scarlet star: see **Guzmania lingulata** var. **major**
Sceletium concavum 303

Schefflera
  actinophylla: see **Brassaia actinophylla**
  arboricola 303
  arboricola 'Variegatum' 303
Schinus
  molle 304
  terebinthifolius 304
Schizanthus pinnatus 304
Schizostylis coccinea 304
Schlumbergera
  bridgesii 305
  truncata 305
Schotia
  afra var. afra 305
  brachypetala 305
Scilla
  natalensis 305
  peruviana 305
Scindapsus aureus: see **Epipremnum aureum**
Screw pine: see **Pandanus utilis**
Sea lavender: see **Limonium** spp.
Sea pink: see **Armeria maritima**
Sea urchin cactus: see **Echinopsis multiplex**
Sealing-wax palm: see **Cyrtostachys lakka**
Sechium edule 306
Sedge, Umbrella: see **Cyperus alternifolius**
Sedum
  morganianum 306
  pachyphyllum 306
  x rubrotinctum 306
  spectabile 'Rubrum' 306
Seegousblom: see **Didelta carnosa** var. **carnosa**
Seeroogblommetjie: see **Hypoestes aristata**
Seeroogkatstert: see **Bulbinella floribunda**
Sekelbos: see **Dichrostachys cinerea** subsp. **africana**
Selaginella sp. 307
Selonsroos: see **Nerium oleander**
Semnanthe lacera 307
Senecio
  cineraria 307
  echinata 307, 308
  elegans 308
  grandifolius 308
  x hybridus 308
  radicans 308
  scaposus 308
  tamoides 308
Sensitive plant: see **Mimosa pudica**
Sering: see **Melia azedarach**
Sering, Gewone: see **Syringa vulgaris**
Serruria florida 309
  vallaris 309
Sesbania punicea 309
Setcreasea
  pallida 'Purple Heart' 309
  purpurea: see **S. pallida** 'Purple Heart'
Seweweeksvaring: see **Rumohra adiantiformis**
Shasta daisy 88, 89
Sheeplaurel: see **Kalmia angustifolia**
Shell flower: see **Alpinia zerumbet; Molucella laevis**
Shell ginger: see **Alpinia zerumbet**
Shrimp plant: see **Justicia brandegeana**
Sickle bush: see **Dichrostachys cinerea**
Sidewinder vriesea: see **Vriesea incurvata**
Sierrissie: see **Capsicum annuum**
Sigaretplant: see **Cuphea ignea**
Siklaam: see **Cyclamen persicum** cv.
Silky oak: see **Grevillea robusta**
Silver birch: see **Betula pendula**
Silver bush: see **Convolvulus cneorum**
Silver carpet: see **Dymondia margaretae**
Silver dollar: see **Lunaria annua**
Silver mimetes: see **Mimetes argenteus**
Silver net plant: see **Fittonia verschaffeltii**
Silver oak: see **Grevillea robusta**
Silver oak, Wild: see **Brachylaena discolor** subsp. **transvaalensis**

365

Silver tree: see Leucadendron argenteum
Silwerberk: see Betula pendula
Silwerboom: see Leucadendron argenteum
Silwerkassia: see Cassia artemisioides
Singapore plumeria: see Plumeria obtusa
Sinningia
 cardinalis 310
 speciosa 310
Sipreskruid: see Santolina chamaecyparissus
Skeerkwas: see Haemanthus coccineus
Skilpadbessie: see Nylandtia spinosa
Skoenlapperblom: see Schizanthus pinnatus
Skoonma-se-tong: see Sansevieria trifasciata
Skoonmoederstoel: see Echinocactus grusonii
Skulpgemmer: see Alpinia zerumbet
Sky flower: see Duranta repens; Thunbergia grandiflora
Sky vine: see Thunbergia grandiflora
Skyrocket: see Ipomopsis rubra
Slender deutzia: see Deutzia gracilis
Slipper flower: see Calceolaria crenatiflora
Slipper orchid: see Paphiopedilum chamberlainianum
Slipper plant: see Pedilanthus tithymaloides subsp. smallii
Slymstok: see Albuca altissima
Small poinsettia: see Euphorbia pulcherrima cv.
Smodingium argutum 310
Snake flower: see Ornithogalum flavissimum
Snake plant: see Sansevieria trifasciata
Snapdragon: see Antirrhinum majus
Snapweed: see Impatiens wallerana
Sneeubessie: see Symphoricarpos albus
Sneeuvlokkie: see Leucojum vernum
Snow-in-Summer: see Cerastium tomentosum
Snow-in-the-mountain: see Euphorbia marginata
Snowball tree: see Viburnum opulus 'Sterile'
Snowberry: see Symphoricarpos albus
Snowbush: see Breynia disticha 'Roseo-picta'
Snowflake: see Leucojum vernum
Soapwort: see Saponaria officinalis
Soe-soe: see Sechium edule
Soetdoring: see Acacia karroo
Soetknoffel: see Tulbaghia simmleri
Solandra maxima 310
Solanum
 capsicastrum 311
 jasminoides 311
 melongena var. esculentum cv. 311
 muricatum 311
 pseudocapsicum 'Pattersonii' 311
 seaforthianum 311
 wendlandii 311
Soleirolia soleirolii 312
Solidago virgaurea 312
Solomon's lily: see Arum palaestinum
Somerlila: see Buddleja davidii
Somersipres: see Kochia scoparia
Sour fig: see Carpobrotus spp.
Southern magnolia: see Magnolia grandiflora
Spaansmos: see Tillandsia usneoides
Spaansriet: see Arundo donax var. versicolor
Spanish bluebell: see Endymion hispanicus
Spanish broom: see Spartium junceum
Spanish chestnut: see Castanea sativa
Spanish dagger: see Yucca gloriosa
Spanish iris: see Iris xiphium
Spanish moss: see Tillandsia usneoides
Spanish reed: see Arundo donax var. versicolor
Spanspekboompie: see Solanum muricatum
Sparaxis
 elegans 312
 grandiflora subsp. acutiloba 312
 hybrids 313
Sparmannia africana 313
Spartium junceum 313
Spathiphyllum x hybridum 314
Spathodea campanulata 314
Spear lily: see Doryanthes excelsa
Speedwell, Marsh: see Veronica scutellata
Spekboom: see Portulacaria afra
Speldekussings: see Leucospermum spp.
Spider flower: see Cleome spinosa; Ferraria crispa var. crispa
Spider lily: see Hymenocallis littoralis
Spider plant: see Chlorophytum comosum 'Picturatum'
Spieëlplant: see Coprosma repens
Spiloxene capensis 314
Spindle tree: see Euonymus spp.
Spinnekopblom: see Ferraria crispa var. crispa
Spiraea, Blue: see Caryopteris incana
Spiraea
 x arguta 315
 x bumalda 'Atrorosea' 315
 cantoniensis 315
Splendid acacia: see Acacia robusta
Sponge gourd: see Luffa aegyptica
Sporrie: see Heliophila coronopifolia
Spotted dumb cane: see Dieffenbachia maculata
Sprekelia formosissima 315
St John's bread: see Ceratonia siliqua
St John's lily: see Clivia miniata var. miniata
St John's wort: see Hypericum calycinum
Stachys rugosa var. linearis 316
Staghorn fern: see Platycerium bifurcatum
Stalked bulbine: see Bulbine frutescens
Standing cypress: see Ipomopsis rubra
Stapelia
 coegaensis 316
 peculiaris 316
 rufa 316
Star flower: see Hypoxis rooperi
Star jasmine: see Trachelospermum jasminoides
Star wort: see Aster novi-belgii
Stars-of-Persia: see Allium christophii
Stenocarpus sinuatus 317
Stenolobium
 alatum: see Tecoma alata
 stans: see Tecoma stans
Sterjasmyn: see Trachelospermum jasminoides
Sterretjies: see Spiloxene capensis
Stictocardia beraviensis 317
Stigmaphyllon ciliatum 317
Stinkkruid: see Pentzia grandiflora
Stinkwood, White: see Celtis africana
Stock: see Matthiola incana
Stoep jacaranda: see Plectranthus saccatus
Stokroos: see Alcea rosea
Stompie: see Brunia nodiflora
Stormlelie: see Zephyranthes grandiflora
Strandroos: see Limonium peregrinum
Strandsalie: see Salvia africana-lutea
Straw-flower: see Helichrysum bracteatum; Helipterum eximium
Strawberry, Indian: see Duchesnea indica
Strawberry, Mock: see Duchesnea indica
Strawberry cactus: see Ferocactus setispinus
Strawberry guava: see Psidium littorale var. longipes
Strawberry tree: see Arbutus unedo
Strelitzia
 juncea 318
 nicolai 318
 reginae 318
 reginae var. lutea 318
Streptocarpus
 cyaneus 319
 dunnii 319
 x hybridus 319
 rexii 319
Streptosolen jamesonii 319
String of hearts: see Ceropegia woodii
Striped draceana: see Dracaena deremensis 'Warneckii'
Strobilanthes
 anisophyllus 320
 dyeranus 320
Strongylodon macrobotrys 320
Strooiblom: see Helichrysum bracteatum
Sugarbush: see Protea repens
Suikerbos: see Protea spp.
Suikerkan: see Protea repens
Sultan's balsam: see Impatiens wallerana
Summer cypress: see Kochia scoparia
Summer lilac: see Buddleja davidii
Sunflower, Thin-leaf: see Helianthus decapetalus 'Multiflorus'
Sutera grandiflora 320
Sutherlandia frutescens 321
Suurberg cushion bush: see Oldenburgia arbuscula
Suurbergsekussingbos: see Oldenburgia arbuscula
Suurknol: see Chasmanthe floribunda; Watsonia pyramidata
Suurvy: see Carpobrotus spp.
Swartoognooi: see Thunbergia alata
Sweet Alison: see Lobularia maritima
Sweet alyssum: see Lobularia maritima
Sweet elder: see Sambucus canadensis
Sweet garlic: see Tulbaghia simmleri
Sweet pea: see Lathyrus odoratus
Sweet pea bush: see Podalyria calyptrata
Sweet scabiosa: see Scabiosa atropurpurea
Sweet thorn: see Acacia karroo
Sweet viburnum: see Viburnum odoratissimum
Sweet violet: see Viola odorata
Sword fern: see Nephrolepis exalta
Sycamore: see Platanus x acerifolia
Symphoricarpos albus 321
Synadenium grantii 'Rubra' 321
Syngonium podophyllum 322
Syringa vulgaris 322
Syzygium
 malaccense 322
 paniculatum 323

Taffeta plants: see Hoffmannia spp.
Tagetes
 erecta 323
 patula 'Naughty Marietta' 323
 patula 'Spry' 323
Tall aristea: see Aristea major
Tall taffeta plant: see Hoffmannia giesbreghtii
Tamarisk: see Tamarix hispida
Tamarix hispida 324
Tapeworm: see Homalocladium platycladum
Tarata: see Pittosporum eugenioides
Tartogo: see Jatropha podagrica
Tassel tree, Golden: see Calpurnia aurea
Tea bush: see Leptospermum spp.
Tecoma
 alata 324
 stans 324
 stans cv. 324
Tecomanthe venusta 325
Tecomaria capensis and cultivars 325
Telopea speciosissima 326
Temple tree: see Plumeria obtusa
Ten Commandments: see Maranta leuconeura 'Erythroneura'
Tetradenia riparia: see Iboza riparia
Tetragonia rosea 326
Tetrapanax papyriferus 326
Thalictrum dipterocarpum 327
Thatching reed: see Chondropetalum tectorum
Thevetia peruviana 327
Thin-leaf sunflower: see Helianthus decapetalus 'Multiflorus'
Thorncroftia succulenta 327
Thrift: see Armeria maritima
Thryptomene sp. 328
Thunbergia
 alata 328
 gibsonii: see T. gregorii
 grandiflora
 gregorii 328
Ti tree: see Cordyline terminalis
Tibouchina
 elegans 329
 granulosa 329
 semidecandra: see T. urvilleana
 urvilleana 329
Tickey creeper: see Ficus pumila
Tierbekvygie: see Faucaria felina
Tierblom: see Tigrida pavonia
Tiger flower: see Tigrida pavonia
Tigrida pavonia 329
Tillandsia
 cyanea 330
 tenuifolia 330
 usneoides 330
Tipu: see Tipuana tipu
Tipuana tipu 330
Tjienkerientjee: see Ornithogalum spp.
Toad flax: see Linaria maroccana
Tobacco flower: see Nicotiana alata 'Grandiflora'
Tongaalwyn: see Aloe plicatilis
Torch cactus: see Trichocereus spachianus
Torch lily: see Kniphofia praecox
Torenia fournieri 331
Touch-me-not: see Mimosa pudica
Tower of jewels: see Echium fastuosum
Towerblom: see Cantua buxifolia
Trachelospermum jasminoides 331
Tradescantia
 blossfeldiana 331
 fluminensis 'Variegata' 331
 sillamontana 332
 virginiana 332
Trailing arctotis: see Arctotis stoechadifolia
Transvaal bottlebrush: see Greyia radlkoferi
Transvaal candelabra tree: see Euphorbia spp.
Transvaal daisy: see Gerbera jamesonii
Transvaalse baakhout: see Greyia radlkoferi
Transvaalse kandelaarnaboom: see Euphorbia spp.
Traveller's joy: see Clematis brachiata
Traveller's tree: see Ravenala madagascariensis
Tree dahlia: see Dahlia imperialis
Tree fern, Common: see Alsophila dregei
Tree fuchsia: see Scotia brachypetala
Tree hibiscus: see Hibiscus tiliaceus
Tree ivy: see x Fatshedera lizei
Tree of kings: see Cordyline terminalis
Tree tomato: see Cyphomandra betacea
Tree wistaria: see Bolusanthus speciosus
Treurwilg: see Salix babylonica
Trichocaulon
 cactiforme 332
 grande 332
Trichocereus spachianus 332
Tridentea peculiaris: see Stapelia peculiaris
Trifolium repens
 'Atropurpureum' 333
 'Purparascens': see T. repens 'Atropurpureum'
Tristellateia australasiae 333
Tritonia
 crocata 333
 disticha subsp. rubrolucens 334
 hybrids 333, 334
 masonorum: see Crocosmia masonorum

Trompetblom: see Bignonia capreolata; Clytostoma callistegioides
Trompetheide: see Erica fastigiata
Tropaeolum majus 334
  pulcherrima
Trots van Bolivië: see Tipuana tipu
Trots-van-Franschhoek: see Serruria florida
Trumpet bush, Golden: see Allamanda neriifolia
Trumpet creeper, Chinese: see Campsis grandiflora
Trumpet flower: see Bignonia capreolata; Salpiglossus sinuata
Trumpet flower, Nepal: see Beaumontia grandiflora
Trumpet lily: see Lilium longiflorum
Trumpet vine
  Argentinian: see Clytostoma callistegioides
  Golden: see Allamanda cathartica 'Hendersonii'
  Violet: see Clytostoma callistegioides
Tuberose: see Polianthes tuberosa
Tuinverbena: see Verbena x hybrida
Tulbaghia
  simmleri 334, 335
  violacea 335
Tulip: see Tulipa hybrids
Tulip magnolia: see Magnolia x soulangiana 'Amabilis'
Tulipa hybrids 335
Tung-oil tree: see Aleurites fordii
Tupidanthus calyptratus 335
Turk's cap: see Malvaviscus arboreus var. mexicanus
Turraea obtusifolia 336
Tussock bellflower: see Campanula carpatica
Tweediia caerulea: see Oxypetalum caeruleum
Twinspur: see Diascia integerrima
Tylecodon
  cacalioides 336
  grandiflorus 336
Typha capensis 336

Uintjie: see Dietes bicolor
Ulex europeus 337
Umbrella sedge: see Cyperus alternifolius
Umbrella tree: see Cussonia spicata
  Australian: see Brassaia actinophylla
Urn plant: see Aechmea fasciata
Ursinia
  cakilifolia 337
  calenduliflora 337
  geyeri 338
  sericea 338

Vaalstompie: see Mimetes argenteus
Vadoekplant: see Luffa aegyptica
Valeriana officinalis 338
Valsakasia: see Robinia pseudoacacia
Valsaralia: see Dizygotheca elegantissima
Valsheide: see Fabiana imbricata
Van Wyk's hout: see Bolusanthus speciosus
Vanda
  x rothschildiana 339
  teres 339
Variegated wax plant: see Hoya carnosa 'Variegata'
Varkoor-plakkie: see Cotyledon orbiculata
Varkstertanthurium: see Anthurium scherzeranum
Vase plant: see Aechmea fasciata
Veerkoppie: see Phylica plumosa
Veldskoenblaar: see Haemanthus coccineus
Veltheimia
  bracteata 339
  bracteata 'Lemon Flame' 339
  capensis 339
Velvet bush: see Kalanchoe beharensis

Velvet plant: see Verbascum thapsus
Vensterplant: see Fenestraria aurantiaca
Venus-hair fern: see Adiantum capillus-veneris
Venus's flytrap: see Dionaea muscipula
Venusvlieëvanger: see Dionaea muscipula
Verbascum
  x hybridum 340
  thapsus 340
Verbena, Lemon: see Aloysia triphylla
Verbena
  canadensis 'Rosea' 340
  x hybrida 340, 341
  peruviana 341
Verbleikblom: see Brunfelsia pauciflora 'Eximia'
Vernonia mespilifolia 341
Veronica scutellata 341
Vetkousie: see Carpanthea pomeridiana
Viburnum
  odoratissimum 342
  opulus 342
  opulus 'Sterile' 342
  tinus 'Lucidum' 342
Vinca: see Catharanthus roseus
Vinca
  major 342
  minor 'Variegata' 342
Vingerhoedjie: see Digitalis purpurea
Vingerpol: see Euphorbia caput-medusae
Vinkel: see Foeniculum vulgare
Viola
  odorata 343
  tricolor: see V. x wittrockiana
  tricolor subsp. subalpina 343
  x wittrockiana 343
Violet: see Viola odorata
  Flame: see Episcia cupreata
  German: see Exacum affine
  Persian: see Exacum affine
Violet-painted petals: see Lapeirousia jacquinii
Violet trumpet vine: see Clytostoma callistegioides
Viooltjie: see Viola odorata
Viooltjies: see Lachenalia aloides
Virgilia
  divaricata 343-4
  oroboides 344
Virginia creeper: see Parthenocissus quinquefolia
Virginian stock: see Malcolmia maritima
Visstertpalm: see Caryota mitis
Vitex trifolia 'Variegata' 344
Vlam-van-die-vlakte: see Bauhinia galpinii
Vlamboom: see Brachychiton acerifolium; Spathodea campanulata
Vlambos, Meksikaanse: see Calliandra tweedii
Vlamdoring: see Acacia ataxacantha
Vlamklimop: see Combretum microphyllum
Vlamviooltjie: see Episcia cupreata
Vlas, Nieu-Seelandse: see Phormium tenax
Vlei lily: see Crinum campanulatum
Vleiknopbos: see Berzelia lanuginosa
Vleilelie: see Crinum campanulatum
Vleiroos: see Orothamnus zeyheri
Vleisalie: see Iboza riparia
Vlier: see Sambucus spp.
Voëlnesvaring: see Asplenium nidus
Voëltjiebos: see Crotalaria agatiflora
Vriesea
  barilletii x *V. carinata*: see V. x mariae
  carinata 344
  incurvata 344, 345
  x mariae 345
  psittacina 345
Vuurbos: see Hamelia chrysantha
Vuurpyl: see Kniphofia praecox
Vuurwielboom: see Stenocarpus sinuatus
Vygies: see Lampranthus spp.

Waaieraalwyn: see Aloe plicatilis
Wachendorfia
  paniculata 345
  thyrsiflora 345
Wallflower: see Cheiranthus cheiri
Wand flower: see Dierama pendulum
Wandelende-Jood: see Zebrina pendula
Wandering Jew: see Tradescantia fluminensis 'Variegata'; Zebrina pendula
Waratah: see Telopea speciosissima
Warszewiczia coccinea 346
Wart leaf: see Ceanothus papillosus 'Roweanus'
Wasbegonia: see Begonia x semperflorens-cultorum
Washington hybrids: see Pelargonium x domesticum
Washington thorn: see Crataegus phaenopyrum
Washingtonia robusta 346
Wasplant: see Hoya carnosa
Waspypie: see Watsonia meriana
Watercrinum: see Crinum campanulatum
Water hawthorn: see Aponogeton distachyos
Water hyacinth: see Eichhornia crassipes
Water lettuce: see Pistia stratiotes
Water lily, Blue: see Nymphaea capensis
Waterblommetjie: see Aponogeton spp.
Watermelon peperomia: see Peperomia argyreia
Watermelon pilea: see Pilea cadierei
Watsonia
  angusta 346
  beatricis 346
  fulgens 347
  hybrid 347
  meriana 347
  pyramidata 347
  pyramidata 'Ardernei' 347
Wattle
  Bailey's: see Acacia baileyana
  Cedar: see Acacia terminalis
  Knife-leaf: see Acacia cultriformis
  Weeping: see Peltophorum africanum
Wax begonia: see Begonia x semperflorens-cultorum
Wax-leaf privet: see Ligustrum lucidum
Wax plant, Geraldton: see Chamelaucium uncinatum
Wax plants: see Hoya spp.
Waxberry: see Symphoricarpos albus
Wedelia trilobata 347
Weduweestrane: see Tradescantia virginiana
Weeping boer-bean: see Schotia brachypetala
Weeping bottle brush: see Callistemon viminalis
Weeping wattle: see Peltophorum africanum
Weeping willow: see Salix babylonica
Weigela florida 348
Western tea myrtle: see Melaleuca nesophylla
Whin: see Ulex europeus
White butterfly lily: see Hedychium coronarium
White cat's whiskers: see Clerodendrum glabrum
White flag bush: see Mussaenda incana
White flowering gum: see Eucalyptus calophylla
White gossamer: see Tradescantia sillamontana
White-haired cycad: see Encephalartos frederici-guilielmi
White karee: see Rhus pendulina
White mulberry: see Morus alba 'Pendula'
White stinkwood: see Celtis africana
White tea tree: see Leptospermum scoparium 'Album'
White thorn: see Crataegus laevigata

White velvet: see Tradescantia sillamontana
Widdringtonia nodiflora 348
Widow's tears: see Tradescantia virginiana
Wigandia urens 348
Wild banana: see Ensete ventricosum (South Africa); Strelitzia nicolai
Wild broom: see Lebeckia cytisoides
Wild cineraria: see Senecio elegans
Wild cotton: see Asclepias physocarpa
Wild dagga: see Leonotis leonurus var. leonurus
Wild date palm: see Phoenix reclinata
Wild fennel: see Nigella damascena
Wild fig, Common: see Ficus natalensis
Wild foxglove: see Ceratotheca triloba
Wild fuchsia: see Halleria elliptica
Wild garlic: see Tulbaghia violacea
Wild gentian: see Chironia baccifera
Wild grape: see Rhoicissus tomentosa
Wild hollyhock: see Sparmannia africana
Wild honeysuckle: see Turraea obtusifolia
Wild iris: see Dietes grandiflora
Wild laburnum: see Calpurnia aurea
Wild pansy: see Viola tricolor subsp. subalpina
Wild pear: see Dombeya rotundifolia var. rotundifolia
Wild phlox: see Sutera grandiflora
Wild pomegranate: see Burchellia bubalina
Wild rhubarb: see Acanthus mollis
Wild rosemary: see Eriocephalus africanus
Wild silver oak: see Brachylaena discolor subsp. transvaalensis
Wild swans: see Asclepias fruticosa
Wilde besembos: see Lebeckia cytisoides
Wilde cineraria: see Senecio elegans
Wilde dagga: see Leonotis leonurus var. leonurus
Wilde floks: see Sutera grandiflora
Wilde iris: see Dietes grandiflora
Wilde kanferfoelie: see Turraea obtusifolia
Wilde katoenboom: see Hibiscus tiliaceus
Wilde malva: see Pelargonium cucullatum
Wildeaarbei: see Duchesnea indica
Wildedadelpalm: see Phoenix reclinata
Wildegeelkeur: see Calpurnia aurea
Wildegranaat: see Burchellia bubalina
Wildekapok: see Asclepias physocarpa
Wildekastaiing: see Calodendrum capense
Wildekatjiepiering: see Gardenia thunbergia; Rothmannia capensis
Wildeknoffel: see Tulbaghia violacea
Wildepiesang: see Ensete ventricosum (South Africa); Strelitzia nicolai
Wildepynappel: see Eucomis autumnalis subsp. autumnalis
Wildevaalbos: see Brachylaena discolor subsp. transvaalensis
Wildevy, Gewone: see Ficus natalensis
Wilgerboom: see Salix babylonica
Willdenowia argentea 349
Willow, Pussy: see Salix discolor
Willow, Weeping: see Salix babylonica
Window plant: see Fenestraria aurantiaca; Monstera deliciosa
Wine cup: see Babiana rubrocyanea
Wine cups: see Geissorhiza radians
Winter buddleia: see Buddleja salviifolia
Winter jasmine: see Jasminum nudiflorum
Winter sweet, African: see Acokanthera oblongifolia
Winterjasmyn: see Jasminum nudiflorum
Wistaria, Tree: see Bolusanthus speciosus
Wisteria sinensis 349
Witkaree: see Rhus pendulina

367

Wit-margriet: see Castalis nudicaulis
Wit moerbei: see Morus alba 'Pendula'
Wit-teebos: see Leptospermum scoparium 'Album'
Witbalroos: see Viburnum opulus 'Sterile'
Witbloekom: see Eucalyptus calophylla
Witbotterblom: see Dimorphotheca pluvialis
Witgemmerlelie: see Hedychium coronarium
Withaarbroodboom: see Encephalartos frederici-guilielmi
Witkatjiepiering: see Gardenia thunbergia
Witsteekbos: see Metalasia muricata
Witstinkhout: see Celtis africana
Wolharpuisbos: see Euryops pectinatus
Wonderlawn: see Dichondra micrantha
Woodbine: see Lonicera spp.; Parthenocissus quinquefolia
Woodland painted petals: see Lapeirousia laxa
Woolly coral tree: see Erythrina latissima
Wormwood cassia: see Cassia artemisioides

Xerophyta viscosa 350

Yam: see Dioscorea bulbifera
Yarrow: see Achillea millefolium 'Rosea'
Yellow bush jasmine: see Jasminum humile 'Revolutum'
Yellow day lily: see Hemerocallis lilioasphodelus
Yellow elder: see Tecoma stans
Yellow flax: see Reinwardtia indica
Yellow ginger: see Hedychium gardneranum
Yellow jessamine: see Gelsemium sempervirens
Yellow leaf dumb cane: see Dieffenbachia maculata 'Rudolph Roehrs'
Yellow milk bush: see Euphorbia mauritanica
Yellow oleander: see Thevetia peruviana
Yellow pomegranate: see Rhigozum obovatum
Yellow wild iris: see Dietes bicolor
Yellowwood: see Podocarpus spp.
Yesterday, Today and Tomorrow: see Brunfelsia pauciflora 'Eximia'
Ysterhout: see Dodonaea angustifolia
Ysterkruisbegonia: see Begonia masoniana

Yucca
 filamentosa 350
 gloriosa 350

Zaluzianskya villosa 351
Zantedeschia
 aethiopica 351
 pentlandii 351
 rehmannii 351
Zebra plant: see Aphelandra squarrosa
Zebrina pendula 352
Zephyr lily: see Zephyranthes grandiflora
Zephyranthes grandiflora 352
Zimbabwe creeper: see Podranea brycei
Zimbabweranker: see Podranea brycei
Zinnia
 elegans 352
 elegans 'Thumbelina' 352
Zonal pelargonium: see Pelargonium x hortorum
Zuurberg harebell: see Dierama pendulum
Zygocactus truncatus: see Schlumbergera truncata